The Morning Side of the Hill

Growing up in Townsville in World War II.

BROLGA

The Morning Side of the Hill

Marion Houldsworth

First published in 1995 by Department of History and Politics, James Cook University

Revised Edition published in 2010 by Boolarong Press

National Library of Australia Cataloguing-in-Publication entry:

Author:	Houldsworth, Marion.
Title:	The morning side of the hill / Marion Houldsworth.
Edition:	Rev. ed.
ISBN:	9781921555473 (pbk.)
Notes:	Previous ed.: Townsville, Qld. : Dept. of History and Politics, James Cook University, 1995.
Subjects:	Houldsworth, Marion--Childhood and youth. Townsville (Qld.)--Biography. Townsville (Qld.)--History. Townsville (Qld.)--Social conditions. Queensland--Social conditions--1939-1945. Queensland--History--1939-1945.
Dewey Number:	994.36042

Typeset by John James

Cover Design by John James

Front Cover photo: John Newman

Back Cover photo: Townsville Bulletin

Published by Boolarong Press, Salisbury, Brisbane, Australia.

Printed and bound by Watson Ferguson & Company 655 Toohey Road Salisbury Qld 4107

ABOUT THE AUTHOR

Marion Houldsworth, Oral Historian, was educated at Blackheath College, Charters Towers, Rockhampton Girls' Grammar School, and the University of Queensland. With her husband and family she lived and worked for many years in the Northern Territory and Papua New Guinea.

Marion has a passionate interest in the history of North Queensland, especially the social history of the people of the Outback and the pastoral industry, and in order to further her work in this field studied Life History at the University of Sussex in the UK.

Her published works include;

Hearts Bright With Hope; a Grammar School Diary; Nova Press, Devonport; 1992

The Immigrant Boy; A Townsville Boyhood, 1912 - 1918; James Cook University Press; 1998

Barefoot Through the Bindies; Growing Up In North Queensland in the Early 1900s; Central Queensland University Press; 2002

Red Dust Rising; The Life of Ray Fryer; Cattleman; Central Queensland University Press; 2004.

From the Gulf to God Knows Where; Men and Women of Australia's Outback; Central Queensland University Press; 2006

Maybe It'll Rain Tomorrow; Living in Australia's Outback; Central Queensland University Press, 2007

The Morning Side of the Hill; A Townsville Childhood, 1939 - 1945; was first published in 1995 by James Cook University of North Queensland as part of the 50th Anniversary Commemorations of Peace in the Pacific.

For

Helena and Bert Stilwell,
Mum and Dad,
who played their part staunchly
in the story of wartime Townsville, 1939-45.

Also Barry, 1929-1990

Many suns arise and set;
Many a change the years beget.
Love the gift is. Love the debt.
Tennynson

Foreword

Reminiscences of childhood are familiar in the form of early chapters in the autobiographical writings of public men, but they are likely to take on a new importance. As a natural corollary of women's studies, attention is beginning to turn to the history of children and childhood. In this new field reminiscences seem likely to be of central importance, whether written by individuals or collected as oral history.

Most readers will open this book out of interest in its picture of the impact of war upon an Australian community. They will not be disappointed, whether older North Queenslanders prompted by nostalgia, or younger Australians curious about a world they never knew. The account of wartime Townsville is remarkable for its clarity, and its rich, concrete and exact detail.

Directly, or indirectly, the war impinged upon every facet of life but only occasionally is it shown as dominating the writer's conscious thoughts. Rather, was it part of the background, always present but impinging directly only as an occasional intrusion upon matters of more immediate moment. News of the first atomic bomb, relayed by a parent with heavy emphasis upon its great significance, is endured politely as an interruption to a fiercely contested game of marbles.

It should be noted here that this is not simply a child's but a girl's view.The writer makes it clear that her brother's direct interest in the war was different.The attention the writer and her friends lavish of their dolls, her brother gives to collecting war souvenirs, mastering aircraft recognition and learning morse code in his ambition to enter the RAAF, before the war ends.

It is well known that shortages of all kinds of everyday necessities were severe in wartime Townsville. The writer recalls even bread and potatoes being unobtainable on occasions; water was at times on tap for only two hours a day. But she depicts a robust, resilient community displaying nothing of the sagging morale officially reported to Canberra.

Much of her depiction of childhood has an interest independent of its wartime setting: schooling and play in particular. Very large classes "sit to attention", chant their "times tables", learn by rote the baffling "parts of the verb to be", and the complexities of arcane units of measurement. The games played in the school-ground and in the neighbourhood are recalled in fond detail; their rules and rituals were exclusively children's property, administered and transmitted independently of all adult authority. Centuries old in some instances, they now seem to have vanished completely.

Equally alien to our modern age is the household economy: wood-burning stoves, bathroom chip-heaters, backyard coppers in which the household laundry was boiled, petrol irons, chook-yards, vegetable gardens and wood-heaps. This was a world closer in years and technology to the Edwardian era than to the present day.

In a narrative written with skill and sensitivity the author does not gloss over childhood miseries. Some of the most memorable pages tell of the desolation of being an outsider in a new school, of fears impossible to tell parents, of nightmares brought on by wartime atrocity reports. Children are wary of adult power, quick to placate, divert. Neverthess no reader will doubt that her memories are of a most remarkable childhood.

B.J. Dalton;

Department of History and Politics, James Cook University.

Preface

Nearly all those mentioned in these pages appear under their real names, but to a small number I have given pseudonyms to avoid the risk of embarrassing innocent parties. I have invented nothing else.

I wish to record my gratitude to the *Townsville Bulletin* for the use of photographs, notices and advertisements originally appearing in its wartime pages; to Annette Burns of the Townsville Central Library for the photographs from its collection; to A'MHara Russell of James Cook University for the use of photographs from the North Queensland Photographic Collection; to Shirley Sellars (nee Ackland), and to Ron and Beryl Quelch for sharing with me their memories of our childhood in wartime Townsville; and to my friend John James, of Sussex, UK, for his inimitable skill and patience in preparing this work for re-publication.

The epigraphs at the head of each chapter are quotations from popular wartime songs. The cover-design, end map and drawings throughout the book were commissioned from noted North Queensland artist John Newman.

Contents

Chapter 1

IN FROM THE WEST

'Run, Rabbit! Run, Rabbit! Run! Run! Run!'

The Old Magazine, Kissing Point

The train wasn't even trying to hurry. It was dawdling. I knew. I was always being accused of dawdling myself. Clunk, clunk! it went, loitering across the plains. We were leaving the west. We were on our way to Townsville.

Chin on the gritty of the carriage window, I stared out at the black-soil paddocks grinding past. Here and there in belts of sun-bleached scrub, sheep rested from heat which hung shimmering over the empty landscape. The fences leaned before the wind and 'roly-poly', the balls of dry bush that bowled for miles downwind, pressed upon them. I wished that we were heading west, too. I wanted to go back to Aramac, to Stainburn Downs station and the animals; Bonzo the dog, all the cats, and Felix, the night-horse that was mine to ride.

I was heart-sick with longing for Stainburn, and I was going to hate Townsville. Mum had explained it all to Barry and me. There was a war. Dad was going to join the army. He had been in the British army in the Great War and thought that now, in this second Great War, army life would be a proper job in a decent town. He knew Mum was tired of living in the outback, the flies, the heat, the dust. He knew that Barry was nearly ten, and it was time he went to a proper school. He had been boarded with an elderly lady in Aramac to go to the school but Mum had been outraged to learn that each afternoon he was sent to the pub to get the old lady her beer and cigarettes. It was the last straw. It was time to make a move. 'And, just think!' Mum had said to Barry and me brightly, 'There'll be the lovely cool sea! You will be able to swim! Your father's got us a nice flat near the beach!' Dad had gone on ahead to join the army, leaving Mum to pack and follow with us.

Packing-up had included a burn-up of my 'cheap and rubbishy' dolls, each of which had been given to me by the station-hands, the stockmen, the rouseabout or the blacksmith after they had been into Aramac on a bender. The dolls were of the cheapest sort, with long, dangly arms and legs and heads of pressed-cardboard with painted smiles, from Cassimatis' Emporium, Aramac's only store, but I had welcomed each one into my doll family and loved them all. Seeing them piled into the rusted-out water tank that was the homestead incinerator, doused with kerosene and burned, had been a lesson in the implacable power of grown-ups.

But now Townsville seemed to be for ever coming. Already we had been nearly two days on the journey. At Barcaldine we had changed trains and again at Winton. Barry and I had been left to mind the piles of ports and cushions while Mum went off to make arrangements. When she had been gone for some time and there seemed no sign of her returning we began to feel at first creeping doubts, then mounting panic and at last complete certainty that she had abandoned us for ever. The whistles and shuntings of trains in the distance had served to emphasize our forsakenness.

Stricken, we had gazed at one another on the empty platform. 'Supposing she never comes back?' I quavered. At this, Barry had tried a bit of bravado, pegging clinker-stones at some crows on the railway line, but I had seen through that at once. He couldn't fool me; he was as alarmed as I was. The muscles round my lip tugged and my eyes brimmed. It was only a matter of time until the crows came to pick our eyes out, as they did at Stainburn to lambs separated from their mothers.

We had reason to be troubled. Once when I was little, Mum had been bitten by a snake. Luckily it was right outside the hospital at Yeppoon or she might have died. It happened at night. Mum had been pulling me by the hand along the edge of the dark road. She felt something strike her ankle and cried out, thinking a sharp stick had sprung up and hit her. When she swung the beam of the torch around, we saw a black snake sliding into the grass.

Mum was in hospital for many months. Hot poultices were applied to her ankle to draw out the venom. For a long time she was frail and ill. We had no relatives in Australia to care for us so Barry and I were put into an orphanage. It was at Parkhurst, just north of Rockhampton, a row of gaunt wooden buildings set high on a windswept ridge, with 'St. George's Home for Orphans' over the gate, to emphasize our abandoned state. Barry had been marched off daily with the older children to the State School in the valley below. I had to stay with the little ones. We were made to play *In and Out the Windows* holding hands in a big circle, but each day when I saw Barry being marched away, the sense of being abandoned engulfed me afresh and I choked on tears and a snotty nose.

But, now, just when I had completely given up hope and had begun a knuckles-in-the-eyes sort of whimpering, Mum returned. She looked different. Something about her hair. It was nicely styled and set in rolls around her face like the fashionable ladies in the McWhirter's catalogue. She looked exactly like the proud queen in the Snow White story.

To fill in time before the train left, Mum said we could walk over to the town and she would buy us some new shoes. Seizing a battered railway-trolley, she piled our ports and rugs and the dilly-bag with the tea things upon it. Heaving and tugging, Barry trundled it along the platform to where the station-master could keep an eye on it. 'She'll be right, Missus. Don't you worry your pretty head about it!' he said. Mum smiled graciously, as an English lady should. She felt it her due to receive compliments. The station-master pushed back his cap and wiped his forehead, staring after us, as we set out on the hot walk into the main street of the town.

At the prospect of new shoes I had brightened marvellously. Until now, new shoes had only been achieved by selecting them from the McWhirter's Mail Order catalogue, making sure to tick second and third choices. Our feet had been placed on pieces of paper on the kitchen floor and Mum had got down on hands and knees to draw the outline, first 'left foot' then 'right foot'.' It was a ticklish process. You dare not move a fraction or the wrong size came in the mail several weeks later and you got the blame for it. 'You must have wriggled!' Mum would exclaim in exasperation. The shoes were usually the wrong colour as well, and would have to be sent back. Barry and I mostly went barefoot, balancing on one foot to remove bindi-eyes and goat-head burrs as necessary. On hot days we scuttled from one patch of weeds to the next on the long walk from the homestead to the shearing-shed and yards.

But now, not only new shoes but shiny black patent-leather ones! I could hardly believe such elegance. Only the beautifully dressed little girls in the McWhirters's catalogue had patent-leather shoes. With a flourish of the wrist, the shop-lady produced the marvellous shoes from the tissue-paper in the box and, kneeling, slid them over my socks. This was a matter of acute embarrassment. How did they feel? I detected a shade of uncertainty on her face. In fact my toes felt trapped and imprisoned after my sandals, but I could not bring myself to say so. Could I tell this lady who had climbed up on a wooden ladder to fetch the box down, that the shoes hurt dreadfully? It would be so rude! How often was I told, 'Oh! Do stop your grizzling!' One word out of me and Mum might get angry. Everything would be spoiled. There might be no new shoes, after all.

'How do they feel? Wiggle your toes! Are you sure there's enough room?' said Mum, in what seemed to me a most challenging manner. 'Are you sure they're comfortable?' I nodded my head up and down vigorously. I seldom spoke unless it was strictly necessary. Mum gave me one doubtful look and then said to the assistant, 'Yes, we'll take them, thank you.' She was enjoying the feeling of power that the money Dad had sent for our journey gave her.

Barry fared better. For a boy he had small neat feet and was soon equipped with black leather lace-ups. Aware of unaccustomed elegance we trailed after Mum to the Acropolis Cafe for chops, beetroot and fried eggs. My feet were burning. By the time we got back to the station for the connecting train I was walking on coals of fire. I managed to get some ease by curling my toes underneath the balls of my feet. 'Do keep up!' said Mum briskly, as we began collecting all the things for the onward journey.

For hours the train crawled across the empty landscape. At intervals it stopped, panting, at elevated water towers where a thick canvas sleeve was swung out on a davit and water taken on for the engine. This was the signal for passengers who had had the forethought to equip themselves with a teapot and 'the makings', as Mum had, to climb down from the little verandah at the back of each carriage and to crunch along the cinders beside the track to the engine. The fireman would fill the teapots from a brass tap near the fire-box in the driver's cab.

Barry returned from these missions gripping the tea-pot ahead of him gingerly, like a loaded firearm. We drank the tea with milk from an empty sauce bottle wrapped in wet cloth, which Mum sniffed at delicately before pouring into our cups. There was nothing else to drink. There was water in a glass decanter in a bracket fixed high on the wall, which sloshed backwards and forwards rhythmically as the train swayed on its way, but it might have been laced with sheep-dip as far as Mum was concerned. 'You never know who's been touching it!' she exclaimed.

At night Barry and I were bedded down, 'top and tail' on the long shiny black seat. At some time during the night I woke up. The train had stopped. I knelt up on the slidy leather seat and peered out. Outside, men in black waistcoats and caps were loading parcels and mail-bags, shouting out cheerfully to one another along the gravel platform. There was the sound of dogs barking miserably. It came from the barred compartment in the guard's van where dogs were locked for the journey. I could tell they were upset and unhappy because every so often the barking turned to squeals of fright as a quarrel broke out among them. I liked dogs. You could trust them. They didn't find fault with you.

Once, at Stainburn Downs station I had got into terrible trouble about a dog. I had let a very fierce blue heeler off his chain, something no-one ever did. He was kept chained up night and day. It made me terribly sad for him. They told me he was savage and would bite. I thought being chained up all the time would make anyone savage. I talked to him and we were friends. One day he made blue heeler grins at me and promised to be good if I would let him off the chain. So I did. But the moment his chain was unclipped he did not lick my hand in gratitude, no! but went like a bullet towards the yards where a mob of horses had just been brought in. Sliding under the bottom rail he began heeling them. Round and round the yard the horses stampeded, nickering and tossing their heads and shouldering one another in fright. The stockmen yelled and cursed. There was a cry; 'Who let that bloody dog off!' 'Get him out of here!' Useless for me to slide away and crouch under the back-steps holding Bonzo close to my beating heart.

Oh, the rousing-at I got! What a dreadful thing to do! What a terrible child I was! A naughty, silly child! What nice little girl would do such a thing! Willful! I was just willful. On and on. Followed by a good slapping. But even so, head hanging in misery, shoulders hunched to make myself as small and invisible as I could, I remembered the joyful sight of the dog flying across the ground in his moment of freedom.

So, now, I watched as on the platform below, the guard peered through the bars of the dogs' compartment. Taking a key off the bunch on his belt he opened the door cautiously. The next moment he was sent staggering backwards. Something large and creamy-coloured leapt out, a huge Alsatian. It balanced for a moment on the guard's shoulder before leaping in a huge arc to go galloping off along the platform, dragging a length of broken chain. Dodging this way and that it looked frantically for a way of escape. 'Block him! Grab the bastard!' shouted the guard. Dropping their parcels and bags, the men spread their legs and arms wide, to block the dog's flight, at the same time mindful that it was an Alsatian and no joking matter. The dog shied past legs and leapt past arms, then, seeing the open gateway to the road, swerved violently, and with a final bound, disappeared into the night. The men stared after him. One of them said, 'Well! I'll be buggered!' and spat on to the gravel. One would have laughed but stopped, on catching sight of the enormous fury of the guard, stomping along the platform. The dog would have had a ticket, a little pink clipped card-board ticket, the same as people had. The guard would be held responsible. 'You useless lot of bastards!' he snarled, 'Get on with your work!' The men quickly resumed loading the mail-bags, sniggering among themselves.

Long after the train had lurched off on its journey under the great blackness of the sky, I shed silent tears for the fate of the dog and chewed the sleeve of my jumper with misery. His owner would never find him; never even know what had happened. Alone and fright-ened in a strange world, he would be lost for ever. Being separated was the hardest thing in the world to bear.

Dad met us at Townsville wearing his army uniform; hat turned up smartly at the side, strap under his chin, khaki shorts and long socks. Because of his service in the Great War he had already been made a corporal. Barry looked at the stripes on his sleeve eagerly. But to me Dad seemed a stranger and I felt overwhelmed with shyness, backing away when he tried to kiss me. 'Leave her,' said Mum, 'You know what she's like. She's been like a dying duck in a thunderstorm the whole the way.' She and Dad moved off through the elegant white-tiled entrance to the station, while I trailed along behind carrying a rug and a cushion. Barry manfully hefted a small brown port, thrusting it forward at each step with one knee. He was seizing the opportunity to establish his importance in Dad's eyes as well as staring in all directions, trying to take everything in at once.

In the wide space before the station, the leaves of the trees had had been trimmed to flat-tened shapes like green breadboards. Green was new to us. Barry and I were used to stunted gidgee, dull grey. Beyond the bread-board trees was the shoulder of a mountain, bare pink granite and brown grass, sweeping upwards to the sky. After the flat plains at Aramac it seemed enormous.

At Stainburn the horizon had been a vast circle about the homestead. Once, when Mum had been teaching Barry about mountains in a Correspondence lesson, she had taken him out on to the back verandah and pointed to a distant mirage shimmering on the horizon.'See!' she had said, 'Mountains are like that. Only they are solid. You can climb them.' Now here was a real mountain before our very eyes. Dad told Barry it was called Castle Hill. On a stony ridge could be seen a circular concrete structure. 'Is that the fort, Dad?' said Barry excitedly. He knew Dad was stationed at the fort at Kissing Point. 'Is that where the war is going to be?'

'No, Sonny Jim,' said Dad, pleased at his eager interest, as he helped the taxi-driver strap the ports and suitcases on to the luggage rack. 'That's the town water supply, the reservoir.

You'll see the fort at Kissing Point, but all in good time. Let's get you home and hosed, first up.'

The flat where we were to live was in Eyre Street, North Ward, set between Castle Hill and the sea. It was a short walk from the army camp at Kissing Point and Dad would be able to slip home often. After all the time out west when Dad had had to take whatever work was available, sometimes being away for months on end, once even as a shearers' cook, we would be together as a proper family. The flat was really half of an elevated Queensland house which had been divided into two. There were front and back verandahs, and a large garden with lawns, coconut palms, banana trees in a clump, bright coloured crotons and red hibiscus. A heady perfume came from the blooms of the frangipani.

Over all was a distant sighing sound which Dad told us was the sea. The sea! So close! Mum clasped her hands in ecstasy and breathed deeply. 'Oh! Smell the ozone!' she exclaimed. This was like an escape for her. She had hated Stainburn, something which she had told Dad frequently. Now she looked at the coconut palms and exclaimed, 'Oh! Before I left the Old Country, Auntie Jessie read my tea-leaves. She said she could see palm-trees! These must be they!' Mum was romantic and loved pretty things. She liked having things go just right, which up till now had not happened very often.

As soon as possible we went for a walk to the beach, Barry running ahead in excitement and I pretending to be. Up a little rise, over some sand-dunes, spiky with wind-blown grasses and there was the sea! We raced to the water's edge. The tiny waves creamed over our feet and we jumped up and down, stamping and splashing, careless of getting the hem of my dress or the bottoms of Barry's pants wet. The waves dragged the sand from beneath our feet so that we seemed to sinking. I squealed and ran from the water, but Barry stood his ground, bravely waiting till he had sunk to his shins. Across the blue of the bay were more mountains that Dad told us were Magnetic Island and Cape Cleveland. The world seemed filled with colour and sparkle. Mum was breathing in the sea air, her eyes closed, her head tilted slightly back, as though she were praying.

A rocky promontory which Dad told us was Kissing Point jutted into the sea. Dad said that it was where his battalion, the 31st Kennedy Regiment, had its headquarters. We could see a cluster of wooden huts among pandanus trees and some concrete gun-emplacements. Barry had thought there would be turrets and crenellations like the Sheriff of Nottingham's castle in *Robin Hood*. He tried to hide his disappointment.

Close to the rocks was a sort of stockyard fence, a wide half-circle of paper-bark saplings within which many people, most of them children, were bobbing up and down in the water. There was no-one swimming outside in the open water. 'This is the shark-proof enclosure,' explained Dad when he and Mum, arm in arm, joined us. 'You must always swim inside it. Never on the outside. There are plenty of sharks about, never fear. A chap got a nine-footer off the breakwater the other day.' At this sobering news Barry picked up some stones to hurl out into the deep water.

I watched the children swimming. The ducking that was going on seemed alarming, I knew that I could not bear to be pushed under the water as these children were doing, but none of them seemed to mind. Two boys had a tin canoe which they were taking in turns to launch, balancing it on the edge of the sand, giving it a push with one foot and scrambling in at the last moment. Again and again the canoe wobbled, filled with water and sank. The one who was sitting in it would go under laughing then bob to the surface flicking the water out of his hair as he dragged it towards the beach. At last one of the boys got it going and leaned forward to paddle with his hands, frowning in concentration to keep his balance. The canoe made a wide circle through the swimmers until one of them grabbed the pointy end and sank it. The boy who had been doing the paddling shouted with laughter as he disappeared under the water.

Other children were bobbing up and down at the edge of the waves, holding their noses to search for shells or diving through one another's legs. They seemed to be as at home in the water as on land and all seemed to be friends, calling shrilly to one another and not always waiting for an answer. Barry and I looked at one another glumly, suddenly aware that we were outsiders.

Barry and I didn't know how to swim. We had never swum anywhere but the dam at Stainburn which was deep and brown, with a bottom of mud which squeezed up between your toes as you waded in and which shelved steeply into deep water. Once I had nearly drowned when I had slipped further and further down the slope until, head well under water, I had held up one desparing arm. Barry had grabbed my wrist and pulled me to the bank. We hadn't told Mum about it for fear of being told we couldn't go to the dam again. But how could we ever go into this swimming enclosure in the sea among all these noisy, splashing children?

'Don't scowl!' Mum told us, 'It will be lovely for you to have friends of your own age when you go to school! And every afternoon after school you will be able to come and swim, too!' Her words were like a doom. School! Who said anything about school! Something else to worry about!

The following day we were marched, in our 'best bib and tucker' as Dad called it, which in my case included the new patent-leather shoes, along Eyre Street to Central School. The school was set among big Moreton Bay fig trees in a fold of two low hills. We stood for a little on the roadside, looking down into the playground. Children swarmed noisily in and out from beneath the buildings, screaming shrilly. At the sight I was overcome with panic. I never liked to see anything that was closely packed together, such as maggots on a carcass, or tea-leaves inside a pot. The swarming children gave me the same sense of aversion. I could not possibly go down there among them! Never in a zillion, squillion years! 'Nonsense! said Mum briskly. 'Once you get used to it you will love it! You'll see! Come along now! And for goodness sake, hold your head up! And don't bite your nails!'

Central was a very old school, with wide shady verandahs with cast-iron railings. The windows of the classrooms were tall and narrow and set high in the walls. At the bottom of each wall was a long wooden flap tied up with a cord to let cool air blow across the children's feet, which were mostly bare. On the walls were rows of iron hooks on which hats and school-bags hung. A busy hum came from within each classroom as we passed by: of multiplication tables being chanted; 'Eight twelves are ninety six. Eight into ninety-six goes twelve!'; of spellings being learned; 'receive. r e c E i v e'; of poetry being recited

I come from haunts of coot and hern,
I make a sudden sally
And sparkle out among the fern
To bicker down a valley.

What were 'cootenhern'? I did't know things like that! Voices of teachers were raised shrilly; 'Stanley Sugden! Come out here at once! Didn't I tell you...'. followed by the whack of a ruler on bare legs. As we filed along the verandah to the Office, I remembered the quiet back verandah at Stainburn where I had sat to do my Correspondence School lessons with the cats for company and Bonzo under my feet. My heart contracted in dread.

The Head Teacher, Mr. Bonham, smoked cigars. He wasn't smoking them when he saw us but Mum told Dad later that she had smelt them on his breath. Barry was asked a few questions which, being the clever one in the family, he answered smartly, standing to attention as Dad had told him to do and saying 'Sir!' after each one. He was put into Grade Five. At nine he was very young for the Grade, but Aramac school had been a small one, with only three teachers. He had been far too clever for Grade Three, so had been put up into Grade Five with children two years older than himself.

Then it was my turn. Overcome with my own inadequacy, I hung my head. My feet, encased in the patent-leather shoes, seethed with pain. When Mr. Bonham said, 'And are we going to like living in Townsville?' in a hearty manner intended to melt my resistance, I remembered Bonzo and Felix and shook my head. When, after a while he changed to 'Tell me about the train journey coming down. That must have been fun!' tears formed in my eyes remembering the Alsatian in the night. I tucked my head down even further in order that they should not be seen. When he said, 'We'll enjoy swimming in the sea, won't we?' I thought of the boisterous children ducking one another in the swimming enclosure and edged behind Mum. Mum pinched my shoulder and pushed me forward.

'Hmm,' said Mr. Bonham, 'Does she know her letters?' He thrust a soft, cloth-covered Royal Reader into my hands. I could have read it with the book upside down or closed altogether. I had recited it from beginning to end to Felix and Bonzo as we rode slowly round the home paddock. I had taught it to to all my dolls. But I could not open my mouth and make words come out for this strange man who wore a suit and a tie and sat behind a desk with his pink scalp shining through grey hair carefully combed across and little bits of hair sticking out of his ears.

'She's tall for her age but I think we'd better put her into Miss Marron's Prep One,' said Mr. Bonham, suddenly anxious to finalize the whole deal. As we were leaving along the verandah, a bare-footed boy came out holding a school-bell by its clapper so that it would not ring prematurely. It was the cheerful boy who had been trying to launch the canoe at the swimming enclosure. With dramatic timing he began to ring the bell just as we were going down the wide steps, putting his whole heart and soul into the task so that his shoulder seemed about to come off. Mum was clicking her tongue angrily at me. 'Why didn't you read nicely for Mr Bonham! For two pins I'd give you a good smack!' she exclaimed. Luckily the clamour of the bell, the sudden eruption of children down the steps and the teacher's admonitions of 'Walk! Don't run! Cliffie Frizwell! Get back here!' precluded any necessity of my having to answer.

The next morning, dressed in a brown box-pleated tunic and blouse, I was made ready for school. A handkerchief was pinned to the front of my tunic, to be neatly tucked in down the front out of sight when not in actual use. Barry had new khaki pants and shirt and a wide-brimmed, straw hat called a 'Donkey's Dinner', which smelt sweetly like warm grass. Each of us had a block of camphor in a little bag pinned to our singlets to ward off germs.

As the time for departure drew near, the muscles around my mouth began to tighten and pull downwards. I was on the point of wailing in a desperation of sheer fright when Mum hastily drew me to the louvres at the side of the verandah. 'There!' she said, pointing, 'See that little boy next door! He's not frightened to go to school!' I gazed resentful-eyed at the boy; clothes starched and ironed, socks neatly turned over shiny shoes, hair swept into a glossy quiff, crouching intently over a game of marbles. Carefully he brushed the ground with the palm of his hand so that the marble would shoot straight. A town boy! I could see no possible relationship between him and my huge reluctance to set foot outside of the door. But Mum had arranged with the boy's mother, Mrs. Quelch, for us to walk to school with him. His name was Ronnie, and when we set out with him, not one of us having the slightest idea what to say to the other, I felt I was delivered into the hands of the enemy.

But Miss Marron was young and kind. The 'Infant's' was a large room with a heavy brown curtain across the middle, on the other side of which another class was noisily at work. I was led to a desk in which another little girl moved over importantly. It was a two-seater with a cast-iron frame and up-and-down seats. There was a knack to standing up so that the seat didn't squeal and flap up with a bang. The other children let the seats slide up the back of their legs, catching them with their bottoms as they reached the vertical. These skills take time to master. My seat squealed and banged. Thirty pairs of eyes stared. Fancy someone who didn't know you got into trouble if you let the seat bang! There were other mysteries, such as how to sharpen slate-pencils.

Every morning, a line of little girls crouched industriously at the edge of the cement gutterings beneath the school, sharpening their slate pencils. They made feathering sweeps with them until the tips had the precision of hospital needles. I pressed too hard. Mine snapped in two, the bottom half dangling by the speckled paper in which it had been wrapped. I wept over it silently. When I had finished, someone looked at me and jeered with disgust, 'You've got a bogie on your nose!' and darted off.

Slate pencils were thin and brittle. They cracked in pieces if dropped on the floor. The pieces weren't to be wasted. There were tin-handles into which they were pushed but which rusted from the heat of your hand and were nasty to touch. They were kept in the press and passed round every morning. Until now a press had been something in the shearing-shed at Stainburn that wool-bales were compressed in; the final stage of the shearing before each bale had 'Stainburn Downs station, Aramac' stencilled on to it and was loaded on to the truck for the railway. Mum had always told us never to go anywhere near the wool-press. She had heard of a child being crushed to death in one. Now, here in this noisy, crowded schoolroom a press was suddenly a sort of cupboard where reading-books, counting-frames and tins of slate-pencils were kept.

Sharpening slate-pencils was something boys never did. They gave them a quick scrape on the concrete of the bottom step and marched into school with snub-nosed ones that screeched horribly. Miss Marron would give them one from the tinful in the press, a tin painted green, with a purple plum cut from the label of Angelina Plum jam pasted on by way of decoration. The slate-pencils in the tin were sharpened every morning by little girls who, bobbing up and down on their toes and clutching the back hem of their dresses behind them as a mark of respect, entreated Miss Marron, 'Please, Miss. Can we sharpen the pencils?' I could only observe these elect and confident pencil-sharpening persons from an awed distance.

I had never written on a slate before. For the Correspondence School we did pot-hooks with pencils. But here each slate was ruled on one side with guide-lines for learning to do Copperplate of thin upward strokes and thick downward ones. The thicker downward ones did for many a finely-tuned pencil tip. The click of a breaking pencil and little cries of anguish would be heard from all over the room. The reverse side of the slate was ruled into three columns, divided again to form nine spaces for working sums.

If you finished the writing lesson, 'M n M n M Meg my', you could turn over and draw a picture. Girls did a house, a regulation square with a pointy roof, smoking chimney and path leading to the front door. The most pleasurable moment came with putting the sun with spiky rays sticking out of it into the top right-hand corner and some petalled flowers along a front path. That everyone in North Ward lived in high-blocked houses with a verandah at the front made little difference to this basic design. Once I tried to draw our proper house. I could see that the posts ought to come downwards, but my mind couldn't seem to make it happen on the slate; instead the posts projected sideways like spider's legs. Miss Marron smiled and sent me with my slate on my chest to show the class behind the curtain.

Boys, of course, drew cars. They hadn't quite got the knack of making the wheels fit within the body of the car and drew them as circles underneath, like balloons. Everyone knew how to draw trees. They were a circle on a stick. The best thing about writing or drawing on a slate was that, with a quick lick of the finger, you could wipe out and amend until you got things perfectly to your liking.

To clean slates everyone had to have a slate rag and a sponge, which had to be washed out at night and held up for display each morning. The boys often forgot. When they opened their sponge-tins their negligence would be betrayed a by frowsty pong. Some didn't have a sponge-tin at all and were spitters, giving their sleeve a quick tug to make it do duty as a dry-rag. They did it furtively, for there was many a hand willing to shoot up with 'Miss! Miss! Andy spitted!'Andy would be hauled out by his shirt-collar and made to stand on the verandah, where he could press himself back amidst the rows of school-bags and shrink with fear lest Mr. Bonham happen upon him.

There were lessons when squares of shiny coloured paper were handed out from which circles, triangles and squares were cut and pasted to form sailing boats or houses. You watched anxiously, hoping to get pink. When you saw yours was going to be the brown or dark green again, your heart sank. Then there was card-threading. You threaded laces in and out of holes around the shape of an apple or pear or bunch of cherries. At the end of the lesson you unthreaded your card and they were put away in the press till next time.

Hardest of all was weaving. Each child had a brown-paper envelope in which were stored a paper frame and paper strips. To do the threading there was a metal rod, which became powdered with rust between lessons. The rust, of course, came off on your hands. Nobody's work was clean. A tall frame which lurked all week in the corner of the room was carried forth and placed at the front of the class. It looked like a giant Stop sign, but was square with strips of serge-material running across. Using bamboo slats, Miss Marron demonstrated the pattern to be done, while the class 'sat up straight', arms folded behind backs, and watched with growing dismay.

'Three over, two under, three over!' Do we understand? Willing fingers, anxious to please, struggle to make paper replicas, counting aloud under the breath the 'threes' and the 'twos', trying to make the metal threader steer a true course. But then, too soon, comes the command 'Hands behind'. You were not quite finished but you must watch the trial-run of the next row. 'Two under! Three over!' proclaims Miss Marron, thrusting the bamboo through the fabric of the demonstration-frame. Then she walks the aisles repeating the pattern mechanically, to urge us on. This has a mesmeric effect. Those still on 'Three over, two under' hesitate, look anxiously from left to right to check their bearings, give up as a bad job and follow suit. Their wefts and woofs change step, mid-row. Row by row stiff patterns begin to emerge. But one mistake, one 'Over' that should have been 'Under' and all is lost. The error is writ plain. The wrongly threaded strip is plucked out. This immediately throws all the subsequent rows into disarray. Although thickish, the paper is only paper. One nervous tug too many and it is bound to part company. You make the discovery that spit has no adhesive properties.

Putting up hands and asking questions is not encouraged. You are there to learn concentration. Esme Purley raises her hand in the air, first calmly, then in agitation and finally clicking fingers, in desperation. Too late! A pale flood oozes along the seat, drips to the floor and forms a spreading puddle. Those nearby distance themselves. No one sneers. They know only too well it could have happened to them.

Mum had adjured Barry to look after me at 'Little Lunch' and 'Big Lunch'. He had agreed because he was obliged to, not because he intended to. Would he be likely to have time for a little sister! He had his own way to make. There were the tactics of 'British Bulldog' to be mastered, as well as the skill of climbing and sliding down the stiff aerial roots of the Moreton Bay fig-trees. The trees were so old that some of the roots had turned to separate tree-trunks and were like plaited wooden ladders into the leafy canopy. Climbing them was strictly forbidden and punishable by being 'sent to the Office' for 'six of the best.' Sometimes these canings took place on parade, in the nature of public executions, as a warning to other miscreants. The boys would hold their hands out at their sides, set their faces stonily, and take pride in bearing up, even when Mr. Bonham raised himself on his toes, the better to swish the cane down harder. They never cried. That was the code. To the watchers there was a sort of awful excitement about the performance. The one thing we all learned was that grown-ups were capable of being cruel and spiteful and it was best to be always on your guard with them.

The best girls' game was making cubby-houses with the fallen red, brown and gold leaves of the Moreton Bay fig-trees, raking them with the sides of their feet into squares and rectangles, pronouncing importantly, 'This must be the kitchen. And this must be the dining-room', parting the leaves to create doorways until a complete house was mapped out. Then the game could begin. 'You must be the father coming home from work. And I must be the mother.' Lesser individuals would be told, 'You must be my little girl', or 'You must be the baby'. The baby knew what was expected. It cried. A lot of smacking went on. Bad children were stood in corners of rooms or were sent to bed without any tea. They cried too. It was very intense.

I would squeeze myself within a hidey-hole of the gnarled fig-tree roots and gaze on enviously. No-one asked me to play. I was not to know the protocol of asking, 'Who owns the game?' and 'Can I play?' It is not easy to come to a school late in the year when everyone has decided who is their friend and who isn't. It is the hardest thing in the world to be one of the Who Isn'ts. It doesn't help that some confident and busy 'mother' glances in your direction and says,

'Stare, stare, like a bear'

or

I made you look, I made you stare,
I made the barber cut your hair!

and, with a forward thrust of her chin for emphasis, sticks out her tongue before continuing busily with her housewifely duties.

These important little girls were frightening because they had power which they didn't hesitate to use. In the play-shed one of them ran into me accidentally, dropping the cream-bun in her hand. We both stared in consternation at the bun, upended in its own jammy creaminess on the asphalt, before, almost spitting in my face, she cried 'I'm telling on you!' and marched in the direction of the Staff Room. I was not to know that the appropriate response was to spit back.

Telltale tit!
Your tongue shall be split!
And all the little puppy dogs
Shall have a little bit!

Lacking knowledge of this play-ground protocol I was overcome with terror, imagining all the teachers pushing back their chairs, getting to their feet and marching down the steps in solid ranks to wreak vengeance upon me. I ran to the nearest garden bed, squeezed in behind a brown shrub and pressed myself flat to the brick wall until the bell had gone.

Then there were the toilets. I had never used a flush-toilet before. At Stainburn we'd had a pit-latrine about twenty feet deep with a boxed seat perched on railway sleepers across the top. I was used to the scorpions that lurked around it and to checking for red-backs under the seat, but I could not get used to the fat green frog known to live in the girls' toilets at Central School. Sometimes one of its transparent pink hands could be seen clinging beneath the rim. The little girls made a game of pulling the chain for the fun of seeing it swim frantically against the onrush of water to drag its fat body back to its hiding place. At this, they would scream and rush from the toilets in a mass, only to do the same thing again a minute or two later. I thought that if I made myself join in the torment perhaps they would like me. I did, but my screams were more real than pretending. I was horrified by the frog's predicament. And it made no difference whether I screamed or not; wearying of the game, they went off in little groups arms entwined, sharing out pink musk sticks bought at the little shop across the road for four a penny, while I stood and watched.

It seemed to me that the secret might lie in having money to spend at the shop. I tried to wheedle a penny from Mum. I was told briskly, 'Money doesn't grow on trees, you know!' and, 'Lollies are bad for your teeth.' Barry and I were not allowed to buy our lunch on Fridays, when a horse-drawn pie-cart parked at the school gate, chimney-pot smoking cheerily, horse asleep between the shafts, head drooping. Threepence bought not only a pie topped with a slathering of mushy peas but a tiny ice-cream in a cone as well. It was a banquet, but Mum said you never knew what was in the pies and whether the people who made them had ever washed their hands or not. Raisin sandwiches from home were far better for us.

Barry and I had started going to the North Ward Methodist Sunday School with Ronnie Quelch. We were always given a penny each to put in the plate. At a certain point of the proceedings the whole Sunday School, standing in a circle, sang,

'Hear the pennies dropping;
listen while they fall,
Every one for Jesus,
He shall have them all...'

while the Collection was taken. I had come to the decision that next Sunday Jesus would have to do without. If he was God's son he could have lots of pennies any time he wanted and I needed one badly myself. So just this one time I would hold out my hand over the plate but not let the penny drop. But, suddenly, out of the blue, wealth was mine.

During the long and lonely Big Lunches I wandered around under the Moreton Bay fig-trees, trying to look as though it was my own choice not to be playing any of the games. The strategy I had developed was to proceed, as though intent on serious matters, from one Moreton Bay fig-tree to another until the bell went and that was half the day over and done with. One day, hidden among the bronze and gold of the fallen leaves, I spotted a dusty handkerchief. My eyes brightened. I knew the protocol for lost handkerchiefs. Finders held them up over the verandah rail on Parade at the end of Big Lunch to be claimed by their owners. I had been awed at the bold daring of these handkerchief-finders, so calm and self-assured, while the rest of the school squinnied their eyes to see. Now, here was my chance for similar importance! I snatched the hanky up. But! What was this! Something tied in one corner. Something round and flat. A penny!

Glancing nervously, to see if anyone had noticed my discovery and was intent on shouldering in on it, I withdrew to the safety of the fig-tree roots. To find a handkerchief was consequential. To find one with money tied in the corner was momentous. I picked at the knot. The penny, brown, sun-warm, weighty with potential, lay in the palm of my hand. I felt a rush of pleasure at the sense of significance it gave me. I, the possessor of a penny! Well, almost the possessor. It was me who had found it. It was mine until the bell went. If it hadn't been for me it would still be lying lost among the leaves. It may have lain there for days. Maybe weeks! Perhaps whoever had lost it had given up even thinking about it? Perhaps they didn't even care? Perhaps they no longer needed it? If they didn't care and didn't need it, why shouldn't it be mine?

I had never heard of *Finders keepers; losers weepers*, but within a very short space of time I had convinced myself that this was so. With great care, I poked the corner of the handkerchief into a crevice of the fig-tree roots and continued poking until the whole handkerchief had disappeared from sight. Then with studied casualness I strolled out from my hiding-place, glanced carelessly around and sauntered without haste but with great determination in the direction of the little shop.

The trouble with good luck is that it seems to come in dollops. Just outside the shop was a group of small girls, heads together, deeply absorbed. They were unwrapping, with looks of anticipation, lollies known as Lucky Lamp-posts. The people at the shop made these small cones of toffee on a stick, wrapped in greaseproof paper. One in hundreds had a silver threepenny-bit embedded in it. At a penny each, Lucky Lamp-posts were a good investment, for even if you didn't get the wonderful threepence, and nobody really expected to, you still had the toffee. Ignoring me, the group of small girls found that they had no marvellous threepenny piece in theirs. Throwing their lolly-papers down carelessly they sauntered off, sliding their lips down their cones of toffee luxuriously.

I went into the shop, slid my penny across the counter and whispered, 'A Lucky Lamp-post, please.' The man took the glass stopper out of the jar, fished round with his hand, drew one out and gave it to me. I took it outside and slowly, pleasurably, but without any real expectation, began to unroll the paper. Then I stared, incredulously. There, embedded within the toffee, seeming to float in the golden heart of it, slightly tilted so that it caught and shone in the light, was a silver threepence! The magic of it was, of course, you had to suck the toffee first to get at the threepence, and even then it yielded only slowly like a reverse Cheshire Cat; first the silver rim, then the half and finally, when all the toffee was licked away and you were sated with sweetness, there was the moment of feeling the threepenny-bit wiggling on the tip of your tongue.

This wealth was soon transformed into four pink Musk Sticks, four Black Cats and a packet of Sherbert Powder to be sucked through a licorice straw, the most intriguing part being that you could then eat the straw itself. None of this brought me the friend I was longing to have but in the midst of the cold-shouldering and the face-pulling, I was strengthened by the secret knowledge that I also had had my hour. The four Black Cats proved too appealing to have their heads bitten off and chewed. They took up residence in an empty Wax Vestas tin under my desk, each swaddled, baby-like, in a scrap of cloth torn from the corner of my slate-rag. They lived to a ripe and mouldy old age and were a great comfort to my lonely heart. I didn't dare take them out to look them, but just knowing they were there was a help.

One day, Miss Marron called me to her side at the table. She smelt pleasantly of Cashmere Bouquet soap and talc and was busily compiling a list of names. 'Now, Dear. Your father is in the army, isn't he?' I nodded. I still had not launched into actual speech with teachers. 'What rank is he?' she said. I stared, owl-like. I tried hard to think what 'rank' meant. I knew Dad came from London, and could sing *Any Old Iron*. I knew he could make Mum mad by grabbing her by the waist and doing, *Knees Up, Mother Brown* around the kitchen table, or singing *Boiled beef and carrots!* I knew that in

'That's the stuff for your Darby Kell; Makes you fit and keeps you well...'

'Darby Kell' meant 'belly', which was 'common' and never to be spoken. I knew Dad could crutch sheep and mend our shoes, but I did not know what 'rank' meant.

Miss Marron persisted gently. 'Is he perhaps a sergeant? No? A lieutenant? What then?' I remembered the two stripes on Dad's sleeve. I could not remember what they meant. Head down, studying my shoes, I whispered, 'It starts with 'c',' making the 'c' like a little cough. Miss Marron looked impressed.

'Do you mean 'colonel'? she said. I hesitated. That sounded nearly right. I wasn't sure, but at least it started with 'c like a little cough'. I was in no position to ask if there were any other ranks within the armed services which started with 'c like a cough'. That would keep Miss Marron waiting. 'Colonel' sounded nearly right. I nodded. Miss Marron wrote something in her book and I went back to my seat.

After that I somehow seemed to be in the ascendancy. We had a spelling test, 'pin', 'pet', 'peg', 'pat' and 'pan', and although I hadn't really got 'five out of five', as the others had, Miss Marron pinned a little ribbon to which was attached a tiny Scottie dog to my tunic. My spelling really did improve then, though I still regarded as interchangeable 'd drags a drum' and 'b like a bat and ball' and gave 'm like a much wider bridge' an extra pothook just to be on the safe side.

On Friday afternoons, just before last bell, the big tin in which boiled lollies were kept was brought down from the top of the press and passed from row to row. You were allowed to peer in for a moment at the lollies, candy-striped pink or purple, in a sugary conglomerate in the bottom of the tin, before you thrust in your hand and plucked one out. When it was my turn, a pink and a purple one came out, stuck together. 'That's all right, Dear. You have them,' said kind Miss Marron. Others were made to put one back.

Mum was far from pleased about this when I told her. 'Oh! Think of the germs! To say nothing of your teeth! Boiled lollies! They're the worst in the world for the enamel! You are not to take one in future. Do you hear! Tell Miss Marron, 'Thank you, but I am not allowed to eat sweets.' Humbly I agreed. I had heard. The following Friday, Miss Marron took a wooden ruler and jabbed it up and down in the tin to break the lollies apart. When it went round I dipped my hand in. The lollies were more than lollies. They were a symbol, not only of respite from the week's toil, but of fellowship, of belonging. I dared not distance myself from the moment of sharing.

'She'll smell your breath!' Barry warned as we trudged home. 'Here! You'd better wash your mouth out.' There was a brass tap on the curb at Short's Corner, opposite the hospital. He held my school-bag while I cupped my hand under it, letting the purifying water stream into my mouth. 'Here, now! Gis a gig.' Which meant 'Let me look.' Barry, aware of the need to disassociate himself as speedily as possible from the precise English spoken at home, was giving himself a crash-course in Central School slang. He checked my face for tell-tale pinkness of lips and tongue. 'You'll do. With a push. Only, make sure you look hang-dog like usual. If you look too chirpy she'll be on to you like a ton of bricks!' I was reassured by his interest. It is comforting to have an ally.

Every afternoon, as soon as we got home from school, we walked with Ronnie Quelch to the beach. Sometimes we stopped to watch a tractor at work in the sand-dunes, dragging a line of wagons filled with sand along a little railway line from the dunes to fill in an area of swamp. At the end of the line the driver would jump down, throwing the lever of each wagon as he trudged along the line. The sand would already be tipping before we heard the 'Clunk! Clunk! Clunk!'

At Kissing Point baths there was always a throng of children bobbing up and down at the water's edge in the shark-proof enclosure. I had got to the stage where I could bravely stand waist-deep and jump up and down with the waves, bobbing down sometimes to my chin to pretend to be swimming. I kept a wary eye open for the seaweed that drifted in the waves like wet scarves, dreading the thought of being touched by it.

One afternoon the waves were rougher than usual, running like surf. One, larger than the rest, rose like a tawny wall, swooshed me up, turned me upside down and dumped me in a swirl of sand and foam at the water's edge. Open-mouthed with fright and discomposure I wailed loudly.

In a moment a motherly arm slid about me and a towel was wrapped around my shoulders. 'Don't cry, Little Girl,' said a voice. To my surprise, it was not a grown-up but another little girl, not much older than I was. Chattering away happily, this motherly little person set about wiping the tears from my eyes, the sand from my ears, my hair, my mouth and my nostrils. As she patted and comforted she told me about her five brothers. 'The baby's Geoffrey,' she said. 'Ánd the next one up is Kelvin. Then there's Colin and then John. The biggest is Max. He's the oldest and I come after him.' She pointed, 'That's Max, there, in the canoe.' It was the important boy who rang the bell at school. 'And my name is Shirley. Shirley Ackland. What's yours?' My heart swelled. I knew that at last I had found a friend.

Chapter 2

BY SAND AND SEA: 1940

'Little Sir Echo, how do you do. Hello! Hello!'

Beach Convolvulus, The Strand

The Ackland boys told Barry they would help him make a canoe. All he would need was a sheet of corrugated roofing-iron and an IXL jam box. Barry didn't have a sheet of roofing-iron. But there was an old chook-house down the end of the back yard. He edged in behind it and gave an experimental tug at one of the sheets of iron. It could have been said to be a little loose and, rather like wiggling a tooth, he kept at it until finally it yielded and fell off of its own accord. Almost.

To get the jam-case it was necessary to approach Mr. Coates at the store and ask politely if there were any jobs he wanted done. Not that Mr. Coates was short of jam cases. Melon-and-Lemon jam was his best selling line. He just liked a show of appreciation. Barry got off lightly. There was no fowl-feed to be humped in from the shed, so he was put to pumping kerosene from a four-gallon drum into empty beer bottles for primus-stoves and hurricane-lamps. When he was finished, Mr. Coates shrugged his head at the back door and said, 'Go on then! Get one off the heap at the back.'

To make the canoe the first thing was to flatten the iron by banging out the corrugations, a pleasurably noisy task at which the boys got busy under the tamarind tree up the back of Acklands' place in Mitchell Street. This was not strictly necessary, but Max said canoes with flat iron looked more professional. The next step was to knock out both ends of the jam case. One end was used for the back, called the stern, and a length split off the other for the pointy end, called the bow. Little Colin was given the job of hammering bent nails back into shape for re-use, squatting industriously over an old brick. Then the sheet of iron was bent into position around the rectangular piece of board and nailed into position. 'You've got to go easy with the nailing, or else the wood splits,' Max told Barry. Then, with crackling thundery sounds, and with everyone talking at once, the other end of the iron was bent over and nailed into position on the thick stick of pine. The whole thing began to look like a canoe.

The most pleasurable part of the job was tarring the nail-holes in the iron and the gaps at the pointy end and the stern. To get the tar all that was necessary if the day was hot enough was to excavate some out from the edges of the narrow strip of bitumen down the middle of Eyre Street. You got tar on your clothes and were in for a big rousing-at at home, of course, but that was a worry for some other time. Now was the time to admire the water-tight canoe.

'So what are you going to call her?' asked Max. The Ackland's was the *Ark Royal*, after the newest aircraft carrier in the British fleet, known to be unsinkable. 'What about *Invincible*?' suggested John.

But Barry had already thought of the name he wanted. The newest ship in the Australian navy was the *Arunta*, a Tribal Class destroyer. 'Mine's going to be the *Arunta* he said. Max looked at him approvingly. They found some green paint in the shed for him to paint the name across on the stern, and as there was still a little paint left, on either side of the pointy-end. They all stood back and admired their combined handiwork. Once it was dry and the tar had set, hard and shiny, the *Arunta* was carried to the Kissing Point Baths for sea trials. Now the proud owner of his own canoe Barry practised hard at getting his balance and leaning forward to paddle with his hands, sometimes even kneeling upright in the sloshy bottom for greater speed. *Arunta* joined the Kissing Point Fleet and was soon taking part in daring sea-battles involving many head-on rammings, broad-sidings and sinkings.

Meanwhile, I was teaching myself to swim. One foot on the bottom for safety's sake, I wriggled parallel to the beach, chin high like a retriever, grabbing at the water with my hands and keeping a wary eye open for seaweed. If I spotted sea-weed drifting in the tawny lifting waves I squealed and ran out on to the beach, hugging my arms around myself in abhorrence.

But now I began to feel pangs of jealousy at being ignored by Barry for so long. We had always just been just us. Now he was always with the Ackland boys. He took no notice of me at all. It wasn't fair. One afternoon I ran to the beached canoe, scrambled in, and clinging to the sides, refused to budge, demanding 'Give me a turn!' Barry would have liked to tip me out bodily, but he thought better of it, knowing the Ackland boys were nice to Shirley.

If he had found some sea-weed and draped it on me it would have sent me running. An empty crab-shell down the back of my togs would have had the same effect. Instead, running the canoe into the water and giving it a mighty shove, he snarled, 'Alright then! Have a turn! And serves yourself right if you get drownded!' Aggravation gave him added strength, and my skinny personage the canoe more buoyancy. It shot across the surface of the swimming enclosure like an arrow, far out into the deep water. Rigid with fright, I gripped the sides and hardly dared to breathe. I knew that canoes turned turtle, dumping their occupants in an instant. The water on either side was green and deep. I saw it only from the corner of my eye, not daring to turn my head the least fraction. I was aware of water slurping along the sides. I willed myself, 'Don't move! Don't move your eyes!' The momentum of the canoe carried it to the paper-bark palings of the shark-proof fence. It bumped and nudged against them for a few minutes before beginning to drift slowly towards the beach, backwards, to bump, at last, on to the familiar sand.

Furious with fright and lost dignity, I unscrambled my skinny legs and escaped to the safety of high, dry sand. I shrilled, 'I'm telling on you! You're getting into trouble!' Wrapping my threadbare towel around me, I stamped, queenly with outraged dignity and thirsting for terrible vengeance, up the beach towards home.

Barry, already scared-looking, now became satisfyingly alarmed. 'Into trouble' meant Dad's razor-strop. It hung in the bathroom; an ever-present reminder against the folly of bad behaviour. It meant, when Dad got home, into the bathroom with him, trousers down, and a good belting. To say nothing of what would become of the *Arunta* and where the sheet of iron that had gone into her construction had come from in the first place.

There are few things in life that are harder to endure than being the bearer of tidings of great import and being pipped at the post by tidings of even greater import. Mum and Dad never did get to hear of my near-death-by-drowning at the hands of my brother. For, hard on my heels, so hard that he was panting, the sister-drowner himself arrived, breathless with News. It was news that would be the headline of next day's *Townsville Bulletin*;

SCHOOLBOYS STUNG BY JELLY-FISH. SERIOUS CONDITION.

Gaspingly, all was told; Max Ackland and Brucie Thomas! Stung bad by Portuguese men o'war! Real bad! Racing down the beach! Dived in! Right on top of them! Screamed and yelled! Rolled on the beach to get the stingers off! Grown-ups rubbed sand on them! Man yelled, 'Get the ambulance!' John went! Grabbed someone's bike! Raced to Coates' Store! Coatesy never charged tuppence to ring on the phone, neither. Done it for free! Ambulance come! Took Brucie on a stretcher! To hospital! Unconscious! Eyes rolling! Like this! (appropriate eye-rollings) Maybe he'd die. Everyone said he was gonna die! Kid died last year by a stinger! It'd be Brucie this year. For certs! Everyone reckoned! Couldn't get stung as bad as that and not be dead! Maxie was stings all over. Maybe he wouldn't die, but! The lady from the C.W.A huts had got him hot tea. He was a bit OK. They made him just sit in the back of the ambulance on the floor. With a blanket round him. The ambulance was ringing a bell when it left!

Hearing all this, I had the good sense to know my cause was lost. Being nearly drownded in the canoe couldn't compete with ambulance bells and crowds of horrified onlookers. It did not help to realize that the electrifying effect of Barry's account was powered by the fright he was in at the thought of having nearly drownded me. Either that or the hiding he would have got if he had. Nor did it help to realize that I had missed all these beach dramatics myself.

After a day or two Max recovered from the worst of the jelly-fish attack but the red criss-cross pattern of the stings on his arms, neck and chest could still be seen a week later. Bruce was in hospital for two weeks. For a while no-one wanted to swim in the shark-enclosure, preferring the rock-pool at the point. But the rock-pool was just a natural crevice in the rocks with a bit of concrete across one end. You couldn't swim in it; just sit in the water up to your chin to cool off, although Mum had told Barry and me not to, saying 'Supposing someone has done wees in it! You wouldn't want to be sitting in someone's wee, would you!' We agreed that, No we wouldn't want to sit in someone's wee. But still we went to the rock-pool with everyone else to cool off. You couldn't not do what all the others were doing. You had to be the same. Wee and all. We probably added a wee or two of our own.

But, on the beach, every time anyone saw the blue-bottle floats of Portuguese men o'war stranded in the dry seaweed along the tide-line, the boys kicked sand on them and squashed the blue floats with their big toes and made them pop.

There would also be kidney-shaped jelly-blubbers, like sandy half-moons, which drifted ashore. They were the egg-sacks of the sea-snails that left scribbly secret messages on the damp sand. Each jelly-blubber contained thousands of eggs which you could see if you held them up against the light. The boys used the jelly-blubbers as ammunition to pelt one another.

Sometimes, there were cowries, and cats' eyes of emerald and tawny gold, which were really the stopper-valves of curly shells, but seemed like jewels glinting among the dried seaweed. There were often long, transparent Chinese fingernail shells which Shirley and I tried to fit on our fingers. Shirley told me that Chinese princesses had such fingernails to show they did not have to do the washing-up.

The beach was littered with pumice-stone which Max said came from volcanoes out at sea, and if the boys saw a stranded coconut that had floated down from the Palm Islands in the north they raced to pick it up. If it made a sloshing sound when they shook it there would be milk in it and it was taken home to be cut open with the axe on the wood-heap. And crab shells that had legs and eyes weren't dead crabs, Max said, but the overcoat a crab had grown out of and thrown away, like snakes growing out of their skins. Max knew everything. He was going to be a doctor.

At low tide the edges of the pools around the rocks of Kissing Point were little worlds of their own, rimmed with salt. In them nobbly mulberry whelks sat on their prey to drill a hole through their shells. Whelks would eat all the barnacles but not limpets because limpets would not sit still while a hole was drilled through their roof. For this reason a cunning barnacle sometimes built its shell on a limpet to escape being eaten. I took some of the neatly drilled dry shells home to please Mum. She made milk-jug covers by sewing them around the edge of her crochet work.

In the deeper parts of the pools, sea-urchins clustered like spiky golliwogs. There were also brittle-stars whose arms broke away if you picked them up and silky smooth pieces of driftwood speckled with toredo worm holes.

Stonefish were something to be really scared of. You tried not to stand on anything that might be one. Stonefish lay so still among the rocks that barnacles and weeds grew on them. You could never have told one from a stone and yet they could kill you if you stood on their spiney back. 'The only cure is to put your foot in boiling-hot water,' said Max, the doctor.

Sea-slugs, which looked like oozy cucumbers on the bottoms of the pools, squirted black ink if you prodded them. Max said, 'The Chinese eat them. They make soup out of them. They call them sea-cucumbers. But the proper name is beche-de-mer. They dry them out first and then make them into soup!' I thought of Mum's pumpkin soup and was glad she didn't know about sea-slugs.

Half-way round the point was a huge slab of rock which had slipped from the cliff above and lay like a slice of toast against the rock-face. The sensible thing would have been to wade around it on the outside but to the Acklands it represented a challenge. The Acklands believed that life was made not only for cheerfulness but for never missing a chance to do something interesting and adventurous. You had not to mind that if the rock slipped you would be squashed to death. You could not let on that you were scared to death. The good opinion of the Acklands, especially Max, was the most important thing in the world. So you had to lie on your back against the main rock and slide and wriggle sideways with the other rock an inch above your nose until at last you squeezed through out into the open at the other end and could see the blue sky again.

Beyond Kissing Point was Rowe's Bay where, at low tide, tawny sandbars, ripple-ribbed like the roof of a dog's mouth and interlaced with shallow channels of shining warm water, stretched for miles towards the pale-blue Palm Islands in the north. Silver-gulls rested in flocks, and dotterels and sand-pipers trotted about briskly, their mottled-brown babies running after them begging for food.

A fish trap like a long untidy fence, built of mangrove saplings and bits of railway line, stretched out into the bay. At high tide it was almost covered; at low tide we could splash out to peer through the rusty wire-netting of the box-trap. There was always something alarming sloshing in the hot shallow water inside; a small shark with beady eyes, a toad-fish puffing itself up, or a couple of sting-rays, thin tails swishing.

At afternoon's end we would trail home around the rocks, thirsty and tired, Shirley encouraging Colin and me, 'It won't be long now! We're nearly there!' But the Ackland boys would take to the water and swim back around the point. Our feet burning on the rocks, snicked by oyster shells, our faces scarlet, we would see them out at sea, their arms rising and falling amidst the coolness of the waves, with never a thought of prowling sharks in their heads.

Little by little, Barry and I began to forget Stainburn and our life out west. I even had a new cat, christened Smoky, a present from the Quelches next door. We began to feel that we belonged in North Ward, to the sea and Central School. With the other children we set out every morning along Eyre Street, gathering others in ones and twos as we went, so that by the time we arrived at school a sizeable group would have formed. Important matters were discussed; someone had squinnied their eye to the cracks in the paling fence around the Lunatic Asylum in Gregory Street and seen them walking around inside; someone's dad had shot three sea-eagles stealing fish from his fish-trap; someone's big brother had been rowing a flattie in Ross Creek and had a bit bited clean out of the oar by a shark; someone else's brother had sailed for the Middle East with the Second AIF. The boy had turned the side of his school hat up like a Digger's. It wasn't long before every boy's hat was turned up on the side.

Sundays were for Sunday school, or maybe picnics. You rode to the Botanic Gardens or Anzac Park on a cushion strapped to the carrier of Mum's bike while Barry rode on the bar of Dad's. Anzac Park meant sliding out along the barrels of the big cannons that had been brought home as souvenirs from the Great War, their barrels polished to a high sheen by the children that had slid along them over the years.

Near Anzac Park, there was a concrete enclosure known as the swimming basin, which was pumped out once a week and then filled again with sea-water so that Townsville people could swim without having to worry about sharks and stingers. It was always full of happily-squealing people enjoying themselves. Mum wouldn't hear of us swimming in it. Heaven only knew what you might catch!

Sometimes, but not often, for it was two and six for adults and half price for children, we went to Magnetic Island, seven miles across the bay, on either the *Melita* or the *Malanda*, to either Picnic Bay or Arcadia. Those who went to one soon became sure that it was superior to the other and grew fierce on the subject.

Going to Arcadia was a journey into paradise. When the boat pulled in at the jetty it leaned to one side as everyone crowded to get off. The wash of the boat slurped among the smooth boulders. Through the cracks between the planks of the jetty, antler coral could be seen in the crystal-clear water. Then came the walk along the track to the beach, everyone with baskets and thermos flasks and rugs to sit on. There was a natural arch where a huge boulder rested across two smaller ones. I wished Mum would not insist that Barry and I pose underneath it for a photo to send to Grandma and Grand-dad Greenleaf in England.

The beach shone, blue and white between headlands covered with pine trees and round boulders stacked like magic castles. Hidden away among the pines and the boulders, the Quelches had a holiday shack of corrugated iron with shutter-windows that pushed out on sticks. Ronnie, Barry and I raced down the hot sandy track to the beach, the air filled with the shrilling of cicadas and the screech of parrots. The water was bright and clear and there were no sharks because a shark-proof fence was strung from one headland to the other on a long steel cable. In the late afternoon the boat gave a long hoot which echoed round the mountain. It was a warning to stragglers on the track back to the jetty to stretch their legs or be left behind. Then came the heavy-eyed journey back across the bay to Ross Creek, the decks of the boat loaded with cases of sweet-smelling pineapples from Horseshoe Bay, into the setting sun and the everyday world.

Ronnie's father worked in the shipping department of Samuel Allens, the big trading firm. He was very gentlemanly. One afternoon he called out to Mum over the fence, 'Mrs. Stilwell! There is going to be a cyclone! My wife feels it might be better if you brought the children over to our place for the night. You would be more than welcome.' They knew Dad was away, helping to establish a new training camp at Miowera, outside Bowen.

But Mum would never show fear. After thirteen years of outback life in Australia she felt equal to anything. On the Dawson Valley farm, living in a tent home, she had often had to hold the ridge-pole at night to stop it blowing away while Dad was away at the dry block with cattle. She was expecting me at the time, so I had come into the world with deep misgivings about storms.

Once, at Stainburn, we had a freak wind-storm, just as we were sitting down to Barry's ninth birthday-tea. The roof of the house had gone whirling away into the darkness. Mum had grabbed us and we had run to shelter in the storeroom, crouching among drums of flour and sugar and bags of potatoes as the rain thundered down. In the morning where the roof had been, a few rafters spiked with rusty nails hung uneasily against the bright blue sky. The birthday cake with 'Happy Birthday Barry' was still sitting the middle of the dining-room table, but the white icing had sunk in the middle and a pool had formed in it. Dad had been away with the sheep that time.

So Mum felt she knew about storms. She told Uncle Les, 'Thank you, but if the worst comes to the worst we will shelter under the big double bed.' The Quelches were now friends whom Barry and I had been told to call Auntie Elsie and Uncle Les. That made Ronnie like a cousin, even though he secretly gave me Chinese burns and horse-bites on my arms when grown-ups weren't looking. Grown-ups always thought Ronnie was such a good little boy; 'such a little gentleman!' He was fussed over by Auntie Elsie because his brother and sister were both grown-up. His brother, Noel, had joined the navy.

So, on the night before the cyclone we stood at the railings of the back verandah and watched the iron-grey clouds lumbering in from the sea. The air was still. Not a bird could be seen or heard. Then a little wisp of wind got up and flicked at the tops of the trees, died again then came back with renewed force, each surge more powerful than the one before it. A few slight branches snapped from trees and went whirling away.

My terror of storms began to get the better of me. Mum said 'Don't be silly! Think of the little girls in England being evacuated from German air-raids and having to carry their own gas-masks, yet still showing British pluck. I won't have you being silly over a bit of wind!'

The time when Barry and I had been in St George's Home for Orphans was never talked about; it was a too terrible. So I could not tell Mum there had been a storm during which I had tried to run to the Boys' House to be with Barry. The clouds had mounted up just like this. All the girls of the Girls' House had been gathered in the doorway watching the storm coming. Suddenly I knew I would only be safe if I could get to Barry. I broke away from the big girls and ran. The wind scooped me up and swept me to the edge of a precipice. Probably the precipice was only a deep gully but it seemed like a precipice. At the very last moment one of the big boys from the Boys' House rushed down, grabbed me up in his arms and staggered with me to safety. For this I got a good smacking from Matron but it did not cure my fear of storms.

But now, Mum went to make sure all the louvres along the verandah were locked. 'Cheer up, Face Ache' said Barry. 'You look like a dying duck in a thunderstorm' That was one of Dad's sayings. I knew Barry was only using it to act big. As the storm worsened Mum made us drag our mattresses and bedding into the lounge and made a sort of nest with them. That was snugly and comforting. Barry had his *Robin Hood* book and I had my koala that had a zippy-place in the back to put a comb and a handkerchief, and Smokey the cat, who tried to get out of my arms and under the blanket.

Underneath our flat was a third flat, partially below ground. The young wife of a private at the Kissing Point barracks lived there with her baby. During the night as the storm raged Mum read to me from *Alice in Wonderland*, which I always found horrifying – the bit about falling and falling down a hole. How terrible! And swimming in your own tears! Disgusting! It was all too awful but it was nice to have Mum all to myself for a change and so while she read I snuggled up to her for comfort, which gave her the impression that I loved the story so that she read it again and again. But suddenly, the lights went out. Next we heard a desperate knocking at the back door. It was the lady from downstairs with her baby wrapped in an army greatcoat. She gasped that water was flooding into her flat 'like a waterfall'. Mum was good in emergencies. She dragged the young mother in from the downpour, dried her off, helped settle the baby down, and got the primus going to make tea.

The worst of the blow came just before daybreak. I'd been asleep but the noise woke me. The wind screamed as though determined to get at us. The house trembled and from time to time shook and swayed. It was reassuring to see Mum get out the four-sided rack on which she made toast, prick the primus, pump it to life and calmly begin to slice a loaf of bread. Occasionally she turned her head to listen as heavy objects slammed against the walls, and the roof creaked and groaned.

In the morning we woke to a watery world. The clump of banana-trees in the back-yard had been flattened. The chook-shed had gone. The road was littered with broken branches and sheets of corrugated iron. The electric light lines sagged in loops along the street. Some of the poles leaned sideways or were broken off. The gutters swirled like flooded creeks, turning Eyre Street into a lake. Before long some of the local boys had their canoes out and were paddling around. Mum had heard of children being sucked into storm-water drains and drowned. She told Barry he could not take his canoe onto the little lake.

'It's OK, Mum!' he told her. 'I sank her on purpose at the baths. Maxie said to.' A lot of boys did this rather than carry their canoes home each afternoon.

The air was full of the roar of the sea and soon we were hurrying towards the beach. As we topped the sandy rise we found everyone grouped in awe. The whole sweep of the bay was a tawny mass of tumbled water. Waves reared like black caves before crashing on to the beach, sending sheets of spray flying. Brown loaves of foam broke off and sailed through the air to flop on to the gardens and rooftops. The shark-proof swimming enclosure had disappeared, leaving only a couple of piles amidst the pounding surf. Barry was glum. '*Arunta* has had it!' he said, giving the sand a savage kick. Beyond the beach the dunes were flattened and eroded into strange gullies, cliffs and canyons. The trunk of a large tree was wedged into where the rock pool had been; the cement wall had been smashed. We hunched ourselves as spray and sand whipped at our legs. In zig-zag fashion, running to avoid the sheets of spray and the surge of unusually high waves, we set off around the bay, amazed at the damage.

Many houses had lost their roofing-iron. Trees lay uprooted. A torrent rushing out of Honeymoon Lane had carved a deep gully across the beach. The Sea View baths had disappeared. They had been privately owned, with living accommodation, but nothing remained except a stove and a refrigerator half buried in the sand, over which the waves swirled. Timber and roofing-iron were scattered along the beach.

Anzac Park was a mess of uprooted trees and sand. The dunes had eroded. The concrete sea-wall had disappeared and the steps down to the beach were now far out in the waves. A big Moreton Bay fig-tree lay capsized, its spreading roots high in the air. Barry and Ronnie climbed through the prostrate branches. The swinging-boats were buried deep under the sand. Of the purple and pink bouganvilleas that had covered the cliffs not a leaf remained.

At school next day all the talk was of the cyclone; where each family had sheltered, how many sheets of iron had been blown from their roof, whose 'dunny-house' had been blown over. (But in our house we did not say 'dunny'. We said 'Little House'.)

By far the most gripping item was that a lady in Cook Street had been killed. The brick chimney of her house had collapsed upon her while she was making a cup of tea. Andy Sugden knew all about it. 'Yeah! Mrs. Halliday, it was! Me Mum and her, they was friends. Mrs. Halliday, she was making a cup of tea when the whole lot comed down on toppa 'er! A big hunk of iron offa the bus sheds, that's what done it. It blewed clean into the chimbley and brung it down!' Andy was making the most of his moment of glory. 'Her son Kennie, he runned over t'our place and banged on the door. Me Dad and him, they nilly busted a gut to get the bricks offa her. But she was a goner.' I had been waiting my turn to tell about the flooded flat underneath our house but I knew it could not compete with a lady killed by a falling chimney.

Mum had told Barry and me many times to come straight home after school and not to dawdle, but that afternoon it was, of course, necessary to detour into Cook Street to look at the scene of so notable a tragedy. The house was a very ordinary low-set pumpkin-coloured one with a latticed verandah like all the others in Cook Street. There were lots of people staring at it, but there was nothing to show that someone had died a horrible death there. I imagined the lady's soul floating out of the kitchen window, past the mango tree on its way to heaven; how surprised it must have been, right in the middle of making a cup of tea. A gaping hole in the roof of the Bus Depot next door showed where the roofing-iron that had demolished the chimney had come from. At the back of the house we could just make out the pile of the rubble of the collapsed chimney.

But suddenly Barry said urgently, 'Come on! We've got the downstairs flat to get a squiz at yet. But don't you let on to Mum that we came round here. She'd fly off the handle.' I nodded. There were things you didn't tell.

Orange and green light from the coloured windows glimmered on the water in the flooded downstairs flat as Barry, Ronnie and I peered in. Cupboards stood open, contents spilling into the flood. The smell of wetness filled the air. The young mother and baby had fled.

Mum had helped her to rescue some of her things and she had gone off to catch the first train down south. Barry and Ronnie eased themselves into the water and began wading from room to room. After a moment's hesitation I cried 'Wait for me!' and followed, feeling the squidgy silt on the lino underfoot as we slish-sloshed around, peering at the evidence of the adult presence cut short; a teapot on the sink, a baby's rattle on the side-board and tooth-brushes in the bathroom. On the rail of the baby's cot a frog was asleep, its yellow throat ticking; another went breast-stroking towards the sofa, passing so close to me that I felt the water sway. In horror, I skidded and sloshed towards the door, wanting only to escape.

Mum had no sympathy for me. It served me right! We should not have gone into the flat in the first place. She had a good mind to give me a good slapping. But she was full of sympathy for the young mother and baby. They would have a difficult journey to the south. The Burdekin had risen twenty-two feet and the railway bridge had been swept away. All trains to the south had been re-routed around the west through Winton and Barcaldine. Mail was being brought to Townsville by the Magnetic Island launch. The Ross River was eleven feet over the dam wall. Uncle Les came over to tell us all this and to see what else could be saved for the young mother.

Barry could hardly wait to add, 'Yes! And do you know what? Doctor Fenton, the Flying Doctor, had to land on the new airstrip at Garbutt because the proper one at the river was flooded. And guess what? He had to stand on his seat when he landed the plane because a four foot brown snake had got into the cock-pit! He killed it with a hammer!' Barry had a gift for remembering odd and wonderful pieces of information and trotting them out at the right moment. He never forgot anything that he read or heard.

After the cyclone Dad bought a Philps' Mantlepiece wireless so that he and Mum could hear the news for themselves. When I announced at school that we owned a wireless, it was with the satisfying knowledge that having a wireless made my family special. Not many families had one.

Barry and I now hung on the edges of the dining-room chairs every afternoon (Barry! Don't swing on your chair! You'll break the legs! Barry!) while the Lone Ranger galloped into our lives on his trusty steed, Silver. Before long, Barry could not leap down the front steps, three at a time, as he did, without whacking himself like a horse and shouting, 'Hi Ho! Silver! Hi! Ho!'

Each time the wireless was switched on, there would be a pause while it warmed up. The News came on to the tune of *The British Grendiers*. There would be the chimes of Big Ben – 'Hear all ye lands; Big Ben still stands.' followed by the very English BBC announcer's voice, 'This is London calling.' It was more than our lives were worth for Barry or me so much as to squeak.

The news of the war in England grew worse and worse; of the nightly blitzes over London, the screaming bombs, the direct hits on streets of ordinary homes, the casualty figures, the evacuations of children to the country for safety. Mum worried about her family in London. Her brother's wife had a new baby girl called Sheila and their home in Kent was right under the flight path of the German Luftwaffe. There was talk about an evacuation of lots of soldiers on a beach at a place called Dunkirk. Dad said, 'The Old Country's having a tough time,' and patted Mum on the shoulder. Mum sat up straight and said, 'Britain can take it!' It was all happening a long way away but people knew Britain had won the First World War and would win this one too.

But I had a new a new worry of my own, more worrying than the war. It hung over me like a black cloud. We were supposed to start collecting for the Combined Sunday Schools'

Annual Picnic. You had to go from door to door up and down the street, knock on doors and ask people to make a donation. At Sunday School we had each been given a penny notebook and a pencil in which the amounts donated were to be written. We had to ask our parents for a tin to put the money in. Dad gave me a Capstan tobacco tin. I thought collecting money was a horrible idea. Why should people give us money? They might not have much. I didn't want to go on a Sunday School picnic, anyhow. Mum said I had to try. She gave me a penny to start my tin off. But after one 'Sorry Dear, I'm afraid I've got nothing to spare this week,'; one 'My Old Man's on the Relief'; two 'We're Catholics'; and a whiskery man who said he was a Calathumpian and couldn't give tuppence for religion, I shrank from any further 'going house to house', as the Superintendent at Sunday School said St Paul had told the disciples to. When I asked Dad what a Calathumpian was, he laughed and said he was a bit of a Calathumpian himself and, in future, to remember the old army advice, 'Never volunteer.'

The Acklands, however, went zestfully about the task and won prizes; *The Last of the Mohicans* and *Seven Little Australians*, for collecting the most Sunday School Picnic Day money.

On Sunday School Picnic day, dressed in our whites, we were piled on the backs of lorries and driven to Pallarenda where we competed against hundreds of children from the other Sunday Schools in Townsville, in three-legged races, wheelbarrow races, egg-and-spoon and sack races. North Ward was a small Sunday School but we won many events because we had the Acklands. In the three-legged race most people jogged along so awkwardly that they tripped one another up and ended up falling over and grazing knees that had to have hankies tied over them to keep the flies off. Not the Acklands. They had practised three-legged racing until they could go as fast with their legs tied as most people could on their own. In sack-racing they knew the trick was to jam your feet into the corners of the sack, grab it tightly under your armpits and run with your legs wide apart. They had practised egg-and-spoon with a china egg out of the chook-yard and for the wheelbarrow race the trick was for Colin to hold his legs so stiff that all Max had to do was to propel him along with his hands hardly touching the ground. Of course, they won!

Almost every race was won by a hugely-smiling Ackland. The Acklands did not believe in losing. Not if they could do something about it.

Dad's regiment was the Kennedy, Townsville's own garrison, based at Kissing Point. They often put on Patriotic Concerts at the Town Hall on Sunday nights. The band played and talented local people performed; a tenor singing Dad's favourite, *Trees*; a baritone, *The Floral Dance;* a basso-profundo, *Asleep in the Deep*. These were favourites that people were glad to hear again and again.

A popular item was always *On the Road to Mandalay*. Someone might recite *Gunga Din* by Rudyard Kipling and follow it up with an encore of *A Private of the Buffs*. A silver-haired lady was certain to sing *Dear Little Child, When You Kneel Down*, convincing me that I was not doing my bit for the brave fighting men who depended on my efforts for their safe return. The evening would finish with Community Singing, for which *Keep the Home Fires Burning* was sure to get people's voices warmed up. Townsville people enjoyed a good sing-a-long. At the end there would be prayers for the King and Royal Family and our fighting men overseas, and *God Save the King*, everyone standing to attention looking determined, the men with their shoulders back and their fists at their sides.

One Sunday night when we had just come home from the Battalion Concert, and Dad was away in camp, Barry said 'Mum, I feel a bit crook.' Mum said, 'Yes, Dear. But please don't say 'crook'. It sounds so common.' Barry looked as though he was thinking of something a long way off and threw up violently. Mum was a VAD in the Voluntary Aid Detachment and went every week to practise bandaging wounds and tying up broken arms. She knew how to take a temperature, giving the thermometer a good shake first to get the mercury down. She took Barry's temperature. It was a hundred and four. He also had a lump in his groin and an angry red streak running up the inside of his leg. It came from a scratch on the inside of his ankle which he had got when his foot slipped off the pedal of some kid's bike, the kind with a row of metal teeth. Now his ankle was swollen and hot to the touch.

The treatment for any kind of inflammation was Antiphlogestine, a poultice of grey paste 'wonderful for drawing'. It was scooped from a tin with a knife, like putty, spread on a bit of clean rag and then held over steam from the kettle to heat. 'The hotter the better!' it was said.

There was general agreement that it was better to err on the safe side; rather a bit too hot than not hot enough. The heat of the Antiphlogistine was always more excruciating than the original pain, the moment of application being accompanied by yells of anguish. Then the poultice was bandaged with strips torn off an old sheet.

Not long before, a little boy in my class at school, Barry Bell, had died after standing on a rusty nail in his backyard. The word had flown around that it had been 'lockjaw', dreaded because there was no cure. Once a sufferer's jaw had locked into place and a fixed smile come upon their features, their case was without hope. 'Lockjaw' was spoken about with fear; never called by its correct name, tetanus. There was no cure. After Barry Bell's death there was not a backyard in North Ward that was not given a thorough going over. Children could be seen at work raking and carting rubbish to be burned, while parents supervised grimly. Very few would have known the connection between 'lockjaw' and the household cows that were kept or the manure that many people went to the Town Common to collect for their vegetables.

Despite the Antiphlogestine treatment, Barry's condition grew worse. Mum changed the poultice hourly throughout the night and sponged him with tepid water to which vinegar had been added to bring his temperature down. His leg continued to swell. He began muttering about 'Stainburn' and 'killing-day' and butchering-knives being sharpened. Alarmed, Mum ran to Quelches' place and hammered on their door.

The Quelches had a telephone, one of very few in Townsville. They also had a friend who owned a Whippet tourer, who drove us, subdued and frightened, to the hospital. I sat on a hard form in the entrance hall of the hospital while Mum disappeared for hours, with only the picture of the King and Queen and the two little princesses in their Coronation robes for company.

When Mum returned she looked desperately worried. Barry had blood poisoning. He was so delirious that he no longer knew who she was. There was talk of having to amputate his leg; it could be either that or his life. Mum had been told to get her husband's permission for the operation, but the Quelches could not get through on their phone. The camp at Miowera was new and not yet connected by phone. In a raging fever, Barry lingered between life and death. When at last Mum got a message through to him, Dad would not give permission for the amputation.

Gradually Barry passed the crisis point and began to rally. He remained in hospital for weeks. At last he was well enough for his bed to be moved out on to the wide hospital verandah. Each morning on the way to Central I could look up and give him a little wave, but when taken to see him I was too shy to talk. He seemed like someone who had been on a long journey. To help pass the time, a Red Cross lady taught him how to knit. He knitted a complete outfit in brown and yellow for my doll.

Townsville Hospital before the war.

At last he came home from hospital but too frail and ill to walk along Eyre Street to school. To help him pass the time, the Quelches gave him the *The Lifebuoy Book of Hobbies*, filled with ideas of things to make. The boys in the illustrations wore shoes and socks and ties and had pally smiles, but Barry was not put off. He had none of the tack-hammers, fret-saws and smoothing-planes recommended, but could hardly wait to get started.

His very first attempt was a doll's house for me, made from four butter boxes. Of very light plywood with a wired lid, butter-boxes were almost perfect cubes and because they fitted together well, people got them from the grocery shop to use for storing food or clothes or as shelves. The diagram in *The Lifebouy Book of Hobbies* showed how to make a doll's house by joining four together, two up two down, and lining the walls of the rooms with newspaper. It said 'scraps of left-over wall-paper', but wallpaper was unknown in Townsville.

The furniture for the doll's house was made from matchboxes glued together. Mum was so glad to have Barry home and getting well again that she bought extra packets of matches and tipped them unused into a pickle bottle, so that he could have the empty boxes; the Quelches and Acklands saved theirs for him as well. Four match-boxes glued together with flour-and-water paste made an arm-chair, six made a settee, which were then covered with fabric. Mum had a scrap-bag into which she put all the left-over pieces from her sewing. Barry turned it out and chose a piece with a pattern of orange flowers. The effect was striking, especially as in real life we had only hard, sea-grass furniture which made marks on the backs of your legs when you sat on it. The most delightful thing about the match-box furniture was a duchess with proper drawers that pulled in and out. The handles were buttons sewn on, the mirror a piece of silver paper, carefully smoothed. The rooms had pretend windows with little bits of lace for curtains. Tiny pictures that Barry had drawn himself and made frames for, with cellophane for glass, were hanging on the walls. I had never seen anything so wonderful. It was the most beautiful doll's house in the world.

The Lifebuoy Book of Hobbies was a gold-mine of ideas. There was a fat-lamp made by putting sand in an empty jam-tin. A strip of twisted rag was embedded in the sand for a wick and melted dripping poured in. When the fat was set, Mum put all the lights out so that Barry could light the lamp in the middle of the kitchen table. It sputtered in a most satisfactory way. Mum said she had often used fat lamps on the farm at Theodore when they couldn't afford kerosene.

There were instructions for making a jam-tin telephone. All you needed were two empty jam tins and a length of fishing line. Dad had some green fishing lines wound on sticks which he kept tucked up in the rafters under the verandah. Barry was sure Dad wouldn't mind if he had a little borrow of one for a bit. All that was necessary was to punch a hole in the bottom of each tin, thread the line through and knot it on the inside. Then Ronnie took one jam-tin and Barry the other and stretched the line taut between them. If they spoke into the tin and then put the tin to their ear they could have a lively conversation.

'Hello?'
'Hello?'
'Can-you-hear-me?'
'Yes-Can-you-hear-me?'
'You stink!'
'So do you!'

until it was time to put the fishing line back where it had come from.

Another idea was for cotton-reel tractors. For these an empty wooden cotton-reel was needed. Normally Mum would have said, 'Certainly not! You must wait until one is empty!' but now she wound all the brown cotton off a nearly-empty reel especially so that Barry could have it. To make the tractor, one rim of the cotton-reel had notches cut into it to give it grip. If you didn't do this it would just spin in one place. Then a rubber-band was threaded through the centre and attached on one side with a small bit of stick. The other side needed a longer stick that could be twirled until the rubber-band was taut. Then it was set down and released. Slowly and purposefully the little engine would trundle itself across the floor. If two boys had one each they could have races and interesting collisions.

The Lifebuoy Book of Hobbies also assured Barry that he could make a lovely vase for his mother. All that was needed was an empty soft-drink bottle, filled to the desired height with sand and some wire. By heating the wire and applying it to the bottle you caused the neck to snap off cleanly. All that was then required was to decorate it and you would have produced a vase which your mother would treasure for years to come. The next time Mum and Auntie Elsie were safely at Methodist Ladies' Afternoon Tea, Barry and Ronnie got a fire going down the backyard. A bit of wire was found among the remains of the old chook-shed.

They had trouble getting the wire to the required temperature. Several bottles cracked in random fashion and Ronnie grew restive. They were his bottles and worth a penny each if washed and returned to Coates' Store. When they had almost given up hope and their faces were blackened and perspiring, a bottle snapped apart just as *The Lifebuoy Book of Hobbies* had promised. Barry lifted away the severed bottle-neck jubilantly. He noted that the edge was quite sharp, licked away the blood from his finger and proceeded to the next step, decoration.

Not long before, Dad had given Mum's stove-recess a bit of a freshening-up with some green paint no longer required at the base-camp. The tin was still on the back landing. Barry prised open the lid, did a quick stir and gave the severed bottle a coat of green paint, then an extra coat for luck. He had meant to decorate the vase with an all-over design of shells, but when he tried to get the shells to stick to the paint all they would do was slide down slowly to the bottom. Not to be beaten, he cut the letters M U M from the heading of the newspaper and glued them on. They looked a bit painty but were the best he could think of. The vase had taken an entire afternoon to create. It did not look exactly like the one in *The Lifebouy Book of Hobbies*, but he was proud and happy. He even crawled in under the front steps of the house and got some red and yellow cannas to put in the vase for the moment of presentation. He could hardly wait to see Mum's face.

It was sad that he did not time the moment of surprise a little better. He ought to have remembered that when the News was on we hardly dared to whisper let alone interrupt. When he appeared at the kitchen door, the wonderful vase that would be treasured-for-ever in his painty hands, Mum was head-bent, listening to the wireless. She did not turn as he began, 'Mum, look what .....' Without so much as a glance, Mum held up one hand for silence. We waited expectantly. Then we heard, beyond the crackling of the wireless, the voice of the King. It was the King himself. He was saying 'This is the Empire's darkest hour'. Far, far away, in the distant land that we knew was called Home, the Battle of Britain had begun. Mum was in no mood for surprises.

One morning not long afterwards, Mr. Bonham announced on morning parade at school, the date of the annual fancy-dress ball: Friday the fifth of September, at the Palais Royal. It was to be called the Patriotic Gala Victory Ball and all the proceeds would go to the Patriotic Fund. A buzz of excitement rippled across the parade at the news. I had no idea what a fancy-dress ball was, but I had seen pictures of Cinderella at the Ball wearing an elaborate gown with her hair puffed strangely on top of her head. I was vastly alarmed. 'What are you going as?' became the sole topic of conversation in the play-shed, each little girl's aspirations fired by the previous speaker's. 'A princess!' was bettered by 'A Fairy Princess' then, 'A Flower Fairy Princess' until finally the matter was settled once and for all with 'A Fairy Queen'. I began to warm to the idea of fairyhood myself.

But Mum settled the matter with 'Nonsense! You are not the fairy type!' and casting around in her mind, came up with her perfect solution. Mickey Mouse! She had had great success in the Dawson River days dressing Barry for a fancy-dress ball as Mickey Mouse. In those days Mickey Mouse had a tail. She had made Barry a tail of fencing-wire covered with black Japan-cloth. Barry's tail had tweaked up the ladies' skirts, causing shrieks of laughter. With his white-gloved hands and his big white buttons he had quite stolen the show. Mum's eyes sparkled as she remembered.

I didn't like Mickey Mouse very much myself, always smiling and being in the right. My favourite was Horace Horse-collar, the sad old horse with ears that poked through his hat, but I didn't dare mention his name. Uncle Horace was Mum's brother, named after Admiral Lord Nelson. It got her goat that Walt Disney had called his mournful old horse Horace. She said it was 'a deliberate insult to our national hero!' and 'Just like the Americans!' I could see that Mum had her mind set on Mickey Mouse. 'You can have a bow-tie and white gloves!' she told me, warming to the task.

Barry declined to go as anything unless it was Desert Army. Mum said, 'Don't be silly! A fancy dress costume should be amusing! Barry said, 'What about an ARP Warden, then?' Uncle Les and Mr. Ackland had just been appointed ARPs – Air Raid Provosts – for their sections of Eyre Street and Mitchell Street. 'If I could borrow Uncle Les's tin-hat all I would need would be an arm-band with ARP on it!' Mum said she would think about it, and began work on the ears and tail for Mickey Mouse.

Then, one day during big-lunch, Miss Marron called to me from the verandah. I sidled up the steps towards the teachers' room, my heart in my boots. What had I done wrong? The room where the teachers had their cup of tea was sacred. To be asked to Wash the Teachers' Cups was a privilege that fell only to the most highly favoured, such as Margaret Robertson, whose father was the Town Clerk. It even ranked above Taking the Roll to the Office. I knew I wasn't being asked to wash the cups. Nothing that wonderful could happen to me. Tiptoeing to diminish the fact of my presence, I crept to the door.

'Come in, Dear', said Miss Marron. It did not lessen my fright to be confronted by a tableful of speculative faces! 'Yes, she is nice and tall, isn't she?' they agreed. Well, then, that settled it! Without further debate I was told that I was to be the conductor of the Central Infants' Percussion Band for the Patriotic Gala Victory Ball. I was sent home with a note to that effect and a diagram of the uniform, which was to be a pill-box hat and shoulder-cloak in the school colours, red and black, trimmed with gold braid.

At this news Mum was flummoxed, uncertain whether to be gratified or put out. Here she was, well along with Mickey Mouse's ears, tail and trousers, and I somehow get myself conducting the band and needing a different costume altogether! So exasperating! She studied the diagram of the uniform. 'Hmm. Let's see. 'Plain red cotton lining' for the cape. Silly lot of Old Biddies! What would they know? Anyone with half an eye could see that red satin would be more appropriate. Costume must catch the light.' When young, mum had won a place at the Royal Academy of Dramatic Art which her father, a very strict churchman, would not let her accept. No daughter of his should appear on a stage! None the less, Mum considered herself an expert on things to do with the theatre. And so it was decided. We would go for the satin. The cap was the difficult bit. Perhaps I wriggled inopportunely. Mum was sure I had and told me so. Perhaps it had been her tape-measure. For whatever reason, the circumference of the cap was somewhat less than the circumference of my head. It perched. 'So it should! It should look jaunty!' said Mum, trying to convince herself. It was just as well the cap was to be secured by elastic under the chin.

The Central School Infants' Percussion Band to this point in time, had consisted of a cardboard box full of instruments dragged from the bottom shelf of the press on Thursday afternoons. The contents were distributed from desk to desk, regardless of talent. I rather fancied myself on the triangle, which gave a soulful little 'ting' much in keeping with my spirits. There were bells on little handles, quite interesting. Tambourines, faded ribbons still in evidence, were well thought of, especially those which still had their little brass rattles. There were cymbals, which could be satisfying. The boys burst buttons off their shirts to be the one to whom the solitary drum was awarded. The fizzers were the black clappers. They did not do a lot: simply went, 'Knackety-knack' when shaken disenchantedly. Even Infants know when they have drawn the short straw.

But now rehearsals began in earnest. Daily, Miss Pask folded back the heavy woollen cover of the piano. She opened the lid, twirled the stool to adjust its height to her short legs, twitched her glasses high on her nose and brought her hands down in a warning chord. Not a knacketty-knack, rub-a-dub, or ting dare precede her.

Miss Marron not only beat time, making generous arm movements, but also mouthed the words. On 'One, two, three, four. ONE!' we all came in, anxious not only to do our bit but to be seen doing it. No-one explained that there was any relationship between Miss Marron's arm-wavings and our instruments. We assumed teachers were always at the front waving their arms. It was useful that she was there to tell us when to start and when to stop. In the meantime it was every man for himself. Those with bell-clusters shook them until their wrists tired. Those with triangles tinged purposefully, sometimes bringing in an interesting dinner-gong variation. The tambourine players, conscious of being the elect, frowned in concentration and tried for vibrato on the little brass rattles. The cymbals clanged in unison, sometimes. Whoever got the drum knew he might not get the chance again so made the most of it. Even the clapper-players knackety-knacked dutifully, only knacking on one another's heads when Miss Marron looked away. The words of the song were,

All the boys and girls are marching, singing as we go,
Holding high our little flags and marching to and fro;
See our little flags a-waving, this is what we do,
For we love our county's colours of the red, white and blue.

We had been intended to sing as we played. This proved ill-considered and was revised in principle. It would suffice if we smiled. Big smiles! Showing our lovely teeth! Many of us were at that time of life when lovely front teeth are lacking. But, hugely, we smiled.

The school was seventy years old. For most of that period there had been pigeons which regarded it as a right to roost on the cross-bars of the Infants' ceiling. The odd dropping or feather had descended upon the slates below. But from this time the pigeons were seen no more. Likewise the stray-dogs whose habit it had been to nose in the rubbish-bins for crusts, decamped yelping, tails down, for St Joseph's Convent down the hill.

On one occasion Mr. Bonham appeared at the door. He nodded encouragement to Miss Pask, hummed along with us for a few bars and told Miss Marron that we were coming along quite nicely. Just a little bit more practice and he was sure we would have it right.

Miss Marron' s smile had a touch of anxiety. She raised her arms and said, 'One, Two, three, four. ONE!' Mr. Bonham departed briskly towards the Big School.

There came the day when I took over as Conductor. The Patriotic Gala Victory Fancy Dress Ball was not far off. The moment could be delayed no longer. Miss Marron stood behind me and showed me what to do with my arms. To start, I must hold them as though for Mum to wind her wool. Then it was, UP! Down! In! Out!

If didn't think about it, I could get it nearly right. Sometimes my arms tended in the same direction or clapped together by chance in mid-air. The band did not care a lot; they had their own concerns. But we remembered to Smile! It all gave Miss Marron a chance to lean on the piano and have a recuperative rest with her head in her hands. It was nice to see how friendly Miss Pask could be. She reached out to pat Miss Marron on the shoulder and to say, 'There! There!'

On the night of the Ball any number of Red Riding Hoods, Butterflies, Sugar Plum Fairies and Gypsy Fortune Tellers swarmed with their proud parents along the footpath towards the Palais Royal. Waltzing Matildas, Captain Hooks and Ned Kellys tumbled off every bus. V for Victory's and Union Jacks climbed from dickie-seats of Austins, and Jockeys, Burglars and Lone Rangers from the backs of utilities and trucks. Strangest of all were the birds: Ducks, Chickens or Canaries with crepe-paper feathers and beak-like head-gear, from beneath which ordinary school-day faces peered expectantly. In the midst of all this spectacle the members of the School Percussion Band looked austere in our black and red capes and pill-box hats. Miss Marron went round adjusting our capes. I was secretly pleased that mine had many more folds of satin and rows of gold-braid than had been strictly required. It was in keeping with my rank.

Then through the door, I glimpsed the interior of the Palais Royal. At the sight of the acres of polished dance-floor glistening under the lights, the hundreds of parents and teachers buzzing with anticipation, I grew faint. Nobody had told us that we had to do it in front of people!

Behind us on the footpath, three hundred Butterflies, Bo-Peeps, Hiawathas, Wattle Fairies and Spider Men were being marshalled into ranks by the teachers. Bib and Bub, in gum-nut hats and gumleaf bloomers, wailed in protest at their costume. Andy Sugden's big brother, Stanley, dressed as the Knave of Hearts, bloodied Cliffie Frizwell's nose for some scathing remark made about his costume, which was really quite nice, a pillow-slip with a hole cut in one end for his head and red paper hearts tacked on the front and back. Stanley tore it off and plonked himself down on the edge of the curb to eat all the nice tarts with which Mrs. Sugden had equipped him.

The Percussion Band was to lead the march in. But how was I know where to turn? At school when we had practised there had been a school-bag laid on the grass to show us this important moment.

'Miss Marron! Miss Marron! How will I know when to turn?'

'Miss Marron! Miss Marron! How will I ..... Miss Marron! ...'

'Miss...'

But Miss Marron was flustering; 'Elsie Clegg! Your mother was supposed to put elastic to hold it on! Andy Sugden! If you don't blow your nose!' and 'No! Esme! Not now!' You should have gone before you came!' and 'Andy Sugden! NOT on your cape!'

Somewhere a band struck up. It was the Lyric Orchestra, specially hired for the occasion, with *We're Going To Hang out the Washing on the Siegfried Line*'. But what were they thinking of! Our band couldn't do that! We could only do, *All the Girls and Boys Are Marching*! We didn't know anything else! Somebody tell them to change! Was it still Four Four time? 'Oh! Miss Marron!'

Someone hissed, 'Well, Go on then!' and gave me a poke between the shoulder blades. I skidded into the doorway, regained my balance and stepped out. The Grand Parade of the Central School Patriotic Gala Victory Ball was underway. It was a big relief that at the last moment four Scholarship boys had stepped out on to the dance-floor as markers to show us where to turn. But so intent was my concentration upon arm movements, baton whirling and getting the left foot down with an appropriate degree of stamp, that I might well have mown the first marker down completely had he not hissed through smiling teeth, 'Geez! Right wheel! You stupid little bugger!'

The Percussion Band marched up on to the stage, formed ranks, faced the audience and launched into the task of accompanying the Lyric Orchestra; '*Up From Somerset*', '*Pack Up Your Troubles*', '*Run, Rabbit, Run*' unrehearsed. We took them in our stride. There seemed no point in half-heartedness. It was just a pity that Bobby Eckersleigh, who up till now had been our best drummer, should have become a little excited and beat so enthusiastically upon his drum that the skin broke, that one of the cymbals should go bowling away across the dance-floor, its player in hot pursuit and that the puddle which wasn't really Esme Purley's fault - Miss Marron ought to have let her go - should trickle slowly across the stage in the direction of the Lyric Orchestra's coats and hats. The members of the Orchestra rolled their eyes in our direction and from time to time took out handkerchiefs to mop their foreheads from the excitement of it all.

The rest of the school were well away with the Grand March. They had practised in the playground every day after Big Lunch for three weeks. First there was marching in a large circle, single file. Then came forming twos with a partner. Twos joined ranks and swung round to become fours, and fours joined fours to make eights. In this compact formation a pleasing sense of belonging prevailed. The older ones knew to take smaller steps to let the little ones keep up. Or should have known. At an appointed moment the ranks began to weave into the intricacies of the Catherine Wheel. One after another each child followed the leader into a whirling circle that looked as though it could never disentangle itself, but somehow changed direction at the last moment and did. The only difficulties experienced were by those who had come with large webbed feet as Frogs, the assorted birds who had similar problems, Bib and Bub who refused to part company, and the Delaney girls, firmly stitched together as Siamese Twins. The spectators applauded warmly, telling one another the Grand Parade was better this year than ever, mothers secretly making up their minds what costume they would attempt next year for little Alma and Arthur, the judges behind their table consulting their notes and deciding who was to be awarded 'Best Dressed', 'Most Amusing', 'Most Original' and 'Most Patriotic' for the evening.

When it was all over, Miss Marron came to help the Percussion Band down off the stage.

By this time we had really hit our stride and would have willingly stayed. It seemed only fair to help the Lyric Orchestra along a bit. 'You have done quite nicely!' Miss Marron told us firmly. To me she said, 'Well done! You kept time all the way through!' What harm could a little white lie do at this stage! The Lyric Orchestra struck up *Somewhere in France with You* for the waltz. The Big School went through their paces: Pride of Erin, Gypsy Tap and Progressive Barn Dance, the parents clapping politely for each. They expected their children to be able to take their place on the dance floor. It was only proper.

At ten o'clock it was the parents' turn. The Mayor and Mayoress led off, followed by Mr. and Mrs. Bonham. After an appropriate pause the parents thronged to the floor which was soon a mass of colour as husbands twirled their wives to '*Oh, Believe Me if All Those Endearing Young Charms*' or showed in the Quick Step that what they didn't know about dipping and reversing hardly mattered.

Mum, in her best pale-green chiffon with a silk rose on one shoulder, would have loved to have danced, but as the wife of an army man on Active Service she knew it would not be appropriate. One foot tapping in time to the music and her fingers playing as though on a little piano, she kept a bright smile firmly fixed on her lips while the couples whirled by. On her lap was a white envelope. It contained two and sixpence which Barry had won as a Special Prize, awarded at the judges' own discretion and contributed out of their own pockets. Barry had gone as 'Hitler After the War', his clothes torn, his head bandaged, one shoe on and one shoe off, one eye blackened, he had staggered up on to the stage, twirled round and round as though hit on the head, and bowed humbly to the judges. It had got a good laugh.

Between dances the boys had sliding competitions on the dance-floor, running to get up speed and skidding to a halt in tumbled heaps, careless now of their costumes and piling feathered head-dresses and pirate swords on to their mother's laps. The girls, less willing to shed their finery, took it in turns to tow one another around the perimeter, one girl squatting on her heels, the other tugging her, monkey-grip, all squealing brightly. In that happy throng each one had already decided, or nearly decided, what costume they would have next year.

But there would not be a next year, nor a year after that, nor after that, for many years to come, or not a year of pleasing certainties such as the Central School Annual Gala Patriotic Fancy Dress Ball. For, far to the north, unobserved by the rest of the world, a group islands, the Kuriles, were being invaded. The Kuriles were peaceful islands, not very big and not very important, near to Japan. But they were in the Pacific. And they were as stepping-stones on the way to the south.

Chapter 3

BRAVING WALKER STREET: 1941

'Wish Me Luck as you Wave me Good-bye,
Cheerio, here I go on my way'

Moreton Bay Fig Tree

Just before Christmas 1940 Dad's regiment moved to Miowera, a practically unknown siding fifteen miles south of Bowen, now to become an important army training centre and staging camp. Dad had been involved in helping to set it up from Headquarters at Kissing Point; now he was to be based at Miowera permanently. He wrote to Mum suggesting that we should all move down to Bowen to live.

Mum folded the letter and sighed. Another move just when we had settled and begun to think of North Ward as home. We had such nice friends in the Quelches and the Acklands. They had become like family. Barry and I were settled at Central; another change of schools was the last thing we needed. She herself was enjoying VAD and Red Cross work. She was exasperated and reluctant. None the less Smoky the cat was handed over the fence to the Quelches, Barry and I, feeling sadly important, asked our teachers for inter-school transfer forms and we set out with all our possessions to start life over again in Bowen.

On the night we left the flat I thought it would seem grown-up and important in Ronnie's eyes if I carried out the little port in which were packed the cutlery, serviette rings and tablecloths. With two hands I heaved it up on to the running-board of the Overland taxi and left it there. All the other luggage was strapped on to the luggage-rack at the back. In the flurry of good-byes no one realized the little port was on the running-board and when the Overland drove off to the station it was flung into the dark.

At the station its loss was discovered. I was in terrible trouble. Why had I interfered? Why didn't I leave things alone! Leaving Barry in charge of all our possessions, Mum rushed back in a second taxi. As its headlights swung round, she saw the little port still lying on the side of the road. Just as the guard was about to blow his whistle she returned breathless. Bundling us into the carriage ahead of her she scrambled in herself. I withered under ferocious looks as the train pulled out of the station and curved away into darkness over the bridge. I was too unhappy about Smoky to care very much.

I couldn't believe that we were leaving Townsville for ever. Watching the rhythmic upward and downward swoops of the moonlight on the telephone wires in the darkness outside the carriage window at last soothed me to sleep.

Dad met us at the station in Bowen, at what Mum called 'some ungodly hour'. He had a pleased, proud grin as he gathered me half-asleep in his arms and took charge of the luggage.

One thing about arriving anywhere at night is that in the morning it is exciting to wake up and look out at a brand-new world. Dad had rented a big high-blocked house with a front verandah set on the side of a stony hill. It hadn't had a coat of paint in years and faced out across a glittering salt-pan. There was a peculiar smell in the air, like killing day at Stainburn, when the carcass was hoisted on the scaffold and the dogs ran in to gollop up the blood. Dad said it was the meat-works at Merinda. He thought we would only notice the smell when the wind was in that direction.

Mum soon made up her mind that she hated Bowen. Her arms became covered in red blotches from sand-fly bites. Dad tried to make a little joke that they liked her English blood, hoping to get her to smile. Mum was determined not to. Barry and I knew the signs. There was going to be a row.

'Barry! You take Marion and go down to the beach and play. Your mother and I have things to talk over,' said Dad. 'Things to talk over' meant raised voices and 'Why had they ever come to this dreadful country in the first place,' and 'Why didn't Dad get a proper job like other men.'

Sometimes it even got around to 'Should have listened to my parents!' and 'Should have married Cousin Charles.' Cousin Charles had a house on the Thames; we knew about that. There were other things which we knew by heart, having heard them through the walls at night when we were supposed to be asleep. Each time the raised voices seemed to us like the end of the world.

With weighted hearts we wandered down to the beach. The tide was in, the waves lip-lopping on the shingly beach. In the sultry heat Barry mechanically picked up pebbles to skim over the water. I looked for 'Victory V' shells, the ones that looked like pennies with a 'V' dotted on one side. Neither of us spoke. It was a school-day and we felt forlorn not to be where everyone else was: in a classroom doing ordinary things. It was hot and, yes, there were sand-flies.

As soon as we dared we straggled back to the house. Dad examined my handful of shells. 'See. The kids like it here already!' he said. Barry and I smiled guardedly. We didn't want to hurt his feelings but we had to face reality. Mum was the one we had to live with. She decided things; we owed our loyalty to Mum. It was also wise to keep in her good books. One good thing about Mum hating Bowen so much was it had taken her mind off my having lost the little brown port.

Plainly, Mum was all for heading back to Townsville. My heart leapt with sudden hope Back to Townsville! Back to Kissing Point and Central! Would we be able to get Smoky back from the Quelches? Mum was saying 'There's Barry with Scholarship next year. We were so close to the Grammar School! There'd be nothing for him here. No future at all!'

Barry and I began to regret having come back from the beach; the argument was still going full bore. It was awful to see Dad, a sergeant before whom grown men stood rigidly to attention, being hauled over the coals like a bad boy. Dad stared out across the salt-encrusted mudflats that stretched for miles in either direction and looked unhappy. We knew that he adored Mum and even we could see how much he had hoped that she would put up with the run-down, shabby little town to be near him. But we could see that he was beginning to feel that Mum was right and that he should never have asked her to come here in the first place. Townsville was a much better place to bring kids up, he could see that now. Bowen wasn't much chop for a woman and kids. Dad had lovely blue-grey eyes, but now a little of the colour seemed to go out of them. He took out his Capstan tin and cigarette papers and began to roll himself a smoke, head down. Next morning he helped us to pile all our things back into the luggage-van of the Sunshine Express, kissed us goodbye, and we went back to Townsville.

Of course, the lovely, airy flat near the beach in Eyre Street had gone to another tenant. Mum took a flat in Walker Street, just round the corner from the station. We hated Walker Street on sight. It was a very old part of Townsville, set under the bony shoulder of Castle Hill with weeds and bindi-eyes on the stony footpaths. Cottages crouched with verandah-blinds pulled down over their faces like caps, huddled together, separated by sagging fences and rows of sour-looking aralias. Walker Street looked the sort of place where no one would ever really want to be. 'Your father will be able to come home for weekends,' Mum told us brightly, determined to put a brave face on her decision. 'The railway station is just around the corner.' Every so often there was a series of whistle-blasts followed by a dull boom. The quarry was also just around the corner.

The front verandah of the flat was enclosed by dark-green roll-up blinds; Barry and I were to have stretcher-beds there, side by side. We knew it was a come down. We were miles from the beach at Kissing Point and Ronnie and the Acklands. We sat on our stretchers staring glumly at one another. 'What do you think?' I quavered. Barry was getting used to life going into reverse just when things were going well. It didn't pay to put too much faith in things; they were likely to fall through just when you least expected it. 'It's up to putty!' was all he said, scowling. We were learning that you can never really go back. Nothing is ever as nice as it was before. Departure alters the pattern of things; they are never quite the same.

We didn't even get Smoky back. 'He wouldn't like it here,' Mum reasoned with me. 'There are too many stray dogs.' There were. A council-man made regular rounds on a motor-bike with a side-car rigged with a cage. He had a pole and net like a large butterfly scoop. He was the dog-catcher. The dogs would gather in a watchful group looking wary, then, at the last moment, flee in different directions, grinning. They had dodging the dog-catcher down to a fine art. The dog-catcher didn't give a hoot. He was off to join the AIF soon.

Now, instead of happily sauntering to school with Ronnie and the Acklands along Eyre Street, Barry and I had unlovely Walker Street to negotiate. It was not so bad in the mornings when I hurried along with Barry, breaking into a trot every few steps to keep up. We paused in front of the Fire Brigade with the gleaming red engines and rows of brass helmets. Each morning a fireman, in gumboots, would be sloshing soapy water across the footpath with a heavy wire broom. At Cobb's Cordial Factory we stopped to watch the bottles, rank upon rank, clinking round tunefully amidst the machinery and we sniffed Cherry Cheer and Creaming Soda on the morning air.

St Anne's School had a picket-fence and trimmed hedges. The girls wore a navy-blue uniform with a wide white collar and instead of buttons their blouses were laced at the front with brown shoe-laces. They wore brown ribbed stockings and panama hats. The air of careless affluence this gave them made me feel mean and inferior as I hurried along after Barry in my brown Central tunic and sandals.

Barry was now in Mr. Krause's Scholarship class, the most important grade of all. He was only eleven and most of his classmates were thirteen or fourteen. Scholarship had been hanging over their heads since they had been in Grade Five. They had got used to the grim reality of getting ready to sit for Scholarship; to more and more homework. Good-bye to pleasant lessons such as pastel books and nature study and singing. Scholaship pupils were never let out of school when the afternoon bell went. Their days of carefree liberty were over. It was taken for granted that the shadows of late afternoon would be slanting across the school grounds before they were set free. This was expected. Barry and his friends boasted about how tough 'Old Krausie' was. 'He knocks the daylights out of you if you muck your homework up!' And, 'The cuts! Krausie's a rip-snorter! Four-of-the-best as soon as look at you!' It was said with pride. Doing 'Scholly' was one of the steps on the way to being grown-up. For many it was the end of their school days. After 'Scholarship' you could leave school and get an apprenticeship in the railways or the meat-works, or, for girls, a nice job in McKimmons. No one expected it to be a push-over. Scholarship pupils walked with the dignity of their own importance upon them.

Now that Barry was in Scholarship I had to walk home alone. Each afternoon I faced the prospect with misery, my heart heavy with dread. Walker Street, parched in the glare of the afternoon sun, had a loveless air. I was sure some of the houses, their timber showing grey though faded paint-work, had dreadful secret things in their past, and watched me passing with spite.

Resorting to cunning, I offered to carry the teacher's flowers home. Each morning, scotty Miss Wheeler was inundated with bouquets of phlox, marigolds and petunias from little girls hoping to win favour. What should she do with such bounty but take it home? But why carry it herself when some willing little menial could be pressed into service? 'Who-oo would like to carry my flowers for me?' she would chirrup sweetly, having been rousing and scolding, even shouting, at us all day long. Up would go my hand, fingers flicking with false enthusiasm. It meant going out of my way to Blackwood Street to where Miss Wheeler's boarding-house was, but the extra distance was worth it. Carrying the teacher's flowers might give me safe passage through the terrors of Walker Street.

Greatest of terrors were the stone-throwing boys, who derived great satisfaction from making little girls cower against the paling fence as they fled past. Once, the stones were lobbing so thick and fast around my feet that I fled in at the front gate of a strange house, pretending it was my home, and hid. The boys jeered tauntingly but sauntered off. At other times they armed themselves with fistfuls of daisy-burrs, spikey prickles on long stems. They flicked them lightly on to the hem of a victim's dress so that they scratched round her legs as she fled.

Their favorite victim was old Johnnie Chinaman, trudging house to house along Walker Street, his bicycle hung with baskets of lettuces, tomatoes, cucumbers and strawberries from the Chinese market-gardens at Aitkenvale. When he mounted the bicycle and balanced on the pedals to get the heavy load going, the boys would run, grinning, up behind him to flick daisy-burrs on to the seat of his blue cotton trousers. 'Johnnie' never showed anger but continued on his way, his sandalled brown feet slim and bony as they worked the pedals, the back of his coat and trousers spiked all over with daisy-burrs. All Chinamen were called 'Johnnies'. There were many around Townsville, most of them with a horse and a cart with a canvas hood.

On the corner not far from our place was the red brick School of Arts. Once I had got that far, I could begin to breathe more easily because I was nearly home. I had only to scurry round the corner into Blackwood Street to deliver the flowers and then double back quickly, to be safe. There was only one more great terror.

Next to the School of Arts was a low-set, weather-board cottage that crouched under a mango tree. A very unfriendly Blue Heeler lived there. I liked Blue Heelers because they reminded me of the one I had been friends with at Stainburn. I had tried to get on friendly terms with this one but he was not interested. He had a way of crouching absolutely still and curling the sides of his lips so that the pink part showed, and whispering a growl. This whispered growl seemed more unfriendly than a full-throated one. His temper had been spoiled by the Walker Street boys who ran sticks along the palings of the fence to stir him up. He had worn a furrow along the inside of the fence running up and down to get at them and had developed big powerful shoulders from thrusting himself along.

One afternoon as I was beginning to sag with the relief of being nearly home, I saw that, with great animal cunning, the dog had scraped a tunnel under the picket-gate and was now lying in wait for its persecutors. Seeing me coming it threw itself into the opening and began scrabbling through, making dreadful squealing growls of anticipation in its throat. It little mattered to it that I wasn't one of the boys who had rattled sticks in its face. It was beside itself with lust for vengeance.

With a shriek, I tossed Miss Wheeler's marigolds to the winds and took to my heels. Too late! With a series of great bounds the dog was upon me. It knocked me sprawling to the stones and snarling terribly, sank its teeth into my thigh, shaking its head from side to side in massive satisfaction. My screams brought people to the rescue. With a boot to the ribs the dog was hauled off, happily before it had worked its way up to my throat. It was dragged away, still chopping with its teeth in my direction.

The owner, a large belligerent lady in slippers and chook-yard hat declared, 'It's the kid's own bloody fault. Had it comin'. Never let up on him. Orlwess giv'in' 'im gyp! No wonder the pore bugger done 'is block!'

My mother, arriving on the scene, was speechless with outrage. She had never met the like for stupidity and vulgarity and told the woman so. Emphatically. 'You will hear further from my husband on this matter. He is staff-sergeant in the Kennedy Regiment and will see that the dog is shot,' she declared, ignoring the rude reply flung at our backs as she led me, wailing, away.

She lit the chip-heater with screwed-up newspaper and put me into a warm bath laced with Condie's Crystals. The brilliant magenta colour of the water was very therapeutic for both body and soul. Sponging me all over, she went on and on about Walker Street, the common type who lived there, and husbands who were always away when they were needed. 'Your father couldn't hit the back end of a barn with a gun! Why he's in the army I'll never know! Just wait till he gets home!' The effect of the Condies Crystals on the bath was to stain it an interesting tea-colour which would not rub off, even with sand-soap and steel wool. It was not my fault but I was made to feel it was.

By the time Dad came home several weeks later the whole incident had almost been forgotten and I was healing quite nicely. Dad dumped his army gear on the back verandah; helmet, kitbag, gas-mask and blue-enamel water-bottle, bayonet, ammunition pouches, haversacks, even down to the tiny calico pouch called a 'house-wife' with pockets filled with pins, needles, thread and a tin thimble. Barry's eyes gleamed as he tried to shoulder the heavy .303. I couldn't even lift it. Barry knelt, and resting the barrel on the verandah-rail took imaginary aim at next-door's rooster, his eyes alight with bloodlust and envy. Then on Dad's 'Righto! That'll do!' the .303 was put away behind the kitchen-dresser with the brooms. Most arresting of all was the gas-mask, with its snout-like tubing and bulbous, vacant eyes. The sight of Barry wearing it was enough to send me squealing through the flat to hide behind the wardrobe in Mum's room.

Dad was home for an important recruiting parade. The Kennedy Regiment was to march along Flinders Street together with a contingent from the RAAF and five bands. Mum was also marching with the VADs.

Barry and I balanced on the edge of one of the garden-beds along Flinders Street to watch the 31st swing past to the regimental march *D'Ye Ken John Peel*, bronzed and fit after being under canvas at Miowera. The 31st was popular with the people because it was

Townville's garrison regiment, their own, so they were getting a rousing reception. 'Dad! Dad!' I called, important with excitement. I wanted people to know that was my father, with his rifle over his squared shoulders and his Digger's hat at a correct angle. 'Pipe down! Stupid!' Barry said, giving me a dig with his elbow, 'Don't you know they can't look! They're 'Eyes front'!' I stuck out my tongue, as I had seen other little girls at school do, at the masculine khaki backs of the 31st Regiment and blew a raspberry. Barry looked at me astonished and I shriveled with mortification, unable to believe I had done such a thing. I could have crept under the acalyphas in the garden-beds with shame. I could not put into words the resentment that had flared momentarily in my heart at that great impersonal force, The Army, which dominated our lives.

Flinders Street saw many such parades, of which Anzac Day was the most important: the day the whole town came together in memory of the Townsville men who had marched away to the Kaiser's war and never come back. For days before, people were asked to bring flowers and ferns from their gardens to the Town Hall. These were made into garlands to festoon the Roll of Honour. On Anzac Day the Town Hall remained open so that the crowds could troop in and out to admire the decorations and pay their respects to the names of The Fallen.

The march started at three o'clock in the afternoon. People lined the streets, three and four deep, to watch. Some, having ridden their bicycles for miles to get there, would lean them against a verandah post and use them to climb on to get a better view. Everyone wore best clothes; their Sunday clothes. It was a very solemn occasion.

The 31st Battalion, the Kennedy, on parade in Flinders Street, November 1939

In pride of place, leading the parade, were the Returned Soldiers, all spit and polish with campaign medals glinting on their shiny Sunday suits, some wearing their Digger hats. They enjoyed showing that they were old hands when it came to marching. They swung along, shoulder to shoulder, bearing banners that proclaimed, 'Ypres', 'Pozieres', 'Passchendaele' and 'The Somme'.

There was profound respect those who marched under 'Lone Pine' or 'Quinn's Post'. Men removed their hats in tribute. Following them came the Garrison Battalion, the RAAF, the Navy and the Volunteer Defence Corps, mostly old Diggers who gave up a couple of nights a week to keep in training. Then came the VAD's and the Women's Defence Corps, who had uniforms of navy-blue serge and a forage cap. Later they became known as the WAAAFs and the AWAASs and had different uniforms. Everyone wore hats and gloves; no woman would have been seen in Flinders Street without her gloves.

St Annes's School, St Patrick's Convent and the Christian Brothers always marched in their school uniforms. The Grammar School had cadets, the smaller boys looking like Puss in Boots in their big army boots and gaiters, but proud to be wearing the Diggers' hat square over their eyes and ears. Bringing up the rear came the Scouts, Cubs, Guides, Brownies and the Junior Red Cross.

I had joined the Junior Red Cross because Shirley had. The meetings were held after school at a house opposite the hospital. We sat in a circle knitting squares that were to be stitched into blankets for Prisoners of War. The Leader read stories about great women such as Sister Cavel, who had said, as she was led out to be shot by the Germans, 'Patriotism is not enough.' Very troubling. We were told patriotism was what was expected of us. When she wasn't reading stories the lady helped me to retrieve dropped stitches. The other little girls clicked away on their needles and could produce several squares each week. Mine grew more and more wayward. Finally, the lady said perhaps I might like to take it home to finish it. Barry said, wasn't I clever to have knitted a map of Africa! But it was worth being a failure at knitting to be able to march in the Anzac Day parade, wearing a white veil with a celluloid Red Cross stitched on the front and a red shoulder-cape over my white Sunday School dress.

It was a bit of a scamper to keep up with the rest of the parade. Every few steps we had to break into a jog-trot to catch up. But we swung our arms 'shoulder high' as we had been told, often the same hand and foot going in time with one another, and kept our eyes to the front like the grown-ups did. We tried not to be disconcerted as the conflicting 'ker-boom-boom-booms' of *Wi' a Hundred Pipers* as the drums of the Townsville Ladies' Pipe Band launched into an attack on *Onward, Christian Soldiers* from the Salvation Army coming up behind. No one smiled or laughed. Anzac Day was the most solemn day of the year.

On the Strand the crowd grouped itself around the War Memorial, allowing children through to sit on the grass in front. The King's message was read aloud: 'Once again the Queen and I join with our people in Australia….' The crowd listened reverently. Then Alderman Gill began his speech. 'It is an honour indeed to address the young people, the tender plants of this Digger Land of ours...' But already my attention would have wandered. We knew about Anzac Day from school.

Each year we had to bring threepence to school to pay for a purple ribbon on which was printed 'Anzac – Lest We Forget' to be pinned to our uniforms. The walls between class-rooms were folded back to make one big room and we were squashed in to sit cross-legged on the floor. Two Returned Servicemen, medals on their suits, told us about The Landing and what it had felt like to scramble up the ridges at Gallipoli being shot at by Johnnie Turk. Dad had medals too. But from somewhere called Ypres and The Somme. It was what being a grown-up man was about. You went away to war and fought battles.

On Thursday nights we often hurried around to the front of the railway station to join the crowd farewelling the Draft. This became the patriotic thing to do and people made an effort to be there. The Draft was the group of young men who had volunteered in response to posters like 'Be an Anzac. Join the AIF' or 'One in, All in! Join up, today!' to go on active service overseas. Sometimes there were only six or seven of them, sometimes as many as fifteen. Some were stockmen down from western stations, some were off cane-farms to the north, many from Townsville firms such as Dalgetty's, Samuel Allens or Burns Philps. They were all young, good-looking and boiling over with excitement to have passed their 'Boards' – medical examinations – and to be on their way at last. Most would be joining the AIF; only a few the RAAF. The appeal of the Digger's slouch hat with its turned-up side brim was irresistible. The forage cap of the RAAF couldn't compete.

The draft would be given High Tea at the Comforts Fund Rooms near the Post Office, then, accompanied by a section of the Volunteer Defence Corps all spruced up for the occasion, and one of the town bands, they would march down Flinders Street to the station. The people gathered to see them off would lean forward to catch a glimpse of these game young fellows who had chucked in good jobs to go off and have 'a crack at the Boche'. There were calls of 'Good Luck, Son!', 'Wade into em, Dig' and 'Don't let the bastards grind you down!' all of which would make the men of the Draft grin hugely, savouring their moment of glory.

The time for the first division of the Southern Mail was twenty past seven. While waiting for the station clock to tick round, the band would play for Community Singing; *Nursie, Come Over Here and Hold My Hand*; *Kiss Me Good-night, Sergeant Major*; *We're Going to Hang Out the Washing on the Siegfried Line* and *Swinging Along the Road to Victory*. Last of all would be *Wish Me Luck as You Wave Me Good-Bye*. As the train pulled out there would be cheers, yackais and cat-calls. But as it curved round over Ross Creek bridge, the carriage lights glittering and snaking in the dark water, the crowd would fall quiet and begin making their way home, speaking in low voices as though coming out of church.

Mum's eyes would always glitter with tears. 'Being young and full of go won't help them when the chips are down. Why is it always the best that volunteer?' Then, giving Barry a quick, unexpected little hug from which he tried to shake away, she would add, 'Thank Heavens, you are too young to be mixed up in this lot!'

One thing about living in Walker Street was that it couldn't have been handier for all these goings-on in town. There was always something happening in Flinders Street: Button Days, Red Cross stalls, parades and War Loan Rallies at the Town Hall, when the mayor and other dignitaries would make stirring speeches from the verandah. There was a large wooden barometer outside the Town Hall on which were painted, in contrasting colours, Townsville's quota for the War Loan and the amount that had already been contributed. The mayor urged Townsville people not to let Mackay or Bundaberg put it over them in being the first in Queensland to fill their quota. The band would strike up with *Run, Rabbit, Run* and *Colonel Bogey*. The centre of attraction would always be a recent example of weaponry, such as a bren gun mounted on a carrier, around which all the men and boys would gather in grave contemplation.

Someone designed and made a huge Victory V flag which was flown from the Town Hall. It had a large red V on a white background surrounded by a blue border. Soon Victory V flags were the fashion, all the shops racing one another to be the next to hang one out. Hotels had Victory V's hanging from their verandah railings. The RSL had a large V illuminated in red lights. V for Victory buttons were sold in Flinders Street and at school.

The Annual Combined Sunday Schools picnic was to be held at Black River. We were to go by train. I made myself a Victory V flag to wave from the train-window, colouring it laboriously in crayon on a torn-off bit of the old sheet which Mum was ripping into bandages for the Red Cross. It was a shame that the red crayon didn't really show up very clearly. Barry attached it to a school-ruler with shoe-tacks and I took it proudly to the railway station. A lady came along the train handing out paper Union Jacks for all the children to wave. She said to me, 'You don't need one do you, Dear. You've got your own nice Victory V flag.' I didn't know whether to smile or cry.

The National Days of the Allied Countries were celebrated with flags flown at mastheads and draped over the verandahs of shops. When Germany invaded Greece, the Greek community organized a fund-raising day. Blue and white flags and palm-fronds decked the fronts of the Bluebird, the Mia Mia and Cafe Beautiful. There was a procession with the women and girls in Greek national costume and decorated floats depicting 'Death or Liberty', 'Lord Byron's Spirit Lives' or 'The Spirit of Greece'. 'The Spirit of Greece' was a long white float several decks high, depicting Athena the Goddess of War enthroned on Mount Olympus with assorted gods, goddesses and attendants at her feet. I spotted Sylvia Manicaros from my class at school, splendid in white tulle, holding Athena's train. Vastly impressed to know someone so exalted, I waved excitedly but Sylvia was too absorbed in her god-duties to notice.

Suddenly the momentous scene ground to a halt. Athena's throne was too high to go under the telephone wire across the street in front of McKimmons. The procession halted. Or some of it did. The front part carried on regardless. Onlookers craned their necks to see what the hold-up was. Someone climbed up on to the float with a broom and tried to lift the wire, but to no avail. The float, Mount Olympus, greenery and all, backed off and made a second attempt, while gods, goddesses, nymphs and satyrs clutched at one another for support. Finally Athena got down off her throne, Mount Olympus was dismantled, carried through in sections and reassembled on the other side. The 'Spirit of Greece' eased through, to huge cheers of encouragement and admiration.

When Hitler invaded Russia there was an 'Aid to Russia' fete with stalls the length of Flinders Street. People were asked to donate warm clothing to be sent. Mum sorted out some cardigans of Dad's saying, 'Well, he won't be needing these for a while.' She added in a skirt and bolero and modish halo-style hat in which she had felt rather chic, a jumper of mine with teddy-bears across the front which one of the English aunts had sent, and Barry's outgrown Sunday school pants. Everything had to be meticulously cleaned, brushed and mended. 'It would be bad enough to be homeless and starving without having to wear shabby clothes,' said Mum.

The shops of Flinders Street vied with one another to mount window displays of the War Effort. Alfred Shaw's showed all the paraphernalia needed in an air-raid; sand-buckets, sand-scoops, stirrup-pumps and dummy bombs the actual size of those being dropped on London in the Blitz. 'They'll never break the British Spirit!' Mum cried passionately as we looked at them. 'The spirit of the British people is more than just old buildings and monuments.' She said this to convince herself and us, having shed bitter tears over a direct hit on the Houses of Commons and the destruction of the Oranges and Lemons church of St

Clements Dane, the week before.

She had just received from Uncle Horace in London an air-graph letter about how things were going with his family. An air-graph was a photographic copy of an original letter, which had to be written on a special form. The reels of photographs were sent out, developed, printed and enlarged to save cargo-space and weight because air-services were being maintained under constant risk of enemy attack. She read the letter out to shoosh us as we argued over whose turn it was to scrape the bread-and-butter pudding basin.

'The Huns keep us all on our toes these days. Your aunt and I and little Sheila have not slept in our bedroom, but in the air-raid shelter, since the middle of last September and even then always in turn-out rig. There isn't time to get dressed when it's a case of incendiary bombs.' 'There!' Mum told us proudly. 'That's the spirit the world admires.'

Heatleys put on a display of the camouflage nets which Mum and other volunteers had been making, using the floor space of the Roof Garden Ball Room. The nets were fourteen feet square and the volunteers had to work standing up for the long hours of knotting the open mesh. Mum would come home worn out, to sink down into a sea-grass chair in front of the crackling wireless in time to tune in to 'This is London calling'.

Mr. Krause expected his Scholarship to be up on war topics in case a question was slipped into the History paper. Barry started a scrap-book, pasting newspaper cuttings over the top of school-work in an All Schools Exercise pad that he had finished, to save paper. He made up some flour-and-water paste in a cup that had lost its handle and began pasting in war photos on the sums and spelling-tests and analysis and parsing on the pages underneath; first of all the capture of Tobruk, then the Siege and finally the evacuation, with the heading 'The Rats of Tobruk' in Old English.

He was silent and thoughtful when the world's largest battleship, the British *Hood* was sunk by the *Bismark*. He outlined the picture in heavy black, for all her crew of fourteen hundred men had gone down with her in one and a half minutes. Everyone was stunned at its loss which Mr. Churchill said was a calamity. When soon afterward the *Bismark* was sunk by the *King George V* and the *Rodney,* Barry exulted 'That'll give them a taste of their own medicine!' He also became an expert on aircraft types and performance and would try to instruct me.

He thought I was hopelessly silly because, copy-cat, I had also started a scrap-book, mainly to use up his flour-and-water paste. It went off quickly in the heat and could smell the house out. But my tastes leaned heavily towards Bib and Bub with little animals dressed in frocks and coats and hats saying 'Quick-sticks!', and Mrs. Scottie with her pramful of puppies. I pasted in pictures of Princess Elizabeth on her fifteenth birthday and of the King and Queen visiting survivors of the London Blitz in the burnt-out rubble of their homes, and, on the off-chance that Mum might just happen to notice when Christmas came, Heatley's advertisements for sleeping-dolls and prams.

On parade at school we were told that we should be proud of the designer of the Australian fighter-aircraft, the Wirraway, because he was a Townsville boy. 'Commander Wackett grew up in Townsville just like you,' Mr. Bonham told us, leaning forward over the wrought-iron verandah rails to emphasize his point. If we too, worked hard at school we could grow up to make our country proud of us. The boys could be brave fighting-men to help defend the Empire and the girls could be nurses, teachers and mothers. We all tried harder at Sums and Spelling that day.

As Barry and I did our homework together at the kitchen table beneath the swarms of flying ants and the occasional stink-beetle that got itself down our necks, he instructed me. 'Hurricanes! They're the fastest thing we've got,' he said. 'And Typhoons! They develop two and a half thou' horsepower! But nothing can match the Spitfire for maneuverability. They can wipe the floor with those Hun Messerschmitts!' balancing precariously on the back legs of the chair in a way that would have brought a sharp rebuke of 'Barry! You'll break your arm! Or the chair, or both!' from Mum if she had been home, and not at First Aid Class.

He said, 'Sometimes I think I wouldn't mind joining the RAAF. They take you at seventeen if you've been through the Air Training Corps. If only I had one of those Morse Practice sets in Hollis Hopkins. You have to be up on your Morse.' He had copied out the Morse code on a little card which he stuck under the pencil-holder in the lid of his school-bag so that he could study it in school.

He and the other boys filled in time during Subject and Predicate or Sum Cards by tapping messages to one another along the six-seater silky-oak desks. He would have liked to practise on me, rapping out dit-dahs on the kitchen table but I never got past 'SOS' which was 'dit-dit-dit dah-dah-dah dit-dit-dit'. Or perhaps it was the other way round?

'V', 'dit-dit-dit dah', was easy to remember as it fitted to the words 'Victory V' and also the opening bit of Beethoven's Fifth Symphony, which Barry told me the BBC in London played every night to encourage the French Resistance.

'Once you've made it into the RAAF you get sent to Canada with the Empire Air Training Scheme. You get your wings; then you get posted to your squadron. Somewhere in the Old Country, most likely. Wouldn't be bad, eh? Flight Lieutenant Barry Stilwell.' He never used his proper name 'Bertrand'. He wasn't really talking to me but gazing past the alarm-clock tick-tocking on the mantelpiece over the stove-recess to some distant point in time when he would be able to join up. 'If only the bloomin' war lasts long enough!'

Instead of the map of the Provinces of South Africa which he was meant to be doing for homework, he busied himself, tip of tongue gripped between his teeth in concentration, with drawing a Swordfish. 'They've got this torpedo under their belly, see.' He drew the Swordfish in a valorously steep dive, blowing a Swastika-bedecked ship to smithereens, funnel, debris and hapless Huns going sky-high. 'Let that be a lesson to them to lay-off our convoys!' he snarled. Suddenly we heard Mum coming up the front steps, home from First Aid Class. Quickly, Barry slid the drawing into his book and began frowning in deep concentration over the Orange Free State's maize-growing potential.

Convoy losses were a constant cause of anxiety in our family. Mum had a nephew Graham, her brother's only son, who although only fifteen was at sea with the British Merchant Navy. He had been at Naval College when the call came for volunteers to replace the heavy loss of manpower at sea due to U-Boat attacks on Merchant Shipping. Auntie Win had been frantic that he should offer himself when he was so young, but Uncle Horace had said that if England had need of him then he must go.

Our prayers for his safe-keeping were unceasing. 'God bless Cousin Graham and bring him safely home,' had to be said before hands reached for serviettes or heads touched pillows. In fact I was bowed beneath a self-imposed burden of prayer, including not only Cousin Graham, but Mum and Dad, the English Aunts and Uncles, 'all our soldiers, sailors and airmen, the King and Queen and all the Royal Family' and any stray cats, dogs or injured minah-birds or willy wagtails which I might have seen that day. The problem was that once I had added someone or something to my list I could never quite bring myself to remove them and so it grew to almost census proportions.

When the ABC News came on Barry and I would be told sharply, 'Ssh!' while Mum listened, head bent in concentration for the dreaded words '..heavy convoy losses..... seventeen of our ships were lost.' Then she would grow tense and silent, imagining fifteen year old Graham and others like him, perhaps adrift, half-frozen in a life-boat in mid-Atlantic or worse, burned to death horribly on a stricken oil-tanker. 'While we're just sitting here taking it easy! I feel so useless!' she would exclaim. Letters from 'Home' seldom mentioned Graham, except obliquely 'The lad is getting a nice tan up', meant he was probably in the Mediterranean, or more ominously after the Arctic Convoys to Archangel in Russia commenced, 'Your Aunt is knitting a nice pull-over for the boy'. We all knew the rules, repeated often enough on Mike Connor's Breakfast Session; not a word must be said about ships or troop movements; 'Careless talk costs lives', 'Loose lips sink ships' and 'Be like Dad, keep mum'.

Sons weren't to write home saying, 'Well, we're off on the *Orsova* next week.' Fathers weren't to let drop, over a beer in the bar of Lowth's, 'My boy's with the Eighth Divvie on his way to Singapore.' Such idle talk was dangerous. Who knew how many German spies might be lurking amidst the chinky-apple scrub or dry spear-grass on Castle Hill!

Chapter 4

SATURDAY MATINEE: 1941

'For the A.I.F. is marching, with a song of liberty;
So keep your chin up, Mother England!
We're Marching on to Victory'

A performance at the Wintergarden Theatre

I was learning the violin and it was all my own fault. There had been a film at the Wintergarden about the about the great violinist, Yehudi Menuhin. Mum herself was very musical and loved talented people. In the film the little Yehudi had played to enthralled crowds on the footpaths of New York. When we came home after seeing it, I thought Mum would be pleased with me if I were a child prodigy, too. I got two school rulers, jumped up on a dining-room chair, adopted a soulful expression and sawed backwards and forwards like Yehudi Menuhin.

Mum's eyes lit with pleasure. I was gratified, and a little surprised. She had always hoped I would show some spark of talent at something. Perhaps I was a great violinist! Perhaps all I needed was tuition! At this I climbed hastily down off the chair and put the rulers away, suddenly wary. Violin lessons! I knew Mr. Kennedy, the music teacher's dark forbidding Music Studio. It was around the corner in the QATB Building in Stanley Street. I had heard the pupils struggling through their scales and pieces and had no wish to join them. But once Mum had an idea she was not easily deterred. The next Saturday morning's edition of the *Townsville Daily Bulletin* carried a small advertisement: 'Wanted. Child's violin. Must be reasonably priced.'

Mr. Kennedy had grey hair and a matching fringe of grey beard that almost formed a circle round his pale-eyed, anxious face. He gazed worriedly at the little violin which Mum had bought, which had grooves cut across the finger-board to show where the fingers were to be put. 'These grooves will significantly alter the tone,' he told Mum. All around the little room were piles of sheet-music sliding off chairs, and instruments in cases shrouded under wraps. One corner was filled with a tangle of music stands. I wished myself well away from it all. 'I gave two pounds ten for it,' Mum was saying, as though that put paid to any further argument on the matter. It was, after all, a third of the family-income for one week.

Mr. Kennedy tucked the tiny violin under his chin and rippled through some experimental arpeggios, his eyes closed. I was awed. Until this moment I had been terribly alarmed by all this purchasing of violins. Even the smell of varnish and resin that rushed out from the case when the lid was opened had served to subdue me. But now I perceived that playing the violin was merely a matter of putting the thing under your chin, looking as though you were tasting Cherry Ripe and working your arm up and down. I already knew how to do the face and the arm bits. All that remained was to get the finger bit right.

Barry and I had made friends with a family called Bensley who lived across the road in Walker Street. Mr. Bensley owned a fruit and vegetable shop in Flinders Street. Mrs. Bensley made wedding bouquets and wreaths for funerals, working in a rubber washing-day apron and standing on an old sack-bag at the flower-filled cement tubs beneath the house. There were two children, Tim, about Barry's age, and Margaretta, slightly older than I was. There was also another girl called Evelyn, a few years older, whom the Bensleys had got from the Children's Orphanage in Warburton Street. She did all the housework and the cooking.

We hadn't expected to become friends with the Bensleys because they were Roman Catholics, which put them on the other side of an almost unbridgeable gulf as though they belonged to an alien camp. We knew by their uniforms that Tim Bensley went to the Christian Brothers' on Melton Hill and Margaretta to St Patrick's Convent on the Strand, to which in Townsville's heat, she wore a long-sleeved navy-blue uniform with a white starched collar bedecked with holy medals.

My friendship with Margaretta got off to a shaky start. I leaned forward curiously and touched one of the medals pinned to her dress. Margaretta started back sharply. 'Don't! Don't touch it!' she cried. 'They're spoilt if a Protestant touches them! Now I'll have to take it to Father Doherty and have it blessed again!' Mum could scarcely contain herself at this.

I began to learn quite a lot about the Catholic religion. One thing was that when you died you stank like a dead horse and went to purgatory, where you stayed put until released by the prayers of a number of Masses. Another was that Protestants didn't go to Heaven, only Catholics. It came as a shock that a Catholic would never enter a Protestant church, not even when, belatedly after the years in the West, I was christened at Central Methodist. And a Catholic would go to Hell for ever and ever if they married a Protestant. As far as Margaretta was concerned, Central Methodist in Stoke Street and Mr. Prouse, who seemed to be on quite friendly terms with God and always started the prayers with 'Heavenly Father', didn't even exist. Worse! Catholics thought the Pope was more important than the King!

Margaretta had a collection of holy cards of saints with rather alarming holes in their hands, but who none the less could manage to smile and to hold lilies or palm-fronds. I showed her my Sunday School tickets which I kept in an empty Capstan tin. They were little cards about the size of a large postage-stamp with text; '*They reap not, neither do they sow*' or '*He careth for thee.*' Each had a robin red-breast, a spray of forget-me-nots, or a scene of Lake Galilee. Every week at Sunday School you were given a new one. When you had six, you handed them in for a slightly larger one. When you had six of these you got a card with a ribbon to be hung on the wall. Finally, after goodness knows how many years of Sunday school attendance, you had six of the largest sized cards and could exchange them for a Bible. John Ackland was the only one I ever knew who achieved this feat, standing up to go forward at a special point in the church proceedings, smiling cheerfully, to be presented with a blue cloth-bound Bible inscribed 'For good attendance'.

There was something of a discrepancy in the way the Bensleys treated their children. Tim was expected to become a doctor so, if his school report from the Brothers was bad, Mr Bensley thought nothing of knocking him flat and giving him a good kicking while he was writhing on the grass. Margaretta, by comparison, was treated like a princess. Everything she had, clothes, dolls, toys, bangles, were the very best. Only children who had slaved their way through Grade Seven to pass Scholarship possessed watches but Margaretta wore one with a neat little gold band and mother-of-pearl face.

She went off regularly to have her hair permed. 'At the cost of a working man's weekly wage!' exclaimed Mum, scandalized. The technique of permanent waving was still not very advanced, so for days afterwards, her arrival would be heralded by what Barry called the 'pong' of scorched hair.

An army friend of Dad's who had slept on the stretcher on the back verandah when on leave bought me a scooter: a very basic model, just two wheels, a foot-board and a handle. I was astonished with delight. No one ever took any notice of me; it was Barry who people liked. I rode the scooter hesitantly along the footpath to meet him after school. The next day Margaretta appeared, flat-footedly propelling the most expensive of models with glittering chrome-work, white inflated tyres – mine had solid ones – handle-grips which sprouted ribbons, sprung footboard and, crowning touch, actual brakes! But instead of being knocked sideways with envy, as I was meant to be, I saw all the classy extras as not only excessive but positively silly. Brakes! Who needed them? You simply pressed your heel down on the back wheel!

Unlike Margaretta's, my scooter became a means of transport. I scootered on messages to the shop, to the library, even to music-lessons, the violin-case swinging precariously on the handle-bar. As other people parked cars or bicycles, I parked my scooter, with grave deliberation.

Ronnie also had a scooter and when he came to play on Saturday afternoons, we pushed them to the top of the Cutting to be able to swoop back down again, the wind singing in our ears, hopeful of right of way across Walker Street as it rushed upwards to meet us.

On Sundays, people with cars headed for Bluewater Creek, ninteen miles north. The Bensleys had a Morris with open sides and canvas hood. They took me with them for Margaretta's benefit. On the way the car would be filled with singing, everyone vying for the chance to call out the next song; *You Are My Sunshine* or *You're the Only Star in My Blue Heaven.* If we passed a dead horse or bullock by the roadside and the stench filled the car so that everyone cried 'Phaugh!' Margaretta would remark imperturbably, 'Sister Selvetia says that's what we smell like when we are dead'. In the sudden silence she would seize the chance to add, 'We haven't done *Out of the Blue Gums* yet.'

At Bluewater, the crowds of people spread picnic blankets under the sparse shade of the ghost-gums, eyeing the ground first to make sure they were not settling down on bindi-eyes, goat-head burrs or a bull-ant's nest. So popular was Bluewater that the Council had even decided to build Male and Female 'conveniences', which were an improvement on having to sidle off into the bush and go behind a tree, or wait till you got home.

Near the bridge was a big paper-bark, with a rope which hung over the water, on which the boys and young men swung, making Tarzan calls which echoed along the creek. Each tried to outdo the other in stunts of daring before letting go of the rope, to jack-knife or somersault into the shining blue water. Awkward belly-flops drew shouts of laughter and catcalls while the hapless youth swam to the bank to drag himself out, grinning to cover his discomfiture. A quick shake of the head to flick the water out of his hair would help him to regain his composure. Girls never took part in these displays of bravado. Boys showed-off; girls admired.

Neither Margaretta nor I could swim, so Mr Bensley ferried us out, one at a time, to a sandbar in the middle of the creek. He would deposit us in the sweet-smelling water to play the hours away until we were scarlet, wrinkled and ravenous. The Bensley's picnics always consisted of delectables from Lanes' Cake Shop; pies and sausage rolls, followed by cream-horns, Neanish tarts, chocolate eclairs and rainbow-cake oozing thick, squishy cream; treats which we never had at home.

Margaretta was very well-read. The Bensley's got *Truth*, every Sunday morning, lobbed over their front fence by a paper-boy who yelled 'Get ya *Truth*' as Mum and Barry and I were setting off for Central Methodist. Mum said *Truth* was a 'scandal sheet'; not fit to clean the stove with, but I looked forward to a resume of its contents next day after school from Margaretta. While she and I busied ourselves with her large collection of expensively dressed dolls and their equipages she would regale me with the juiciest bits of the scandal and murder for the week.

In this way, I learned of the Pyjama Girl in her charred silk pyjamas, who had been murdered many years before but ever since kept in a bath of formalin because she had never been identified. 'Just imagine her lying there staring, staring,' said Margaretta. I did. The bath-tub at the flat had iron feet like the claws of an eagle holding a ball. I could well imagine the half burned body of the Pyjama Girl, still in its silk pyjamas, lying in the bath staring up at me. I could hardly be persuaded to clean my teeth after that, let alone have my hair washed over the bath on Saturday morning. I knew the Pyjama Girl's eye could be staring up at me from just below the plug hole.

Barry's and my reading was less theatrical. Barry had bought, for a shilling, from the corner store, an album called *The Nestle's Book of Knowledge*. It had general knowledge information with blank spaces in which to stick the coloured cards which came in Nestle's penny chocolates. From *The Nestle's Book of Knowledge* we became familiar with the Seven Wonders of the World – Barry could name them off by heart; also how steam-engines worked; the Relief of Mafeking and the Sword of Damocles, which showed Damocles at a feast, horror-struck to find he was seated directly underneath a sword hanging by a single hair above his head. But how silly of him to sit there in the first place! You couldn't have missed seeing a thing like!

Barry was an avid collector of Nestle's cards, investing every penny that came his way in Nestle's chocolates to build up his album. In my class at Sunday school we had just had the story of the Wise Virgins and how they hid their money away. I quite liked their attitude. I would hide my money away too. I had a hidey-hole I had discovered behind a loose rock in the foot-path. There was a stone which slid out neatly, leaving a little space behind. It was my Ali Baba's cave. I had a penny hidden there which gave me a pleasurable sense of importance. Sometimes I took the stone out just to see the penny lying there.

Barry got to know of my hoard. 'Now, Skin,' (short for 'Skin and Blister', London rhyming slang for 'sister'; but in my case, short for 'Skinny Legs'), 'You know I'm saving these *Book of Knowledge* cards for your sake as much as my own. Don't be Ikey. I know you've got a penny stashed away somewhere. Fair goes! Cough it up!' I felt the weightiness of being asked, not unlike Queen Isabella of Spain giving Christopher Columbus the gold for his fleet. I led Barry to my secret hiding place and drew out the stone. There lay my penny in all its grand consequentiality.

'Ha!' said Barry, snatching it out without ceremony. No courtly bow, velvet cap in hand, for queenly largesse. Off he dashed full pelt towards the corner shop. I trailed behind, uncertain whether my greatness-of-heart had been acknowledged. Clinging to the idea that it was I who was funding this important purchase, I craned my head next to his as the new card was revealed; 'The Mausoleum of Halicarnassus'. 'Pigs!' said Barry, in disgust. 'Already got it!' He broke the chocolate into two bits, gave me the smaller and sauntered off, hands in pockets, whistling.

Sometimes, if the shop-keeper was busy with a customer, weighing out sugar or biscuits or chook-feed, Barry would place himself off-handedly near the counter and, pretending to be reading the old newspapers placed there for wrapping purposes, would unobtrusively go through the box of penny chocolates, sliding the red wrappers back just far enough to see which card each contained. If he found one he didn't have he would deftly replace it with an unwanted double of his own. This process required nerves of steel as he was liable to a good kick in the pants if detected.

In this way he built up *The Nestle's Book of Knowledge*. It was the only encyclopaedia we ever owned. Barry knew it off by heart and would quiz me. 'Who was it that asked for 'more'; 'What's the difference between a stalactite and a stalagmite?' I could never remember. 'Stalactites hold on tight. See?' I didn't, but I was impressed that he did.

When we listened to the Quiz Kids on Sunday nights, Barry knew as many answers as they did. 'If only we could send you to a good school!' Mum would sigh. But Barry had no desire to be at a 'good school'. He was now a member of a little gang of Walker Street boys, the Mark of Zorros. For their headquarters they had a nest in the long guinea grass at the foot of the hill behind the High School across the road from our place. Barry was beginning to feel he belonged. The Mark of Zorros had chosen their name in honour of a matinee hero. Each Saturday afternoon at the Wintergarden, Zorro could be seen in a very hot and itchy-looking black costume with a mask and sombrero hat, righting wrong and overcoming the wicked. The Baddies always ended up with a mark from Zoro' s sword intended to scare them into better behaviour. Walker Street had one great advantage; the Wintergarden Picture Theatre was just around the corner.

Mum didn't like us going to matinees; they were 'coarse and vulgar' and 'did nothing to improve one's mind' but she took us to *Gulliver's Travels*, *Pinocchio*, *Tom Brown's Schooldays* and *The Bluebird*. I cried all the way through '*The Bluebird*', longing for the love of grandparents I had never seen. When the children in the film ran through the woods to their grandparents' outstretched arms in the Land of Memory, I knew without being able to express it in words that the children of immigrants are sadly short-changed of love.

As Mum adored anything to do with romance and gaiety we got to see *New Moon* with Jeanette MacDonald and Nelson Eddie. For weeks afterwards, Mum pegged the sheets on the line or cut up the tripe and the onions for dinner humming dreamily *Softly, As in a Morning Sunrise*, or *Lover, Come Back to Me* and Barry marched me along Walker Street in step to *Give Me Some Men Who are Stout Hearted Men.*

Dad came home and we went to see Charlie Chaplin in *The Great Dictator*, which had Hitler falling over his own flat feet and going through doors that banged shut on his nose. The management of the Roxy Theatre was so sure of the value of *The Great Dictator* to the War Effort that they wanted everyone in Townsville to see it. If people couldn't afford tickets, all they had to do was bring a letter from their minister at church and they could get in free.

Dad liked George Formby and took us to see *Call a Cop*. As he had once played the mandolin himself he took us right through *When I'm Cleaning Windows*.

'The blushing bride, she looked divine,
The bride-groom he was doing fine,
I'd rather have his job than mine,
When I'm cleaning windows.'

Lacking a mandolin, he would do the appropriate twanging through his nose, click-clacking two spoons on his wrists, elbows and knees for rhythm, all the while executing little music-hall dance steps around the dining-room, his eyes sparkling with fun. He would also take us through our paces on *Hands, Knees and Bumps-a-daisy* and *Doing the Lambeth Walk* at the end of which there had to be a shout of 'Oi!' After a few impatient 'Really! Bert!'s Mum would take herself disapprovingly out to the verandah to dampen-down the ironing or water the ferns, distancing herself from such Cockneyfied goings-on.

But on Saturday afternoons we longed to be like other children who swarmed to the Wintergarden for the matinee, with sixpence to get in and threepence to spend on a Violet

Crumble Bar. It didn't matter what the programme was; tastes were simple. There should be Goodies and Baddies. There should be towns with wooden sidewalks and saloon-bar doors that swung in and out, lots of empty barrels standing about and a dusty main street along which the final shoot-out would take place. Horses had to be able to gallop for miles without knocking-up and be able to come to a halt sliding on their haunches. The hero's hat should never blow off.

It was also a requirement at some point of the proceedings that a driverless coach bearing the heroine must be about to plunge over a precipice. The heroine must never do anything useful such as seizing the reins, or jumping clear while the going was good. She must stifle a scream with pretty hands and reach out with helpless arms. Over the skyline at that moment must ride Gene Autry, Roy Rodgers or The Lone Ranger. It little mattered which one. But he must take in the situation at a glance, reach a shared decision for utmost speed with Beauty, Trigger or Silver, and, hat still in place, gallop to a last minute rescue.

It was a remarkable feature of these cliff-edge rescues that the wheels of the coach always spun in the opposite direction to that in which the coach was travelling, and continued to do so even after it had bounced the required number of times down the ravine, to lie, an irrecoverable loss to the coaching company concerned, in the gulch below.

Barry explained to me that the wheels spun backwards because in the filming they moved faster than the rate at which cameras could film. I listened, but doubtfully. I knew he knew such things. But I also knew that there was a really-truly Cowboy Land where wheels did move backwards, where boulders were always stacked in piles ready for Baddies to ride through while Goodies jumped on them without either missing completely or breaking a leg. Goodies could also receive terrible bangs on the head with the butt of a Baddy's revolver and recover completely by simply shaking their heads, looking more resolved than ever and putting their hats back on. There was also this strange thing in Cowboy Land that miles from anywhere, an orchestra would strike up, and the hero, who up till this point had been a shining example of courage, horsemanship and common-sense, would spoil everything by suddenly taking off his hat, gazing into the heroine's eyes and bursting into song.

This was the signal for pandemonium to break out in the audience, as boys took the opportunity to thump their neighbours, to kick the person in front of them or to give one another Chinese-burns or horse-bites on the arm. Girls rearranged one another's hairstyles, read Fantail wrappers aloud, told secrets and beat off boys who, intent on showing affection, made raids on hairclips or ribbons.

Should the manager with his strong torch-beam stroll at a masterful pace down the aisle, it was sure to have a composing effect. Seats were magically reoccupied and calm restored. No one wanted to find themselves frog-marched out to the reality of a hot sunlit Saturday-afternoon in Sturt Street.

The high point of the afternoon was the serial; *Tarzan and the Apes*, *The Lone Ranger*, *Jungle Jim*, or *The Dead End Kids*. The only episode of *The Dead End Kids* which I ever saw came to its end just as the boys were trapped at the bottom of a lift-shaft with the lift descending down, down, down upon them. Then 'To be Continued' came of the screen, to loud groans and another outbreak of elbowings and hair-pullings at the thought of having to wait till next Saturday to see what happened.

Each serial continued for about thirteen weeks. There were swinging bridges over chasms that broke when people were half-way across. There were crocodiles that slid into the water when the hero was swimming to the heroine's rescue. Frequently, villains stepped into swamps and were sucked down, leaving only a hat that floated on the surface. Every episode concluded at some nail-biting point; the heroine tied to a stake in a jungle clearing, while the flames gained around her and the savages danced.

When I begged Margaretta to tell me the fate of the Dead End Kids in the lift-shaft, she said off-handedly 'Oh, at the last moment there was this little side-door that opened. They all got out.' Margaretta was calm about such crises. She knew the rules. Goodies didn't get killed. Only baddies.

She herself was a Deanna Durban devotee. She had seen every Deanna Durban film, not once but two or three times, following them with the faithful Evelyn, from the Roxy to the Olympia, the Regent in Hermit Park or the South Townville Talkies. She knew all the songs and dialogue and directed me in long Saturday afternoon re-enactments of the plots. 'I must be Deanna Durban. You must be waiting for me at the stage door. Now, help me on with my furs. Then we must go to a night-club. You must call the waiter and order champagne.' The champagne was water tinted pink with red crepe-paper and came in an old tomato-sauce bottle. The expensive caviar supper on the silver salver was some nasturtium flowers on a Sunshine Milk tin lid.

Margaretta saw to it that I learned all the Deanna Durban songs, *Cherry Cherry Bim*, *My Heart is Singing* and *It's Foolish But It's Fun*. Deanna Durban had dimples. Margaretta pressed her fingertips into her cheeks to acquire dimples. Once Deanna had been kidnapped and, though locked in a dreadful dungeon, faced her captors with her dimpled chin held up bravely. Margaretta and I spent an entire sunny afternoon crouched under the wash-tubs to prove that we too could be dauntless in adversity.

Despite Mum's poor opinion of them, Saturday afternoon matinees had a wonderfully positive outlook. No matter how bad things might seem, they were bound to turn out all right in the end. Good always triumphed over evil. Though the war news about which the grown-ups talked in worried tones was gloomy, it was taken for granted by the children of Townsville that things would turn out alright. Our side was going to win. That old Hitler hadn't a hope! Anyone could see that he was a Baddie!

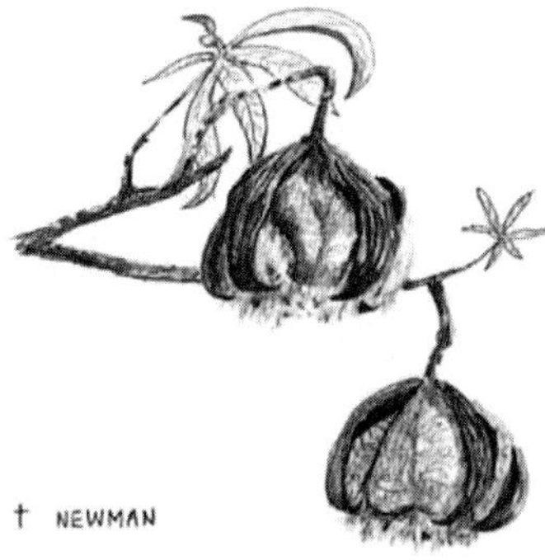

Chapter 5

PATRIOTIC TIMES: 1941

'There'll be Bluebirds over the White Cliffs of Dover,
Tomorrow, when the world is free.'

Central State School

Suddenly I could read. Not just the Queensland School Reading Book, but proper reading, like grown-ups. The School Reading Books had black and white illustrations of children in button-up boots, with girls in pinafores and boys in sailor-suits. Kevin Clegg said his grandma had told him they had had the same books in her day. The stories made you anxious. The fluffy little chicken that didn't come when Mother Hen called in *Obey Your Parents* was torn to pieces by a hawk. It made you scamper full pelt from the cubby-house at the first sign of being wanted. Barry had built us a cubby-house down the back-yard and a stray cat had her kittens there. Each afternoon we crouched watching the little bullet heads butting into the mother's damp pink fur, deciding on names and which ones were our favourites. The ugly one that no-one loved became my special one.

Another Reading Book lesson was *The Stone in the Road*, in which a good little boy went about moving stones out of the way of passing horses and carriages. A rich man rewarded him by hiding a gold coin under a stone for him to find. I picked up stones off the bitumen along Walker Street for days, not once coming across a gold coin placed for my pleasurable discovery.

In Miss Wheeler's Grade One we had Reading after Little Lunch. The purple Reading Books were taken out of the press and slapped down four or five at a time on the ends of the desks. One reached energetically, hoping for a cleanish one, not one with the cover missing and 1934 stamped on the ragged pages.

For Reading it was 'seats back' so that we could stand smartly when it was our turn to read. Everything was done to numbers. 'Stand!' We stood. On 'Seats back! One!' those at the end of each form got a grip on it but knew not to do any actual lifting until 'Two!' They knew well enough to hoist and deposit with feather-touch quiet. Any banging and half the lesson could be spend practising to Miss Wheeler's hissed commands 'Seats in! One! Two! Seats back! One! Two!' until even she, tiring of it, would screw her eyes tight and whisper the final command, pretending to be surprised at how very quietly it had been done.

For Reading, the class sat, backs straight, feet flat on the floor holding the open book on the palm of the left hand and pointing to each word as it was read aloud, with the 'pointing finger' of the right. Woe betide any child who forgot himself and curled a careless thumb over the bottom edge of the book to keep the pages flat. It was always a boy. The fan-shaped grubbiness at the bottom-centre of each page was a give-away. Miss Wheeler would have the offender out into the centre-aisle and, hoiking up the back of his trouser legs as far as knee-length tight serge would allow, administered sharp slaps. It was not unknown for her to finish the admonition by bringing the defaced Reading Book sharply down on the miscreant's head.

At the end of this small distraction the one whose turn it was to read next would go ahead smoothly as though nothing had happened. The chance to read came but once a day. It was best to make the most of it, enunciating every consonant with an audible click of the tongue and remembering to count for punctuation marks: two for a comma, four for a full-stop. 'There was once an old woman whose only son, (one, two) Jack, (one, two) was very lazy.' (one, two, three, four). As each paragraph was numbered it was possible to tell which would be yours when the time came. Silent rehearsal was not only feasible but advisable. Some paragraphs would be short, a mere: 'Yes', (one, two) said the boy, (one, two) with a willing smile. (one, two, three, four)' Some were several sentences long. This never seemed fair. I always seemed to get a short one and never be discovered in full and eloquent flow when Mr. Bonham, passing along the verandah, paused at the door.

But beyond the School Readers I could not read. Mum could not believe such a dullard. She bought me *Tiger Tim* and *Rainbow* comics, but the merry little moppets in the pictures seemed to have nothing to do with Walker Street, Central School and the fearsome Miss Wheeler. Reading was something you did after Little Lunch and then left well alone.

But when Mum went to the Library in the School of Arts I went with her, so I knew that there were tall shelves lined with books covered in shiny black linen, with the titles lettered in white ink. There was a shelf at the far end of the room reserved for children's books, also covered in shiny black linen and lettered in white. One day, crouched on the linoleum in front of this shelf, I made the discovery that each book had a dramatic full-colour picture at the front and five or six equally intriguing ones throughout; a gorilla, beating its chest and snarling with rage was bursting out of the jungle upon startled campers; a woman clutching a fair-haired child was fleeing from a castle; school girls were kneeling in a dark cellar examining a hoard of jewelry. Who were these people? What were they doing? And Why?

'Mum', I whispered nervously, fingering Mum's dress as she waited at the Librarian's desk, 'Could I have a book, too?' Mum no doubt thought it was money down the drain. She had just about given up on me and my lack of any discernible abilities. None the less, she paid over the threepence and I went home with a book.

I curled up with it on a sea-grass chair on the back verandah with a wary eye on the green tree-frog, its yellow throat ticking, asleep in a nearby maidenhair-fern. I intended to study the pictures and to pose looking grown-up and absorbed. To my surprise I found I could pick out a few words here and there. I had no inkling what the repetitious 'katydids' on the first page were all about, but somehow the sense of the story began to present itself to me. Soon, the disagreeable proximity of the frog, the discomfort of the ridged sea-grass chair, the narrow back verandah and Walker Street dissolved. I was somewhere in a not-to-be-defined Other Place, listening eagerly, all unobserved, as two sisters argued about their holidays. There were problems about money. I knew about those! I was at one with them and yet they didn't know I was there. It was magical.

Mum's call 'Set the table, please. Barry will be home from school at any minute!' went unheeded. My mumbled, 'I'm reading!' met with a sharp, 'Don't be silly! You know you can't!' until curious, she appeared from the kitchen. 'Go on, then! Let me hear you!' she said. Clearly and with that high-pitched sing-song enunciation which the clever little girls at the top of the class used for Mr. Bonham's benefit, I began to read aloud from *What Katy Did.* Mum was astonished. It was better than a win at Bert Brown's Casket Agency, she told me, giving me a quick congratulatory hug. I knew that I had shot up enormously in her opinion. I had also shot up in my own.

I could hardly wait for Barry to come home to tell him the news, but when he did come, heaving his school-bag down on to the back verandah, he had more important tidings of his own. The Combined Schools' Patriotic Concert was to be Friday week at the Wintergarden and Mr. Penphrase had told them that boys had to have long-sleeved white shirts and shorts with a white belt and maroon tie.

For weeks we had been treated to regular previews of *Up from Somerset* and *Drake's Drum* from Barry under the shower. 'He takes after your father,' sighed Mum, pausing in the midst of making dumplings for the stew while the cubby-house cat, now an indoors cat and christened 'Mumpuss', twined ingratiatingly in and out of her legs. 'Your father used to be a choir boy at St Paul's Cathedral. He had a lovely voice. He used to sing at all the shipboard concerts on the *Border* when we were coming out; *Little Grey Home in the West* and *Smiling Through.* Her eyes were soft with the light of remembering. Barry from the bathroom would be just hitting his stride with *Hearts of Oak.*

When he and the Mark of Zorros went chasing the goats on the ridge of Castle Hill above the reservoir, pausing as they galloped through the brown grass to aim with their 'gings' or shanghais at the bony rumps of the fleeing herd, the shouted refrain of *Excelsior* would come floting down.

'Try not the pass,' the old man said.
'Dark lowers the tempest overhead,
The roaring torrent is deep and wide.'
But still that valiant youth replied, 'Excelsior! Excelsior!'

They relished the octave drop between the beginning and ending of each line which gave them the chance to show how strong and manly their voices were becoming. They shouted it, poised on the pink granite boulders high on the ridge, with the goats bounding and leaping before them over the skyline.

Mum bought a maroon tie from Stan Shorts, The Menswear Specialist. It was one of the clip-on variety with a permanent knot at the front. This was a disappointment to Barry as he liked to stand posed in front of the mirror of Mum's wardrobe, going through the masculine ritual of putting his tie on, even though it often ended up well below his belt or far too short, displaying shirt buttons that were not meant to be on view.

'But you'll have to make do with your school belt.' said Mum. I'll give it a coat of white paint. Perhaps we'll be able to clean if off again afterwards.' Painting my school shoes white for the Sunday School Anniversary had worked, but it didn't seem to work with Barry's belt. Mum gave it two coats as it swung, pegged to the washing line. For some reason the paint refused to dry. Mum, not to be beaten, lit the oven and tried to bake it dry. The belt stayed tacky. On the night of the concert Barry emerged from the bathroom, his hair gleaming with Spruso, clutching his pants, demanding, 'What am I supposed to do for a belt?' Mum, a look of desperation in her eyes, cried 'Its no use! You'll have to use your father's! Quick! Get it from his lowboy!' Dad's belt was ample enough to wrap around Barry twice. 'It will have to be cut!' cried Mum in desperation, 'Oh! Well! There are more ways of killing a cat than choking it to death!' She sliced Dad's good civilian belt with the bread-knife and punched a new hole with the prong of the carving-fork.

When we arrived at the Wintergarden the gravel area outside was a seething mass of parents and white-clad children. Clouds of insects swirled around the lamps under which the Townsville Ladies' Pipe Band in tartan kilts and black velvet jackets, and the Central State School Fife and Drum band in white sun-helmets were drawn up, taking it in turns to get the Patriotic flavor of the evening going with *Sussex by the Sea* and *Pack Up Your Troubles*.

Boys, aware of their unaccustomed ties and ear-scrubbed spruceness were dashing after one another among the palms and croton-beds. Girls intoxicated by crisp white voile, new socks, patent-leather shoes and Shirley Temple curls acquired by painful hours in curling-rags, chattered shrilly and unnecessarily, telling one another with shiverings and clutchings, how nervous they were, all the while glancing round artfully, to see if the boys were noticing their miraculously-enhanced appearances. All were intoxicated at knowing themselves to be the stars of the occasion.

There was a sudden hush as teachers, also dressed to the nines, began marshalling the children for the start of the performance. The different schools eyed one another jealously, each feeling confident that its contingent looked the best, as, subdued and expectant, they were marched off.

Inside the theatre the rows of reclining canvas seats were packed with parents, grandparents, aunts and uncles. Last to arrive before the lights dimmed was the Official Party: the Mayor, the Lady Mayoress in tight cerise, the Chief Inspector of Schools, Mr.Walton and, of most singular interest to the entire gathering, the Director of Education, Mr. Edwards.

Every head turned to catch a glimpse of this august presence whose name evoked awe from every parent, teacher and pupil.

It was he who could raise the school-leaving-age to fifteen if he desired, who knew what questions were on the Scholarship papers and who, once they were set, kept them under lock and key in his own office: a being, in short, superior to any that most of them had ever clapped eyes on. Not a heart among the assembled parents but breathed a half-prayer that the evening should go well in the presence of such personages. No cock-ups! No bungles! And if someone was going to fall off a form or sing the wrong note, let it not be their own Elsie, Beryl, Raymond or Eric.

Then the heavy maroon velvet curtains stirred and began to rise, revealing tier upon tier, shoulder to shoulder, the white-clad ranks of the Townsville Combined Schools' Patriotic Choir, faces stiff with fright, lips strained into well-trained smiles, eyes searching, searching beyond the footlights for Mum and Dad, Grandma and the family. Barry being tall was in the middle of the back row, hands clasped tightly behind. Mum observed with relief that his black belt was obscured behind the well-frizzed hair of the girl in front of him.

A dramatic pause, a moment of hushed expectation, then Mr. Penphrase, who for weeks might have been observed riding his push-bike from school to school for rehearsals, strode on to the stage, resplendent in full evening dress and with the solemn tread of one who knows the moment of fulfillment has arrived, that the success or failure of the venture is in his own hands and that the eye of the Director of Education is full upon him. After a seemly pause, enter also Miss Pask the Accompanist, posy of pansies at her shoulder, who crosses the stage in silver evening shoes with quick, competent steps. After her, trails a bespectacled girl who thinks to make herself invisible by hunching her shoulders sufficiently. She is to 'turn over' for Miss Pask.

A chord was struck. Mothers and fathers clambered out of the canvas deck-chairs and helped Grandmas to their feet. All stood to attention, squared their shoulders and threw hearts and souls into *God Save the King*. The Patriotic Concert got underway. *Wandering the King's Highway* was followed by *Keep Right On To The End Of The Road*; *Sea Fever* by *Rule Britannia* and *Hearts of Oak* by *Men of Harlech* and *All Through The Night*. During *Excelsior* Barry's face was wrapt and intent, very different from his derisory goat-hunting yodellings.

A slight fair-haired girl came forward and sang in crystal tones *It's a Lovely Day, Tomorrow* and *The White Cliffs of Dover*. People were reaching for handkerchiefs before she climbed, to appreciative acclaim, back to her seat. 'A little Vera Lynn!' said the stout lady behind us, blowing loudly. Several boys clambered down from their places and grouping themselves at the front of the stage with only minor re-adjustments of place, belts and ties, launched into *D 'Y e Ken John Peel* as a compliment to the Garrison. 'There's Maxie Ackland!' I hissed in a stage whisper, not at all unwilling to have people near us know that we were acquainted with such talent.

For a change of pace there was Verse-Speaking: *The Bugles of England* followed up by *My Country* :

'The bugles of England were calling o'er the sea,

As they had called a thousand years; calling now to me'
and
'Though earth holds many splendours, wherever I may die,
I know to what brown country my homing thoughts will fly.'

The words of popular patriotic songs were printed on the back of the programme for Community Singing, though most of them were known by heart. The audience, mindful of Townsville's reputation for music, cleared its throat and looked to its collective laurels. *Old Father Thames* rolled off sonorously along Sturt Street; *There'll Always Be an England* could have been heard from the railway-shunting-yards, but when it came to *Land of Hope and Glory*, I glanced nervously upwards to make sure that the great inverted duck-pond bowl of the Wintergarden ceiling was still firmly in its place.

The success of the Patriotic Concert stood Barry in good stead at home for many weeks to come. These days he always seemed to be in hot water. Cries of, 'Just you wait till your father comes home!' would follow him as he fled to the Mark of Zorros' lair at the foot of the hill.

Mum had always taken great pleasure in making all her own clothes, studying styles and patterns in the glossy fashion manuals in McKimmin's haberdashery department, deliberating over materials and trimmings. Dress-lengths for new frocks and matching bloomers for me usually came from the remnants table. She took fierce pleasure in being able to cut out a garment from less material than was recommended in the printed instructions, getting down on hands and knees on the lino with the fabric spread on an old sheet, putting and taking pieces of flimsy tissue-pattern with murmurings of, 'Let me see. Selvedge here. Aha!' and, 'Where there's a will there's a way. They always tell you to cut to waste!' pleased at having outwitted 'them' once again.

One afternoon she was just starting to work on our Show frocks. Everyone in Townsville had to have a new outfit for the annual Pastoral and Agricultural Show, the huge day of the year, which was looked forward to for months, events being dated as having been 'before the Show' or 'after the Show'. My Show outfit was to be a pleated skirt with bib and braces in a Royal Stewart tartan, with waistcoat and forage cap to match. The little girl in the illustration on the pattern looked pert and sunny. Mum was hoping that such an ensemble might do something to perk me up a bit. Everything was cleared off the dining-room table, the bright red fabric spread out ready for the moment of 'cutting-out'. For Cutting Out, Mum had a pair of special dress-making scissors. No-one but herself dare use them. No pictures for scrap-books, no brown paper for school-book covers. No string. No cardboard. Nothing! Mum's dress-making scizzors were sacred. As important as Dad's tin of campaign medals in his lowboy drawer. Things you never touched.

But, now, slowly, in the very moment of making the first cut into the Royal Stewart, her face contracted to a frown. Whatever was wrong with her scissors? She made a few experimental chops in the air. They even felt different; somehow heavier and slower. Gone was the razor-sharp response which was the thrill of starting her task; the instant keenness of well-honed steel. Whatever could be wrong with them!

I knew what Mum did not know. Mum did not know that the craze at school was for gat-guns. Every boy, including Barry, had a laboriously carved piece of wood shaped like a revolver. The ammunition was rubber bands. The best rubber bands were rings cut from bicycle inner-tubes. If your mother just happened to have a very good pair of scizzors, sharpish, so much the better, and of course, the Mark of Zorros were blood-brothers who shared. Weren't they? The laboriously cut rubber-bands, crisscrossed decoratively on the wooden handle of the Mark of Zoro's guns, provided not only professional-looking hand-grips but ready supplies of ammunition. If a boy got the length of his barrel equal to the stretch of the rubber ring, he had a formidable piece of playground weaponry. 'Ouch!'es, 'Ow!'s and 'I'm telling on you!'s resounded in and out of the aerial roots of the Moreton Bay fig-trees, around the brick posts under the school, in the play-shed, even during Religious Instruction! Stanley Sugden was hit in the eye and was doubled off on the bar of a Scholarship boy's bicycle to the ambulance, his eye poulticed with cold tea-leaves to relieve the pain.

That was the final straw. The Infant's School was marched to the Big School for a special parade. We gazed up in awed fright as Mr. Bonham paced the verandah, his brows drawn ferociously. Then, gripping the wrought-iron railings, he leaned outwards, the more to strike terror to our hearts, and said, pausing between each word, 'If.. it ..comes.. to my .. attention.. that.. any .. one.. of.. you (by 'you' he meant the boys. The girls were just giving up hop-scotch in favour of skippy) so ...much...as...even..THINKING of rubber-guns..!' Long pause. 'Then it will be the WORSE for him!' An even longer pause ensued here while Mr. Bonham gave every row of boys on the parade the full benefit of his eye. The boys kept their eyes to the front, not even daring to blow away flies crawling up nostrils. They heard the words, 'Six-of-the-best', 'kept in for a month', and 'pick up rubbish for the rest of the year' and wriggled their bare toes into the gravel. Old Hambone's cuts were no joke! Mr. Bonham swished the side of his trousers with the cane to emphasize his point. The girls looked smug. The boys were copping it and a good job too! There was not a girl who didn't bear red welts on her legs, arms or neck inflicted by rubber bands. They rejoiced as one; silently, viciously.

Mum knew nothing of this. So, now, material spread before her, she made a few more experimental chops in mid-air with her scissors. Where was the rapier keenness gone! How grinding, how reluctant they felt! She got a scrap of material from the scrap-bag and gave a tentative cut. Toothless, the blades chomped up and down. On Mum's face, bewilderment turned to dismay! Dismay to suspicion; suspicion to terrible suspicion; terrible suspicion to realization! Barry!

At that moment the front gate clicked and, coming up the path was Dad, smiling cheerfully, kit-bag over one shoulder, home unexpectedly from Miowera. Quietly, I eased myself down the back steps and fled along Walker Street. I would meet Barry and warn him. Behind me I could hear Mum's voice raised in recriminations that suddenly included Dad as well; '...needs a man to handle him… a father that's never here…getting completely out of hand ....wretched Army!

Weighed down with foreboding, I lay in wait for Barry at the School of Arts corner. Here he came, school-bag over one shoulder, 'Donkey's Dinner' on the back of his head, abstractedly kicking a bottle-top along the gutter ahead of him, whistling *Colonel Bogey* as he came. Seeing me, evident harbinger of ill-tidings, his face fell. 'Oh! you're in for it!' I breathed. 'Mum knows about the scissors! And Dad's home.' I made my face sympathetic, loyal page to doomed knight. Was there not also, beneath the sympathy, some slight satisfaction at being the bearer of such dire news, some tiny shiver of anticipation at the drama to come?

'Pigs arse!' said Barry, dragging the gat-gun from his waist-band. 'Here then! Get rid of this! Shove it up under the roof of the cubby. Don't let on!' Squaring his shoulders and firming his chin he brushed past me and marched home, every bit the recaptured Prisoner-of-War being dragged before the Camp Commandant for summary execution.

Rhythmic wallops with Dad's razor-strap resounded from the bathroom. Barry didn't cry. Britishers never broke under interrogation. This only served to make Dad crankier. He had been in a perfectly good mood when he had arrived home, but what man wants to come home to this! Wife up in arms, and flaming kids getting out of hand.

Barry, face taut and guarded, pushed past me. The last thing he wanted was sympathy from me. He ducked under the hessian doorway of the cubby-house, reappeared with the gat-gun and, holding it by the barrel as an act of surrender, marched back up stairs. There was a loud crack. The gat-gun, in two pieces, arced out over the verandah-railing and landed in the back yard, pink rubber rings bounding in all directions.

'Stick the flaming thing in the bin!' Dad roared, thoroughly worked up now. Barry, taking two steps at a time, crouched, chin on knees, gathering up the pieces. Under his breath he muttered, 'Yes, Sir! No, Sir! Three bags full, Sir!' which is what the boys at school said after they had copped a belting from Krausie. Now, glancing cautiously over his shoulder towards the house, he eased a few more of the rubber bands off the broken handle and scattered them with studied carelessness into the grass. Who was Dad to come barging in busting up a bloke's things? He would be gone back to camp on Monday and good riddance, too!

Mum was mollified by Dad putting a razor-sharp edge on her dress-making scissors. He was a dab hand at most things, having become, like most men who went through the Great Depression, a Jack of All Trades. He honed Mum's scissors lovingly, glancing along the blades in the light and putting the finishing touch by stroking them firmly across the neck of a glass bottle to smooth any roughness. Our outfits for the Show were finished in due time.

The suit which Mum made herself for the Show was navy-blue slub-linen with a floral motif on the shoulder and pocket. For accessories she chose a red felt hat, pulling it well down over her face in Greta Garbo style, and navy shoes, handbag and gloves. She had made a tartan bow-tie for Barry to match my tartan kilt, cap, and waistcoat. Barry wasn't having a bar of it. 'Come off it, Mum! Fair goes! Face Ache's enough to make the Black Watch sound the Retreat, as it is!'

I took this for what it was, a compliment, and tended to strut as we set off for the bus-stop at the Great Northern. My pleated skirt kicked out nicely over my knees as I walked. My hair in Shirley Temple sausage-curls on either side of my forage cap bounced rhythmically in time with my step. Most wonderful of all I had new shiny patent-leather shoes from Fostar's Shoe shop, the one with the big rocking-horse to ride while you waited. I also had a handbag on a shoulder strap with my handkerchief and sixpence inside.

The bus-driver greeted me; 'Hello, Scottie! Aren't we all dolled up!' Unfortunately he was the one who, on a former occasion, had tried to put his hand up the leg of my bloomers when the bus was empty and I wasn't sure at which stop to get off.

'You might smile a bit!' Mum said impatiently as we took our seats. 'Why do you always have to put on that down-in-the-mouth expression when someone speaks to you?' A cloud began to edge over my day.

The shadow deepened when, in the Exhibits' Hall at the Show Grounds, it was discovered in the School Work section that Margaretta had won First Prize for 'Transcription, with Decorative Heading; Ten years and Under'. There amidst the 'Maps of Queensland showing Physical Features', Model Compositions on 'Magnetic Island' and exemplary Geometrical Drawing books, her Exercise Book lay, shiny blue ribbon attached, the product of Margaretta's own hands for all the world to startle back from in admiration and wonder, showering honour upon not only herself but St Patrick's Convent.

'I do wish you two would try a little harder!' said Mum. Then, studying Margaretta's masterwork more closely; 'I don't know. It seems very good for an eight year old. I wouldn't put it past those Bensleys to get Evelyn to do it for her. Or maybe even one of the Nuns! You can never tell with RCs, what they'll get up to.'

Perhaps if I had won a prize for school work, which wasn't very likely as Miss Wheeler hadn't thought to enter any, I might have got the dear little pinch-faced monkey-on-a-stick that I had my heart set on. No amount of wheedling and dragging my new patent-leather shoes in the dust would budge Mum from her conviction that such things were not only a sheer and utter waste of money but harboured every germ under the sun as well. Certainly the flamboyant Show-dolls with kewpie smiles, unaccountably stuck together legs, gauzy skirts and spangles where their singlets should have been, were entirely out of the question. They cost too much money. I knew that. Margaretta had them right around the mirror in her bedroom and across her curtains.

Mum bought me a balloon which I knew to be beneath the dignity of one wearing the Royal Stewart, forage cap and all. I resolved to get rid of it at the very first opportunity. My plan was that, upon its demise, I would burst into inconsolable tears. Tenderly, to soothe my distress, Mum would purchase the first little monkey-on-a-stick she happened upon. I trailed the balloon in the bindi-eyes, stroked the prickly flanks of the Champion Large White Boar with it, fluttered it over the display of pineapples from Horseshoe Bay and allowed it to become entangled in the wheels of a pramful of twins. The balloon was one of the determined type and intended to weather the most exacting of People's Days at the Show.

Somewhere a big drum was booming, 'Ker-thum-thum-thum!' It was Jimmy Sharman's Boxing Troupe, the boxers looking tired and bored on a plank high above the heads of the crowd. Mum hurried us briskly past. Nor were we afforded any opportunity to study the faded canvas banners outside each of the tents in Side Show Alley: Fifi, The Tattooed Lady; The Snake Pit; The Laconas, Aerial Gymnasts Extraordinaire; Shirley Thomms, The Yodelling Songbird; Ubangi, 24 inches of Savage Warrior, or the Crazy House with the laughing mechanical sailor beckoning and nodding.

Barry spent his sixpence on two consecutive rides on the Flying Horses, bucking his mount to make it swing far out almost level with the striped awning, tie flying over his shoulder. Having recently seen *Forty Thousand Horsemen*, he was riding with the Light Horse somewhere in the Western Desert towards Benghazi. I spent my sixpence on a Hoadley's Show-bag and shared out self-importantly the Violet Crumble Bar, Ladybirds and Bachelor-Buttons. I discovered one of the basics laws of sharing; pleasurable while you are doing it but tends not to leave much for yourself.

While other families were hoeing into pies with mushy green-peas, saveloys that dripped tomato-sauce down their chins, waffles oozing cream, toffee-apples and fairy-floss on sticks, we had a nice healthy little lunch of egg-and-lettuce sandwiches prepared for the occasion by Mum.

She had even brought an enamel cup so that we wouldn't have to put our mouths to the drink-bubblers, a certain source of impetigo. We spent a healthy outdoors afternoon beside the Show Ring, watching the distant Fat Cattle being judged, the Figure of Eight Races and the Working Dog Trials, the tranquillity only slightly marred by the distant shrieks of laughter and squeals of enjoyment from the crowds on the Merry Go Rounds, Big Dipper, Slippery Dips and Knock 'Ems.

During the High Jumps a stray balloon bounced and wobbled across the ring, causing the competing horse to shy violently. The rider lurched forward over its neck and but for grabbing the mane would have been thrown. Though the crowd murmured in sympathy, the bell rang dismissing horse and rider. Everyone looked to see whose balloon it had been. Pale with consternation I clutched mine and held it in front of me visibly, as though to ward off a vampire-attack, willing people to see I still had mine.

After darkness fell there were fireworks, culminating in a huge pink elephant which lit up the night sky and lingered high above the upturned faces of the crowd as they breathed, 'Ah!' We had gone home well before then but I heard about it at school. The Show and all its wonders were the only topic of conversation in the play-shed at Big Lunch: how many rides people had gone on; how many Show Bags they had bought, which side-shows they had been to. Everyone had seen Ubangi the Warrior. Esme Purley had been sick on the Octopus. All the boys had seen Jimmy Sharman, or said they had. Everyone was sunburnt. Everyone had had a wonderful time.

It was well that the Show of 1941 gave pleasure to be long remembered; that the gravel and bindi-eye expanse of the Show Grounds knew such spendthrift gaity; the parading of best-dresses, suits and ties; the thrills of dodgem-cars and octopus-rides; of tattooed ladies; boxing tents; sunburnt faces; fairy-floss; show-bags; kewpie-dolls; squeals and laughter. The eager photographs taken by the Show photographer would be exclaimed over and placed in albums, carefully lettered, in white ink, 'Townsville Show 1941 Uncle Arthur, Auntie Mavis and little Doreen'; down-payments of happy memories against the who knows of the future. Merry-go-rounds would cease to turn, boxing-tent drums to boom, laughter fade as a willy-wagtail feather of dust. Any escaped balloon that bounced its way across the empty Show Ring would do so in a silence that brooded as though in portent.

For, long before next Show Time came round again, with the rumble of heavy vehicles, the tramp of marching boots, the barking of orders, the roar of dun-flanked aircraft overhead, Townsville Show Grounds would have become one vast, grim-jawed military encampment.

Chapter 6

BARRY IN TROUBLE: 1941

'For a while we must part, but remember me, Sweetheart,
Till the Lights of London Shine Again'

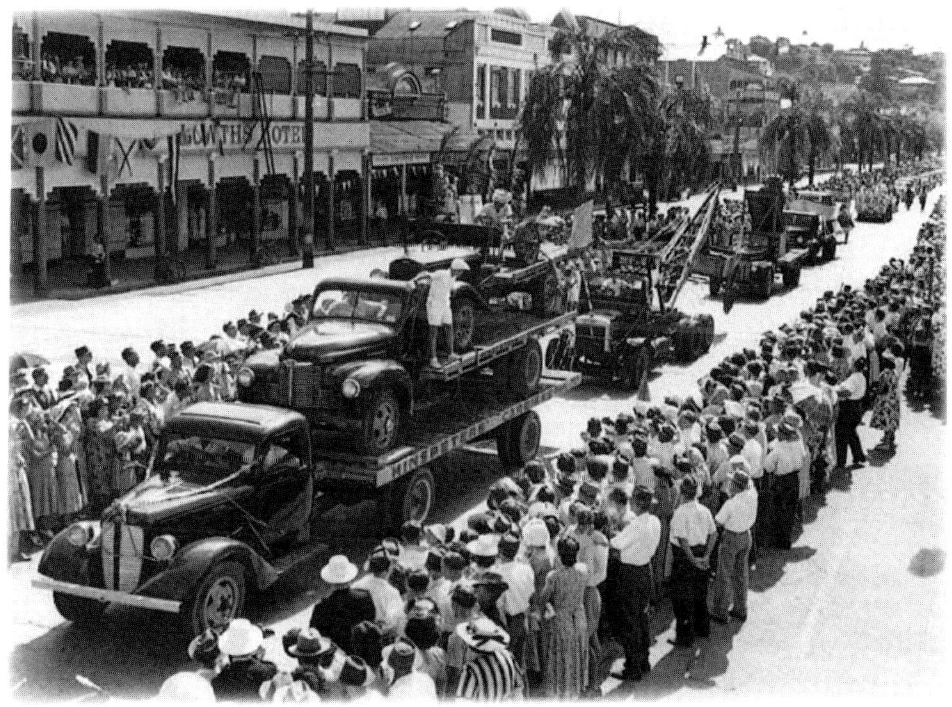

Patriotic Parade in Flinders Street, 1941

The government announced that Child Endowment payments would begin in July 1941. Mum exclaimed, 'It's like the song we used to sing on the *Border*, coming out! *Pennies from Heaven*!' All the mothers were pleased – more than pleased – delighted, because the money was to be paid directly to them, not to the father. As very few women worked outside the home, Child Endowment would give them some money in their own hands. The second child in each family was to be paid five-shillings a week; children after the second were to get seven and sixpence.

I was impressed by my sudden importance as 'second child'. Barry demanded, 'Why is she getting it and not me?' Mum said, 'Don't be silly, both of you!' and explained that the payment was not for any child individually but to improve the health of families in general. 'It is to go towards fruit and milk and shoes and school-needs,' she said, adding that she didn't doubt there would be those who would squander their Child Endowment on beer and tobacco and 'the Dogs'. 'The Dogs' were one of Mum's pet hates. Whenever she saw a working-man exercising his two or three greyhounds along Walker Street – and Walker Street was that kind of street – she would exclaim, 'Just look! Dogs eating good steak while his children make do on bread and syrup!' It was an established fact that greyhounds ate only steak. Or the ones in Walker street did. She was sure of it. But, greyhound owners or not, on the first Child Endowment Day, the Post Office was the most popular place in Townsville, a queue of excited women stretching along the pavement as far as the Town Hall.

Townsville was an expensive place to live; the most expensive in Queensland. Uncle Les said so, telling Mum that the cost of living had risen since the beginning of the war by forty percent. That was because food and other goods had to be hauled such long distances. There was a weekly fruit train but fruit and vegetables were beyond what many families could afford. 'You children don't know what a good apple tastes like,' Mum would sigh, squeezing a wrinkly specimen. Her eyes would shine at the memory of Cox's Pippins, picked straight from the garden in Kent.

She believed that a child should eat an apple after every meal. But apples in Townsville had become a luxury. So when she saw in the paper that the many Chinese fruiterers were vying with one another for custom, her eyes lit up 'Look! At Sang Chong Wah's, apples are fifteen for a shilling. At Mee Hoo's and Goon Chew's one gets only a dozen!' But then Mee Hoo went one better. He would give a discount of ten percent to all families of servicemen.

Mum cried, 'If Mee Hoo is patriotic enough to give ten percent off, he deserves our custom! But how to get out to Mee Hoo's? Now, Barry! Supposing you had a bicycle!' Suddenly Barry was all interest. A bike! Most kids only got a bike when they passed Scholarship! He was all ears as Mum continued. 'If you had a bicycle you could ride out on a Saturday and get the greens for us! Would you promise never to ride no-hands like that boy who was fined two-and-six last week?' Eyes gleaming, Barry promised solemnly. He would have promised to ride standing on his head at the sudden prospect of getting a bike. The visions of manly freedom it evoked!

A brand-new one from Pages' Cycles cost five pounds, nearly a week's army pay, so that was out of the question. Mum studied the 'For Sale' notices in the *Bulletin* until she found one that seemed to fill the bill: 'Gents bike. Good condition, 25/-'. She wrote a letter to the Box Number provided, asking to view the bicycle in question. When the bike arrived, ridden by a burly water-sider in a flannel undershirt, the Gent's Bike turned out to be as old as the hills, weighed a ton and had no mud-guards. Mum was doubtful; she suspected the coat of black paint might well have been hastily applied to cover up some deficiency. But Barry was beside himself with anticipation. On he hopped and peddled off furiously along Walker Street to show that he could handle it. He tried not to let on how incredibly heavy it was to push. Neither did he disclose that it had no brakes. Mum didn't want to disappoint him and there were all those cheap apples out at Mee Hoo's so she paid the man the money and he departed, no doubt straight to Lowth's to celebrate having got rid of his old grid for half the price of a new one.

The following Saturday, Mum's string shopping-bag over his shoulder, Barry set off for Mee Hoo's. Mum hummed to herself while she waited his return, filling the washing-up bowl ready to scrub the wealth of apples she would have at such generous prices. Then Barry returned, his face glum. The ten percent discount was only for families of servicemen away overseas.

Mum was beside herself with indignation 'Of all the frosts! What does he mean, 'Overseas'! Away is away! Not every man in the services can be at the Front! The army has to have a base!' That was one of the army principles that Dad had drilled into us, 'First consolidate your base.' Another was, 'Often the best means of defence is attack.' Mum said, 'I've a good idea to go out there and give him a piece of my mind!'

Luckily for Mee Hoo, Mum couldn't ride a bicycle, not one that weighed a ton, had no brakes and a tendency for the chain to keep coming off. Mum went back to buying her green-groceries from Bensley's. They were expensive but at least they weren't pulling swifties. Besides, they did take me to Bluewater just about every Sunday. Barry didn't give a hoot one way or the other. He still had the bike.

I now rode to school, church and Sunday School in style, doubled by Barry on the bar of the bike. I learned to keep my head down so that he could steer over my straw school hat, to sway in rhythm with his laboured pedallings, to hold my legs out stiffly, ankles crossed, to avoid the anguish of a heel caught in the front spokes and to ignore the numbness occasioned by prolonged perching on the bar. 'Doubling' was against the law but everybody did it. It was the only way for families to get around. Who had cars! If you knew someone who had a car it was worth mentioning casually in conversation as somehow reflecting lustre upon yourself.

But to be frugal was patriotic. The Government was urging housewives to be thrifty so that the money they saved could be invested in the War Loan. Posters showed young Diggers boarding a troop-ship with their kit-bags and rifles; the message was; 'Our boys are going away to fight. Help them fight with your money!' There was a poster of a young soldier lying dead, still clutching his rifle; 'Today at the Front he gave his life for you! What have you given for him?'

Mum said 'If the women of England can put up with Stukas dive-bombing their homes, the least I can do is to scrimp every penny I can out of the House-keeping for the War Loan!' She had a battery of thrifty strategies from the Depression years, when the rule had been 'Use it up. Make it do. Do without'. In the *Bulletin* were cartoons of over-loaded shopping-bags out of which a hairy Squanderbug was grinning. The warning was, 'Don't be bitten by the Squanderbug! Save for Victory!' Housewives redoubled their efforts; nothing was wasted.

Behind our kitchen door hung the String Bag; something like a laundry-bag on a coat-hanger, embroidered with a cottage garden scene of hollyhocks and wall-flowers. It had different-sized pockets, into which all kinds of things were put to be used again and again. The large pocket at the bottom was for brown paper and brown-paper bags, which were smoothed and folded for future use. Lunch-wrappers were used for several days. In fact lunch-wrappers were a luxury. Many children's school lunches, which they called their 'bit', normally just bread and jam, or bread and dripping, were wrapped in newspaper.

The string around parcels was never cut, but carefully unpicked, given a quick figure-of-eight twist around finger and thumb, tied with a half-knot and tucked away in one of the smaller pockets of the String Bag. Corks also had a special pocket. They were for when Mum made a batch of Heenzo, a cough syrup with a base to which were added honey and lemon-juice, giving three large bottles for two-shillings. One nice thing about feeling a cold coming on was being dosed with Heenzo.

Instead of buying new bed-sheets Mum 'turned' the old ones, cutting them lengthwise and hemming the outer edges to the centre. She made pillowslips from calico and hung them to bleach on the line. Calico was also used to make my school bloomers; I got used to the sandpapery stiffness. When Lord Baden-Powell died, Barry needed a Scout hat for the big memorial parade but he had to make do with an old army hat of Dad's. Old saucepans were given a new lease of life with 'Tops', little metal discs pushed through from one side to the other and fastened. The saucepan never sat quite squarely on the stove again, but it was 'doing ones bit' for the War Effort.

As no lady ever went to town, or anywhere, without stockings, Mum mended the ladders in her silk ones, using a smooth wooden darning mushroom and a single thread of silk drawn from a discarded stocking so the darn was almost invisible. Darned stockings became a sign of thrift to help the War Effort. Some ladies resorted to using painted-on stockings, but it was hard to get the seam at the back straight, which gave the game away, and in any case, it didn't feel ladylike, not having proper stockings on. Like going out without a hat! Or gloves!

Letters from 'Home' told of Mum's uncles and aunties suffering constant bombing raids in the London Blitz. Great Aunt Kitty's house had received a direct hit. The doughty old lady had been dug out of the rubble with just her handbag and the pet cat. Very strict food rationing was being enforced due to U-boat attacks on merchant convoys. Having to queue for long hours in the cold was also taking a toll. Grandma Greenleaf, a diabetic, had difficulty getting her insulin supply and diet. To make things worse, England was having its worst winter for decades, with snow fifteen feet deep in some places and parts of the English Channel frozen over. 'How can they fight that madman Hitler on two ounces of butter a week, a couple of spoonfuls of tea and not enough meat to feed Mumpuss!' cried Mum. She swung into action to send them all food parcels. There'd Always Be an England while she could do something about it!

Now, when Mr. Shields the Grocer made his weekly call, his calico apron firmly tied round his hips, pencil behind his ear and note-book at the ready, Mum dictated impressive lists. 'Tea? Yes. Definitely! Billy Tea with the kangaroo on the packet. They will like that. They must have tea! These dreadful air-raids night after night! Sugar? Yes. Trufood Milk. Some Nestle's Condensed as well. Cocoa. Corned Beef. Some tinned apricots for a little treat. And some of that nice dark chocolate, Old Gold.' She also added in a few medical items such as Bex powders, Vicks Vapor Rub and Eumenthol Jubes.

When Mr. Shields delivered the boxes, I helped to stack and sort the groceries on the kitchen table. It was better than playing shop. The sugar was measured into draw-string calico bags which Mum had sewed, because in previous parcels, brown-paper bags had been wet and ruined. For the same reason glass bottles of Indian Head Coffee Essence were no longer included. They smashed. When everything was ready the parcels had to be stitched up in calico and addressed with indelible pencil, the sort that would not write unless licked, making the tongue purple, or more properly, dipped in water, when they wrote with a thick squishy line that, once dried, would not come out. Goodness only knew what desperate situations each parcel might have to go through before it reached its destination in 'The Old Country'.

The man at the Post Office was very strict about weight: five pounds per parcel. A fraction of an ounce over and Mum would have to take the parcels home and repack them. She would deliver him a stinging lecture on London in the Blitz and how easy Australians in general and those in Townsville, especially some in the Post Office had it, by comparison. There would also be some allusion to the possibility of some people being Fifth Columnists for all anybody knew. This bodyline approach did little to lessen the Post Office man's intransigence. Mum, with tears of vexation and weariness, would hump the whole load back to Walker Street, unpick the calico, remove a tin of fish-paste or a cake of Pear's soap and start all over again.

She would make a note of the date of posting because at times, a small ominous paragraph would appear in the *Bulletin* to the effect that all mails posted between certain dates had been lost at sea due to enemy U-boat action. When this happened Mum would scan her list and heave a sigh of relief if her mail would have got through. Sometimes parcels went missing and never did turn up on the doorsteps of grateful aunts, uncles and cousins; they would have been stolen en route.

At school we were issued with envelopes for the collection of Patriotic Funds: anonymous so there wouldn't be any 'My Mum giv' more'n your Mum!' Even so it was possible to tell whose envelopes had coppers and whose had silver or even a ten-shilling note. The money went to the Red Cross and the Comforts Fund.

'You'd think I did enough for the Comforts Fund,' Mum would sigh handing Barry and me our sixpences. She spent several hours each week at the Comforts Fund Rooms, cutting out and making pyjamas to be sent to military hospitals, altering soldiers' uniforms and sewing on chevrons for the newly-promoted. Sometimes it was just a matter of making cups of tea and handing out stationery. Sometimes she helped soldiers who hadn't had much in the way of education to write letters to their wives or mothers.

Patriotic Fund collections were also made door to door on a weekly basis. Each household was expected to contribute at least sixpence. The results in each area were published in the *Bulletin*. At first there was a degree of competition between suburbs and people tended to dig a little more deeply into their pockets to boost their own suburb. After a while it became apparent that well-heeled areas such as Stanton and Melton Hill were always going to be outright winners. After that the fun went out of it and it was just a matter of having the sixpence ready when the collector came around, or hiding it under the pot-plant if nobody was going to be at home.

Then the Red Cross announced a Fund Raising Amateur Hour Competition. There would be a competition each week for six weeks at the Theatre Royal, and an overall winner would be announced. Mum, whose very being lit up at the mention of anything to do with the theatre, tried in vain to pressure Barry and me to enter. 'Oh! Barry! You could recite *The Charge of the Light Brigade*. Just think!

Theirs not to reason why; theirs but to do and die!
Into the valley of death, rode the Six Hundred'.

She clutched her heart and threw one arm out passionately to demonstrate. Barry asked if he could finish off the custard. So she tried me. 'Oh! Snookie! You could do one of your violin pieces! 'Minuet in G' is starting to come along quite nicely!' This lacking conviction, she tried another tack, 'Couldn't you and Margaretta sing a duet? You could do *Little Sir Echo* together so nicely.'

'Margaretta is doing a tap-dance' I said, and knew at once it had been a tactical error. Now I had a lecture on being shy when there was no need for it, and that if only I would go along with Margaretta to dancing lessons I would enjoy it and make some nice friends as well.

Margaretta was one of a bevy of little girls who every Saturday morning clattered their way in tap-shoes along Flinders Street to the Glenda Norris School of Dancing in the AWU Hall. They learned to become marigolds with frills of orange crepe-paper tied under their chins or gypsy-girls with brass curtain-rings dangling on loops of cotton from their ears. Margaretta had even been known to hurry along to 4TO Radio's *Saturday Morning Talent Time* and, unfazed by being On Air to hundreds, possibly thousands of unseen listeners, tap her way briskly through *Lazy Bones Sleeping In the Sun* and to follow it with an unsolicited encore of *Don't give up the Ship, Boys* to the astonishment of the announcer.

For the Red Cross Fund Raising Competition she was going to tap to *Umbrella Man*. I had already seen her pink frilly costume and the frilly umbrella around the rim of which she was going to peep shyly at the audience as she danced. She knew how to stretch her eyes to make them look large and to pucker her lips into a pout, having once been a runner-up in a Shirley Temple look-alike competition. With such artistry I knew I could not hope to compete. Even Mum knew when she was beaten. She simply couldn't imagine how she had come by such lack-lustre progeny.

Both Barry and I had War Savings money-boxes which Mum had got from the Town Hall for us, a piece of flat cardboard, which when folded, inserting correct tab into correct slot several times, became a money-box. When the box was filled, the money was to go towards the purchase of a War Savings Certificate. Neither Barry nor I had any money and not much prospect of coming by any. On the one or two occasions when Dad brought any of his army friends home, we produced our boxes and placed them conspicuously in the hope of extracting a few coins from the visitors.

Then Barry heard of a wonderful way making money. Bottle-ohing! There were boys at Central who went on Sunday mornings scouring Anzac Park for empties left behind by Saturday-night drinkers. Each bottle was worth a penny when returned to the Ozone Cafe across the road. 'Y'kin git a sugar-bagful!' Mick Ivory told him, 'The drunks leave 'em. Jíst on the grass waiting to be picked up! A kid found a quid once! Even a watch, one time! An' false teeth! Them old booze-artists get as shickered as cut snakes when they're on the grog!'

Barry was awed by the prospect of such easily come-by largesse. He explained it all to Mum as she mashed the pumpkin. He discreetly left out the part about watches and false teeth. Mum had been frying three nice bits of bacon to accompany the liver for tea. These now frizzled themselves into oblivion while she told Barry that bottle-oh-ing sounded to her like the mud-pickers that got down into the Thames at low tide and poked about in the mud for lost coins and even – shuddering as she said it – false teeth! Only common, working-class people did such things! And what on earth would his father would think of her if she allowed such an activity, to say nothing of the Quelches and the Acklands.

Barry, standing tall, his face shining with loyalty to King and Country replied, 'Dad would reckon I was doing my bit for the War Effort!' He knew Mum would fall it. But I knew, and he knew that I knew, that what he was really after was a Spud gun, which Hollis Hopkins had in their window, for twelve and sixpence each. The day of the Gat Gun was over; Spud Guns were now the thing. For ammo they used pellets extracted by pressing the tip of the barrel into a raw potato.

He had tried to badger me into parting up with some of the contents of my War Savings money-box, saying it was for the War Effort. 'Just think! I can be practising for the army! Think how much money it will save the Army when I join up!' I was not to be wooed by such honeyed talk. But to Mum he put his case very persuasively. Collecting empties on the Strand was every bit as patriotic as taking sixpences in an envelope to school for the War Effort! Mum caved in. I think she even quite looked forward to seeing how much of this unexpected bounty he would come-by with the prospect of adding to the collection of War Loan Certificates she kept hidden under the newspaper-lining of the towel cupboard.

The following Sunday Barry got up quite early and peddled off, a sugar-bag on the handlebars for all the empties he was going to collect. However, as it is with early birds and worms so also is it with bottle-ohs and bottles. The Strand and Anzac Park had been thoroughly worked over long before Barry got there. There might never have been a Saturday night reveller within miles. Not a solitary empty was to be seen. He came across only one, wrapped in brown paper at the base of the War Memorial, a port bottle stamped 'Non Returnable'.

Barry never did get the Spud gun, but then, at the cost of twelve shillings and sixpence each, the craze for them was bound to be short lived, and before very long the potatoes on which they relied for fire-power were to become a rare and precious commodity in Townsville. Housewives would queue to obtain a meagre packet of potatoes as a treat to accompany a Sunday roast, or be granted one as an under-the-counter favour by a friendly greengrocer. Would they be likely to waste a precious spud for ammunition for a tom-fool toy gun! Spud guns had their day before they even got fairly started.

But, oh! Well! There were other things for a boy to think about. A crocodile, officially given as five feet in length, but which in the healthful environs of Kissing Point quickly grew to a more robust eight, had been seen basking in the sand dunes near the CWA huts. Barry feigned an appointment with Dr Trembath, the dentist, wagged the afternoon off school and rode his bike to track the monster down, or to at least catch a glimpse of it. He was somewhat taken a-back to come face to face with, not a saurian of challenging proportions, but a police constable perched on the concrete remains of the rock-pool wall under the cliff, making a roll-your-own, a shot-gun casually across his knees.

The constable, perhaps bored with his long and fruitless vigil, not only overlooked the fact that Barry was not at school, but also told him quite chattily that the croc was probably migrating from somewhere up near the mouth of the Bohle or Bluewater and on its way down to the mangroves south of Ross River to breed. Nonetheless, to be on the safe side the police were going to patrol the beach each day before dawn.

But as he had wagged the afternoon off, Barry thought he might as well avail himself of the chance to inspect work on the new City Baths. He pedalled along the Strand and watched the work in progress. 'They're getting a go on!' he told me. 'All the sides and the bottom are done. There's a space inside the sides of the walls for pipes and things and reinforcement spikes sticking out all over the place. The men reckon us kid'll be using it next year.' Neither of us could imagine it. Only film-star people like Ginger Rogers and Fred Astaire had swimming-baths.

But no news about either crocodile or swimming-baths could hope to compete with that wild-fire news around the play-ground at school next day. Davo, the Magician, was dead. Not only dead, but murdered-dead! How could he be! The only people that got murdered were gangster men in gangster matinees. Davo was well known to all Townsville school-children, one of several entertainers whom the Department of Education allowed to go round the schools putting on shows. The children would bring their three-pences, the teacher would tick their names off in a book and when the appointed day arrived, the folding doors between two rooms would be pushed back, the desks and forms shoved against the wall, the children marshalled; little ones sitting cross-legged on the floor at the front; bigger boys standing aloft on the desks at the back, arms akimbo to show that really they didn't go for this sort of thing any more and could see through old Davo's tricks anyhow.

There were rope tricks, Davo working a lasso into wider and wider circles before leaping in and out of the sinuous whorls, leather chaps flapping, foxy red face perspiring and high-heeled cowboy boots clunking noisily on the timber floor.

Now he was dead. How could people just be dead. Before such a fact the imaginations of seven-year olds were brought up short. They could only deal with it in terms of the tricks they remembered Davo doing the previous Friday afternoon at Central. 'Remember when he brung them coloured hankies outa his sleeve?' 'Nah! It was flowers he brung outa his sleeve. Them flowers, they was in his pocket.' 'What about how he got the two-bob from Wally's ear?' There was laughter at the memory of that. 'But the best one was the pigeon outa his hat! The way it flew round the room and done a poop on Miss Poultney's table!'

I had not seen Davo the Magician on Friday. When, on arriving home, I had broached the subject, I had not been suprised to have Mum retort sharply. 'A sheer and utter waste of money! If it was for something worthwhile, like the Red Cross, I wouldn't mind. But a magician! In school time! I don't know what Mr. Bonham is thinking of!' So on the morning of the Davo the Magician Show when Miss Wheeler was ticking off the names of those who had brought their threepences, I had to state publicly, 'I'm not allowed.' I tried not to let it show how much I minded. Everyone in the class looked at me with mingled pity and scorn. To be 'not allowed' made you different. It meant you were not one of them, an outsider, the worst possible thing to be.

When the time had come for the rest of Grade One to march off along the verandah, all expectation, to crowd into Grade Five for the entertainment, I and about four other 'Not Alloweds' parked ourselves on the roots of the fig-trees. We were joined by the 'Forgot m' threepence's, which is what those too poor to be able to afford one had to say. We all listened forlornly to the distant laughter and tried to pretend that we didn't give a hoot. We repeated to one another what our Mum's had said about magicians, school-time and Mr. Bonham, and assured one-another that it was nicer to be outside anyhow.

As though to deepen my gloom, I saw, as I trudged homewards along Walker street, the goats on Castle Hill being rounded-up. Some, too wily to be caught, had bounded along the ridge and were even now making off over the skyline. The remainder were trotting obediently down the hillside under the direction of a couple of scruffy but determined kelpies. One mother-goat, with twins at her heels, thought to turn and make a dash for freedom. The kelpie dropped to a crouch and fixed her with a steely look. The nanny thought better of it and shouldered her way in among the herd, her kids pressing close to her flanks. The owner of the kelpies came striding down the hill leaving all responsibility to the dogs, apart from an occasional long whistle. Some goats had bells and there was a metallic tinkling as the herd flowed shoulder to shoulder down the stony ridge, into Blackwood Street, the dogs tailing them. When I told Barry he said, 'They've taken them to the pound. The silly beggars keep hanging round the top of the quarry and knocking goolies down on the quarry-men. One bloke nearly got clobbered.'

'But what will they do with them?' I quavered, remembering the mother-goat with the twins. He said, 'Maybe people will buy them for milkers. The ones with the bells, they belong to people over on the South-Side, mainly. The ones the dogs couldn't get round would be the wild ones that live up the hill.'

After this the Mark of Zoros had to find other adventures on Saturday afternoons instead of goat-chasing. They took to prowling along the railway-line. There were often sugar-cane-trains coming down from Bamberoo and Helen's Hill, laden with cane for the mill at Giru. The eight-foot lengths of cane were chained across open trucks. Sometimes a stick would slide out of the load and could be picked up from the side of the railway line. Sometimes the boys ran beside the track and gave a loose stick a bit of help. The tough outer skin of the stick could be peeled back with the teeth and the inner pulpy mass chewed and sucked for the sugary-sweet juice.

'All that sugar will ruin your teeth!' cried Mum, 'To say nothing of the damage to your enamel!' She would have liked to put her foot down on these goings-on, but how could she keep a tight rein on a boy whose father was away in the army? He needed a man to pull him into line.

One evening there was a knock on the verandah steps. A police-constable stood there silhouetted against the street light. Mum, her face filled with apprehension, took off her apron and hurried through. The constable was very polite, almost apologetic. Did she have a son, Barry Stilwell? Was she aware that her son, Barry Stilwell, had been illegally on the premises of the Townsville Technical High School? It seemed that her son, Barry Stilwell, had been involved with some other boys in the removal of a certain quantity of lead roofing-nails, the property of the Technical High School, from the premises of said Technical High School.

Listening fearfully in the background, I knew this to be true. On Saturday Margaretta and I had been playing Orphanages in her back yard. We had all her dolls arranged in rows under a canopy of a baby-shawl strung between two bushes. I was Matron of the Deanna Durbin Home for Orphans which was funded by the generosity of Miss Deanna Durban. Miss Deanna Durban was coming to visit the orphanage and I had to have the orphans all spruce for the occasion. It was somewhat awkward because I also had to double as the handsome escort who helped Miss Deanna Durban in and out of her expensive limousine and took her arm as she made a stately entrance to the orphanage. None of Margaretta's dolls looked like orphans. They were all exquisitely turned out, still wearing the original tulle and satin frocks, petticoats and bonnets in which they had come from the shop, unlike my dolls, who had to make do with outfits made from the sleeves of old cardigans with holes cut to poke their arms through and nappies made from worn-out singlets.

During Deanna Durban's visit I had been aware that the Mark of Zoros were making their way, Commando-fashion, on their elbows, through the pumpkin-vines down the back. Reaching the fence they had hauled themselves up, and from there scaled on to the roof of one of the sheds of the next-door Technical College. It had been a simple matter for them to drop stealthily to the asphalt school-ground.

Their Commando Training now stood them in good stead, for all hell broke loose. There was obviously a German machine-gun nest on the top floor of the main building where the Dressmaking Rooms were. The 'jjinng!'s of ricocheting bullets and the 'eh-eh-eh-eh's of return fire could be heard as the combat-toughened troops raced for cover. Barry was hit and clutching his heart pitched forward, his weapon still in his hand just like the War Loan poster. Fortunately it was not a mortal wound. Rolling to one side he began to drag himself to cover, still firing gamely from the hip. One of his companions, more die-hard than the rest, raced forth shouting 'Keep me covered!' and seizing him under the armpit, began to drag him to safety. A dust-bin was upturned. Its lid wobbled noisily into the centre of the play-area and flopped. This seemed to be the signal for a general, 'Cease Fire!' The Commandos fell into a heap laughing.

Then suddenly there was deadly quiet, followed by excited exclamations. 'Jings! Get a load of these, will you!' and 'You little ripper!' and 'You beaudy!' They had discovered an area between two close-set sheds that was used to dump old bits of steel piping and off-cuts of corrugated iron. Amongst these was a pile of lead-headed roofing nails. 'D'y reckon they would melt down?' said one. 'Yeah! Make ripper sinkers!' said another. 'I seen me uncle doing it. Lead's not hard to melt,' said a third. 'C'mon! Grab some! Let's give it a go!'

They fell on the pile and stuffed their pockets till their pants were sagging on their hips, then, forgetting they had arrived as Commandos, sauntered forth casually, climbed back over the fence and disappeared across Walker Street towards our place. 'Boys are so stupid!' said Miss Dianna Durbin in a bored voice. 'Come! Now you must help me back into my car.'

Mum being known to be on roster at the Comforts Fund Rooms, the Mark of Zoros got a fire going down behind the cubby-house, and in the cast-iron pot that was the drinking-bowl from the empty chook-yard, managed to melt the lead nail-heads to a sludge. They lined up some old house-bricks and used the hollows for moulds. With awed cries of, 'Oh! You little snifter!', 'Cripes!' and 'Holy Cow' they poured off a set of ingots. One each. Curious and disquieted, I peered around the edge of the cubby-house. 'What are you making?' I said. 'A wigwam for a goose's bridle,' snarled Barry, hot, sweaty and flushed with achievement. 'Clear off and play with your dolls!'

So now here he was in real trouble. Looking unaccustomedly scared, he was sent to fetch his ingot from the cubby-house. The constable examined it, head on one side, the better to let the light fall on the gleaming metal. He gave a low whistle under his breath that could have been admonition or admiration.

On a certain date, the Mark of Zoros were required to appear at the Children's Court. Barry, dressed in his Sunday School clothes, hair Sprusoed, shoes polished, maroon clip-on tie just so, went off under escort by Mum, very grim of face. She wore her best navy Show outfit and Greta Garbo hat. Any hopes she may have had of thus prevailing upon the magistrate's better feelings were to no avail. He did not forego the opportunity to upbraid the parents of the boys, who, he declared, 'should exert better influence and stricter control over their sons. There was altogether too much laxity. Parents were not taking their responsibilities seriously enough.' They were each fined six shillings.

Mum and Barry returned home in complete silence. Without so much as taking off her hat Mum turned round briskly and marched out again. Barry sat on the edge of the bed and slowly began removing his tie. His shoulders sagged. A tear squeezed itself out from beneath his eyelashes and he brushed at it angrily.

'Where's Mum gone?' I quavered. There was always the possibility that she might get so fed up one day that she would walk out and leave us for good. Barry gave his nose a quick wipe on the sleeve of his Sunday School shirt. He stared out at the dusty glare of Walker Street. 'Gone to see about a house,' he said. Then, ruefully kicking the edge of the mat, he added, 'We're leaving.'

Chapter 7

THE HOUSE ON THE HILL: 1941

'It's a Lovely Day, Tomorrow,
Tomorrow is a lovely day!'

The House on the Hill

We loved the house at Alexandra Street. It was very old, set on the side of the hill in North Ward, with an enormous yard terraced with pink stonework and overgrown garden-beds amidst the rocks and grass of the natural hillside. The house was built into the slope of the hill at the back with very high concrete posts at the front, giving it a whimsical, non-conforming appearance. There was a very long front verandah onto which the rooms opened one after another and from which there were magnificent views of the pink granite precipices of Castle Hill.

As soon as we arrived, Barry and I tore off all round the house and yard, ignoring Mum's calls to help carry in the rolled-up bedding, the wireless, her hat-box and other things.

It was an astonishing house. Perhaps it had been added to over the years; perhaps it was two older houses joined together. It didn't have the plan of the usual Queensland house: front verandah, central corridor with rooms opening on either side and verandah at the back, off which were bathroom and kitchen. In the Alexandra Street house the rooms went off one another or opened out on to the front verandah. The verandah was in two sections, one part much wider than the other. Some of the rooms had ceilings with elegant mouldings and ornate circular vents; some had no ceilings at all, just bare rafters and the corrugated iron crackling in the heat.

The greatest astonishment of all was that there was no connecting door to the bathroom, to get to which you had to walk outside round the end of the house and enter by a separate door. There was no bath or chip-heater, just a cold shower and a shelf on which to place a jug and basin. I was very alarmed to see, clinging to the corners of the shower recess, two green frogs fast asleep with their throats pulsing, giving every indication of being permanent and long-term residents.

There was a big poinciana tree in the front yard and, at the back, a tall ironbark and a bloodwood. Barry decided the bloodwood would be just right for a tree-house. There were a couple of thousand-gallon tanks to collect the rain-water off the roof and stone steps which led down to the underneath part of the house and the lower terraces. There were lemon-trees, pawpaws, a custard-apple, a mulberry-tree and a big purple bouganvillea which spilled over from the top terrace to the lower.

There was an outdoors Little House, painted pink with a jaunty chimney. Close beside it, so close that you had to turn sideways to squeeze through the gap, was an enormous boulder which must at some time in ages past have bounced down the hill and come to rest just there. Barry said it was a good thing no-one had been in the Little House at the time.

We found signs of the children who had lived there before us: a small metal car with no wheels in one of the garden beds; a tumbler that had been covered with shells and lacquered as a Mother's Day gift on the laundry shelf and chalk writing on the rafters under the house. We wondered about these children and whether we should have liked then if we had known them. For a moment we felt a little shy at intruding into their private play-world but we were glad they were gone and that all this was now our domain. It was our first proper home.

As there were rooms to spare, Barry and I were each to have our own bedroom. I would have much preferred the one that was to be his, which was small and snug with a sloping ceiling and a door of its own that opened out on to the hill at the back. It seemed to me to be a very splendid thing to have your own door. There was a similar one next to it that I wheedled to have, but Mum had it firmly fixed in her mind that colonial daughters should have rooms that opened out on to front verandahs through French doors.

From the moment I entered the room that was to be mine I was filled with nameless dread. It was large and Mum had gone to a lot of trouble to decorate it in pink and green. There was a pink three-quarter-size iron bedstead made up with a white counterpane, the dressing-table Dad had made me with a pink and green flounce and a pink framed mirror. On the floor was a large linoleum square with a floral pattern and across one corner of the room was a pink and green floral curtain behind which to hang my frocks. White lace curtains at the window moved softly in the breeze.

'Well! Do you like it?' Mum exclaimed expectantly. She had been busy all week while we'd been at school. I nodded, my flesh creeping with inexplicable terror. 'Well! Can't you show a little enthusiasm!' she cried, exasperatedly. How could I possibly tell her that I knew there was presence in the room that did not want me there, an unpleasantness which saw me as an interloper and wished me gone. I sensed it as a coolness of the flesh at the sides of my neck, in a breath of touch to my hair, and in the darkness of the pink framed looking-glass mirroring the timber of the opposite wall blankly, and yet not quite blankly.

'Can't I have the little room next to Barry?' was all I could think to say. Clicking her tongue in exasperation, Mum cried, 'Well! If you're not the giddy limit! After all the work

I have put in to make it nice for you! And all the thanks I get is a hang-dog look!'

Before we could move in, the house had to be properly furnished. Mum was anxious about this because the Quelches were advising caution. To the north, they pointed out, the Japanese were over-running the Malayan Peninsula. Better to wait a while and see how things turned out. Mum wrote to Dad. His response was a cheerful, 'Go ahead! The Nips will never take Singapore, the Gibraltar of the East. Just let them try and they will get their fingers well and truly burnt! Our Eighth Divvie boys are there. The Japs will never be game enough to take them on!' He told Mum to get her furniture, adding, 'As Mr. Menzies said back in February, 'Better to come out of the whole shooting-match stony-broke than not to come out of it at all!'

Mum had a wonderful time at Carfoot's, 'The Furniture Specialists' in Flinders Street. She had never owned her own furniture before. But first, the floors of the house had to be covered with congoleum, a less expensive version of linoleum. The man at the shop told her to lay plenty of newspaper on the floors first, since they were very old and not all that even. We crawled around on our hands and knees laying old copies of the *Bulletin* saved for us by the Quelches and Acklands, no doubt to the sorrow of the children as they were worth threepence a bundle at the fish-shop.

We spread the papers in thick layers, overlapping the edges and putting saucepan lids, bars of kerosene-soap or jars of Mum's green tomato pickle on the corners to stop them flying up when the breeze came through. It was a constant temptation to read *Bib and Bub* and *Ginger Meggs*.

'Cripes! Listen to this!' Barry would say, crouching over a photo on the page in front of him, 'This New Zealand bloke; he crawled out on the wing of a Wellington at twelve thousand feet to put a fire in the engine out. Geez! He got the VC for it, but!' I would be more engrossed in a Heatley's ad for dolls' prams although I knew that the one I longed for, with metal sides and folding cover, was out of the question.

Even Mum herself would get caught. 'Do you know,' she would exclaim, sitting back on her heels, in the sea of newspaper, 'In London all the shop-windows have been boarded up! There's just a little peep-hole space for people to look through. How dismal Regent Street must seem!' She would sigh and then catch herself and urge us to lay the papers the wrong way round; 'That way we won't be tempted!' But, only a moment or so later she would add, 'Oh! Dear! How terrible! A baby was buried alive for three days in the rubble of a house. Its dead mother's body had protected it! Dear Heavens!' Then, in exasperation, 'Oh! We'll never be finished at this rate!'

When the congoleum was laid it gave the house an exciting rubbery smell. The pattern was of smoky-grey and blue rectangles, making the rooms look bright and spacious. There were places where the uneven floor-boards showed through in parallel ridges where we should have put more newspapers.

Then the furniture truck with *Carfoots* on the side arrived and backed into the driveway. The men scratched their heads as to how best to negotiate the steep terrace to the front verandah. There was quite a drop over the edge. Neither of them wanted to be the one to be nudged over by a careless shove at the other end of the new dining-room table.

They especially watched their step with the kitchen cabinet which had the fashionable arctic-glass bow-front, resting it frequently on its end legs as they edged their way up the front path. Mum, watching it wobbling and swaying, was like a cat on hot bricks. When at last it was safely installed in the kitchen she clasped her hands with pleasure, opening and shutting the drawers, the storage cupboards and the built-in bread bin. She knew that most people, including Auntie Elsie, still had old-fashioned kitchen dressers. She immediately set about putting her silverware and the serviettes, doilies and fancy jug-covers, into the drawers, sighing with pleasure as she did so. The bottom bit of the legs of the chairs, table and cabinet had all been sprayed with green. 'You could choose from red, green or blue,' she told me. 'But I quite like the green, don't you?'

Three rooms, the kitchen, the dining-room and Mum's big bedroom each had floor-coverings and a suite of furniture for £45/10/- to be paid off at seventeen shillings per week. As a bonus there was a setting of split-cane furniture for the verandah, made from lawyer-vine. It was excessively uncomfortable to sit in and only the cats or unsuspecting visitors ever used it.

Mum had paid £5 extra for a Mawson ice-chest, not one with a drinking-tap on the side like the Bensleys had, but still an ice-chest, a wonderful improvement. Up till now Mum had tried to keep the milk cool by covering it with muslin and standing it in a bowl of water, to cool by evaporation. After this, it became Barry's first job every morning to bring in the ice which was delivered to the front step by the ice-man, wearing a leather-apron and gripping the ice in a pair of metal-tongs as he ran with it to the front step. Barry would race it at speed the length of the verandah and through the house to thrust it into the top section of the ice-chest, then dance around for a few steps flicking his hands to get rid of the numbness. It became my job to empty the drip-bowl underneath the bottom flap which caught the melted water. If this job was forgotten the water oozed in a puddle across the floor. The drip-bowl was a big china basin that once a year was brought out and used to make the Christmas cake. No-one ever opened the ice-chest unless it was an absolute necessity. At sixpence a block for ice, the cool air was far too valuable.

On the first night in the new house

Mum let me sleep with her in the big double-bed. Perhaps she was a little nervous herself. Perhaps she sensed my unspoken terror of the Pink Room with its softly moving curtains and dim stillness. As Mum and I luxuriated in the large double bed, the old house began to settle down for the night around us. It seemed to sigh as the heat of the day seeped out of the timber. There were clicks and the occasional creak. 'What's that?' I whispered nervously. 'Just the floors and walls. Old houses always talk to themselves at night' Mum said. This was not as reassuring as she meant it to be. I lay straining to hear and yet not wanting to hear anything. The corrugated-iron roof ticked as it adjusted to the night air. Flying-foxes squabbled and shrieked in the mango-tree next door. From the hillside came the repetitive mournful call of a storm-bird, a run of notes, each a fraction of a semi tone higher. 'Do we? Do we?' From far off another answered. 'There must be rain on the way' said Mum unaccountably whispering. 'Thank goodness we got all the furniture in.'

I was just beginning to drift off to sleep when there was a soft click of the verandah gate and the sound of a stealthy footstep on the floorboards. I felt Mum tense and grip my shoulder. Neither of us dared to breathe. We heard it again; footsteps very soft but very assured, the catlike tread of someone or something that had been this way many times, the verandah boards creaking slightly as they made their way along. Was it someone who knew that a woman and two children were alone in the house, unable to protect themselves?

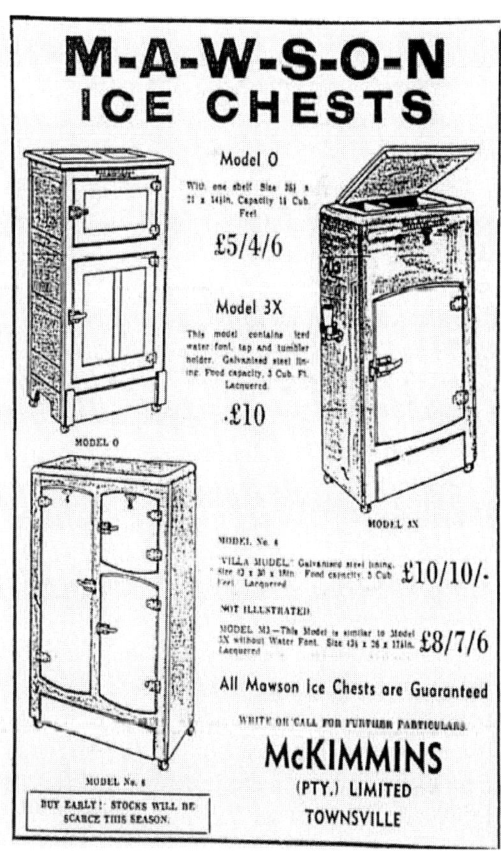

Mum fumbled at the side of the bed for her torch. The footsteps paused, then as slowly and assuredly as before, continued along the verandah. Whenever Mum was frightened her temper took over. Once, on their farm she had nearly blown Dad's head off with a shot-gun when, coming home late one night, he made ghost-noises for a silly trick. So, now, with a cry of 'Who's there!' she leapt from the bed, brandishing the torch and banging it to make it go on. In her haste she forgot that she didn't know where the switch for the verandah light was. She stumbled over a box of shoes that had been carried in. Shoes went everywhere. The footsteps ceased.

At last Mum found the switch, which was really a pull-cord. The verandah was flooded with light. Gripping the torch she flung herself through the door. There was no one to be seen. The verandah was littered with the tea-chests and packing-cases that our belongings had come in, and the big stag-horn and crows-nest ferns that Mum had bought from the previous family. She searched but there was no-one there. She peered over the verandah rails but there was a twenty-foot drop to the rocks below. No-one could have escaped that way.

She came back to bed slowly, looking troubled. 'I'll just leave the verandah light on for a while, shall I?' she said. Eventually we both fell asleep exhausted.

Next day Mum got herself prepared well before nightfall. She sent Barry down to Coates' Store on his bike for new batteries for the torch. She told him to fetch the handle of a broken mattock that had been waiting some time to be mended and placed it beside her bed. As darkness fell she went round and locked all the windows and slid the bolts on the doors shut. They were stiff from disuse; some had been painted over. No one in Townsville seemed to lock their doors.

There was no way to lock the verandah. It was open on all sides with only a low gate on a latch. Mum told Barry to construct a booby-trap. His suggestion was for an axe to be suspended over the verandah gate by a piece of string. 'If anyone tries to come in the string will break and it'll smash their head in! Like the Sword of Damocles!', he said with relish.

His next idea was to stick the bread-knife and carving knife by their handles into the cracks, with a trip-wire, so that the intruder would fall on them and impale himself. Mum explained she meant only something that would act as an alert system if anyone tried to come through the gate, at which point she herself intended to rush out and deal them a sharp crack with the mattock handle.

Barry's masterpiece was to tie all the lengths of string from the String Bag together and join them on to the verandah light pull-cord, so that if Mum heard anything, she would be able to pull the string and the light would go on. He constructed a booby-trap by placing the broom and the mop across two empty buckets and balancing all the empty metal containers from the kitchen; saucepans, frying-pan and milk-billy on them. He tied a spoon inside the dipper and hung it on the verandah gate for good measure. This was all so exciting that we could hardly wait for it to be night-time to catch our midnight prowler. Or so we felt while it was yet daylight. Once night had fallen it was a different matter.

It didn't help at all that Barry remembered the name of a scary radio serial, *It Walks By Night* and kept saying it over and over in a spooky voice because he knew it was getting on Mum's goat. 'You can go to bed if you haven't got more sense than that!' she told him sharply. The house was very hot with all the windows shut. Eventually we all went to bed, after cleaning our teeth over the high verandah rail rather than going out round the side of the house to the bathroom.

I must have been asleep some time, when I felt Mum tense. There was the faintest possible click of the verandah gate latch and then the sound of the slow measured footsteps along the boards. Mum pulled with all her might on Barry's string, unfortunately just a little too hard. It parted company. The footsteps paused just as they had the previous night, before continuing along the verandah. Beside herself with outrage, Mum seized the torch, gripped her mattock handle and flung open the door. 'Who dares to enter my house!' she cried in a voice that would have terrified me if I had been an intruder.

But again there was no one there. Barry, who had come running, Dad's claw-hammer in hand, joined in the search. No one was hiding behind the stag-horn fern. No one had slipped over the verandah railing, though Mum threw a bucket of water which she had left there for the purpose, just in case.

Mum looked thoughtful. 'I think I'll make us all a nice cup of tea; I could use one myself.' We all sat on her bed and talked about it with all the lights on. 'Mum,' said Barry, blowing into his cup thoughtfully, 'Do you reckon this place could be haunted?' Mum shook her head at him in a threatening manner, but he went on. 'You know Frizzie Frizwell, at school. He reckons they lived here once and it gave his mother the heeby-jeebies.'

'Having five rowdy boys like Mrs. Frizwell would give anyone the heeby-jeebies!' said Mum, decisively. 'Now! No more talk of ghosts. Such nonsense! We're here now and we're not moving. All the lino! All the furniture! And houses getting harder and harder to come by, with all the servicemen bringing their families north.'

Gradually we came to accept the sound of the nightly footfalls along the verandah. We still slept with the windows and doors locked. We still listened half in fear, half in terrible fascination but we did grow used to them. Then Dad came home on leave from Miowera. When we told him about the ghostly footsteps in the middle of the night, his eyes glinted. 'A ghost, eh! Well! We'll soon see about that!' adding, because he knew it would get Mum's goat, 'As the Old Maid said when she waved her wooden leg!'

That night he sat up against the bed-head smoking quietly while he waited for the ghostly footsteps that had troubled us. Sure enough at the usual time, came the familiar soft tread. At the first stealthy footfall Dad was out of bed like a shot, the mattock-handle at the ready. 'Bert! Be careful!' whispered Mum, but Dad's blood was up. On went the verandah light. There was a pause. Then, 'Well! I'll be damned!' and, with a shout of laughter, 'Here's your flaming ghost!'

Mum, Barry and I crowded in the doorway. Peering though Mum's arm, I saw an enormously fat green frog gulping stupidly in the light. Then, as we watched, it continued on its heavy way along the verandah, plomp, plomp, plomp, the boards creaking softly beneath its weight. Reaching the stag-horn fern it stretched up and pulled its corpulent body into the green fronds, turned so that just the tip of its head was showing over the edge of the pot, closed its eyes and settled down for the night. Mum and Barry joined Dad in the laughter.

'No wonder there was nobody when we searched!'.

'What about my booby-trap! And the Sword of Damocles axe!'

'I'll shift the whole kit and caboodle outside under the tree, first thing in the morning,' said Dad.

Suddenly they were all looking at me. I was the only one not laughing. 'What's the matter, Snookie?' Dad asked. 'You look as though you've seen a ghost!' 'Oh, leave her!' said Mum, 'You know she hasn't got much sense of humour.' But what I was secretly thinking was that now Dad was home and had settled the mystery of the scary footsteps, I would have to start sleeping in the Pink Room all on my own.

I was spared the ordeal for one more night. The following evening it was announced that there was to be a Gala Opening of the new Drive-In Theatre at the Sports Reserve. The new Drive-in would be the only one of its kind in the world outside America. Those people who had cars would be able to view the whole performance from the comfort of their car. Those who didn't would be able to bring rugs and cushions and enjoy a cool evening under the stars or in the grand-stand, while they watched the picture. The programme was to be *Wings over the Navy* and *Fifty-Second Street* with war-news showing the historic meeting of Mr. Churchill and President Roosevelt in mid-Atlantic.

Mum made a thermos of tea and a tin of Cockles. From the previous family at the house she had bought three folding beach-chairs with padded seats and back-rests. The Sports Reserve was just round the corner so we set off carrying our rugs, canvas chairs and picnic. The ads were already showing by the time we arrived so we had to find a place on the grass in the dark. Unfortunately, the Sports Reserve was also used for Dog Racing on Saturday afternoons. Mum became convinced that she could smell dog. One of us had trodden in something nasty, she was certain. All the time that Cornel Wilde was making decisions about being a Navy pilot, Mum was hissing, 'I'm sure I smell dog-dirt! Barry! Check the bottom of your shoe! Marion! Have you trodden in anything?'

Apart from that it was lovely sitting in a family group on our picnic-rug under the stars, sipping hot tea out of our bakelite mugs and seeing other families that we knew from school doing much the same thing. It didn't seem to matter that the soundtrack did not always match what the actors were saying or that all the words were slow and heavy in parts or then spurted ahead suddenly and sounded like Donald Duck. It was still nice to think that we had the only Drive-in Theatre anywhere in the world except for America, right here at the North Ward Sports Reserve. Though not many people did much actual driving-in.

The time while Dad was on leave became a festive occasion. We went to Mount St John Zoo, catching the bus from the front of the Post Office. We gazed solemnly through the wire fence at the crocodiles asleep under a veil of green slime. Though we watched for a long time they did not so much as blink an eye. We gazed respectfully at the rock-python wrapped in slumber round a stump in its enclosure. I felt a rush of pity towards the tawny dingoes which paced in agitation inside the wire of their cages. When one of the monkeys in the monkey-cage turned its bright crimson bottom in our direction I felt Mum's hand on my shoulder, pulling me away. 'Why did it do that?' I wanted to know. 'Do what' said Mum innocently, adding 'Oh! Do look at the beautiful peacock showing his feathers! Isn't he splendid!'

That night we all sat round the wireless to listen to the Victory Show; two hours of entertainment by Gladys Moncrief, Harry Dearth, Jack Davy, Bob Dyer, Harold Williams and other well-known entertainers. I knew Harold Williams because he was 'Orpheus the Singer' on the ABC Argonauts' Club in the afternoons, who often sang *The Green-Eyed Dragon*. For the Victory Show he sang *Keep Right On To The End of The Road.*

Between songs there were speeches by important people in the army, the air-force and the navy. Mr Forde, the Minister for Defence, said that the evening would go down in history as a high spot marking Australia's determination to win the war. By the time the programme was finished I was asleep and Dad carried me to bed, so that I slept the first night in the dreaded Pink Room without knowing anything about it. But after that bedtime became a time of dread.

I lay flat in the middle of the pink iron bed, hardly daring to breathe, terrified to make the slightest movement lest the It, which I knew dwelt in the room, should turn its malevolence upon me. I sensed that as long as I kept perfectly still and did not turn over it would extend cold tolerance of my presence. I particularly associated the horror of the room with the circular carved vent in the ceiling which stared down like an eye.

Early on the morning of the day Dad had to go back to camp Mum shook us. 'Wake up and open your Christmas presents so that your father can see them.' It was only October. I tried not to let it show that half the fun of Christmas presents was finding them in the pillow-slip at the end of your bed on Christmas morning. It wasn't the same being told just to open them, without having looked forward to it at all. My present was a china tea-set in a box with a lid that opened by pulling a ribbon. There were six cups, saucers and plates, a tea-pot, sugar basin and milk-jug. Best of all was a cake-plate with handles exactly like the one Mum used for Sunday night tea. I was overwhelmed with delight and spent the morning fitting the pieces in and out of the exotic box.

It was very apparent what Barry's present was even before he opened it. Bicycle mudguards look like mudguards even though wrapped in paper with Merry Christmas printed on it. He was inclined to be disgruntled and would have liked to head back to bed. There was a second present for him to open which looked almost as though it could be a watch. It was the right size and shape. Quickly he ripped the paper off, but it was only a tin of bright pink Gibbs' toothpaste. 'I thought you would like to have your own special tooth-paste!' cried Mum, when she saw the disappointment on his face. Luckily there was also a tool-kit to strap under the seat of his bicycle and this saved the day.

After Dad had gone back to camp Mum decided that she would give up working such long hours at the Comforts Fund Rooms. She continued to make pyjamas for the military hospitals bringing the material home, cutting out on the dining-room table and sewing them on her Bluebird machine. She said she would confine her war-work to the VADs in future. Then came the news that the VADs were to be posted overseas and be entitled to wear the curved 'Australia' badge on their epaulettes like the AIF. Mum was wild with envy 'Oh, to be young!' she cried. Disconsolately she stirred the mango chutney she was making. 'I was too young for the last war and too old for this!' she sighed. She was thirty-two.

But her training as a Voluntary Aide came in handy one night. Mrs. Woodward, up the hill from us, choked on a fish-bone. Her bachelor son Clive, who had a chemist shop in Flinders Street, should have known what to do; instead, he panicked. Having seen Mum in her blue VAD uniform, he rushed to the fence calling 'Mrs. Stilwell! Mrs. Stilwell! Come quickly! Mother is choking!'

Choking on fish bones had not been part of the VAD course but Mum was resourceful. She induced the old lady to swallow a raw egg. The glutinous albumen wrapped itself round the fishbone and drew it free. Mrs. Woodward was convinced Mum had saved her life and sent Clive later with a lovely Doultonware plate with a haywain scene that had been a gift to her on her wedding day more than fifty years before. Mum treasured the plate and used it only on state occasions such as Christmas and birthdays. It was the only occasion on which her ability was ever recognized.

Then it was nearly November and very soon it would be Guy Fawkes Night. During the week the excitement at school had been mounting. All the boys talked about was crackers. The window of Coates' Store was full of them. Boys selected carefully, brought their purchases to school and, squatting on their hunkers under the fig-trees, made bright red piles of Tom Thumbs, squibs and bungers. There was exchange of expertise in the capabilities and caprices of various types: Flower Pots, Ink wells, Roman Candles, Catherine Wheels; Well only rich kids from Melton Hill and Stanton Hill had them! Or maybe girls. Squibs? They were for chucking behind sheilas to make 'em squeal. Bungers? Them? You stick 'em in a letter-box and run like blazes. To make the crackers last longer the strings of cotton that bound them together were meticulously unpicked. The conical piles in front of each boy grew as the week progressed. They ran possessive fingers through their ammunition, avid for the night to come.

There was much talk about the Guys they were busy making, calling them Guy Foxes, like 'flying-foxes' – nothing to do with Guy Fawkes. The Guys were made out of sugar-bags stuffed with grass and leaves and sawdust, and dressed in old cast-off trousers and shirts that had been saved for months for the occasion. A well-turned out Guy even had a hat. When he was ready he was propped up in an old pram or billy-goat cart and pushed round the streets from door to door. He was parked in a gateway and grouping themselves together round him the boys would chant,

Guy! Guy! Stick him up on high!
Tie him to a lamp-post and there let him die!
and
Remember! Remember!
The fifth of November!
A penny for the Guy!

If householders came out and gave them a few pennies, they galloped off to Coates' Store to buy more crackers. Most people would give them something because it was the tradition. They themselves had done the same thing as kids. Guy Fawkes Night was a favorite with everybody even though a few grass-fires were accidentally started every year, or a few children had to go to the Ambulance with burns. The excitement of the previous weeks, the building of bonfires, saving all the rubbish and stacking it in a cleared space in a wigwam-shape, adding to it bit by bit: rubbish from the chook-yard, broken fence-palings, driftwood from the beach, anything that would burn; then at last, hoisting the Guy on top with crackers in his hat and pockets, ready for the night to come, made it all worth while.

But Barry and I were not allowed to have fire-works. Mum had put her foot down. Not only were they a wicked waste of money but she herself had a horror of them, having been badly burnt by a fire-cracker as a little girl in London. It had exploded down the front of her dress and her throat had a network of scars that she tried to keep hidden by wearing high-necked frocks or frilly blouses.

But now, on this Guy Fawkes Night she had gone off to VADs for the special farewell parade for the young volunteers going overseas. We had had our orders; To get our homework done. Not to waste time listening to *First Light Frazer* and to be in bed before she got back. Instead we sat on the front steps, rebellious and feeling hard-done-by. Why should we be different from all the other kids? They had crackers. Why shouldn't we? Bet if Dad was home he would let us! All the other kids' fathers let them! Why should we be the only ones missing out? It was always the same! Mum gets some bee in her bonnet and spoils all the fun!

The mosquitoes whined around us in the warm darkness. From down the street we could hear the plubs and hisses of squibs and bungers going off. A sky-rocket fizzed up from beyond the Sports Reserve. Barry watched it appraisingly. 'That could be Frizwell's. Frizzie said they had four rockets.' With five brothers to collect the Penny-for-the-Guy money, the Frizwells were able to do it in style.

Our end of Alexandra Street was dark and quiet. Only three other families with children lived nearby, the Browns, the Hindleys and the Flynns, all Catholics. Catholics knew that Guy Fawkes Night was a Protestant celebration. 'If only we had a bit of money!' cried Barry fiercely. 'I could rip down to Coates, and get some Tom Thumbs and bungers! They don't shut till nine. What have you got in your War Savings Box?' 'Three and six.' I said, 'But Mum knows. She had to borrow it the other day to fix the ice-man up.'

'We could get some you know!' said Barry fiercely, slapping at a mosquito on his knee. 'Remember that picture? The one about the kid that played the violin. Remember how he played on the corner of the street and all the people chucked money in his case! Well, if we went into town, you could play your violin. People would chuck money. They know it's for Guy Fox. Some of your pieces don't sound all that bad. That Minuet thing's nearly OK.'

'But what about Mum? She'd go us!' I cried, terribly alarmed. Barry said, warming to his plan, 'Mum's not to know! Look, all we've got to do is go into town. You play a few pieces. People chuck money. I'll whiz down to Coates' and get some crackers. We let them off down the gully. Mum needn't know a thing about it. If Dad was here he would have let us; bet your boots!'

'Yes, but... '

'Oh, don't start, 'Yes, butting'. Come on! What do you say we give it a go?'

'Supposing Mum comes back early!'

'She won't. They never finish that VAD stuff on time. They gas-bag. And do broken-arms, and things.'

'But what about your homework?' Scholarship was just around the corner.

'Bugger my homework. We only had a compo; 'A character from *We of the Never Never*.' I'll do the Quiet Stockman. Krausie likes him. I can do it standing on one ear. Come on! There's only one Guy Fox Night a year. We'll miss out to if you don't get a move on!'

Terribly alarmed but not wishing to spoil the good opinion of me which Barry suddenly seemed to have, I allowed myself to be persuaded. The vision he held out, of coins showering into my violin-case while I held the crowd enthralled, had a definite allure.

Barry wheeled his bike out from under the house. It had no torch as there was never any need for him to go out at night. Clutching my violin case in one hand and music stand in the other, I perched on the bar. Barry thrust *Pieces for Little Fingers* and *Dancing Days* down the front of his shirt. Heaving manfully on the pedals he got us started towards the Cutting and town.

We set up shop on the corner of Walker Street outside the School of Arts: familiar territory and not too alarming although the building seemed strangely dark. We didn't know the RAAF had taken it over and that the Library had been shifted to the Town Hall.

Walker Street was deserted. Kids with crackers had used them up and drifted away, though the acrid pungency still lingered in the air. Barry set up my music-stand under a lamp-post swarming with flying-ants. He clipped *Pieces for Little Fingers* into place. We didn't know whether to be glad that there was no one around to see us get started, or not. 'They'll show up once you get going, like it was in the picture. At first there was no-one, then they all started coming around. Then they chucked the money.'

I began the ritualized rubbing of the bow with resin which at home I could spin out for a good quarter of my practice hour. 'Skip that! Get on with it, or we'll miss Coates' Store,' said Barry. He was a little more vehement than he intended to be. Even he was beginning to sense that this was no longer the good idea it had seemed on the verandah steps at home.

I tucked my chin firmly on to my violin and began. *Minuet in G* scritched its way on to the glassy surface of the night. 'Don't play your best stuff first! Wait till people start to come!' hissed my manager. In the picture the expensively dressed crowds hurrying past to night-clubs and theatres had been drawn almost against their will to the young Yehudi Menuhin. Passing taxi-drivers had stopped their cars to listen. Stall-holders had left their stalls unattended. Patrons had come forth from restaurants. My *Golliwogs Dance* seemed not to have the same effect. 'Do something else,' ordered Barry. I switched to *Fairy Pleasures* and *Tripping Lightly.*

Flying-ants from the overhead lamp rained down on my music. Nervous and dispirited, I decided to dispense with the formalities of counting time and to play straight ahead, without the niceties of three-four, four-four or any-other-sort-of-four time. That way I could get up the speed that added a certain flair to my performance.

Across the road a fox-terrier began a startled yapping. Another joined it. Down the road a larger dog bayed, baritone-chested. At this, the pair of foxies turned treble in excitement. They had been frightened out of their wits earlier by the crackers. Now was their chance to give vent to their indignation. Soon they had every dog in Walker Street roused. Only one, more sympatico with a lone violin, began a long sostenuendo howling.

Suddenly there was shout from a low-set worker's cottage across the road. 'Hoy! Youse kids! Git over here!'

At last! The long awaited moment! Someone acknowledging our efforts! With relief, Barry said, 'Quick! Get your gear! Even if he only gives us threepence, let's just take it and get. There might still be crackers at Coates's and even if there aren't, we can always put it into chocolates for *The Nestles Book of Knowledge*.' We hurried across the road, eager to accept our earnings and be gone.

In the light streaming from the doorway we could see a burly figure leaning against the verandah-post, arms akimbo. 'Looks like a wharfie,' said Barry under his breath. 'They're rolling in dough! He might be good for two-bob, even!' We gazed up expectantly.

'Youse kids,' the voice from the doorway said, 'If youse don't put a bloody sock in it and bugger off, I'll be out there and give youse a bloody-good clip round the bloody ear-hole; the pair of you! Now clear off!' He scratched his backside with the satisfaction of having got that off his chest and, finger to nostril, blew his nose over the railing.

Silently, humbly, like Arabs melting into the night, we folded our tents and departed. Pushing the bike, we trudged up the Cutting in silence.

Barry said, defiantly, 'There wouldn't have been any need to, if Dad had been home. Dad would have given us a couple of bob for crackers; bet your boots. But that stingie old coot! We should have chucked a couple of goolies on his roof and run for it! That would have shown him!' Then, suddenly scared, he said, 'You won't let on to Mum, will you!' He didn't have to see me shake my head in the darkness. He knew I wouldn't.

Those warm November nights when merry, bare-foot children went chanting through the quiet streets of Townsville, pushing 'Guy Foxes' in billy-carts, with cries of, 'A penny for the Guy!' and 'Remember! Remember! The fifth of November!' would soon be but sepia-toned memories of long-long ago for children and adults alike. The hisses, pops and bangs, the rockets that lit the night skies and startled the flying-foxes out of the mango trees of Townsville on Guy Fawkes Night, 1941, were the end of an era. They would never come again. The calm, silvery Pacific dawn of Sunday, 7th December, was at hand.

Chapter 8

AIR-RAID SHELTERS: 1942

'We're off to see the Wizard,
The wonderful Wizard of Oz'

HMAS Sydney

HMAS *Sydney* had been lost. The Quelches had friends in Hermit Park, the Youngs, whose son John was missing. 'Oh! It's so dreadful for them. They keep hoping to get word from the Navy that he's safe, but every day that passes there's less hope.' Auntie Elsie was a composed, placid lady but as she told Mum this, over afternoon tea in the Botanic Gardens, tears formed in her eyes and she reached into her purse for a handkerchief.

Mum said feelingly, 'It would be the not knowing one way or the other, that would be the hardest part. To grieve, or to go on hoping when all hope was gone.' Auntie Elsie nodded, pressing her lace-edged handkerchief to her lips. 'It could be our boy!' Noel was now on HMAS *Canberra*. 'I live in dread of a telegram. Constant dread! Every time the gate clicks, I think it could be the telegram-boy with a message from the Navy. There's never an hour goes by I'm not worrying about him. Never an hour!' Mum reached and laid a comforting hand on her arm.

Mum had planned this afternoon tea in the Botanic Gardens to lift Auntie Elsie's spirits. As the two women talked in low voices, I sat, chin propped on the picnic table, legs swinging, eyes fixed vacantly on the cliffs above, my mind drinking in every word.

There was an art to listening-in to grown-ups' conversation. First you made yourself invisible. You never looked at them directly or appeared even to be aware that they were there. Next you looked listless, not the slightest bit interested in what was being said. You stared at the snow scene on the lid of the cake-tin in front of you; you folded and refolded your handkerchief on your lap into 'baby-in-the-cradle's or 'rabbit's ears'. You might possibly examine the most recent gravel-rash scabs on your knees and elbows, though this was risky; any movement might attract attention; 'Tchhs' of impatience and the adult code-word 'Little pitchers' – short for 'Little pitchers have big ears', grown-up talk meaning 'children are listening'. Though you kept your face carefully blank, you were as tuned-in as any French Resistance radio-operator, gathering information, opinions, attitudes and prejudices.

It was not mere curiosity that made me burn to hear what grown-ups said. It was the need to inform myself. The adult world was frightening. I grasped for some key to understanding what the mystery of being grown-up was all about. Like the man on the wireless who sang, *Ah! Sweet Mystery of Life at Last I've Found You!* perhaps there would come a moment of 'Ah!' for me, when I would know what life was about. If it could be understood perhaps it would not seem so threatening.

But now, just at the absorbing moment of Auntie Elsie's tears, Mum became aware of my presence. She frowned. Reassured by my expressionless face – carefully maintained for there was always the future to consider – she said, 'Why don't you go and play on the swing-boats?' Docilely, as though only waiting for her permission, I slipped away.

Barry, Ronnie and I climbed into the swinging-boat under the Moreton Bay fig. 'Mum's crying, isn't she?' said Ronnie. Importantly, I was able to tell them, 'It's something to do with a ship, the *Sydney*. I don't know what it's about, but. Do you?' Barry had been balanced on the back of the swinging-boat, heaving on the chains to work it high enough to make me squeal. Now he let it slow down under its own momentum.

'Well, there was this German raider, the *Kormoran*, see? The Huns doll her up to make out she's a cargo-ship so that she can sneak in off the West Australian coast, spying. But she's heavily armed. The *Sydney* catches her right in the act, and signals to ask what she's up to. Before you can say 'Jack Robinson' the *Kormoran* opens up, point-blank. Then the *Sydney* gets in a couple of beauties and the *Kormoran's* a goner. She sinks. The *Sydney* goes off full-steam over the horizon. Then she just disappears.'

'But why? Ships are big! They can't just disappear! Can they?'

'They can if a shell lobs in their magazine. Ker-boom! Like the *Hood*. The *Hood* went down in five minutes. All hands lost, eleven hundred of them, except about five that got picked up. Anyway! No one knows what happened to the *Sydney*. They've only found one float. No survivors. Seven hundred blokes gone west. That's why Auntie Elsie's down-in-the-mouth. She's thinking of Noel on the *Canberra*.'

Ronnie looked troubled. But he said, 'Daddy said to look on the bright side. The *Canberra* is here in the Pacific. There aren't any Germans here. Noel will be alright, Daddy says so!'

But now Barry was gazing upwards, studying the massive branches and aerial-roots of the Moreton Bay Fig. The tree was very old with limbs as broad as horse-backs to sit astride on or walk along. I could bravely make it to the very lowest, to sit calling, 'Mum! Mum! Look! Look at me!' hoping she would think I was daring. Some of the aerial-root systems, at ground level, were ropey and pliable and could be swung on. Others had matured into separate trunks, with toe-holds and crevices for bare-footed boys to haul themselves up to explore the sun-dappled upper reaches. I was wary of these knotty columns; while the crannies provided good hand-holds, they were also cool and dark and favoured by lurking frogs. What could be worse than reaching for a hold and feeling the nose of a frog!

Ronnie and I watched in admiration as Barry threw himself into the task of scaling the heights, balancing with careless ease along the broad limbs, hauling himself up the woody pillars of roots until at last he reached the top and stood, one leg and one arm stretched out in X formation high against the sky. He did not give a Tarzan warble to celebrate the moment. He knew Mum would come down on him like a ton of bricks. We were here to show support for Auntie Elsie. We had to be on best behaviour. We had to show respect. Also, Barry was supposed to be saving himself. Tomorrow Scholarship started!

As Mum had been recently telling him, not once but over and over, when he was discovered listening to *First Light Frazer* or *The Green Hornet*, Scholarship could decide the rest of his life. It decided whether he would go on to Townsville Grammar School or not. His whole future would be decided by the results. Tomorrow was the first day of the two day exam. He had been told to take things easy at the Gardens and not even to swing on the maypole. He had to save his energy for tomorrow and the long bike-ride out to West End School.

When it was time to leave, Barry and I set off on his bike, hoping that with a bit of luck we could get home in time for the start of *The Search for the Golden Boomerang*. It was our favourite serial, about a family travelling in the Northern Territory. They had one peril after another; crocodiles, herds of stampeding buffaloes, bush-fires and ferocious Aborigines. In the latest episode the eldest boy in the family had been staked out on a bull-ants' nest and left to be eaten alive. Although he'd had many close-shaves before we didn't hold out much hope for him this time, knowing bull-ants.

Barry's legs pumping, we raced along Alexandra Street, getting extra speed from the hill near home. At the bottom of the hill was a gully crossed by a little bridge. The previous rainy season had scoured out a deposit of gravel and dumped it on the far side of the bridge. Barry's strategy for getting through the gravel was to get up speed. Sheer impetus had always worked before. But this time something went wrong. The handlebars skewed, the front wheel skidded. A sheet of gravel flew up like foam. Barry and I went sailing over the handlebars and described arcs through the air.

I landed, positive I was killed but comparatively unharmed. Immediately I opened my mouth as far as it would go and set up a howl. Barry had landed at the edge of the gravel where it formed a thin layer over the bitumen. He skidded for some distance. The bike lay in a heap, its wheel spinning.

He picked himself up and dazedly, struggled to get it on its wheels, kicking the pedals round to get the chain back on. 'Geez! She's buckled to hell! Mum'll kill me! I gotta get out to West End tomorrow!'

I stopped my caterwauling long enough to snivel, 'Never mind the bike. Look at your leg!' Only then did Barry realize that he was gravel-rashed from ankle to thigh, the length of his left leg. His right arm was bright red from wrist to elbow. His jaw was bleeding. 'Oh! Geez! What'll Mum say?' he groaned. At that very moment we heard the brakes of the North Ward bus squeal as it turned into Alexandra Street.

Mum overtook us as we trudged sorrowfully homewards pushing the bike. Horrified, she cried. 'What happened? Oh! For goodness sake, Marion! Take his school-bag! Can't you see how badly hurt he is?'

Barry brightened perceptibly at this. He had expected to be in terrible trouble for riding recklessly. Now he sensed he was going to be treated as Walking Wounded. His shoulders straightened a little. I dragged along behind, thinking, 'Well! She might have noticed my knee! And my elbow!'

I tried an experimental grizzle or two. Mum, hurrying on ahead, called, 'Now don't you start! Look at Barry! Half the skin of his leg missing and as brave as a lion!'

Barry needed all the courage he could muster for the treatment that lay ahead. First the injuries had to be bathed with Condies' Crystals to swab away all the fragments of gravel, grass-stalks, even a little bit of stick, that were embedded. He sat on one kitchen-chair with his leg elevated on another while Mum sponged gently with an old piece of torn sheeting, catching the drips in the enamel basin from the bathroom.

Then she uncorked the iodine bottle, holding it against the light to judge how far the contents would go. There would not be enough to do the whole length of his leg. Only the deepest areas oozing globules of clear fluid would be able to be done and the worst part on his elbow. 'Grit your teeth, now,' she said. Barry gripped the edge of the kitchen chair and set his jaw. Mum poured out the viscous brown fluid from the bottle. Despite himself Barry gave a snarl of pain in the back of his throat. His face screwed in agony. The fluid from the bottle might as well have been liquid fire. To have iodine dabbed on the merest scratch or splinter was agonizing: to have it poured over an area of torn flesh, excruciating. Barry' s eyes glittered with pain, but he did not cry.

Mum hovered anxiously, then she fetched an old sheet from the linen-cupboard and began tearing it into strips. She kept her shoulder turned to Barry in case he wanted to cry without her seeing him. But he didn't. To me, hanging doom-faced over the kitchen table, she snapped, 'Well! Don't just stand there staring! Put the dipper on! Make a cup of tea! Be useful!'

There was an aluminium dipper to be filled with tank-water from the tap out the back, into which an immersion-heater called a plunger was thrust. I had never been allowed to use the plunger before, so this was a step forward to maturity. (At a later date I nearly set fire to the house by hanging the plunger back on its hook on the wall without switching it off first. It scorched a very interesting spiral pattern into the wall before the smell of burning paint raised the alarm.) But now, importantly, I set about making a pot of tea.

Mum arranged a couple of dining-room chairs in front of the wireless and helped Barry to get his leg as comfortable as possible. She gave him a hot cup of tea with lots of sugar in it and let him finish off the Iced VoVo's. 'If your father was home he might have doubled you in to the Ambulance Station. Whatever are we going to do about your bike? How on earth can you get out to West End tomorrow?'

Barry finished his cup of tea and hauled himself up on to his good leg, 'I'll just go down and have a squiz at her, Mum.' he said. 'Indeed! You'll do no such thing!' exclaimed Mum distractedly. 'If only there was someway to get in touch with your father! Why is he never here when things happen!'

Despite Mum's protests Barry hobbled off down the back steps, hunch-shouldered with pain. Shortly we heard him banging away down under the house. When he came back, his bandages were the worse for wear and beginning to slip down. 'I reckon she's a goer, Mum. She'll do to get me out there tomorrow, at any rate.'

Next morning Mum and I stood on the front steps and watched Barry ride off to sit for Scholarship. He held the bandaged leg out stiffly to one side while he worked the pedal with the other. The buckled part of the front wheel scraped repetitiously as he ground his way slowly along Alexandra Street, up the hill and out of sight.

'Oh! What a thing to happen to him!' cried Mum, clasping her hands to her mouth. 'Such promise! But how can he sit for an examination in that state! And your father not even knowing! Still, he is very young! Not thirteen till January. If he doesn't get through he could always sit again next year.' Neither she nor I could begin to imagine how Barry would get up the Cutting, let alone down the other side, with only one good leg. 'Oh! I hope he remembered his protractor box!' she cried, adding, 'Oh! I think I need another cup of tea! It's really all too much!'

Not very long after this, Mum turned on the wireless early one morning for Captain Hatfield's Daily Dozen. Until Barry's accident, we always had to do this exercise programme of what Barry called 'Physical Jerks'.

It was always the same formula, starting with running-on-the-spot for a warm-up, then touching-toes twelve times, and arm-flings to correct any tendency to round-shouldered-ness. All these were done to the cheerful military commands of Captain Hatfield; 'Knees higher! Higher! Higher! Beautiful morning! Good to be alive! Swing those arms! Higher! Higher!'

Mum tried to ignore the bad grace with which Barry and I slouched through the routines. At the end the pianist played sweet tinkly music while Captain Hatfield exhorted us to keep our shoulders flat, fill our lungs and breath ; 'In!'; 'Out!' Barry and I would hunch as much as we thought we could get away with and take shallow sniffs. Mum lined us up along the verandah-railing, a look of determined well-being in her eye as she drew deep breaths, 'filling the lungs' and gazed up at the morning hawks slowly circling over Castle Hill.

To cook the morning porridge in the heat of summer, Mum used a primus instead of lighting the fire. In early December there came a morning when the wireless was on but a News Broadcast had replaced Captain Hatfield. Mum had stopped pumping the primus to listen. She held her hand up, saying, 'Shush! Listen! This is important!' The announcer's voice was solemn. '....The Japanese have attacked Pearl Harbour...over 2000 United States personnel have been killed... the *USS Arizona* has been sunk... installations are blazing ... President Roosevelt has addressed the nation...America is now at war...'

The primus burned on, the flame sharp and blue with no porridge saucepan on the top of it. In the hissing silence, Mum said, her voice tense with dread, 'Where on earth is Pearl Harbour? Who has ever heard of it! Where is Hawaii, for goodness sake!'

'I'll get my atlas!' said Barry, limping off. We peered over his shoulder. Hawaii was hard to find because it was marked 'Sandwich Islands' with 'Hawaii' in tiny print underneath.

'Oh, Dear! Oh! Dear! Such a little place! How can it be so important!' cried Mum, 'So many lives lost! And Mr. Churchill says that if the Japanese attacked the USA then Britain would declare war on Japan within the hour. He would not go back on his word. This means England will be involved, too. Oh! Is there no end to all this fighting!'

At this moment the ice-man came. 'Not good, is it!' he said. 'Getting a bit too close for comfort! Reckon I'll be off to join up before too long!'

Next morning's *Bulletin* had a banner headline right across page three, where the news started, in huge letters, 'JAPAN BRINGS WAR TO THE PACIFIC'. There was a full page of photographs of Hickman Base with smoke pouring up from the installations and the wreckage of ships in the harbour. Mum and Barry read every word, their heads close together over the kitchen table. There was a fold-out map of the Pacific which Barry stuck up on the wall of his bedroom

One small paragraph of the *Bulletin* had caught Mum's eye. The three Japanese laundries in Townsville would be closed down. They would be open from 10 a.m. to 2 p.m.to enable people who had clothes being laundered to pick them up. A heavily-armed military guard would be on duty while this was going on. Auntie Elsie had always sent the white linen suits that Uncle Les wore to the Japanese laundry. 'However will she manage?' said Mum. 'Fancy having to do all those heavy whites herself!'

'Jap laundrymen! Huh!' said Barry. 'They've probably been spies all along! Just pretending! I bet they've been snooping round the aerodrome and Kissing Point, taking photos and making maps and everything!' Barry's favourite book just now was '*The Riddle of the Sands*' so he knew all about spies

Breaking-up Day at school was when there were class picnics under the Moreton Bay fig-trees, each class to its own tree. There were egg and lettuce sandwiches, or Burdekin duck sandwiches, or Windsor sausage sandwiches; special treats from home for the occasion, and cakes and water-melon – 'No water-melon fights! 'Who threw that! No throwing!'– and, as the finale, after a lot of 'Line up! Line up!'s and a lot of shufflings into place and 'No pushing!s', a large canvas cylinder whose presence until now had dominated proceedings, every child knowing with an anticipatory thrill what it portended, was wheeled forth and, steaming dry-ice smoke, was opened. Ice-creams in little cardboard tubs were produced and given out, to be scraped and licked to the last drop with tiny wooden spoons. Ah! The sweet satisfaction! And then, as though there was no end to the largesse of the occasion, paper-bags of boiled lollies were produced and presented, one to each child, good or not good, clever or not clever. To everybody! A benison of boiled lollies! And when there was one packet left over, the satisfaction of it, when, who should Miss Wheeler present it to but Andy Sugden! Which was only fair. We all knew it was fair. His sufferings had marked the school-hours of our year and still he smiled a hopeful, sad little smile to anyone who might smile back.

But this year, before the class picnics could get started, there was to be a special parade. Class by class, we were marshalled to the gravel parade-ground, and sat, avoiding the bindi-eyes as much as possible, cross-legged, gazing up at Mr. Bonham on the Office verandah. Frowningly, he ran his eye over the ranks to settle us down. Then, drawing himself up proudly, he began; 'I have a very important message to read out you. You are to listen hard – That boy in the back row! Come and see me afterwards! Yes! You! You know who I mean! – Now! All of you! Listen hard! And you are to tell your parents what I am about to say to you!'

The important message was from Mr. Forgan Smith, the Premier of Queensland, about the holidays. He knew we had looked forward to them but we might have to go without some of the pleasures because for the first time, the shores of Australia were under threat from an enemy. Then he said something that I knew would make Mum's eyes light up when I told her; we had to learn to follow the example of the children of the Motherland, who had learned to do their duty with a song on their lips, and as we were of the same stock, he was sure we would be able to learn to do so too.

Sitting there on the hot gravel, squinnying our eyes against the glare, we had no idea what the important message was all about. But we felt serious, and dignified by being told it, and assumed grave faces.

When the message finished with the instruction that we were expected, in the years ahead, to set an example of high British courage, so that with God's help, victory would be ours, and Australia a free country; Well! We almost felt we wanted to arm ourselves on the spot and go marching off to war.

Barry did arm himself. He made a rifle from a piece of wood, carving the butt lovingly and adding small nails from Dad's work bench for sights and a trigger. It looked authentic, especially when he added the finishing touch of a strap fashioned from a broken trunk strap to carry it over his shoulder like a Digger.

I hankered to carry arms in similar fashion. Barry made my rifle from a length of bamboo which had a very pleasing angle just where the butt of a rifle would be. In one way it was superior to Barry's; being bamboo it was hollow, like the barrel of a rifle.

I was more than satisfied with my weapon and carried it constantly. If I had to scooter down to the store for Mum, I slung my rifle over my shoulder before setting out. Who knew? A Japanese platoon might be advancing through the bush, bayonets at the ready, along the edge of Landsborough Street! Perhaps the sight of a brave little Australian girl riding dauntlessly on her scooter might be enough to turn them back!

A lot of official instructions were now issued by the Town Council. The ones for Air Raids said to 'Keep Calm!' There is something about being told to keep calm that has a most unnerving effect. It makes you wonder what everybody else knows that you don't.

The next instruction was to turn off the gas. Like most kitchen stoves in Townsville, ours was a wood stove, so that didn't apply to us. Next you had to see that the bath and sink were filled as a reserve supply of water to put out fires started by bombs. We didn't have a bath, only a shower; or a sink – we washed up in an enamel basin and threw the water on to the papaw tree, so that didn't apply to us either. Keeping off the streets hardly applied, as we were almost in the bush on the side of Castle Hill. There was only one instruction that Mum was able to do much about. It was to keep a supply of food in a receptacle that would not be affected by glass splinters. With her expertise in sending parcels to England, Mum soon got that organized.

Barry was sent to the store for a butter-box into which she packed tea, cocoa, sugar, condensed milk, Sao biscuits and Dino. Instead of making the usual Christmas cake she baked one in a large Trufood milk-tin with a press-on lid. This was then sealed and packed away too.

Trenches were dug by the Town Council in parks and recreation areas. The ones in Queen's Park were the zig-zag kind. Barry said this was so that the blast from bombs wouldn't travel along them. The ones in Stokes Street were very deep. When you looked into them they were well over a man's head. Some parts were covered over with railway sleepers and soil; the sides were lined with corrugated iron to stop the dirt sliding in.

The men who had been working on building the City Baths on the Strand were set to digging trenches. Gradually the new baths half-filled with greenish water and stayed that way with bits of rusty iron and rubbish sticking out.

It was a terrible shame about the baths, because they were badly needed. Another little boy, aged eight, had been killed by a Portuguese Man o' War when he was paddling at the water's edge at Rowe's Bay. People said, 'Flaming Japs! Spoiling things. Needn't have happened if we'd had the baths!'

The Council said it would not be possible for them to provide air-raid trenches for all citizens so householders would have to make their own. Sand would be deposited in front of every house and people had to collect it and store it themselves. It was for putting out incendiary-bombs. A pile of creek-gravel was dumped at the front of our place. We got an extra large load because there were two more houses up the side of the hill from us, Woodwards and Browns. They never did collect their allowance so Ronnie and Barry had a very nice sand-pile to make roads and tunnels for cars, before the rainy season set in and it began to wash away down the hillside.

A bucket of sand had to be placed by both the front and back doorway, together with a spade and a rake, for putting out incendiaries. There was also something called a sugar-bag poultice for extinguishing incendiaries. Mum made two on her Bluebird sewing-machine, 'tch-tching' angrily to herself over how the bagging caught in the needle. To make the incendiary-poultice the instructions were to sew four lines of stitching at intervals down the length of a sugar-bag, leaving one end open so that the sections could be filled with sand. Then it was to be sewn across the top, a task that was not accomplished without a certain amount of spillage on to the precious Bluebird, the floor and Mum herself. The Japanese came in for some comments.

The idea of the sugar-bag poultice was that you were to use it as a body-shield in approaching an incendiary-bomb and then throw it on the bomb to extinguish it. Barry was avid for all this excitement to begin and had a small practice on Mumpuss. She was very offended and ran to hide herself under the low part of the house, licking her hind leg furiously to re-establish her sense of worth.

In fact, Mumpuss thought the buckets of sand had been placed at the doors for her convenience and used them appropriately, balancing gravely in the elevated position, closing her eyes for delicacy's sake if she thought we were looking. While the sand was available, Mum also took the opportunity to re-pot some of her ferns.

When the Quelches announced that they were going to sell their home in Eyre Street and move to Hermit Park, we were devastated. Auntie Elsie thought their house was too close to the fort at Kissing Point which might become a bomb target. There was also talk of evacuating invalids and the elderly. The people of South Townsville living near the wharves were told to be ready to leave. Hubert Wells Power Station was another possible target. Anyone who owned a car was asked to report to the Police to help with evacuations.

Barry could not get over the news of the loss of the *Prince of Wales* and the *Repulse*, sunk by Japanese bombers. 'The *Prince of Wales*! But she was brand new! It only goes to show that these big battleships have got to have air-cover! They've got to have a carrier with them!' he said angrily. Mum shed quiet tears for the young lives wasted, 'Poor old England! The best and bravest being wiped out. She is taking such a battering! This could mean the end of her days as a sea-power! Britannia can't rule the waves with such terrible losses as these, especially here in the East.' Not long after this, the Government let it be known that a protective screen of mines was being laid along the Australian coastline.

A new order from the Town Council was that bulbs had to be removed from verandah lights, nor were there to be lights in any of the shops in town. 'What's the point, when the lights from the houses on Stanton Hill and Melton Hill can probably be seen from miles out to sea!' said Barry as he got up on a kitchen chair under Mum's direction to take the bulbs from the lights on the long front verandah.

On the Friday before Christmas Mum took us into town. Santa Claus was going to be at McKimmins at three o'clock and also Donald Duck. At McKimmins we found a wall of sandbags eight feet high had been built across the entrance, extending right back up to Stokes Street.

'Cripes!' said Barry, very impressed. 'Oh Dear!' said Mum, 'This reminds me of the

Zeppelin raids over London when I was a little girl!' Out in the middle of the street, work was underway on the concrete pill-boxes which Barry told us were called Hanlon's Hide-outs. One was already complete, a second one under construction.

We didn't linger long at Santa Claus's grotto because he was very obviously only a pretend Santa Claus with red cotton pyjamas and a beard made of cotton-wool. Anyone could see through him. He had a tin of boiled lollies that he allowed each child to dig their hand into in turn. Mum hissed in my ear, 'Don't you dare! Think of the germs!'

Barry and I went off to buy our present for Mum. Barry decided that if we went fifty-fifty we could get her a proper one instead of just the usual cake of soap and a hankie. In Penny's there were bread-boards with a fancy design around the edge for two-and-six, but in Carrols' we found just the thing, a doily-press with a poker-work pattern of poinsettias on the front and a silken cord to fasten it with. Mum loved her collection of doilies, most of which she had embroidered and crocheted herself while she sat by the wireless at night. ('The devil finds work for idle hands!') Every vase and ornament in the house had a starched and ironed doily under it and when special visitors such as Mr. Prouse, the minister, or Auntie Elsie and Mrs. Ackland came, the cakes were served on doilies as well. So Barry and I spent two-and-ninepence on the doily press and found we still had enough money left over for eau de cologne in a tiny bottle shaped like a crown.

Barry then announced that as he was the older he would give her the doily-press and I could give her the bottle of scent. The arithmetic of this quite eluded me but I was sure I was being diddled and said so. It didn't seem fair to me because he already had the wooden pin-tray he had made for Mum in wood-work at school, as well as the nail-box for Dad.

We argued all the way back to McKimmins' Corner where we had arranged to meet Mum. If Barry hadn't pointed it out to me I would have completely missed the fact that some of the shops had butter-muslin glued on their windows to stop glass-splinters when the bombs were dropped and that the ends of the garden beds had been painted white. 'That's so that cars can see them in the black-out when there's an air-raid on,' Barry explained. He was thoroughly enjoying the mounting tension that preparations to meet the enemy generated and could scarcely wait for the action to start.

I didn't get the pram for Christmas that I had so longed for; I got a triangular-shaped tin of toffees with Mickey Mouse on the lid and a blackboard and easel. I set these up on the verandah, arranged my dolls on the uncomfortable split-cane chairs and proceeded to give them the best possible of Grade One educations. I gave them what-for round the legs when they got their sums wrong.

Another present was a pair of twin china dolls, each small enough to fit in the palm of my hand, whom I christened Peter and Paul. Barry hid Paul under the cushion of one of the split-cane chairs to tease me. When Ronnie flopped down in the chair, an audible crunch announced Pauls's untimely fate. My heart-broken sobs subsided to hiccoughs only when Mum spent all of Christmas afternoon painstakingly sticking together with Tarzan's Grip all the bits that hadn't turned to powder. But ever after Paul was rewarded with losts of extra love for being an invalid.

Barry's presents were a new school-port to start at Grammar and a smart fold-over pencil-case. It contained pencils, rubber and a ruler and clipped shut with a button. He got a game called 'Air Ace' which he and Ronnie played non-stop until the dice bounced off the verandah to the rocks below. He also got a new pair of swimming-togs, the black woollen sort with a white belt, having worn out the seat of his old ones sliding over the rocks around Kissing Point with the Acklands.

Dad wrote that it looked as though Old Winnie was right when he said we were in for a tough time. The *Bulletin* published an identification chart of Japanese aircraft which might attempt to fly over Australian territory. Barry studied it and went around the house muttering 'Mitsubishi Transport,' 'Mitsubishi Naval Bomber,' 'Kawanishi four-engine flying boat,' screwing up his eyes to visualize the outline of each on the chart and be able to name its characteristics. The year ended with a stern warning from the police that no leniency would be extended to perpetrators of breaches of the order prohibiting letting-off fireworks of any description on New Year's Eve.

On the second of January, 1942 Barry turned thirteen and began work on our air-raid shelter. We had an enormous yard, but it was very steep and rocky so there was really only one place for the shelter to go: down at the bottom of the lowest terrace against the fence, next to the wood-heap and the chook-yard.

If a raid came in the middle of the night, which seemed likely, we would have no little difficulty negotiating the two sets of uneven stone steps down from the house without the benefit of a torch which we would not be allowed to use because of the black-out. Mum said, 'No doubt they will come on moonlight nights which will make it easier.'

For tools Barry had the axe, a shovel and the mattock, the handle of which he bound with all the string from Mum's String Bag before starting work. First he cut out a rectangle about ten feet long and six feet wide among all the weeds and then with the shovel laid the area bare. The bright bare earth looked quite impressive.

Mum brought the water-bag down from the verandah and hung it in the lemon-tree nearby. As well as drinking from it, hooking it over one arm to lift it to his lips the way men did, he sometimes ducked his head and poured water over his head and neck to cool off.

A little later when Mum came down with some cups of tea and slices of his birthday cake, the shelter was already five inches deep all over and the pile of soil mounting. Barry had a row of interesting blisters across the palms of both hands. Mum said brightly, 'Here! Let me have a go! I used to be a dab hand with a shovel when we had the farm!' But only an extra inch or two was added to the depth of the shelter before she too had blistered hands. Blisters or not, Barry was determined not to be beaten. He worked on stolidly all the through the heat of the afternoon, even though Mum kept coming to the verandah-railing and calling down, 'Come on, Son! Give it away for a little while, now! It's your birthday! You can do some more in the cool of the evening.'

There was a diagram in the *Bulletin* showing how to make an air-raid shelter but it was very complicated. That night, after Mum had dressed his hands by drawing a needle through the blisters, then dabbing them with methylated spirits, Barry pored over the descriptions of how to space joists, two-inch bearers and spreaders. 'The trouble is, we haven't got any of that stuff: 'Timber for the joists' What's a 'joist', anyhow? Must be just another name for

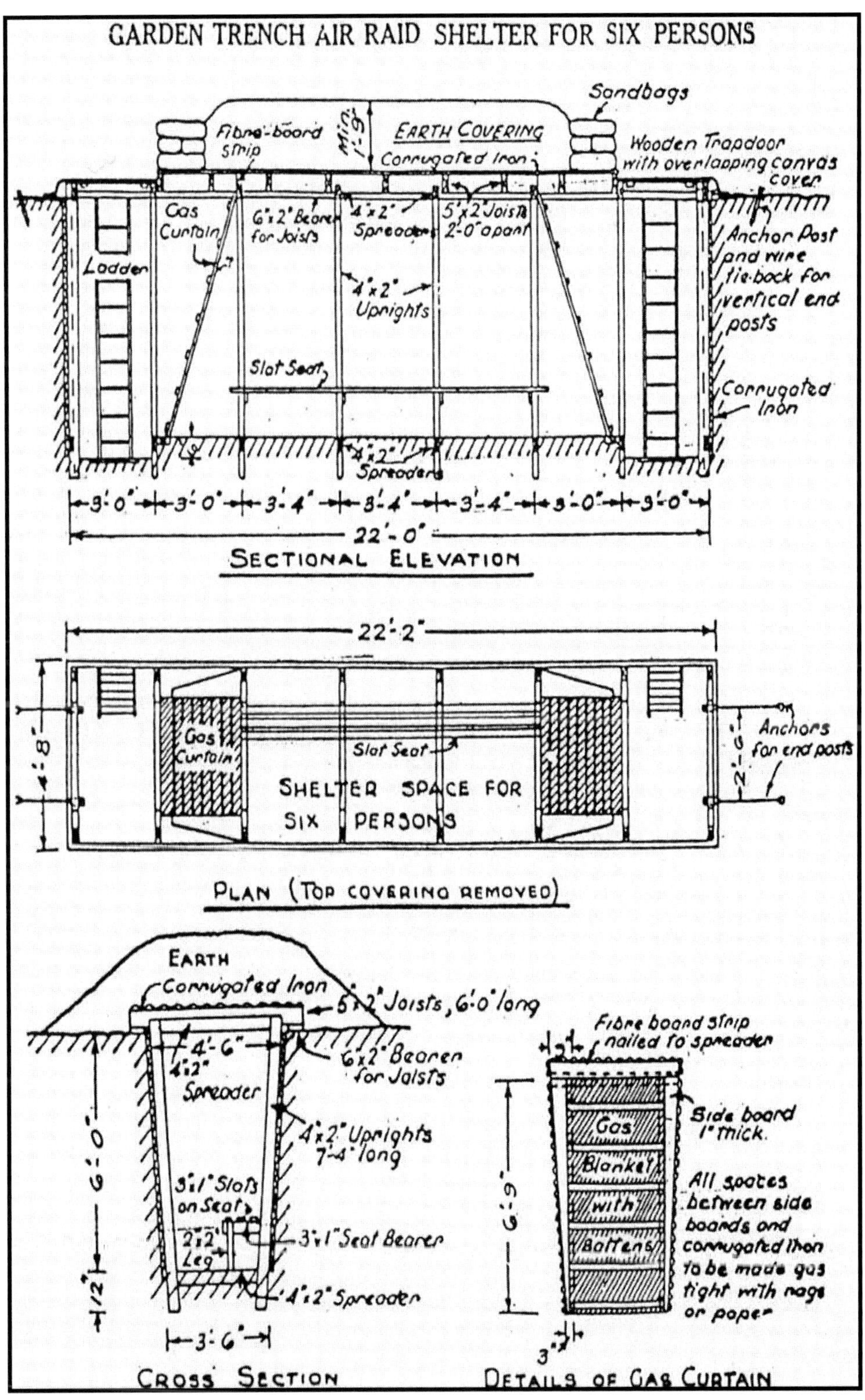
GARDEN TRENCH AIR RAID SHELTER FOR SIX PERSONS
Sandbags
Fibre-board strip
Min. 1'-9"
EARTH COVERING
Corrugated Iron
Wooden Trapdoor with overlapping canvas cover
Gas Curtain
6"x2" Bearer for Joists
4"x2" Spreader
5"x2" Joists 2'-0" apart
Ladder
4"x2" Uprights
Anchor Post and wire tie-back for vertical end posts
Slot Seat
Corrugated Iron
4"x2" Spreaders
3'-0" 3'-0" 3'-4" 3'-4" 3'-4" 3'-0" 3'-0"
22'-0"
SECTIONAL ELEVATION
22'-2"
4'-8"
Gas Curtain
Slot Seat
Anchors for end posts
2'-6"
SHELTER SPACE FOR SIX PERSONS
PLAN (TOP COVERING REMOVED)
EARTH
Corrugated Iron
5"x2" Joists, 6'-0" long
4'-6"
4"x2" Spreader
6"x2" Bearer for Joists
4"x2" Uprights 7'-4" long
6'-0"
3"x1" Slots on Seat
2"x2" Leg
3"x1" Seat Bearer
4"x2" Spreader
1'2"
3'-6"
CROSS SECTION
Fibre board strip nailed to spreader
Gas Blanket with Battens
Side board 1" thick.
6'-9"
All spaces between side boards and corrugated iron to be made gas tight with rags or paper
3"
DETAILS OF GAS CURTAIN

'joint' but you have to saw it out, by the look of it. But, cripes! Our old saw's as blunt as billy-oh! You couldn't cut butter with it!'

'And, look! You've got to have corrugated-iron to shore up the side walls to stop them collapsing in! And look at this! There's got to be a ladder at both ends and a trap-door to keep out gas and a canvas cover over that. Where am I supposed to get all that stuff?'

A major problem was that, being on the side of Castle Hill, there were some sizable rocks to be moved. He was able to build up another level of rocks right round the edge of the nearby garden bed. A couple of larger ones that were really small boulders, just had to stay were they were with the possibility of being used as chairs and tables when the shelter was finished.

It was an exciting moment when after days of heavy labour the pit, for such it was rather than a trench, was deep enough for the next step: being roofed over. Scowling manfully, Barry set about dismantling the old chook-house so that its materials could be used for the air-raid shelter roof. 'Watch out for old nails!' Mum warned from the kitchen door. She didn't want him getting lock-jaw.

With a great deal of clanking, the roof of the chook-shed was torn off and tossed in a pile. Rusty nails were drawn from the lengths of timber. Nails that snapped off or wouldn't budge were belted into the wood. Then the beams were laid across the open pit and the corrugated-iron was laid across these. At this stage we all got down into the dark interior for a foretaste of what it would be like. The iron from the chook-house was full of holes and the sun shone through in interesting patterns. There was a strong earthy smell. Barry had cut a little shelf into one wall for Mum to put cups and things on. He showed this to her proudly. The steps were also cut out of the earth; there wasn't enough timber to make a ladder.

Next came the task of covering the iron with loose dirt from the excavation. The instruction in the *Bulletin* was that the roof should be covered with soil to a depth of not less than one foot nine inches. This was the exciting part. Mum and I helped as best we could, half-filling buckets of soil and carrying them between us to be tipped on. Before long we were all gloriously dirty. Then Barry, wiping the sweat from his face and giving himself an earth-moustache in the process, said, 'Hang on! I reckon that will have to be about it. She won't take too much more.' The roof was beginning to sag under the weight of the soil.

We all climbed down inside again. Now in the close, earthy darkness, the roof overhead could be seen bulging downwards ominously. 'Are you sure it's safe?' I quavered. Mum looked dubious. 'I'm sure it will be just splendid as long as we don't get a direct hit. Even those new shelters in Flinders Street can't take direct hits.' 'Yes, they can,' said Barry wearily, 'They've got reinforced concrete fifteen inches thick. They can cop a five hundred pound bomb to within fifty feet'.

'Yes, but they are for fifty people each. And they have got all the men who were working on the swimming baths doing them. A shelter for a family is bound to be a much more simple affair. Especially if the father is away in camp.' Mum was doing her best to cheer Barry, who after all his valiant labours for the last six days, could see that the results were not really up to scratch. 'It wouldn't have hurt the army to check on families where the men are away and to come good with a bit of help,' she added.

Barry said to me, 'You could play cubby-houses down here if you like, you know. I wouldn't mind. As long as you were careful and didn't touch the roof.' I was gracious enough to pretend that I thought this a good idea.

The Ackland family were also having a bit of trouble with their shelter. Being in Mitchell Street only one block back from the beach, the soil in their backyard was very sandy. Although there were three big boys to share the digging and Mr. Ackland at home to supervise, the soil slipped in as fast as they dug it out. Not long before, there had been a terrible accident in Mitchell Street when a back-yard well had collapsed, killing the man digging it. Mr. Ackland was Air Raid Warden for his section of Mitchell Street. He thought the people would be better off not trying to dig trenches in the loose sand. His own family would be safer under the big slate-lined billiard-table in the front room, he decided.

The family next-door to them, whose father was the manager of Humes Pipes, made their shelter by sinking concrete pipe-sections into the sand. The Bensleys, of course, didn't attempt to make their own shelter. They simply got a contractor to come in and make one for them. It was superior quality, with built in bunks and a suite of lounge furniture. Margaretta and I played in it quite a lot, feeling very grown-up to have a play-house all of our own, until after a while we found the dank smell of concrete, the dim greenish light and the sense of being cut off from the warm everyday world up above too overpowering. We went back to our familiar cubbies under the house, or out in the sunshiny garden.

About a week after Barry finished our air-raid shelter it began to rain during the night. The storm-birds had been calling more and more insistently for days, 'Do we? Do we?' on and on. Then down came the rain, thundering all night on the corrugated-iron roof. Mum had to put bowls and billy-cans under several places where leaks dripped on the lino. In the morning we woke to a strange new sound, the roaring of water down the gully. From the verandah we looked up at Castle Hill, waterfalls cascading in splendor down the bright rocks.

The stonework of our back steps had also turned to merry little waterfalls that gurgled and tumbled, bearing sticks and leaves as they went, straight down into Barry's air-raid shelter. We hurried down to peer in. The water-level was just below the roof, a foam-covered expanse that reached back into the darkness. No one spoke. Then Barry said, tiredly, 'I should have put a drain in. It said you had to put a drain, but I forgot.'

Barry's was not the only air-raid shelter to fill with water after that night of torrential rain. The trenches in Queen's Park, the ones in Sturt and Denham Streets and the trenches dug along all the bus routes so that passengers would have somewhere to shelter if the bus was caught in a raid, were all brimming with frothy water. As there were only the piles of dirt that had been excavated, to mark the locations of these, the Council put white marker-posts so that no one would fall in and come to an unfortunate end.

The mosquitoes soon found these to be wonderfully provided new breeding places and took to them with gusto. Before long, we were pumping mosquito-spray round all the rooms as night fell, then lighting 'Tiger' coils and sitting as close to them as we could get, while we listened to the ABC Argonauts' Club and Mum made the pyjamas that the hospital was stock-piling for the casualties when the raids started.

One day in the middle of January, Mrs. Woodward called down from her verandah higher up the hill, 'Mrs. Stilwell! Mrs. Stilwell!' Mum rushed out, thinking it must be a notification about the evacuations which everyone was talking about. Woodwards had a telephone and we hadn't, so serious news had to be called down the hillside like this. But this time it was good news. 'Clive has just rung from the shop; the Scholarship results are out. They're in the *Bulletin*. Tell Barry that he has passed! That must be a very clever little boy you have there. Only fifty-nine percent of children in the whole of Queensland got through!'

Mum was overjoyed; she valued brains and ability above all else. She went into her bedroom and brought out from where it had been hidden in her hat-box, the Conway Stewart pen and pencil set that was to be Barry's present for passing Scholarship. This is what she had dreamed of! Now he would go to Townsville Grammar and grow up to be an educated English gentleman. It was her reward for the long years of exile. And wouldn't it be one in the eye for her overbearing old father in England! Telling her that Bert was not good enough for her and that it would be madness to immigrate! And never to come crying back home to him if she did. Him and his 'You make your own bed and you lie in it!' The hard old man! Well, here was Barry with a Queensland Government Scholarship to Townsville Grammar School! Now he could too could study law and show the hard-hearted old devil a thing or two!

Barry had gone to Coates's for the bread. She could hardly wait for him to come home. Excitedly we watched the road. We saw him pedaling like mad down the hill. Here he came, going like steam! Mum slid the Conway Stewart pen and pencil set into the pocket of her apron and hissed 'Stop jumping up and down! You'll spoil the surprise!' at me.

Barry, charging in at the front gate, leapt off his bike, threw it into the maiden's-blush vine and came bounding up the terrace. 'Mum! Guess what! Guess what!' Mum, her face glowing with the joy of the moment, cried, 'Yes, isn't it wonderful! Just wonderful! You've passed! You passed Scholarship! Oh! Well done! I'm so proud of you!' She reached out her arms to embrace him.

Barry paused, but only for a moment. 'Oh, that!' he said, off-handledly, sliding past. Then, breathlessly, eyes alight with fierce wonder, words tumbling over one another in his excitement, he cried, 'You'll never guess what I've just seen! Americans! The American Army is coming! They're here right now! They've landed on the beach!'

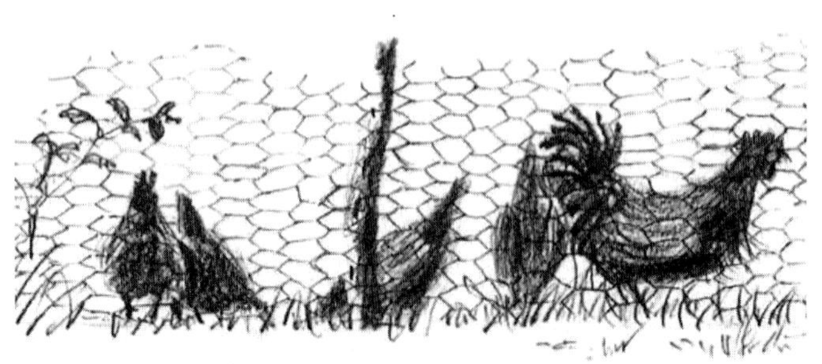

Chapter 9

AMERICANS ON THE BEACH!

'We're all together, now, as we've never been before,
The Aussies and the Yanks, and we're gonna win the war'

American LST's, Kissing Point, February 1942

Americans on the beach! I wanted to see them too! Soon we were flying at breakneck speed in and out of the sand and gravel, down the dirt track that was called Landsborough Street. Suddenly, thundering towards us we saw a long line of military trucks. Barry skidded the bike to a halt and pulled over quickly into the spikey shade of a pandanus clump. A convoy! We stared and stared, as the huge trucks roared past, engines thundering, canvas hoods flapping, one 'Vvrrrhhoom' after another, grit flying, roadside grass flattening, and then, grinding through gear changes, turned into the gravelly paddock of the Grammar School.

'It's the RAAF! They're RAAF trucks!' cried Barry, his face alight. Inside the school grounds the trucks had drawn up in ranks. Khaki-clad figures with navy-blue air-force caps leapt out and began heaving equipment to the ground. 'Jings! They're setting up camp!'

He was due to start at the Grammar School at the beginning of February. The idea of having a RAAF encampment in the grounds of his new school was ripper! In the excitement we almost forgot about the arrivals on the beach.

'Come on!' he ordered, and we were off again, full pelt to Kissing Point. At the sand-hills he dumped the bike among the beach-vines and we raced over the burning sand. Normally this was a performance of galloping from one patch of vines to another for a moment's relief for bare feet; today we simply flew across the hot sand yelling in excitement, for there, between the base of the cliffs and the shark-enclosure, were three huge steel ships, American landing-barges, drawn up side by side, their bow-doors gaping. They looked like stranded whales with wide-open steel jaws. It was terrifying to see them there, in possession of the little curve of bright sand that was ours by right.

The sailors were like flying-ants round the lights at night. Or green-ants when the nest is blown down. All energy and purpose. They swarmed. They were everywhere. So these were the Americans!

Each of the big stranded ships had a steel ramp, up and down which officers in bossy-boots strode, shouting and flinging their arms, giving orders drowned by the roar of trucks thumping up and down the ramps and the scream of winches. Strips of steel matting with rows of holes had been laid to make tracks through the dunes on to the sand-flats. As the trucks drove over them the ends the each strip bounced up and thumped down again, sending the sand spurting.

The trucks were stacked high with crates and boxes. Barry was sure he could see weapons; Max Ackland was certain he had seen ammunition in steel cases. Everyone agreed the rolls of khaki canvas were tents, hundreds of them. There were steel drums stacked one on top of another in long rows. The sand-flat was a sea of equipment. Men with whistles directed the lines of trucks. Others showed them where to back and turn. Yet others swarmed upon them and began unloading, adding to the stacks that grew even as we watched. Small vehicles that were just four wheels with canvas hoods and no sides revved through the sand as though not needing a road. Strangest of all were large vehicles like tractors with a huge blade on the front. 'They're called bull-dozers,' Max told Barry with the authority of having arrived at the scene an hour before us. Shirley added importantly, 'The busy little ones are called 'Jeeps'.

The work went on at a furious pace. The blazing sun and the heat, striking up off the sand, meant nothing. Closer at hand some sailors worked on a fence, belting steel pegs into the sand with sledge-hammers: two doing the swinging, taking it in turns, another kneeling to hold the post, head turned sideways, eyes screwed shut. Others kicked rolls of mesh along in front of them; others followed, wiring the mesh into position. 'We aren't going to be able to go to the rock-pool anymore!' I said. The others looked at me and at one another in consternation! Not be able to get to the rock-pool! But it was ours! It was our special place! But here was a six-foot barrier being built to fence us out!

Grouped in the scribbly shade of a casuarina, we studied the Americans intently; tattoos of eagles and Stars and Stripes on bare muscular arms, round white caps perched on backs of heads – how did they stop them falling off! – spiky hair-cuts, strong white teeth in friendly smiles. It was *Wings Over the Navy* come to life before our eyes. We half expected that amidst all the confusion and din, Cornell Wilde and Errol Flynn were also doing their bit. The sailors knew they had a fascinated audience. We heard words that had previously only been part of a matinee. 'Hot Diggity!', 'Crap!', 'Dang!' and 'Son of a Gun!' Once, someone gashed his hand with the wire-cutters and let fly with 'Son of a bitch!' The others scowled and told him, 'Hey! Guy! Watch your mouth! Kids here!'

One of the sailors drew out a thick roll of money from his hip pocket, studied it for a moment, made a laughing comment to the others, then flicked out a red ten-shilling note. Sauntering over he asked Max if there was 'someplace handy' where he could run to buy them some 'soda'. Coates' Store wasn't all that close: it was two blocks back from the beach and along Eyre Street, but both Max and John, good runners in their own age-group on Sports Day, set off, sand spurting from beneath their feet. I watched them, thinking, 'That will show these Americans that we can run!' I was prickly with resentment about these newcomers to our beach and not at all as ready to accept them as the others seemed to be.

The sailors had also asked Max and John to get some 'ice-cones'. When the boys returned, faces red with heat, they held the ice-creams in front of them like relay batons melting over their wrists. The Americans laughed when Max held out he sticky change. 'Keep it, Kid! Have yourself a soda!' Max hesitated. Six shillings was a huge amount, nearly a day's pay for an Australian soldier, but the sailors had already lost interest.

I didn't like it that the American had called Max, 'Kid'. Max wasn't a 'Kid'. He was important. He was in Grade Six; nearly in Scholarship. Who were these Americans, to be coming and taking our rock-hole and calling Australians 'Kid' as though they were boss-cockies. This was our place, not theirs!

But with casual charm the Americans set about making friends with the gathered children. They wanted to know everyone's names, what 'Year' they were in at school, whether they got 'good grades', how old they were, in fact everything about them. North Ward's children had never been made to feel so important. They were more used to being told to make themselves scarce, to keep their noses out of things that didn't concern them and to clear off. Soon everyone was pushing to the front trying to get a word in edgeways; 'My Dad's a ganger on the railway! He rides a pumper up and down the line to Julaga.'; 'My little brother felled outa the mango-tree and broke his collar bone!' 'My Dad come home full and busted Mum's lip!' That was Andy Sugden.

The Americans listened with interest, asking questions, kidding people along, but never once stopping work on the fence. They sent Max back to the store for cigarettes and again he was told to keep the change.

Once the security fence was complete, there was never any lack of volunteers hanging about on the outside of it. Everyone wanted to run to Coates' store for the Americans. No one any longer was quite so willing to do errands for people in their neighbourhood. What was the point of slipping down to the store for a half a pound of bacon-bits for old Mrs. Thistlethwaite over the back, who might come good with a penny, when they would be missing out on the chance of being told by the Yanks to 'keep the change' from ten-bob or a quid! The value of money had changed.

The Landing Craft on the beach at Kissing Point became the focal point of North Ward. There was so much to see, as truckload after truckload of stores, armaments and equipment were unloaded and ferried away in convoys. 'They're setting up a big base out near Kurukan.' someone said. For once I was able to add my pennyworth. 'Yes! I've seen the tents!' Margaretta and I had waved from the car last Sunday on the way to Bluewater. A vast encampment stretched for what seemed miles among the stunted scrub.

The LSTs were moored to the beach by long hawsers, each about as thick as a man's arm. With the rise and fall of the vessels the ropes tautened and slackened, dipping lazily up and down in the water. It wasn't long before all the local boys were swimming out to sit perched along the thick rope like gulls, as it rose and fell. The off-duty Americans lined the ship's-rails above and tossed coins into the water for the boys to dive for. There would be a flurry of arms threshing the water, then legs kicking up in duck-dives. The Americans laughed to see them trying to catch the coins before they winked their way to the sandy bottom. The boy who grabbed the coin would burst to the surface grinning in triumph and flick the water out of his hair with a shake of his head. The others trod water, looking up hopefully for the next coin to be thrown. All day, yells and laughter sounded around the steel hulls. I watched with grave, disapproving eyes, feeling it very undignified. Australian boys shouldn't dive for money! Especially from Americans! Where was their pride? 'It's only a bit of fun!' soothed Shirley, always a peacemaker.

I was not the only one to disapprove of the boys perched, dipping up and down, on the rope. Nobby Clarke, the old fisherman who had thrown his lines for years off the Kissing Point rocks, could no longer get round to his favourite possie. He had taken to fishing off the beach. With a practised hand he swung the line round his head until it gathered momentum, then, released, went curving out into the deep water with a tiny plop. Then he dug a couple of sticks into the sand, attached his lines and sat down to make a roll-your-own, keeping an eye on his fishing-lines, the activity around the LSTs and the boys on the rope. 'Silly young coots!' he grumbled out loud to all who passed. 'They oughta be inside the shark-enclosure!' They ought to have been too. No one seemed to worry about sharks anymore. All anyone thought about was the Americans. The amazement of it! The excitement of it! The Americans themselves dived from the sterns of the barges and sky-larked around in the water, never inside the shark-enclosure. Nobby Clarke watched them, stoney-eyed and spat into the sand. 'Bloody clowns!' he muttered.

The sailors played a game like rounders on the beach. They called it base-ball. Sometimes they batted the ball far out into the water. One of them had a large black dog named Tex who firmly believed that he was in the navy. When the Americans were at work Tex was there leaping in and out of the trucks, hanging out of the window, tongue lolling, to help judge backing-distance. He was masterful at judging clearance on to the ramps.

Tex pulled quite a bit of rank at the rounders game, streaking after the ball, sometimes returning it with an obliging wave of his tail, tossing his head up and down to keep his grip, sometimes making off in the opposite direction, looking waggishly over his shoulder. When he was sure they were after him he tucked his tail out of reach and bounded ahead until at last they had him cornered. This was the signal for him to roll over and waggle his legs in the air joyfully. When the ball was hit into the water, Tex was there like a shot, paddling furiously with yips of excitement to get to it first.

One afternoon there were masses of clouds piling along the horizon. The day had been a scorcher and the bay lay like a sheet of plate glass. A group of Americans raced down and dived into the water's edge. When the sailors hit the water and struck out, Tex was right behind, his paws working furiously to keep up. The whole group swam further and further from the shore. Magnetic Island seemed luminously close in the pre-storm stillness.

Watchers on the shore began to think they might be going to try to swim the channel and wondered if they realized that it was seven miles.

One or two shaded their eyes in concern. Just then, along the beach came old Nobby, fishing-bag over his shoulder. When he saw what was happening he threw down his bag, gollied up some phlegm, and spat into the sand. 'Gawd Almighty!' he cried, 'One of them Yanks is gunna get took! You can lay a quid on it! I'm telling yer, there's some big mongrel-thing out there! Been hangin' about for a bit now. It's took that many of me catches!' Digging into his fishing-bag he dragged out the head of a large trevally, snapped off clean behind the gills. 'Git a load of this, will yer! Can't 've bin more'n twenty minutes back. Chop! Somethin' bit it clean in half! Right offa me line! I'm givin' it to yer straight! Them Yank mugs out there need their bloody heads read!'

At this the people on the beach began to shout to the swimmers, now far out in the bay. Calls of 'Come back!' 'Shark!' went echoing over the water. There was no reply except the excited yips of the black dog.

Some of the men on duty came across and joined in the shouts of warning, stretching their lips in shrill whistles At last one of the swimmers hesitated. We could hear him call to the others, treading water. The scattered swimmers regrouped and without any great show of urgency began the long haul back to the beach. At last, to the relief of the watchers on the shore, they reached the shallows and waded up the beach, joking and grinning at the worried onlookers. Then one turned to glance over his shoulder. 'Where's Tex? Where's the dawg?' There were whistles and shouts. 'Come on, Tex!' 'Get here, Dawg!' Everyone stared at the flat, shining water of the bay. Not so much as a ripple disturbed the surface. The black dog never made it back to the beach. 'Tell yer!' said old Nobby in the shocked silence, 'Them mongrel flamin' things! They can smell a dog in the water a mile off! I knew a big bugger was hanging about!'

Shark lines were set from the sterns of the LSTs, with the usual bait, a sting-ray with one flap cut away so that it could only flounder helplessly. It was not long before a grey-nurse shark nine feet in length was caught. When Barry and I arrived breathless at the scene, there was already quite a crowd gathered, watching silently as the shark was snigged to the top of the beach by a Jeep. The shark's eye still seemed to have an evil gleam. As it was dragged past our legs it seemed to be measuring them for size. We all dropped back instinctively. No one wanted to touch or be touched by the sandpapery hide.

When the jaws were propped open with a stick they were massive enough for a person's head to fit inside. One sailor had a camera and asked if any of us would kneel down and put our head inside for a photograph. There was silence. No one was willing, though having your photo taken was a rare event. The rows of razor-edged teeth were too vicious-looking. The sailor was disappointed. 'Aw! Shucks!' he said. 'They tell me this dang critter is a Cleveland Bay shark. And me, I'm from Cleveland, Ohio! Best little ole hometown in the You-nited States! I sure woulda liked to show my folks back home this big Cleveland Bay fella's teeth! Ain't no-one up for it?'

I had been half-hiding behind Shirley, but now she stepped forward. 'I will!' she said firmly, smiling an Ackland smile. To the wonderment of the whole crowd she knelt down in the sand and thrust her head inside the open jaws of the shark while the photograph was taken. The Ackland family were like that, always braver and better at doing things than anyone else.

Later, when the belly of the shark was opened, the collar of the black dog was found amongst the stomach contents. The sailor had promised Shirley he would give her a copy of the photograph but he never did, because within a few days the great LST landing barges had backed off the beach and sailed away.

For Townsville people, news of the British withdrawal on the Malayan Peninsula was the beginning of a time of tense anxiety. Wild rumours flew around. The schools might not be re-opening; no children reaching school-age would be enrolled; attendance at school wouldn't be compulsory; parents had to muster at the schools to dig air-raid trenches. Finally an official proclamation! No school on the coastal side of the Great Divide would re-open! Some form of education by Correspondence Lessons would be introduced and teachers would be employed in Brisbane to issue and mark them.

No school! Terrible! What a shock! At the end of seven weeks of long hot Christmas holidays most children were more than ready for school. First Day Back with the excitement of new classrooms and new teachers was looked forward to with anticipation. The big question was always, 'Who will we get?' meaning, as a teacher. The merits and undesirabilities of last year's teachers; who was a push-over, who had favourites, who was fair, or mean, were discussed with renewed interest. Even the boys would have admitted that, in a way, they didn't mind all that much, the thought of strolling off in groups, each of them in a new 'Donkey's Dinner', for First Day Back in the new school year. There were always Red, Red Rover Rover, British Bulldog and Bedlam. And who knew? This year they might even get to be Bell Boy, or Ink Monitor! The news that the schools would not re-open was met with blank stares from both children and parents.

Mum had no sooner adjusted herself to the thought of having me home all day and having to teach me herself, when there was a worse shock. Townsville Grammar would not re-open; it had been requisitioned by the RAAF, not just the sports grounds for their encampment but all the buildings for the Headquarters of Fighter Command. Mum was aghast. All her plans for Barry to go to Townsville Grammar come to nothing! She wrote to All Souls' School, in Charters Towers. Back came the reply. All Souls' had been requisitioned for the duration; the boys would be under canvas on the banks of the Burdekin! 'Why can't it be the servicemen who are under canvas?' Mum cried, in a desperation of disappointment.

In Malaya, Singapore was under siege. The Australian Eighth Division was there, many of them young and inexperienced. On the fifteenth of February, the thing that had seemed impossible, that Dad had said could never happen, happened. Singapore, the impregnable British fortress defending Australia from the Japanese, fell. It was impossible! But Singapore was in enemy hands and the young men of the Eighth Division were marched off into captivity.

Then came the bombing of Rabaul and Port Moresby. People stared at one another in dismay. Port Moresby wasn't far to the north, was it? Up till now Townsville people thought of Port Moresby, if at all, only as the destination of the Thursday Lockheed service from the aerodrome. But now, the Japanese were bombing it!

Suddenly the war was on the doorstep. Then the *Perth* was sunk in the Sunda Straits and hundreds of young Australian sailors drowned. A Qantas flying-boat from Darwin was shot down and all the passengers killed. It was probably one of the ones we had seen on Sunday afternoons, landing out on the bay. How dreadful to think of it going down in flames, passengers screaming. The Empire Air Service was suspended.

The War was no longer just jokes about far away Adolf Hitler and Tojo with his buck-teeth. The little yellow men with the goggle-eye glasses in the cartoons were coming to life and heading our way with death and destruction.

There were stories of atrocities in the places that had already been over-run. Refugee ships leaving Singapore had been bombed and strafed. The water had been covered with charred and blackened bodies of women and children. A flying-boat filled with women and children that had escaped to Broome was strafed and many killed. Broome! That was over in W.A. wasn't it? That place they get the pearls? In our own country! In Australia!

A businessman who had escaped the massacre in Rabaul told how he had been marched into the jungle with all his mates and had watched as they were bayonetted one by one. He himself, though wounded, had crawled to safety. Barry and Ronnie talked about these things in low tones. They were not supposed to let me know about them. Of course, they did.

Mr. Forde, the Minister for the Army, made a wireless broadcast. Mum and Barry listened, their heads bent close to the silk-pleated front. Mr. Forde warned; the attack would come soon; when it came Australia would be ready! Wherever the enemy was found we would fight them! We would never give in.

'Mmm!' said Mum, resuming her fancy-work, 'Trying to sound like Mr. Churchill!' Then to Barry and me she said, 'What you have to remember is that your Grandparents, Uncles and Aunts have been putting up with nightly raids by the German Luftwaffe since 1940. What they have had to endure, we most certainly can, with as much spirit! Never forget you are British!'

Major-General Gordon Bennett who had escaped from Singapore after the surrender – though Dad said his place should have been with his men – said that an attack on Australia would be made very soon and it was only a matter of time, not months but weeks. When it did, he said, victory would depend on every man, woman and child. I particularly liked the part about 'child', feeling that it referred to me personally. I was determined to acquit myself valorously when the time came.

On 19th February the Japanese bombed Darwin. Who knew how many casualties there were? Uncle Les said, 'When they tell you officially it was fifteen, you can bank on it there were many more!' The Post Office in Darwin had received a direct hit and the staff had been killed. Almost immediately, work on dismantling the Clock Tower on the Townsville Post Office began. No use making it easy for the Little Yellow So-and-So's!

Mr. Curtin, the Prime Minister, made an announcement that from now on, under new war regulations, everyone in Australia was at the service of the Government whether they liked it or not. 'Well,' said Mum, 'I'll believe it when they make a clean sweep of all those racing-dogs! The reason the Germans and the Japanese have got the edge on us is because they have been strong and self-disciplined and denied themselves frivolities. There are no racing-dogs in Germany or Japan!'

Everywhere there were signs of preparation for the attack to come. Three shifts a day worked on the concrete air-raid shelters in Flinders Street. Dad wrote that from the air the pill-box shelters would probably look like platoons of soldiers marching and would draw fire. We were to avoid using them. Slit-trenches were dug in the grass on the town side of Victoria Bridge, more in the Botanic Gardens, at the Railway Refreshment Rooms and along Denham Street. The Town Council announced that it had provided shelter for six hundred people. As well, business houses had to provide shelters for their own staff: Samuel Allen's in Cleveland Street, Dalgetys' and the Customs House in their basements.

Barry came in one day with a bolt out of the blue. Chook Charlson's father had it from someone in the know! The Government intended pulling out of the north! They were going to give everything north of Brisbane to the Japs and fall back. Chook's father had it on good authority! It stood to reason! It wouldn't be possible to defend the whole of the Queensland. But they could use the big industrial towns down south as a base to hit back at the Japs. The best they could do would be to defend the 'Brisbane Line'.

Beatie Babcock's uncle had it straight from the horses' mouth! The plan was to fall back behind the Great Divide. Move all the civilians out. The Japs could have the coast.

Ernie Eklesten's big brother had the Real McCoy! He was part of a team that was going to fall back ahead of the oncoming Japs and blow all the bridges! Some of the bridges were already mined! It was supposed to be top secret, but! So not to blab about on about it!

The talk went round and round. There had already been Jap landings up in the Gulf! And on Cape York Peninsula! The Japs could be here any day! The Charlsons were clearing out on tomorrow night's train. They were just locking their house and taking off down south.

Dad wrote that this 'Brisbane Line' talk was a load of tommy rot; that it was scare-mongering and that you always got 'Know-all-know-nothings' that were a pack of 'gutless-wonders.' He told us that Major General Durrant, Commanding Officer for the North, had told the Thirty First that Townsville had to be defended at all costs. It was important as an Allied Base.

Next came confusion about the evacuation. Would there be a general evacuation or not? A committee of ladies said they would organize it. Then the Department of Public Instruction said that the School Inspectors of each area would be in charge. Then the Government sent a special officer from the south to take control. Everyone was told to have a port packed ready: only a small one because you could only take what you could carry.

Mum got out the little port I had lost on the night we went to Bowen and gave it a good shine with brown shoe-polish. She packed a few essentials for each of us. As well as socks, singlets and jumpers she included the little leather-bound copy of *Macbeth* which she had won as a school-prize and a tiny folding brush-and-comb made of horn, which had belonged to Grandfather Greenleaf as a child.

In the midst of all this worry and confusion I had the additional sorrow of the final demise of Paul, the invalid doll, whose glue came unstuck. Even I could see that his case was hopeless. I had a new friend, Audrey Saunders, from the house at the back. She and I gave Paul a moving funeral down at the back fence where there was already a cat-cemetery of deceased kittens. We outlined the new grave prettily with frangipani flowers. We had plenty of practice as undertakers as we conducted services for all the double-bar finches that died of fright if the cats pounced at them.

When Mum told me I could choose one doll to take with me to be evacuated, I chose Eskimo Doll because she was flat-faced, hopeless at sums and not liked by any of the other dolls. I thought if I didn't look after her, nobody else would. So Eskimo Doll, a sponge bag, hand-towel and a drinking-cup went in my school-bag ready to be evacuated. I took *Little Women* to read, even though I was still smarting with indignation at the discovery that Jo March was a girl.

Barry took *The Riddle of the Sands*. We knew we would need things to read because we were told that evacuation trains were shunted on to sidings for long hours to make way for troop trains heading north. Barry also took the flat tin with Dad's War medals from the Great War and an especially good pocket-knife given to him by one of the American sailors off the LSTs whose name had also been Stilwell.

The worst thing about the evacuations, as far as I could see, was the animals. The instructions were that birds like budgerigars and canaries could be let go as long as they could fly. Horses could be turned loose but cats and dogs were to be destroyed. 'Destroyed' for most people meant putting them in a bag with a stone and throwing them into Ross Creek at high tide, to save the fee at the lethal chamber in South Townsville. Mum said that Mumpuss was capable of looking after herself and could catch lizards and frogs. At least that would be better than going in a bag with a stone into Ross Creek.

The order for a general evacuation did not come, but, almost nightly, we went into the railway station to see off friends who had made the decision to leave. Most nights two or three divisions of the Mail left, though there were some nights when there were as many as four. We would go in with little parting gifts such as a brown paper bag of Anzac biscuits or a jar of Rosella jam. On the night the Fornos left, Mrs. Forno had her own little girl Beryl, her own baby, Ray, and two little cousins as well; Bobby, who was about five and Dawn who was just a toddler, being taken to safety because their mother was sick. The carriage was an old uncomfortable one with straight hard seats, but Mrs. Forno, calmly and efficiently, was settling the four children into her corner with rugs and cushions. They were going to Stanthorpe on the Darling Downs. Their minister's wife and children were in the same carriage, so they would all be able to help one another on the long journey ahead.

On the night we saw off the Quelches we were all very down in the mouth. Auntie Elsie, though not a real relation, was the only Auntie we had ever known; Ronnie was like a cousin. On the platform the crowd milled around, passing luggage on board, putting rugs on seats to show that they were taken, stowing baskets with food and thermos-flasks on the luggage racks.

Husbands and wives gave one another last minute instructions. Auntie Elsie told Uncle Les he must promise that the very first thing he would do in the new house was to get in a man to dig an air-raid shelter; she wouldn't rest content until she knew he had one. Ronnie,

Barry and I squeezed through the crowd to see the engine which stood panting quietly, its cow-catcher snout pointing towards the south. The driver was on the footplate tapping gauges. The fireman scrunched along the cinders, oilcan in hand, peering at the piston-rods. There was a momentary glimpse of leaping flames in the fire-box as the door was opened and a shovelful of coal tossed in. In the air was the sting of hot metal and polished brass.

When we got back to the adults, Ronnie was pounced on by his mother. 'There you are! Where have you been? The train is about to leave!' He was bundled into the carriage. We barely had time to pass in the *Film Fun* and *Magnet* we had bought him for the long journey; the *Magnet* because the schoolmaster at Greyfriars School was Mr. Quelch and *Film Fun* because everybody's favourite was Fatty and Skinny.

There was a slamming of heavy wooden doors. The guard put his whistle to his lips and raised his arm, and amid tears and calls of 'Good-bye!' 'Good Luck!' the evacuation train pulled slowly out of the station and curved over the bridge into the darkness. We waved until the red rear-lamps could be seen no more. 'Goodness knows when we shall all meet again,' murmured Mum. Already, behind us, the crowd for the next evacuation train at nine o'clock was gathering, tense and anxious to be gone.

In the end we didn't evacuate at all because you had to have a letter from a friend or relative in the south to say they would give you accommodation. Once you had this you took it to the Chief Air Raid Warden in your area, who for North Ward was Canon Cue, and he gave you a free rail-pass on an evacuation train. Of course, as Mum and Dad were English we had no relatives in the south, so that was that. Mum put a brave face on it. 'Someone has to remain here to back up the troops when the time comes!' she said. 'At least all that VAD Training won't have been for nothing!' She was probably also worried about the houseful of furniture, still to be paid off.

One of the good things about not being evacuated was that Mum and I got to go to all the auctions that people were having to sell off their possessions before the Japs got them. Daily, columns of 'Auction' notices appeared in the *Bulletin*, each headed politely, 'Favoured with instructions from Mrs. So-and-So' followed by a list of all the items for sale; dining-room suites, cots, ice-boxes, meat-safes, galvanized-iron wash-tubs, mangles, bicycles. People just wanted to sell up and get out while the going was good. There were all those stories of Japanese atrocities in the north to spur them on.

Mum would study the Auction Notices, underlining in pencil those items she thought would be worth having. In this way we came by a bow-fronted china-cabinet, a Shelley tea-set, blinds for the verandah, a china red-setter dog's head to hang on the wall and the complete works of Balzac.

I often hankered for things that were being bid for, such as doll's dressers and walking dolls going for a few shillings. Once Mum bought me a table and chair set for three shillings. 'I could have got a piano,' she sighed, 'Only five pounds! But I didn't have the money. You have to remember to keep enough to pay the man with the utility-truck to bring the things home.' She got Barry a chest of drawers for his room. Two of the drawers had false fronts and were really one large drawer in which to keep a top-hat. For Dad there was a smoker's stand about which Mum was very pleased as she paid only three shillings for it and they had been over two pounds in McKimmins at Christmas.

The auctions were also a good opportunity to buy garden tools which were no longer available in shops as they were now under the control of the National Service. The best of all purchases as far as I was concerned was a narrow green wooden bed with a pattern of rosebuds on the bottom rail. It was placed in the corner of the front verandah, the mosquito net was hung on the bamboo tester and I never had to sleep in the hated Pink Room ever again.

Barry, with no school to attend, was out and about on his bike all day long, and kept us wonderfully supplied with up-to-the-minute information. Did we know that they think spies have been at work? A secret radio must have been in contact with the enemy! Information that hadn't yet been broadcast in Australia was being published in Japan. But the Military were on to them! At night he stood out on the verandah in the dark, scowling up at the heights of Castle Hill, willing his eyes to pick out any tell-tale signalling.

Did we know the hospital was getting twenty-two water-tanks, one-thousand gallon ones, in case the reservoir was hit by a bomb? He'd been talking to the men who were putting them in, this arvo! He'd also seen the nurses shifting people out of the hospital into huts in the grounds so that there would be plenty of beds for bomb-casualties. Shelters had been dug in the hospital grounds, but they reckon that, when there's a raid, anyone who can't be moved will have a mattress plonked over their bed! That was to protect them against bomb-splinters and flying glass.

Did we know that the Queen's Hotel had five thousand sand-bags around the front? Five thousand! And talking of sand-bags; Cliffie Frizwell's mother reckoned there was a bloke out at Mango Avenue selling sugar-bags for five bob a dozen. Did Mum think he ought to ride out and get some to make sand-bags? Off he rode with a precious ten-shilling note from the house-keeping, but by the time he got there it was too late. Everybody else had had the same idea. A few sand-bags round the place would do no harm, when all was said and done.

Did we know that the police had steel helmets now? With 'P' on the front? And the Air Raid Wardens, theirs had 'W'; Mr. Ackland had one! And a gas-mask and a gas-warning rattle! Mum wanted to know what the general public were supposed to be wearing while the Air Raid Wardens were wearing their gas-masks and rattling their rattles. But she conceded, 'The wardens have the greater need. They aren't allowed to take shelter during a raid but must be out seeing about fires and incendiary bombs. I suppose we will just have to make do with wet towels wrapped around our faces.'

One day, Barry flew into the house, wild with excitement. The ARP were asking for boys to volunteer as runners. Each boy would get a helmet and an arm-band! All Mum had to do was to sign this consent form. He thrust the paper at her, together with the pen from his Conway Stewart set, already primed with the cap off. Mum put her glasses on, pulled out a kitchen chair and sat down to read the form. Barry hovered in an agony of suspense. 'It says here, that boys must be turned fifteen and a half,' Mum informed him. 'You are just turned thirteen.' Barry's face fell, but not by all that much. He had known all along that he didn't stand much chance of pulling the wool over Mum's eyes. He had one last try. 'Well,

I'm taller than most of them!' he told her earnestly, 'And Dad would want me to do my bit!' Mum told him, 'Dad would want you to be here during a raid looking after Marion and me. You are the man of the family while your father is away.' That put it in a better light. He squared his shoulders. He was a man that had womenfolk to see to. It was a pity about the helmet and arm-band, but!

For a few days doing Correspondence lessons at home with Mum was fun. First thing, after the breakfast dishes had been washed and put away and the floors swept, Mum would say, 'Now, about these lessons!' We would get out the brown paper envelope in which they had come from Brisbane. We would sharpen the plain unpainted pencil that was issued and set up school at the little table on the verandah. It was like being back at Stainburn Downs again, but instead of flat plains shimmering in the heat, now there was Castle Hill to gaze out at. I chewed the end of my pencil and wondered what was the remainder when seventeen was divided by four. 'If the pupil does not clearly understand have him divide seventeen used matchsticks into four bundles of four sticks each and note the remainder.' (The 'pupil' was always a boy) But was that a wallaby far up on the hill, poised on a rock? And look, a hawk with something in its claws, something with a tail that hung down. It didn't take long for Mum to suspect that either I was not very bright or had little aptitude for learning. Barry had been so quick! Impatiently she cast on for the sleeve of a khaki jumper she was knitting for Red Cross Prisoner of War parcels.

Sighing, she waited for me to decide if a boy had eighteen marbles and gave seven of them away how many he would have left. My mind was trying to imagine anyone I knew giving marbles away. Barry wouldn't even let me borrow his big Tomboler. Audrey had given me her celluloid baby-doll once but her mother had made her come over and get it back.

But, I soon realized, Mum did not know how to conduct a Copy Book Lesson. She never shouted, 'Feet flat on the floor! Backs straight! Pencils sloping over your shoulder! Com-mence!' the way Miss Wheeler had, but let me lounge on the edge of the table, chin on hand, squinting sideways at the Copy Book as I wrote.

Finally, Mum would exclaim in exasperation, 'Oh! Let's have some reading!' But she didn't know about counting four for full-stops and two for commas. She herself would read aloud from *Hiawatha* or *Lamb's Tales from Shakespeare* until the Falls of Minnetonka and the Big Sea Shining Water were firmly established in my mind as being within the Forest of Arden. Kabibinoka, the Terrible, clad in his wampum belt, took up residence behind the Little House boulder, and lurked ready to leap out at me at night. A wampum belt was a superior kind of singlet, I was sure.

Then there was, 'Write a letter to a friend describing an interesting sight you have seen recently'. I wrote to Ronnie in far away Warwick, telling him about a stick-insect I had seen or that the mangoes were finished. It never occurred to me to mention the preparations for enemy attack that were going on all around.

The Correspondence Lessons were returned from Brisbane after two or three weeks, marked in exquisite red ink copperplate writing. By that time you really didn't care if you had got the legs in the diagram of an insect coming out of the wrong bit or not. What was a 'thorax', anyhow? The letters to Ronnie were never actually posted, but came back also, mysteriously corrected in red ink.

After a while the system was changed and we had to go to Central School on Friday mornings to hand in one lot of lessons and collect the next. Even the smell of a proper classroom now had infinite appeal. The empty blackboards stirred longings for a time when all was ordered. One, on which was still drawn a Christmas Tree with presents and candles and 'Merry Christmas, 1941' seemed to be from another time long ago. Clutching our packets of lessons, we scattered away quickly lest we be caught alone and far from home in that dreaded event, the first air-raid.

There were several false-alarms, caused by short-circuits. The first one was on a Sunday afternoon. People dived for their shelters, just any-old-how. The wardens were in the gardening clothes in which they had been cleaning out their chook-yards or snoozing on the verandah. After that, everyone was told to learn to recognize the correct air-raid warning. The proper siren would last for three minutes, rising and falling. The All Clear was going to be one continuous blast for two minutes. Mr. Butler, the Chief Warden, said he had been amazed at the complacency of Townsville people and that there was nothing to warrant foolish optimism just because the Americans were here.

So there were regular black-out practices. All street lights were switched off; all suburbs plunged into darkness. The ARP wardens rode round on push-bikes to make sure that no-one was being slip-shod. 'One light can cost a thousand lives.' Cars, which had to have their headlights masked so that only a slit of light showed through, had to pull over to the kerb and turn off their lights. They had to have a strip of white paint right round the edges of their mud-guards and running-boards to make them easier to see.

During the blackouts Mum, Barry and I sat on the verandah keeping our voices low because it wouldn't have seemed right to talk in ordinary ones in the mysterious darkness. Mum's knitting needles clicked away, as though she could help win the war by knitting. Only an occasional flying-fox swerving overhead on canvas wings or a frog calling 'Frank, Frank, Frank' disturbed the stillness.

Sometimes we would hear the siren wail to end the blackout. Sometimes not. It depended on which way the wind was. Then you would see streets of lights going on one after another as people got fed up with waiting. We had an eagles's eye view from the side of the hill. When the lights came on, we blinked our eyes at the return to normality and Mum saying things like 'Clean your teeth now, ready for bed.'

The rest of the time there was a 'brown-out', when you could have one light on as long as your windows were covered with brown paper or painted over with a water-based black-out paint. Mum used up all her collection of brown paper from the String Bag to brown-out our windows. 'There! Keep a thing seven years and it is bound to come in handy!' she said. 'But won't it be the devil's own job to get it off once this is all over!'

Barbed wire entanglements were built right around the curve of the beach and in all the streets of North Ward. They were a surprising shape because Barry and I thought they would be like the ones in the Great War which Dad had told us about; just coils of wire. The ones in North Ward were like tent-shaped fences, strung on steel posts spaced at regular intervals, high wires at the centre, lower ones on either side. The one in Alexandra Street came right down the street at the edge of the bitumen and stopped right in front of our house at the foot of the hill. There was an overlapping part just near the gully bridge, with a gap for us to walk through to get to the bus stop. Mum said, 'For the life of me I can't see that it wouldn't be just as easy for the Japanese to walk through the gap too!' But Barry said, 'There will be a machine-gun post up on he hill going eh-eh-eh-eh-eh- at them, remember!' We had seen the soldiers, stripped to the waist, digging slit trenches up on the hill, swearing when they hit a rock with a clang of their shovel and taking it easy on the dirt-pile to have a smoke.

One night early in March a special blackout practice was to take place from quarter past eight until half-past nine. All VAD members had to be at their posts. Mum, looking smart and excited in her uniform, gave us last minute instructions about cleaning teeth and being in bed by nine, as she pulled on her hat and gloves. But our clock was slow and she was caught in the blackout. The siren went; the lights went out. 'Oh! I'm late! I'll miss the bus!' she cried in a frenzy, rushing out.

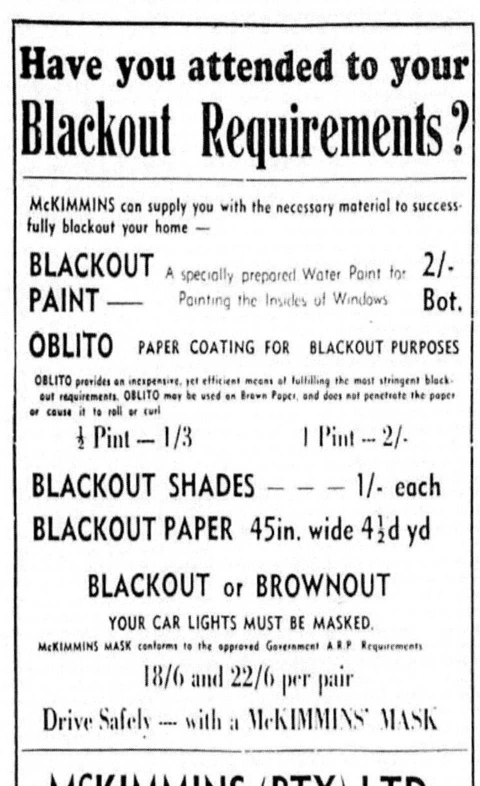

Alone in the dark she misjudged the gap in the barbed-wire fence; or forgot that it was there. Barry checked next morning when he went to look for her VAD hat. He said in her rush she must have forgotten. Her hat was yards from the gap. But alone in the darkness, with no-one to give a warning shout, Mum tripped and fell headlong into the barbed-wire entanglements. Goodness knows how she managed to extricate herself. She staggered back to the house, blood streaming down her face from the gash in her forehead, her wrist swollen, her uniform torn, her stockings ruined.

With me shielding the candle so as not to break the blackout, Barry doctored Mum's injuries. Tears of pain and distress filled her eyes. 'It was an important parade! Whatever will they think of me for missing it!' she wept. Barry said, 'Crikey! Mum! It was the barbed-wire! And the blackout! You're a casualty! A war casualty! You're probably the first civilian casualty of the war in the whole of Townsville!'

Very soon the Acklands, Barry and I and the few other children who hadn't been evacuated, became quite adapt at negotiating the barbed-wire entanglements around the streets of North Ward and down to the beach, each child in turn holding one wire down with a foot and lifting the one above, as we slipped nimbly through. Our frequent passage wore well-defined little tracks where the barbed-wire entanglements sagged visibly. Soon even the most bandy-legged, buck-toothed, be-spectacled of Japanese invaders would have had little trouble following in our blithesome footsteps up from the beach.

Chapter 10

TO THE CORAL SEA: 1942

'I'm telling you, and you'll agree with me,
We're in this fight for the sake of Liberty!'

North Ward

The Acklands were a remarkable family, sunny-natured, affectionate, generous. Their nicest attribute was that they took as much pride and pleasure in one another's accomplishments and successes as in their own, sharing in the gladness of a gift, a prize, or an achievement with eyes shining with delight for one another's moment of happiness.

This generosity of spirit acted like a magnet on children for miles around. There were always bicycles propped against their front fence. As soon as anyone was let out to play – because you had to be 'let out', asking politely 'May I go and play now?' not just taking it as a right – all the neighbourhood children would want to head to Acklands'.

Mrs. Ackland was gentle and loving and Mr. Ackland stood no nonsense. Other people's children got pulled into line just as quickly as his own. In fact, realizing that there was line to be toed was one of the charms. It was reassuring to know that there was a strict adult who would not tolerate nonsense. Any spitefulness and squabbles and the instigator would find himself out of the front footpath, disentangling his bike and on his way home.

The sunlit hours were for getting better at doing things; being busy, useful, having fun. Acklands' back yard had places to practise all kinds of skills; hop-step and jump, high-jump and pole-vaulting. There were condensed-milk tins sunk into the grass for golf-putting. There was a tent to sit in if you wanted to read. There was a big tamarind tree ideal for a tree-house, or tree-mansion; the Acklands' tree-house was not the rudimentary three-bits-of-plank-and-a-bag-roof that Barry and I had in our bloodwood tree.

The Acklands' tree-house had rooms beyond rooms, landing-stages and verandahs with wooden steps nailed to the branches for access from one part to another. If you wanted to come down in a hurry, which the boys always did in furious games of tree-chasey, there was a knotted rope down which to slide hand over hand.

There was a longer rope with an old car-tyre tied on to it, better than any swing.

There was another old tyre inside which you took your turn to curl up while one of the others bowled you round the yard. This may sound easy enough to do, but there is something about feeling your head going down and your feet coming up and the ground beginning to go past at an increasing speed that makes it almost impossible not to squeal and to want to flop out sideways on to the grass.

Shirley didn't squeal. Shirley never squealed. She could do everything that the boys could do; walk on her hands, with her dress tucked into her bloomers for modesty's sake, walk on stilts, hang head down from high branches 'no hands', ride on the handles of a bicycle, hit a 'home' for rounders, run three-legged races. This came from being the only girl in a family with five brothers. But she was also motherly and sweet-natured and looked after the little ones; standing for no nonsense, wiping eyes and noses and soothing upsets in a way that made the sufferer suddenly think, 'I feel better now!'

It was not all play. Often, there was work to be done. Portion of the huge backyard was given over to flourishing beds of carrots, beetroots, spring onions and spinach. These were harvested and sold to neighbours along the street, or taken over to old Mrs. Howie who kept a cow in her backyard in Eyre Street, in exchange for a half a bucket of frothy milk. The children took it in turns to be the one to collect it, for Mrs. Howie rewarded whoever it was with a pannikin of fresh milk.

The cow, Bridie, was as tame as a kitchen-cat. Everyday she was taken by Mrs. Howie for casual strolls around North Ward, so that she was never short of green-pickings, snatching mouthfuls of petunias or nasturtiums that had unwisely poked their heads through the paling fences along Mitchell Street and Honeymoon Lane. Bridie's milk was blossom-sweet.

There was also a large fowl-yard, with eggs to be collected, cleaned and stored ready for use or for sale to the neighbourhood. The military camps which had sprung up all around Townsville had first call on all commercial supplies of eggs, milk and vegetables so those which people could produce for themselves in their own backyards and share with their neighbourhood became increasingly valued.

Every year Mr. Ackland bought one hundred and fifty day-old chicks from one of the poultry farms out at Aitkenvale. These were kept in large flat cardboard boxes with strips of old flannelette hanging down so that the chickens would think they were under a mother hen's wings. When they started to develop a few feathers in their wing-tips they were past the danger stage. Then they were raised until they became pullets that were put in a special yard to turn into layers, or cockerels for whom a more histrionic end was in store.

When the cockerels were ready for culling, and sufficient orders for a nice plump Sunday lunch bird had been taken, Mr. Ackland would don his working clothes, Mrs. Ackland and Shirley their hessian-aprons, and Doing the Cockerels Day had come.

First the copper would be well stoked up and put on to boil. Mr. Ackland would hone his knives. Mrs. Ackland would put white enamel bowls on the back steps for the giblets. Any dogs that had arrived with visitors would be hauled by their collars out to the road and the gate shut on their noses. Then Max and John got into the cockerel yard to herd them towards one corner. Sensing untoward happenings they would give cockalorums of perturbation. This was not wise, as he who protested the loudest was likely to be the first on the production line. He would find himself seized by his handsome neck and borne by his heels, uttering 'brarrks' of dismay at this sudden turn of events.

Mr. Ackland had a very humane way of dispatching the cockerels; not the woodblock and the chippy-choppy axe for him. He would take the legs of the bird in his left hand, grasping the wing tips to prevent them fluttering then, almost caressingly, he would take the head in his other hand, his palm facing downwards so that the bird blinked its eyes, reassured. Then with a sudden jerk of the wrist, its head would be snapped sharply backwards, the neck instantly dislocated. Wings fluttering in the frenzy of death, it would be tossed on to the pile ready for plucking.

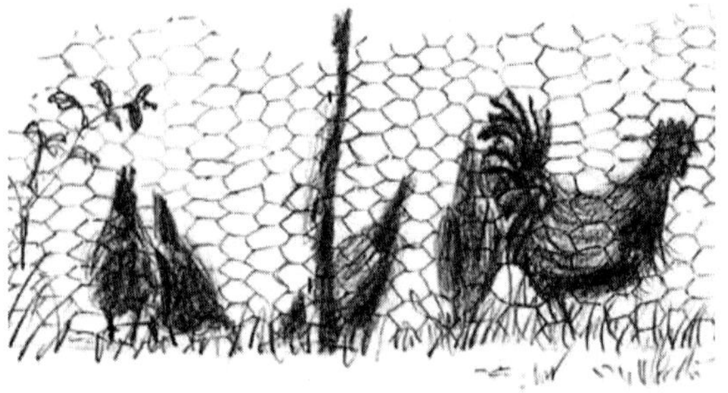

There was a production-line at the wash-troughs. Max's job was to dip each of the freshly killed birds into the boiling copper, holding them by their legs above the steam. Oh! The nose-wrinkling smell! Phaugh! Everyone pulled faces. But the hot water made the feathers easier to pluck. The strong wing feathers were ripped out by Colin and John who also tried to stuff fistfuls of wet feathers down one another's shirts when their father was looking the other way. The partially cleaned birds were then passed on to Mrs. Ackland and Shirley, who attacked the tiny pin-feathers, the hardest of all to extract.

Mr. Ackland would attend to drawing the entrails, tossing livers and kidneys into the waiting bowls on the back steps. The carcasses were sluiced out and the feet cut off and tossed aside. Last of all the gizzards would be slit, turned inside out and rinsed. These also went into the giblet bowls for making soup. It was a matter of morbid interest to inspect the contents of the gizzards to see what the cockerel had eaten for its last supper. Any corn was waste; you didn't feed chooks the night before they were due for the chop. It was also fascinating to play with a pair of chopped-off feet, making them walk in the dust, and scratch, making 'brrrrkk' noises. Once all the work was done and the feathers burnt, the notebook in which orders had been placed was consulted and the dressed birds were delivered around the neighbourhood to housewives eagerly awaiting their arrival.

Having a roast chicken only happened on special occasions, such as Christmas or Easter. 'Chookie for dinner!' made people sit up to the table with sparkling eyes and a sense of expectation. Mum usually saw to it that I managed to get the wish-bone. But roast chicken was a luxury. More frequently Mum would buy an 'old boiler', a hen past laying, and simmer it very gently for a couple of hours in a pot on the back of the stove with a parsnip, carrot and onion, to be served with parsley sauce.

Wishbones had to be broken under the corner of the table by crooking your little finger, though it was possible to cheat on this by substituting finger and thumb. When the bone snapped in two, the person with the larger section got the wish. Wishing had to be done secretly. It was a known fact that telling your wish spoilt the magic. In some families all the wish-bones for the year were kept hooked over the nail on which the calendar from the local store was hung. They were cracked on New Year's Day for good luck in the coming year.

Soon there were army encampments all over Townsville, in school-grounds, on sports fields, in parks, and in the Botanic gardens. Townsville's population grew from 31,000 to over 90,000 in a matter of weeks. The camps spread far to the west in and amongst the Chinee apple scrub.

It was considered helping the War Effort to have a vegetable garden and fowls. There was a poster showing a man's boot pushing a spade into the soil with the slogan, 'Dig for Victory'. The Government said every patriotic household should have its own garden to boost food production. Of course in the middle of the dry season in Townsville, all that most back-gardens could produce was billy-goat burrs. The problem was the water supply.

Townsville's one weir, filling as it did only once a year during the rainy season, had never been adequate. As military personnel poured into the town, doubling and then tripling the population, the strain on the water-supply grew critical. Townsville people were used to water restrictions during the Dry, and to taking it easy with water. They knew by second nature to take frugal showers, or share bath-water, and to clean their teeth with just a cup of water.

But the Americans and the southern troops thought nothing of washing down army vehicles with the hose going full-pelt, or laundering their clothes by tossing them in a heap on the concrete floor and letting the shower run on them. This, in a town where the citizens were issued with 'Don't waste water' labels to stick on the stove recess next to the notices 'What to do in an Invasion' and 'What to do in an Air Raid'! People were outraged. Then tempers flared.

Before long many of the other basic needs of life were in short supply. The trains coming north brought troops and supplies for the troops, but very little for the civilian population. Many of the Flinders Street stores, McKimmins, Heatleys and Inglis Smith had so little to sell that they began closing for long lunch-breaks. They placed notices in their windows telling customers that they would be happy to serve them once again when normal supplies became available. Even cornflakes were not to be had. They were too bulky to transport. It was almost impossible to buy fruit, vegetables, milk, eggs or ice or even the firewood on which most of the housewives of Townsville depended for cooking. But more than any of these, what worried Townsville people most was the closure of the schools.

Then Townsville parents learned that the schools in Brisbane had re-opened. That was it! Brisbane always got preferential treatment! Immediately, a public meeting was called. If Brisbane children were back at school, why shouldn't Townsville children be too? If Brisbane schools were having staggered hours, then so could Townsville schools! It simply wasn't possible to keep kids on a quarter-acre block for twenty-four hours a day. Most parents would know that! The children would be better off at school under supervision. In an air-raid at least parents would know the where they were. As it was, many of the boys were just hanging around the army camps or getting up to mischief. With all the military traffic on the roads, most of the drivers going like half-axes, it was only a matter of time before some kid got knocked off a bike and killed! Children were allowed in at the pictures, weren't they? And at Sunday School! Then what was the point of keeping the schools shut? If the authorities wanted air-raid trenches dug then the parents would do it. They'd form working-bees and turn up with picks and shovels. But the way things were going, the kids of the North would be falling behind the ones down south in their school-work. That would look good in the Scholarship results, wouldn't it? Or was that what the Government in Brisbane wanted?

But Central School was now ARP Headquarters; Railway Estate, Hermit Park and West End schools had been converted to Military hospitals; Mundingburra was an army camp. After a lot of discussion it was decided that Grades Six and Seven could return, part-time. So off Max Ackland went, because it was his Scholarship year. How envious we all felt of his school-bag and books and pencil case and his air of being called to higher things.

Mrs. Ackland still had Shirley, John and Colin to teach at the table on the back verandah. When Mr. Ackland was busy in his Watkin's Products' office in the front room, the children worked with earnest concentration. When he was away, her sweet nature was sorely tried. They played tricks, asked unnecessary questions, or told her that that wasn't the way things had been done at school. When there was some talk that Grade Five might be allowed to go back Mrs. Ackland thought it was too good to be true. It was; the military said 'No'.

In March the Grammar School announced that it would be re-opening in Rosslea, a colonial house in spacious grounds at Hermit Park. It was ironic that, although the roof of the proper Grammar School could be seen from our verandah, Barry would have to ride five miles there and back in the heat every day. Nonetheless Mum could hardly get to the Grammar School secretary's office in Flinders Street fast enough to pay the first term's fees and get the list of things he would require; grey school suit, blue shirts, grey serge trousers, grey school hose – meaning socks – with the school colours on the turn-overs and the black and gold school tie and hat-band for the grey felt school hat. She ticked the items off the list as the salesman in L.S.D Mercers placed them on the counter. This was her moment! Barry was about to become an educated gentleman! And not a moment before time! He had been coming home lately with some of the most frightful Americanisms 'Yeah!' 'You're telling me!' 'Right on!' 'Say, Folks!' – and, anathema!- 'Momsie'. The sooner he was within the walls of the Grammar School, even temporary ones, learning Latin and French, the better she would like it!

American Servicemen at Arcadia on Magnetic Island

Up till now, Mum had always cut Barry's hair – Dad's too when he was at home – with hand-clippers which were kept in a box on the bathroom shelf. Barry would sit on a kitchen chair out the back, a towel swathed round his neck and tucked under his chin. He squirmed further and further down on the seat, uttering, 'Ow's, 'Quit it!'s and 'You're pulling!'s while Mum frowned in concentration. But now, to commence at Townsville Grammar, he was given two-shillings from the Housekeeping and sent into town to get a professional 'short-back-and-sides' at the barber-shop.

When he returned, you could have heard Mum's face fall a mile away. There he stood, grinning just a little too bravely, with an American GI crew-cut! Mum's outrage and indignation knew no bounds. 'What have you done! Oh! Barry! How could you! Whatever will Mr. Whight, the Headmaster, think of you!' she cried in shocked dismay, adding grimly, 'Just you wait till I tell your father!' Barry didn't give a hoot. Dad was far away now down south in Geelong at a big army training base and who knew, who cared when he would come back!

But he explained that most of the crowd in the barber shop had been GIs getting crew-cuts. It had seemed a good idea to get one too. The barber had even said he'd almost forgotten how to do a 'short-back-and-sides'. 'Leastways, Momsie,' he said, in the American drawl he could do so well, 'It'll work out plumb cheaper in the long haul.' Mum banged down the saucepan she had been scouring with ash so hard that Mumpuss leapt for safety through the stove-recess window. Barry was lucky that it hadn't been banged on his head.

'You look like a ...' she searched her mind for the most scathing comment '... like a damned Yank!' Barry's eyes gleamed with what could only have been satisfaction. He went into his bedroom and, ducking his head to see into the mirror, ran his fingers across his short spiky hair. He was humming, the Marines' Hymn;

'From the Halls of Montezuma to the Shores of Tripoli
We fight our country's battles over land and over sea.
Admiration of all nations; we're the finest ever seen.
And we glory in the title of the United States Marines.'

So when he rode off on his old black bicycle to start at the temporary Grammar School out at Rosslea, wearing his new Grammar School hat and tie, Mum and I saw him off from the front step. 'I don't know!' said Mum sadly, more to herself than to me, 'Why is it that things never seem to turn out the way you want them to.' I felt that somehow I was included in her vast disappointment.

Other private schools were also opening in surprising temporary places;

St Anne's, in Walker Street, had been taken over by the Women's Auxiliary Army Corps so the girls had been moved away to Ravenswood to an old gold-rush hotel. St Patrick's on the Strand had been requisitioned by the Women's Australian Air-force Auxiliary Force, the WAAAFs, so the school had moved to St Mary's in West End. All the private schools in Charters Towers had also become either hospitals or officers' quarters.

World War II Fort, Magnetic Island.

Once Barry was at the Grammar School, eagerly swapping information with like-minded mates, it wasn't long before Mum and I were regaled each night, over shepherd's pie and rice pudding, with the most up-to-date of inside information. If ever we saw two red flags on sticks, we were to go for our lives because that was how unexploded bombs were to be marked. There had been two, no three unidentified planes over Townsville lately, very high. Japs, of course. And, what-d'ya know! He had seen ladies wearing trousers – yes! Trousers! – in Flinders Street! American nurses, for certs, because of the cow-horns hair-styles. And, get this! There were a couple of battalions of Negroes out near Wulguru. One of the chaps (Mum was pleased about that 'chaps'!) had a father at the Experimental Station at Oonoonba; he'd seen them setting up camp. They would be building aerodromes, and things; they wouldn't be allowed to come into town.

Oh! And another thing! Mr. Blank told them in Chem (she liked that 'Chem', too) that the Japs had these incendiary leaves made of celluloid impregnated with phosphorus so that no matter what you did, you couldn't put them out! You had to cart them on a shovel to an open space and let them burn themselves out. It was the Japs' way of setting the bush and all the cane-farms on fire. Mum made a mental note to make sure the garden shovel was placed handily by the back door.

The nightly de-briefing went on to the accompaniment of Mum's 'Please don't gulp your food!' 'Pick your serviette off the floor!' and my indignant cries of 'Barry's flying!' – not keeping his elbows in to his side while he cut and slashed hungrily at his food.

Barry had taken to Grammar School life like a duck to water. He liked being called 'Stilwell' like an air-force officer. He liked Chemistry and Physics and went around the house muttering 'H2S04, Sulphuric acid' and 'HCl, Hydrochloric acid', eyebrows scowling in concentration. He locked himself in his room to do experiments. One night there was a loud thump. Alarmed, Mum cried 'Barry! What are you up to? Are you getting on with your homework?' When there was no answer, she went to the door, drying her hands on her apron, and listened. There was a smell of chemicals. 'Barry?' When there was still no answer she ran around the outside of the house and peered through the window. There was Barry, slumped on the floor. Mum was always at her best in an emergency. She hauled herself through the window, threw open both doors and dragged Barry on to the back path. He revived in the fresh air and was given a cup of tea and a lecture. No more experiments! 'Supposing you burnt the house down! Supposing I had been at VADs?'

Lots of Barry's energy went into taking part with the Scouts in house-to-house collections for essential war-needs. Australia did not produce paper, rubber or aluminium. Civilians were asked by the Government to donate whatever they had in their homes so that it could be re-used for the War Effort. The aluminium was needed to make fighter planes and bombers. Telegrams were sent to the mayors of every town telling them to appeal to householders to donate the aluminium articles in their kitchens for aeroplane production.

House-proud Mum kept her pots and pans in the tall, three-sided saucepan rack that stood in the corner of the stove-recess. She polished them up with wood-ash regularly. It was hard to be asked to give them to be melted down for aeroplanes. She arrayed them on the kitchen table sadly, as though parting with old friends. It was particularly hard to part with the big aluminium kettle; rain or shine, it had sat at the back of the stove, quietly simmering away with warm water for washing-up and cups of tea.

'But some women have given their sons!' she sighed. 'If aluminium is needed to stop these monsters in their tracks then so be it!' There had recently been terrible reports from General Stilwell in Burma of the Japanese using Prisoners-of-War for bayonet-practice, and of women prisoners being raped and massacred. Nurses on an island called Banka had been herded into the water and machine-gunned. Only one, Vivian Bullwinkel, had survived to tell the tale. Mum said resolutely, 'When is your group coming to collect, Barry?'

The suburbs were divided into blocks of streets, and different areas were allocated to each Scout Troop, then certain streets to each Patrol. Before the collection started on the following Saturday, Mum took all of the articles down to the wood-heap and gave each of them a whack with the axe. 'It's not that I don't trust people, it's that I like to be on the safe side. I don't mind my kettle going towards the War Effort, but I'd hate it to end up on someone else's stove!'

When a rubber collection was announced, Mum said, 'Well, we don't own a car, and you've got to have your bike to get to school. I don't see that there is much that we can donate.' Barry said, 'There must be something, Mum! Don't you know that ninety-seven percent of the world's rubber production is now in Jap hands? What about your bathing-cap! And Marion's? They're rubber, aren't they? And the hot-water bottle! How often do we use that!' (Only when we had colds. Then it was comforting to be put to bed with one.) I had a very small one of my own shaped like an elephant. Surely, it didn't have to go to be melted down! 'Yes! Everything!' declared Barry.

He explained patiently, 'They melt all the rubber down and then they add equal parts of other things like the sap they are extracting from poinsettias. Stacks of other things, too. Mangroves and Moreton Bay figs. And that rubber-vine that grows round the Court House and at Rowe's Bay. They reckon they could get rubber from that if they got it going. They're thinking of starting plantations up round the Charters Towers, Mr. Blank reckons.' Mr. Blank, Barry's chemistry master, was rapidly assuming the mantle of authority in most matters where Barry was concerned.

When Barry and his patrol came round the following Saturday with their billy-carts, going house-to-house, off went all our rubber things, even the mat from the bathroom that was to stop us skidding on the tin floor and the rubber corks from the string bag which Mum used when making ginger-beer; even her rubber wash-day apron.

Amidst all the garden-hoses and gum-boots that had been donated, were a toddler's rubber rabbit and a smiling Squeeze-me kewpie doll. If I could have distracted the Scouts' attention I would have rushed to their rescue. It was terrible to watch as they were wheeled away in the billy-cart, smiling bravely, unaware of the combatant role in store for them.

The next time I went to Acklands' to play, the old tyre from the swing and the tyre they had bowled one another in around the yard had gone to the rubber collectors too, to make tyres for planes and army trucks. In all, the Scouts collected nearly two thousand old tyres, three thousand bicycle tubes and one hundred bags of assorted scrap, among which would have been my elephant hot-water bottle and the brave little rabbit and Squeeze-me doll. Later, it was announced that Townsville had beaten every other town in Australia at collecting rubber and had come top of the list. So that made it feel better.

Barry got the idea into his head that he could make rubber. He went off on his bicycle to the Common where there were clumps of rubber-vines among the lantana and ti-trees around the lagoons. Completely unfazed by the thought of the brown snakes that might have been lurking, he got in among the rubber-vines and tapped the sticky sap, using the little tins that Nestle's Cream came in to collect it. He managed to milk enough sap to make a ball about the size of a baldy tennis ball, which he showed to Mum and me proudly. Although it came complete with bits of bark and twig and grit, it did seem to be rubber because it bounced stickily. He took it to school to show Mr. Blank. Soon, collecting rubber-vine sap to make balls became a craze.

That year there were no Easter Eggs. Barry and I each got a glass cup and saucer of toffees. It wasn't long before glass cups and saucers were all that was available. As china ones broke, or were deliberately smashed if they had 'Made in Japan' on the bottom, glass ones were all that could be had. You had to remember to leave the spoon standing upright while the tea was poured so that the heat went up the spoon. Otherwise the glass would expand too quickly and crack. The handles of glass cups also had a habit of coming off, depositing the contents in suddenly animated laps.

There was no Anzac Day parade. The Government thought it wouldn't be a good idea for people to crowd together into Flinders Street in case there was an air-raid. In fact people were told it was not sensible to be in town on Saturday morning to do the shopping, straggling all over the street like Brown's cows. But Townsville people liked to do things the way they had always been done, even though Flinders Street was now a sea of the silvery-khaki of American uniforms.

Suddenly the familiar Digger-khaki of Australian troops, and their clumpy boots and puttees looked bushy and ugly. Just look how nice the Americans looked in their shiny lace-ups! They could almost be going to a party, or at any minute might start to tappity-tap like Fred Astaire 'dancing cheek to cheek'. And they wore ties, too. Australian soldiers had open-necked shirts. Only the Australian officers got to wear a tie. But all the GIs wore ties that they tucked smartly inside the front buttons of their shirts, and dressy caps worn appealingly on one side of their shiny hair. They knew how nice they looked and it made them smile and be all charming.

It didn't take long for the more enterprising of Townsville boys to realize that there was money to be made from the Americans' shiny shoes. They got themselves an IXI jam-box, cut it down into a Shoe Shine box, and took up their stations outside Lowth's Hotel, the Great Northern or the Shamrock. They squatted cheekily on the foot-path raking in money, learning American slang and maybe even getting hold of a GI cap. A boy with a GI cap never rode with his hands on the handlebars of his bike but with arms folded or even in his pockets, such raffish confidence did this sign of GI friendship confer on him.

It became almost impossible to get a table at the Bluebird Cafe or the new cafes with names like 'Miami' or 'Florida' or 'Golden Gate' that had opened. They overflowed with American serviceman swinging back on their chairs and calling for Lime Spiders – glasses of soft-drink with a scoop of ice-cream on the top, and Nut Sundaes, at two shillings, luxuries ordinary people couldn't afford.

Mum was impatient with the milk bars which gave themselves American names. 'You would think Australians would have more pride in choosing names! Whatever happened to 'Boomerang' or 'Kookaburra'? The Americans will despise people who ape them so slavishly! Now, the Salvation Army! They have the best idea! That large wooden kangaroo on the footpath, with 'Hop in' on it! That's the spirit!'

Everywhere prices soared. Apples which had been a penny each were suddenly threepence. Watermelons, which at Bensleys' had been two shillings, were now one pound. It was accepted that the Americans didn't bother too much about whether they were handing over a one pound note or a fiver and that many shop-keepers didn't feel it was up to them to point out the difference.

But people felt hard done by about being done out of the Anzac Day March. Some thought it was a sign of weakness not to have held the march just because of the Japs. We should have marched just to show them! So people made their own floral tributes and heaped them on the War Memorial in Anzac Park. One, made from hibiscus, frangipani and iris, depicted the Stars and Stripes. Weren't there some rows about this! It was not the Yanks' memorial! It was for our boys! The Anzacs! Barry said, 'Mr. Blank reckons we are lucky to have the Americans here. He says the Japanese fleet is moving south.'

The Japanese fleet moving south! So scary sounding! What did it mean? Were we all going to be killed? Marched into the bush and bayoneted like the men in Rabaul? Barry had not spared the details of what a bayoneting was. 'They give the blade a twist before they pull it out so that some of your guts comes out too!' Or the nurses on Banka Island machine-gunned in the water? If it was me would I be able to duck under at the last minute and hold my breath like brave Nurse Bullwinkel? Who would protect me? Would Mum be there with me? What would happen to Barry? Would he be marched away with the men? Nightmares became a regular occurrence; little men with bucky teeth marching down Alexandra Street with their bayonets at the ready.

Early in May the Ackland children came to our place to sleep overnight. The big ones had planned to climb Castle Hill and wanted to set out early in the morning. At sundown we lined the verandah rail, gazing up at the heights still bathed in the last golden light. Max, Barry, Shirley and John planned the route to take, which rocks to explore, which gullies looked the most climbable. There were certain ravines with pockets of dark trees. Might there be pools of water there, perhaps the drinking places of the goats and wallabies? They must drink somewhere! But better carry our own water-bag!

After tea there was time for a game out on the street before bed. I would have liked 'Pins and Needles'. There was magic in lining up, under the lamp-post in the street, to wait for the caller at the front to tell you what action you had to perform before you could take another step towards the finishing line; 'Thread the Needle', 'Spit in the Bottle' or 'Lamp-posts', feeling shivery as your turn drew near. Anyone who didn't want to do as they were told, such as having to 'Take a rotten egg!'which meant to go back to the beginning again, was told 'I'm boss of the game and no back answers!' But the boys were avid for something more reckless. 'Pins and Needles! Hooey!' said John, 'I vote 'I Ackey!' That did it! All the boys wanted 'I Ackey' and Shirley voted with them out of habit.

'I Acky' was nearly the same as Hidey, but quicker; 'Three out; all out'. Our hillside was perfect for it. In the half-dark, there were warm rocks and tree trunks to hide behind and dry brown grass to lie in. Bounds were set – Look Out Rock up the hill, the gully-bridge in the other direction; 'Spuds' were counted, holding out our fists – 'One potato, two potato, three potato, four!' – to see who would be 'in', then, hearts fluttering with something not quite fear, yet more than excitement, we were scattering in all directions to hide.

I was filled with the dread of the hunted as the searching footsteps drew near. But in 'Quick I Ackey'; we were hardly recovered from the racing 'Home! One! Two! Three!' of one game before the 'Five! Ten! Fifteen! Twenty!' for the next had begun.

It was always little Colin who thought of the most daring hiding-places, lying flat as a lizard on top of the water-tank, hanging by his fingers on the outside of Look Out Rock or bracing himself between the cross-beams beneath the gully bridge. The hiding and searching went on, the warmth of the day giving way to chill, before a long call from Mum summoned us in.

The coals of the kitchen stove were glowing; perfect for making toast on the long wire fork, as we drank cocoa and played a last game of 'Up Jenkyns'. You sat along both sides of the kitchen table in two teams, Barry the captain of one and Max the other. I glowed with pleasure when Max picked me. It was lovely to be chosen! And horrible to be the one left till last as I usually was.

For 'Up Jenkyns' you had to pass a penny along under the edge of the table from hand to hand without the other side guessing who had it. The opposite team would watch and listen like hawks. When they thought they knew who had the penny, their captain called 'Up Jenkyns!' Then you had to hold up your fists. Sometimes John or Colin acted silly, pretending they had the penny when all the time they didn't. The captain gave 'Down' calls; 'Open windows!' was hands brought down on the table with fingers flat; 'Creepy crawlies' was creeping your fingers forward. 'Honey-pots' was hard to do. It was creeping your fingers forward with only the tips of them on the table. 'Slams' and 'Smashems' were the best. You banged your hands down so hard that the noise covered up the sound of the penny. You tried very hard not to be the one who gave the game away by letting the penny be heard.

The game grew louder and louder with the excitement of it all until Mum insisted we must shoosh the noise or we would be disturbing Mrs. Woodward. So, before bed, we had a nice quiet game of Happy Families.

Next morning, in the brightness of an early dry season May, we set off, carrying our supplies in our school-bags. Shirley had the frying-pan for the eggs, each wrapped in newspaper, which Barry carried in the billy-can. The tea and sugar were in little calico bags which Mum had made. The salt was in a screw of newspaper. Most important of all was the water-bag. Max carried that.

The two big boys set a course towards the shield-shaped rock which could be seen from our verandah. Long before we reached it we were wading thigh deep in spear-grass. Its matted clusters of seeds latched on to our clothes. 'Don't let them get near your eyes,' warned Max. 'The minute they're wet they start burrowing. They dig themselves right in.' It was true. He spat in the palm of his hand and showed us. The moment the snaky head of the spear-grass seed felt the moisture it seemed to come alive and began thrashing its three-inch tail. I wondered what the poor goats did if they got one of them in their pale, silly eyes.

A flight of rainbow lorikeets flashed raucously overhead calling to one another to keep in touch, very much as we were doing as we scaled the ridge towards the skyline. Two drowsy wallabies got to their big hind legs, stared at us with deerlike faces, before loping off unhurriedly through the sparse shadows of the ironbarks.

Just below the summit we stopped for dinner-camp. There was a bulging rock escarpment against which the boys stacked some stones in a half-circle to make a fire-place. As the pale blue smoke drifted upwards and the flames licked around the billy, we were all glad of the deep shade of the rock-wall. Shirley put a eucalyptus twig across the billy so the tea would taste like proper billy-tea.

On the satiny white bark of a nearby gum, a trail of green-ants hastened up and down, each telling the other that it didn't have time to talk, but nuzzling feelers all the same, before pressing on. High overhead, where the leaves played with the light, could be seen a colony of their globe-shaped nests made of leaves sewn together. I wondered about the doings within these ant-dwellings until, with a squawk, I realized that green-ants had invaded the back of my collar. Shirley dabbed the stings with a wet hankie and murmured soothingly. She could make people feel better just by being nice.

But the boys were only interested in the ships in the harbour, which rank upon rank, stretched like a palisade, across the width of the bay. I knew about palisades from Barry's *Robin Hood.* A palisade was a fence to fire arrows and things from; or throw boiling oil over. So the ships in the harbour were like that, a protective fence in front of Townsville. It made me feel safe and comfortable just seeing them there. The boys counted them in fives and tens. 'I make it forty-eight,' said Barry. 'No, I reckon fifty-six!' said John. You've missed the ones out near Cape Cleveland.' All the boys agreed the ships were waiting in the bay to form convoys to go north to New Guinea with a naval escort.

Max's class had been doing the Spanish Invasion of England in Drake's time. 'It's an Armada!' he said. Even in Grade Two we knew about Drake playing bowls when the Armada was in sight, just to show he was not scared. I suddenly felt quite courageous. We had an Armada, just like Drake, and it was a palisade. There was nothing to be scared about.

When we reached the summit, we ran from one look-out to another making 'Cooees!' to the people far below, in the houses planted casually around the skirts of the hill. If someone waved back it was a moment of companionable sharing across the void. We studied the distances to Melbourne, Perth and Princess Charlotte Bay on the bronze plinth on the highest look-out and studied the military block-house that had been built into the northern cliff-top. We could see the sentry on guard behind the barbed wire fence.

'Get a load of the harbour!' said Barry, 'The wharves are jam-packed with ships, too!' He added darkly, 'You can bet your boots those Japanese laundymen got photos of all this!' Even from this height we could hear the cranes unloading. We could see a train curving in across the mangrove flats and a convoy of military trucks raising the dust as it sped towards Armstrong's Paddock where there was a huge encampment. It lay baking in the heat, acres and acres of tents and huts and the huge igloos that were the work-shops for repairing planes. Scattered about in a pattern like the blades of a windmill blown down in a willy-willy, were the broad strips of air-fields, in and out of the chinee-apple scrub, heat shimmering on them. Everywhere in the world below us was war-busyness and activity, yet on the summit of

Castle Hill there was nothing between us and the dome of the sky but the wind as it lifted our hair and cooled our faces. The pastel-coloured distances of bony hills and straggling creeks were quilted with cloud shadows.

We took the easy way home, down the gravel track that was the road. As we stared towards the aerodrome into the glare of the western sun we could see, bank on bank, heavy war-planes lumbering to line up, wing-tip to wing-tip. The air throbbed with the sound of massive engines being revved, decelerated and revved again.

Even in the late afternoon, when the Ackland children had packed up and ridden off home on their bicycles, the air still throbbed with reverberations from beyond the hill. The drumming of engines continued far into the night.

Mum had bundled all the used sheets from the children's visit into a pile and early the next morning she got up to boil them in the copper. In the dawn light she stood, copper-stick in hand, watching flight after flight of aircraft go over the house. 'Barry! Do you want to see this?' she called out. In our pyjamas we hung over the verandah-rail to watch, as yet another formation crossed overhead, wheeled like a flight of pelicans over the lagoons and headed into the pale gold of the breaking day.

'Geez! B-17s! Flying Fortresses!' yelled Barry. 'And B-26s! Marauders! Holy Cow! There must be something big on! Look at them!'

Hands shielding our eyes, we watched the formations soar into the shine of the morning sun. Our roofing-iron trembled. Mumpuss, who had been sunning herself in the bright warmth of the gerberas, flattened to the ground and streaked for cover under the house. Other people down the hill came from their houses and, shading their eyes, gazed upwards. Boxer Bliss, the miniature Foxie three houses along, began a shrill barking.

Barry boiled with excitement. 'That's it! Mr. Blank said the Jap fleet was heading south! These bombers must be going out to intercept them! To have a crack at them!' Squinnying his eyes, he stared till the last plane was a dancing speck that could be seen no more. He was hardly there within himself at all, but had gone riding on the wings of the morning into battle with the brave squadrons. Mum had to tell him three times to get the stove going for breakfast and to start getting dressed ready for school.

We were not to know, and did not know for many weeks to come, that what we had seen in the early May morning was a day in history. We had been watching the opening stages of the Battle of the Coral Sea.

Chapter 11

AIR RAIDS: 1942

'Moonlight becomes you, it goes with your hair,
You certainly know the right thing to wear'

Anti Aircraft Gun, The Strand.

An official Air Raid Precautions notification went out; there would be house-to-house inspections of all Air Raid equipment and shelters; not good news for Mum. We were OK as far as buckets of sand, rakes and shovels went. But, oh! The air-raid shelter! And, oh! The stirrup-pump, which every household was required to have.

A stirrup-pump was something like an old-fashioned car-pump. It had foot-rests at the bottom, a handle that went up and down, and a length of hose, the other end of which went into a bucket of water. The idea was that you rushed to the fire caused by an incendiary-bomb, somebody pumped up and down like mad and somebody at the other end kept up a supply of water for the bucket. Stirrup-pumps cost thirty-seven and sixpence, about as much as the week's housekeeping money, so Mum had propped at the expenditure. It would be just as simple to throw the bucket of water on the fire in the first place, she was sure.

Barry and she had several hot disputes on the subject. Firstly, the families of all the other chaps at Grammar School had stirrup-pumps. Secondly, he liked the idea of being the one who heroically played the stream of water on to the flames. He felt vindictively pleased that Mum was going to be caught out by the ARP inspection and given a rap over the knuckles. They would make her go to go to the Town Hall and buy one.

As for the Air Raid shelter! We had given up any pretence of using it in the event of air-raid. A crop of weeds flourished in the entrance; frogs and toads lurked within its depths. The soil on the roof had long since been used as a landing ground for playing paratroopers. Barry had it on authority that paratroopers, landing with all their equipment, hit the ground with a force equivalent to leaping from a height of twelve feet. The lowest branch of the bloodwood was not twelve feet, possibly only seven or eight, but it felt impressive to launch from it, shouting, 'Hi! Ho! Silver!' and to fly through the air, being sure to land with a roll the way paratroopers did. This was a game that could only be played when it was certain Mum was black-leading the stove, altering a dress or doing the English mail, otherwise there were likely to be peremptory calls of 'I hope you're not gallivanting all over that air-raid shelter!' The answer was always, 'No, Mum. Just fixing the tree-house up a bit!'; giving a couple of bangs to make it convincing.

Mum fretted over the impending inspection. She imagined having to report to the Air Raid Precaution authorities to give an account of herself. But when Mr. Hindley, the warden for our end of Alexandra Street came round, he was sympathetic. He rubbed his chin thoughtfully as he regarded our shelter and remarked that some nice top-soil seemed to have washed down into it. 'Quite good for your gladdies when it's dug out after this lot's over.' He was quite a gardener himself. But you couldn't grow much on rocky soil like this. All the goodness was gone out it. As for the stirrup-pump. Well, he had one himself and something seemed to be wrong with the blessed connection. Kept coming off whenever a bit of pressure was applied. To his mind they were just good money down the drain. One of those notions that the top brass get a bee in their bonnet about. He couldn't see that it wouldn't be just as useful to throw a bucket of water on the incendiary thing in the first place.

On that note he and Mum parted on friendly terms. His final words of advice were that in the event of an air-raid he expected we would be quite safe if we just slipped in under the big double bed.

So, when the first raid came, that was what we did. The siren went with a series of short blasts then a rising and falling wail that lasted for three minutes. It was the sort of sound that makes the back of your neck go all prickly. Outside it was a brilliant moonlit night. The air was like crystal so that, unlike many of the false alarms and practice-alarms, we heard the siren quite plainly right across North Ward, echoing round the hill. But Mum had to wake Barry up. He would have slept right through it and missed it and she knew he would never forgive her.

Mum dragged the mattress off the bed in the Pink Room and threw it on top of her own. Then she got the mattress off my bed on the verandah and told Barry to bring his too. With these she made walls along both sides of hers. Then she told us to crawl in. We had all our blankets because it was freezing. My teeth were chattering, but as much from the strangeness of it all as from cold.

'Have you got the torch?' said Barry, trying to regain a little of the authority he felt he had lost though having to be woken up in the first place. We waited for something exciting to start happening. From Uncle Horace's letters from London we knew that in air-raids whole blocks of buildings started going up in flames. We knew there should be dive-bombers screaming, the crump of high explosives and search-lights fanning across the sky. Then fire-engines and ambulances should pick their way through smouldering rubble, sirens wailing and bells clanging. Meanwhile the ack-ack should be putting up a terrific show and tracer bullets lighting the sky. With a bit of luck, the King or Mr. Churchill should come around in the morning to say 'Well done!' Barry and I waited for these things, or some of them, to start happening. After a while when nothing did, Barry said, 'Blow this for a lark! I'm going out to have a look!'

'Oh! No you're not!' said Mum, but Barry wriggled out from under the bed like a goanna, with his blanket around his shoulders because of the cold.

After a moment or two, Mum and I slid out too, not wanting to miss anything. We lined up like Indians in our blankets along the verandah railing. In the white moonlight the houses and trees of North Ward had turned to silver, the roofs glistening like Christmas cards. The bloodwood tree looked like a Christmas Tree with its crystal leaves. The search lights on the Strand, Kissing Point and Stanton Hill pencilled across the sky, sometimes stabbing across one another the way boys play at sword fighting. Mum said it reminded her of the spotlights at Drury Lane.'Ssh!' said Barry. 'Listen!' 'Listen to what?' said Mum. 'Aircraft! Very high!'

I listened. I heard the Bliss family's little Fox Terrier, Boxer, being trodden upon in their black-out haste giving an indignant yelp.'Listen! Explosions! Over near the wharves, somewhere'

Again I listened. Very high above, there was a layer of lacy clouds. When the search-lights cut through them they were like knight's swords with ladies' scarves upon them. It was very cold.

From somewhere far away, we heard a rattling like a boy dragging a stick along a paling fence. 'Machine guns!' said Barry tensely. Saunder's rooster crowed, mistaking the brilliance of the moon for dawn. Another in Paxton Street answered it. 'Oh! I'm freezing!' I chattered, letting my teeth rattle for emphasis. 'Then hop back into bed.' said Mum.

I went in and climbed on the doubled-up mattresses. I was reminded of the princess who lay on twelve mattresses because she was so used to luxury. I eyed the ceiling. Twelve mattresses and you would be touching it. I wondered whether I should have got Mum to take me to the Little House while we were up, or whether I could last until morning. I pulled the blanket over my head to breathe in my own warmth. Soon I was fast asleep.

That was my first Japanese raid on Townsville. It was Saturday, 25 July 1942.

Of course, at Grammar School on Monday, Barry and the other boys pooled experiences and came up with a group account much more riveting than any of them could have experienced in person. Someone had seen two raiders briefly in the search-lights. All agreed it had been the search-lights that had forced them to climb. There had been a hissing sound as the bombs fell, then there had been one long explosion. Others had heard four separate blasts. There had been an orange-coloured flare. Someone had seen the bomb-craters. The sister of one boy had been at a dance at the Flying Squadron Hall. In the shelters they had all sung, *The Aussies and the Yanks are Here.* Barry came home disconsolate at living in

North Ward where none of these ripping things had taken place.

The authorities in Brisbane said that Townsville had been fortunate to have a real attack without suffering any casualties and that now all Queenslanders knew that the enemy meant business and would be prepared for much heavier attacks.

Mum left the doubled-up mattresses in position on her bed for a day or two then she got tired of the disarray and made all the beds up nicely again. She put some old *Townsville Bulletins* under the mattresses for additional warmth because of the cold weather. One night at tea she told Barry and me that she had realized during the raid that had things been more serious, she would have had to report for duty at her VAD post, leaving us on our own. It had made her realize her first duty was to her family so she had decided to resign.

No sooner were all the rooms put to rights than there was another raid. At two in the morning the wail of the air-raid siren echoed round the hillside, setting dogs barking. Again we scrambled all the mattresses on and around the double bed in Mum's room. Then Barry put on Dad's old army coat and was off, out the front verandah gate.'Where do you think you're going!' cried Mum.'Only up the hill a bit, I'm not missing it this time!' 'Oh! No, you're not!' said Mum, but he was already gone.

There were two flights of stone steps which passed our place, leading to Woodward's and Brown's. Beyond that the bush started. 'Boys are so lucky,' I thought. 'They can get away with anything!' Mum and I wrapped ourselves in our blankets and waited on the verandah to see what would happen. I had never been awake so late, or only at Christmas when you keep waking up to see if it's time to wake up. The moonlight was dimmer and gentler. In the ironbark tree near the Little House a possum coughed and growled. Search-lights stabbed left and right. Very high above could be heard the drone of an aircraft, so faint that it could have been a mosquito.

We heard a distant thud that could have been a rock-fall on the hill. On very cold nights rocks did that. Then more thuds. Beyond Stanton Hill there were some flashes of light. Then I heard Boxer Bliss being trodden underfoot again. Mum said, 'You go back to bed. I'll just listen for Barry to come back'

After this raid the boy in Barry's class whose father worked the Experimental Station at Oonoonba had the best of it. He was able to give a graphic account of how one of the bombs had lopped off the top of a palm-tree and blown out some fence posts. He also had a sliver of shrapnel to display. 'It was concave on one side, about a quarter of an inch thick; and heavy!' Barry told us. 'The bomb crater was big enough to put a truck in!'

North Ward's martial reputation hung on the fact that the ack-ack emplacement on the Strand had gone into action and there had been tracer bullets. Barry had made a great deal of this; he never spoilt a good story by neglecting graphic details.

When the sirens went again the following night Mum shook Barry awake and said, 'The siren has gone! Do you want to get up?' Barry had had a footie match against Town Tech during the day. He just grunted, turned over and went back to sleep. As far as he was concerned, this bloomin' Tojo thing was a big let-down!

Mum didn't even bother to rearrange the mattresses into a shelter. I got into bed with her and that was that. This was the occasion on which the enemy raider was intercepted by two American fighters, fired upon and forced to jettison its bombs over Cape Pallarenda. It had been one of the Kawanishi flying-boats that Barry had been at such pains to learn to spot over the Christmas holidays. Barry cut out from the *Bulletin* the photos of the two American pilots who had driven it away and pasted them into his war scrapbook.

Mum went into town specially to buy the Atikon Bomb-blast protectors that McKimmins were advertising. They were supposed to protect your ear-drums, brain and lungs and improve morale during a raid. Barry said the ear-plugs were just like the gunners in the RAAF wore. But Mum found that the bomb-blast protectors were only plugs to put in your mouth and ears and a waste of money. She decided that she could make some herself from clothes pegs and cloth.

After these raids Townsville was placed on more of a war footing. All the open-air picture theatres were closed down. North Ward no longer had The Only Drive-in Theatre in the World outside of the United States. The beam from its projector might be too much of a give-away. The Olympia Theatre in town, where Townsville people sat in deck-chairs under the starry skies, closed for the same reason. Children under fourteen were no longer allowed in to places of public entertainment, which meant no more Saturday afternoon matinees. Another wartime regulation that was, in Barry's words, 'a fair cow', was that radio stations 4QN and 4TO had to close transmission at sundown so that enemy aircraft could not use their signal to beam in on Townsville. Barry spat chips at not being able to keep up with *First Light Frazer* and *The Green Hornet*.

Most people mourned the loss of *Martin's Corner*, about the everyday doings of a family that owned a grocery shop. People discussed the Martin family's ups and downs as though they were real people or friends that they knew. There was general sorrow at the thought of being cut off from their goings-on.

The brown-out was now strictly imposed; according to Barry so as not to create a sky-glow against which Jap subs could target coastal shipping. 'They'd be sitting ducks!' he said. Our evenings became very subdued. Each household was allowed only one light, a low-wattage bulb. After tea we sat round the dining-room table, Barry doing homework and Mum knitting, fancy-working, or letting out the seams of Barry's school clothes because he was growing so quickly. Clothing was now rationed and things had to be made to do, as our clothing coupons had to last until next June.

In the dim light I liked to pull two sea-grass chairs opposite one another to make a boat in which I could sit with the cats and my dolls, imagining we were survivors from a torpedoed vessel. One ship, the *Benares* evacuating children from London to Canada was torpedoed by the Germans in mid-Atlantic. Seventy-three children were drowned. They had been put on a life-raft which capsized, throwing them into the stormy water. But the cat and the dolls on my raft were survivors. I liked to be the one in charge who issued out the sips of water to the others, bravely doing without any myself and inspiring them to courage and fortitude until bedtime came.

Water had become terribly important. After the raids, Mum said that we must do something about our tanks, because if the town water-supply was bombed we could be cut off entirely. Our tanks had been there since pussy was a kitten, she said. They were at the stage of oozing patches of green slime through the leaks.

Pioneering life on a farm in Australia had made Mum practical, though she often sighed 'To think I left a beautiful home in the Old County for this!' None the less she knew the way to fix leaky tanks. It was to insert slivers of pine wrapped in old rag into the suspected hole. When the wood was wet it swelled and blocked the hole. It worked; most of the time. You could tell how much water was left in the tank by tapping the rungs with your knuckles. Above the level of the water, the tank echoed 'boing! boing!' like a drum. Below the waterline it made a dull watery thud, 'doum! doum'. If it was a thousand gallon tank and your tapping showed it to just under half full, you knew you had about five hundred gallons of water left and felt reassured.

It was critical to know how much water you had. Water was now being cut off to each suburb in turn for most of the day. When the water was switched back on in their suburb, people filled every receptacle they owned; buckets, wash-tubs, the copper, the baby's bath. Who knew when it would come on again? There was always the chance that it might be never. It was the now the middle of the Dry and the weir was low. A crocodile had even been seen sloshing around in the mud.

Mum got Barry to siphon the precious rainwater from our top tank into the lower one. Then he squeezed through the manhole into the top one to clean it out. He fussed a bit over the fact that there were two resident frogs. This surprised me as I thought I was the only one who didn't like frogs. As he captured each one in turn he sent it sent it flying through the manhole into the midday sun. 'Don't hurt the poor things!' Mum cried. Barry said something that sounded like 'Bloody things!' Mum pretended not to hear. The frogs sat in the middle of the gravelled terrace blinking in astonishment then hopped resignedly under the tank-stand. This was my opportunity to run squealing to the big boulder beside the Little House and climb to the top. From this vantage point I could survey the work of cleaning out the tank, without actually having to be involved; Mum, passing old towels and the bucket and Barry's voice sounding like sound-effects of the gods on Mount Olympus, in the ABC Argonauts' Club.

After that, every time the water was switched on to North Ward, the hose was looped up and let run into the clean tank. Of course, the water from the weir was muddy, but it was water. In this way we came by two full tanks of water, two thousand gallons of the precious stuff, when water was the scarcest thing in Townsville. Mum put a half a cup of kerosene into each tank to stop mosquitoes breeding.

People had been told to store water in a forty-four gallon drum supplied to each household for putting out incendiary bombs. That was all very well but many forgot about putting kerosene on the water in them, so that as the weather grew warmer there were plagues of mosquitoes. Everyone smelt of Citronella oil rubbed on to keep them at bay. But it wasn't long before there were outbreaks of dengue fever. The nightmares of my dengue fever delirium were always the same, a long road along which Japanese soldiers, bayonets fixed, were bearing down, tramp, tramp, tramp. I stood in their way transfixed. My legs would not move. I knew that their bayonets would stab my throat and my stomach but I could not move or run. My hands clutched at the mosquito net and broke the tester from which

GENERAL NOTICES

TOWNSVILLE CITY COUNCIL

WATER SUPPLY

IN ORDER TO CONSERVE WATER RESOURCES AS FAR AS POSSIBLE, the Council has decided to LIMIT CONSUMPTION TO ONE MILLION GALLONS PER DAY.

To distribute this water equitably amongst the whole of the people dependent upon the Water Supply System, Water will be turned on in the mains for ONE PERIOD ONLY PER DAY.

The City is zoned for distribution purposes, in order to ensure that persons living on higher levels or at the extremities of the mains will receive their share of the available water. The time at which water will be turned on in the various areas will be advertised as the zoning areas are established.

As far as can be arranged, water will be supplied between the hours of 6 a.m. and 8 a.m., but in some areas the time will be later than this.

It is essential that every person in the City Area must make every effort to reduce to a minimum the use of even the small allowance permitted under this scheme.

The following Methods of CONSERVING WATER should be Strictly followed:—

1.—When the water is on, do not Wash, Shave, or Clean Teeth under a running tap.

2.—While using a Shower open up the valve Only Sufficiently to permit of a Small Trickle from the Shower. This will be found adequate to give a satisfactory shower.

3.—Do not store Water in Baths, Wash Tubs, or other Receptacles, which may be required for use. Apply to the Council for an empty Bitumen Drum. It will be delivered Free of Charge.

4.—Collect all Waste Water from Baths, Wash Tubs, etc., and use for Flushing Pedestals. If this water is comparatively clean, it may be put into the Flush System above the pedestal. IN doing this, do not stand on the pedestal or pull on the flush system. Both are frail and may collapse. The pedestal may be flushed in a simpler, but not quite so effective manner by pouring half a bucket of water quickly into it.

5.—The person who Wastes Water in the present emergency is depriving you of portion of your share of the water available.

REPORT ALL CASES OF WASTE TO THE COUNCIL.

A. ROBERTSON, Town Clerk.

TOWNSVILLE CITY COUNCIL

WATER SUPPLY

WATER will be turned on in the mains in the following areas as shown in this schedule. In those areas not mentioned, the times will remain unaltered until further notice is given through these columns.

Zone.	Times during which water will be turned on in mains.
Pimlico, Aitkenvale, Hermit Park, South Townsville, Railway Estate.	6 a.m.—8 a.m.
Oonoonba.	9 a.m.—11 a.m.

A. ROBERTSON, Town Clerk.

it hung.

People who hadn't taken forethought about their water would find themselves having to call out over the fence to a neighbour, 'I've got this nice big Queensland Blue pumpkin coming on. I'll go you halves for a couple of buckets of water.' A child whose father worked at the meat-works might appear on a neighbour's step with a newspaper-wrapped parcel; 'Mum says she'll swap you these sausages for a copperful of water.'

There was talk about Japanese secret agents having been landed from submarines along the coast or on islands along the Barrier Reef to spy on shipping. Japanese submarines were operating off the coast; that was a fact. In June three midget submarines had penetrated Sydney Harbour and made the first enemy attack in history on Sydney. They had torpedoed and sunk a converted ferry, the *Kuttabul*, killing a number of young naval recruits who were sleeping on board. Then they in turn were sunk by gunfire and depth-charges. Sydney had a night of wild excitement, thinking an air-raid was in progress. Afterwards Townsville people who were evacuees in Sydney thought 'Well! Blow this for a lark! We might as well go home to Townsville!' And they did, as soon as they got the chance of a seat on a train.

A Japanese submarine was sunk off the coast from Sydney. Barry knew all about it. The pilot of the coastal-defence plane spotted it cruising on the surface. He missed it on his first bomb-run and the sub crash-dived. On his second run he lobbed six explosives right along its deck. As he circled above, he saw its bow sticking up vertically, gushing oil. So that was one in the eye for them! Sneaking round inside Australian waters!

Stories like this helped to buck people's spirits up after the loss of Tobruk in the Middle East, which had been a symbol of thumbing the nose at Hitler. The 'Rats of Tobruk' had stood for Aussie guts and determination. The fall of Tobruk after eight months of holding out against Rommel's Panzers was a terrible blow. Barry tried to put a brave face on things, telling us, 'The RAF made a thousand-bomber raid on Essen and Cologne! That should've blown a few Boche out of their beds!' which only made Mum sigh for the beautiful cathedral and the pointlessness of it all.

There was also the loss of *HMAS Yarra* with nearly all hands, trying to save the convoy she was escorting to Australia. They encountered three Japanese cruisers in the Sunda Straits. The *Yarra* gave the convoy the signal to disperse and then charged 'Full Steam Ahead' at the enemy to give the cargo ships a chance to escape. After a three hour battle *Yarra* was sunk. The worst of it was that her heroism was in vain as the Japanese cruisers then chased and sank the three cargo vessels. One was an oil-tanker and her all crew were incinerated. In Australia we did not produce any oil of our own. All supplies were brought in at great risk so petrol was strictly rationed and for 'essential services' only.

People who owned cars put them up on blocks under their houses or had charcoal-burners fitted on the luggage-rack. Charcoal-burning cars chugged around at a very sedate pace, belching and fuming, but people with charcoal-burners got a slightly larger petrol ration to encourage them.

Although there were no casualties in the raids on Townsville, people were injured on the dark streets when they were knocked off bicycles by army vehicles. And a little girl in Alexandra Street, Peggy Phillips, lost her mother. Mrs. Phillips had been ill in bed and had got up on the cold nights to struggle to the air-raid shelter. Her illness turned to pneumonia and she died. Peggy went to live with elderly aunts in a big old house hidden behind bouganvilleas and travellers' palms in Alexandra Street and seemed to me just like Anne of Green Gables. She came to my next birthday party, bringing me a *Girls' Own Stories* from which the fly-leaf had been neatly removed and my name written on the cover. I understood that was what you had to do if you didn't have a mother any more because of the air-raids.

One morning there was a letter from Dad, worried that at a time like this we should be on our own. A friend of his had a mate whose wife and married daughter had gone up north to be near him, but because of the housing shortage they hadn't been able to find a place to live. Didn't Mum agree that it would be the decent thing to share our house with them for a bit until they found somewhere of their own? And it would be a weight off his mind if he knew she had a couple of other women with her. And, as it happened, the women were already known to her. They, too, had been soldier settlers in the Dawson Valley days. He was sure Mum would remember; Jack Ruse? His wife was a decent little woman, remember? Not much of a looker but a nice little woman. The daughter had been a bit of a mouse, but she was married now with a baby.

Anti-aircraft guns, the Strand, 1942

Mum gave an exclamation of sheer dismay. A baby! As though having two strange women in the house wasn't bad enough! Where did he get these ideas from? '…a weight off his mind,' indeed! Nonsense! As though she wasn't perfectly capable of looking after herself, whatever happened! She moved around the rooms, picking up an ornament and placing it down again carefully, touching a book here or adjusting a curtain there. 'That's the trouble with men. They have a few drinks in the Mess with a couple of friends, and before you can say Jack Robinson they have some hare-brained notion to solve the problems of the world!' She peered into a fern pot to see if it needed watering. 'They never stop to think! What about tea, sugar and butter rationing? Would these women have their own coupons? And what about the water supply? We were only just holding our own with the tanks, as it was! As for the Little House! With only one service a week, it could be disastrous!' She sighed heavily. She knew that it would not be possible to refuse. This was wartime; people had to share. The people of England had opened their homes generously to those who had lost theirs; we had a big house and here were two nice women with none. And a baby.

She sat down at the little table on the verandah and wrote to Dad. Mrs. Ruse and her daughter and child would be most welcome.

Among the evacuees who returned was my friend Audrey Saunders who lived over the back. Audrey and her sister Alwyn were the last of a large family of about twelve brothers and sisters and had inherited great wealth in the form of sleeping-dolls, doll's-cots and dolls' clothes. Four posts under their house had been partitioned off for their cubby house and floored with lino and rugs superfluous to the needs of the household upstairs. Instead of dolls' tea-sets Audrey and Alwyn had proper tea-pots and jugs, lacking only something minor such as a handle, which gave a touch of sophistication to their tea-parties.

The three of us held concerts, using the stone steps in the orange trees for stage and seating, one performing and the other two applauding. These concerts were meant to be public performances in aid of the War Effort, to which people were invited by a notice nailed on to the cascara tree at the bus-stop. Bobby Skau on behalf of the public drew a skull and cross bones with blood dripping down, adding 'Ha Ha'. It was the public's only response.

A wide rocky gully separated Audrey's place from mine. We devised a system of flags for signaling whether or not we were allowed out to play. Audrey's flags hung from the bamboo wireless aerial in their chook-yard. As our ground was rocky, my flagpole was a stick in a kerosene-tin filled with stones. Most of the fun was putting the signal flag up. Whether the other person ever read them or not was a matter of small concern. When we were 'allowed out' we simply cooeed across the gully.

Audrey and I wandered together over the slopes of Castle Hill, giving names to the gullies or interesting groups of rocks; 'Burdekin Plum Rock', 'Wallaby Rock' or 'Waterfall Rock'. There was no waterfall of course, only a place where the rocks were glassy from the rush of water when it did rain. If there were caves within a rock-pile we would crawl in and sit, feeling remote and adventurous although the houses below were only a few hundred yards away. We always kept an eye out for boomerangs because Ross McKenzie at Sunday School had found one, very silvery pale and fragile, on the hill behind his place in Warburton Street. We never stepped over a piece of quartz, with which the slopes were littered, without picking it up to see if it showed signs of 'colour'. I was convinced it was only a matter of time until I would find the piece that would lie in my hand beribboned with gold.

Mr. Saunders, a retired jeweller, had a little workshop underneath their house in which he engraved the bracelets and other gifts with which Americans liked to shower their girlfriends. His souvenir bracelets made from threepences and florins were very popular. For Audrey and me he made silver identity disks from shilling-pieces, grinding off the king's head from one side to make room for the writing. This was strictly illegal but the bakelite ones which were issued to civilians were so ugly and had to be worn on a strip of leather, just like military personel, and were called dog-tags. Audrey's and my silver disks were engraved with our names, addresses and ages and we wore them with pleasureable showy-offness. A lot of grown-ups ordered identity bracelets from Mr. Saunders so as not to have to wear the ugly bakelite disks. But silver bracelets were not officially approved. In an air-raid, arms and legs could be blown off and then who would know who the bits and pieces belonged to? It stood to reason, didn't it! As Barry pointed out.

Audrey's brother, Victor, was fighting in New Guinea, so Mr. Saunders spent much of his time in his rocking chair on the verandah following the war-news in the *Bulletin*. Sometimes he would read bits aloud to us, to which we listened politely. War was something that grown-ups went on and on about. You had to seem interested. Afterwards you might be told you could pick a mandarin off the tree down near the chook-yard. So we knew that after being turned back from landing in Port Moresby by the Battle of the Coral Sea, the Japanese had landed their forces at Buna and Gona and were attempting to force their way across the Owen Stanley Range. If they took Port Moresby they could use it as a base from which to attack North Queensland. There was heavy fighting going on to hold them back. Australian wounded were carried to safety over the Owen Stanley range along the Kokoda Track. The New Guinea natives who carried them became a legend as the Fuzzy Wuzzy Angels. There was a poem which became very popular as a recitation at concerts and Wog Afternoons.

Many a mother in Australia, when the busy day is done,
Sends a prayer to the Almighty for the keeping of her son,
Asking that an angel guide him, and bring him safely back;
Now we see those prayers are answered on the Owen Stanley Track.

To raise money for the war effort, Wog afternoons became the thing. Even the Methodist Ladies held them, although normally anything to do with dice would have been frowned upon. But Wog wasn't really gambling, was it! And it was all in a good cause! In Wog the numbers on a dice stood for the various parts of an insect. Six for a body, five for a head, four for a tail, three for each leg, two for a mouth and one each for the eyes.

Each player had to throw a six before they could start drawing. Then the ladies' heads would be down, eyes intent and little exclamations of triumph or exasperation heard as the dice cups rattled fast and furiously. Suddenly, there would be the cry of 'Wog!' followed by a barrage of 'Oh! I only needed an eye!' or 'One more leg and I would have been finished!' Afterwards there would be a nice afternoon tea and perhaps a talk by someone in one of the Services. Then there were interludes for solos; songs or recitations of the inspirational kind: *Beyond the Sunset*, or *Just for Today*. When Mrs. Sheafer stood, one hand on the piano, ankles nicely placed together, to sing *The Stranger of Galilee* she turned her eyes to the picture of Jesus on the wall, tall and blonde, knocking on a door: *The Light of the World.* Her eyes shone with love at the words;

And He walks with me, and He talks with me,
And He tells me I am his own,
And the joy we share, as we linger there,
No other has ever known.

Walking home afterwards Mum said, to herself, rather than to me; 'Well, it's just as well she as the Lord to turn to. Mr. Sheafer is certainly nothing to write home about!' Thin-sandy Mr. Sheafer was in Gentlemen's Underwear in McKimmins with a tape-measure around his neck.

Margaretta, who had been evacuated well out of harm's way to Melbourne, returned, flying in of course, very much the Dianna Durban of her dreams. Mum said Mr. Bensley must have had to pay through the nose for her ticket as seats on planes were as scarce as hen's teeth, but that 'money always talked.' With Margaretta's return my social life stepped up a notch or two. The Bensleys did not like to miss out on anything going on. Mum made cutting comments about people who had petrol to burn when it was brought in at the cost of human lives. But she did not prevent my going out with them, even to the rodeos.

To entertain the thousands of troops and give them something more to do than the endless two-up games, rodeos were organized at Mt St John. To give the contests more zing, they were usually 'Aussies' versus 'Yanks'. Sometimes there would be fun items such as two Americans coming out of the chute on one bullock or an Australian riding backwards. The barracking was deafening. There was one well-known buck-jumping stallion named Wild Jimmy. It was claimed that he had never been ridden. Both the Americans and the Australians wanted to be the first to ride him.

Week after week Wild Jimmy would come storming out of the chute, back arched, head down, snorting fire and brimstone. If he hadn't got rid of his rider within the first few moments his indignation knew no bounds. He rushed at the fence and tried to wipe him off on the railings. Failing this he had other cards to play; great stiff-legged bounds in the air, in the middle of which he would suddenly corkscrew. Then there was rising on back legs and going down on stiffened front ones. It usually took only three or four seconds for that week's rider, American or Australian, to go hurtling through the air. Once they hit the dust Wild Jimmy pranced around as though to trample them underfoot. Clowns in baggy costumes raced in, flapping sack-bags in his face. Sometimes Wild Jimmy turned his attention to the clowns. They would race to the fence to escape his teeth.

There was a Tex Morton song about a buck-jumper called *Mandrake* and a new chum who rode him 'just two seconds, one up, one coming down' of which there was a Townsville version;

Screw down the saddle, make it good and tight,
Back from the rails, please. Ask him if he's right.
Pick up your mate, Lads, he's had a nasty fall.
They're all the same to Jimmy, Yankee Dudes and all.

When an American was thrown, the roar from the Australian troops and the shouts of 'Beaudy, Jimmy! Little ripper!' could have been heard at the top of Castle Hill.

The Bensleys also went to Mt. St John Zoo frequently. It was always crowded with American troops taking photos of one another scratching the wallabies or in front of the crocodile pool, especially at three o'clock which was feeding time. Once there was a huge crowd to watch Mr. St John Robinson punt out in a dinghy to where the female crocodile had a nest in reeds in the middle of the lagoon. When he tried to remove some eggs, the crocodile lashed her tail and charged. He fended her off with one of the oars. Everyone applauded, but I was on the mother crocodile's side.

Another big attraction was a twenty-five foot rock python that had swallowed a calf at Bamberoo. The farmer had discovered the mother of the calf, lowing piteously as she stood over the snake. It was too replete to move. Mr. St John Robinson had bought the python and placed it in an enclosure with a ten-foot long companion. Before long, the ten-foot companion disappeared and the newcomer had developed not only a suspicious paunch but a rather too satisfied expression. It was felt a trip to the zoo was well worth while for the chance to observe this barefaced scoundrel.

But no matter where you went you had to wear your hat; everyone, grown-ups as well; men and ladies, not only children. You had a school hat, a play hat and a Sunday hat. A Sunday hat was very special. It gave a sense of occasion to getting ready for church or Sunday School. There came the moment when the hat-box was pulled down from the top of the wardrobe and the Sunday hats were taken out.

Mine was a crisp white straw, rather more like a bonnet than a hat, edged with blue satin, with blue satin rosettes on the brim, fastened under my chin with a blue satin bow. It had taken a lot of sighing and wheedling to achieve this delectable Sunday hat. Audrey Saunders had one almost identical, except that her trimmings were pink. As I was now going to the Presbyterian Sunday School in Warburton Street with Audrey, it had been a matter of life and death to have a Sunday hat exactly like hers. I could scarcely breathe for fulfillment when Mum took me into Carrols, instructed the shop-lady to tie one on my head, stood back, head on one side and said, 'Well, Yes! Perhaps it helps her look less sallow', and bought the wonderful Sunday hat for me.

One Sunday afternoon at the zoo, Margaretta and I had been round all the enclosures. The wallabies were flopped on their sides in the shade. Americans were trying to lure them with bits of chocolate. Emus stalked up and down the wire, looking auntyish. The cockatoo clung to his wire cage and thrust his head through to be scratched. Blue Mountain parrots shrieked. We studied the sleeping python for any indication of its notorious banquets. I contemplated morbidly the anguish of the smaller snake knowing itself about to be eaten and not being able to scream for help.

'Come on!' said Margaretta, 'Let's go and see if the monkeys are being rude!' In front of the monkeys' cage was a low railing to keep people back from the wire. I leaned over this, pivoting backwards and forwards on my elbows as we watched the monkeys. They were clustered at the top of their threadbare tree, grooming one another and stretching their mouths in monkey grins. Suddenly, without warning, one of them made a huge leap. It landed on the wire mesh in front of me, thrust its thin, monkey-arm through the wire, seized my Sunday hat, blue satin ribbons, rosettes and all, and squealing in triumph made off with it, leaping and bounding, to the top of the monkey-tree.

My scream could not have been more stricken had I fallen into the crocodiles' pool. People came running. Nobody laughed. Everyone stared dumb-founded as the monkey, perched on its branch, first tried to put the Sunday hat on its head, then decided in favour of ripping the ribbons off. Another monkey pounced possessively, snatched the hat and made off with it.

This was the signal for a monkey free-for-all. Backwards and forwards the white hat flew, snatched at, ripped and tossed, from paw to paw. Then the original monkey-phief decided enough was enough. Pouncing decisively he seized it and swung to the top of the tree, waving it like a banner.

There, baring his teeth to keep the rest at bay, he squatted and began methodically to unpick the long continuous piece of straw from which the hat had been fashioned. When he had finished, the length of straw reached from his high perch to the concrete below and the hat was no more.

'Don't cry, Little Girl!' said a kind by-stander. An American soldier offered me chewing gum which Margaretta accepted on my behalf and popped into her mouth. My tears were no longer for the wonderful hat. I was crying with sheer fright at the thought of having to go home and present myself hatless to Mum. If only I could get run over by an American truck, like little Patsy Flynn, down the road from us. The Americans had sent her down south in a special military aircraft and she was spoken of in tones of compassion. If only something like that could overtake me! Anything! Anything rather than face Mum!

The dreaded moment came when, exhausted with fright, feet dragging, face woe-begone, I clicked my way in at the verandah gate. I told my tale, accompanied with freshly-brewed tears, although by now I was all cried out of genuine ones. I knew the reasonableness of an appropriate show of sorrow, of observing through my knuckles its effectiveness and raising or lowering the flow accordingly.

My amazement could scarcely have been greater and my knuckles were stopped in their tracks, to have Mum burst into laughter. The monkey had snatched my hat! Incredible! He had tried to put it on its own head and pulled the straw to shreds? Well, the hat hadn't done much for me in the first place! It had been a complete waste of money! She should have had more sense than to buy it in the first place! It had looked ridiculous on me! I was not the bonnet-and-ribbon type! And of course Margaretta should not have accepted the chewing-gum. One must never! And she never wanted to see me chewing gum like an American. How vulgar! Only cows chewed in public!

Artie Shaw & American Navy Band concert, The Strand, Townsville.

Underlying my relief at having been let off so lightly was a sense of something very like outrage; a proper mother would be smacking and scolding! There was also a tinge of resentment. 'Well! If I had known that this was how she was going to take it I would have been saved a lot of trouble. All that crying! What a waste of effort!'

If I cherished any illusions about being bought a replacement for the delectable Sunday hat, I was sadly disappointed. Mr. Kennedy, the violin teacher, had written to Mum to say that the little violin with the grooves to show me where to put my fingers would no longer do. I must have a better violin. So the entire family income for one week went on a lovely honey-coloured instrument, which even to my ear had a honey-voice to match its appearance. The little old one was bought by Mr. Kennedy for his museum of strange and unusual instruments.

Barry, inspired by Artie Shaw and Benny Goodman, had started to learn the clarinet. He had got to the 'Blue-squeak-bells of grunt-Scotland' stage. It was a noticeable coincidence that at about the same time as Barry and I began practising each evening, Mr. Woodward next door would open his grand piano and begin to play also. He could only play two pieces, *The Rustle of Spring* and *Devotion*, but without fail they were played, forte, as a sort of accompaniment to the anxious strains emanating from our house.

One evening, just as all three of us were about to launch into our musical rigours for the day – Mr. Woodward would have known by the melodic little preliminaries on my tuning-whistle that the moment was at hand – there was a crash from the kitchen. Mum gave a cry, 'Oh! No!' Barry and I rushed in. Mum was sitting at the kitchen table, her face drained with shock. 'Mum! What's wrong?' Barry said.

'Oh! Poor Elsie! Poor Les! Oh! How terrible for them! How dreadful! Whatever will they do? That lovely young man! Only a boy! So full of promise!' was all she could say.

Barry and I slid on to the kitchen chairs. Mum grew calmer. She looked long into Barry's face, as though seeing him for the first time after a long absence. She reached over and put her hand on his arm as though to feel the warmth of his flesh. She said, 'It was on the News, 'The Department of the Navy regrets to announce…' Oh! It is too dreadful! All those young lives!' She wiped her eyes, and told us. 'The *Canberra* has been sunk!'

Chapter 12

CHRISTMAS IS BANNED: 1942

'There's No More Room Down in Our Air-raid Shelter,
There's Mum and Dad, and Aunt and Gran and me'

HMAS Canberra, sunk 9th of August, 1942.

The first thing to do was to pay a formal visit to Uncle Les Quelch. Next day Barry was kept home from school. Mum and I dressed in our best clothes, Mum choosing dark colours in case the news was bad. Barry wore the whites he wore to church. Mum got up early to make a casserole for Uncle Les's ice-box; a vegetarian one because he was diabetic. She knew that in the circumstances he would not be likely to cook anything himself. She also made a boiled fruit cake for the other visitors he would be receiving.

Soberly we caught the North Ward bus. It was aggravating that it would have to be one of the old open-air ones from the early days so that we were thoroughly wind-blown just when we wanted to look our best. The atmosphere at Quelches' place was subdued. There were people from their church seated gravely in the lounge, the men rising to shake hands formally with each new arrival. The photograph of Noel in his naval uniform stood on the piano. Someone had placed a vase of freshly cut gerberas beside it. The flowers made me feel uneasy, as though Noel were definitely dead.

Barry told me 'There are usually some survivors. Noel may have been picked up. He could have been one of the lucky ones. It doesn't have to be like the *Perth* when they were all lost.' The people in the lounge were saying much the same thing. Everyone was trying to put on a brave face. No one could bear to think of all the bright young men full of hopes and dreams for the future who would have gone down with the *Canberra*.

Mum helped the other women make tea and pass around the cups and saucers, glad to be doing something. It was awkward trying to think of things to say that were neither too mournful nor too bright. Barry and I hung over the railings of the back steps wishing we could be gone. It seemed strange to be at Ronnie's place and to see his cricket-bat and marble-bag hanging from the rafters and he himself so far away.

That night all we had for tea was Windsor sausage. Mum said she was too wrung out to be cooking; but for us Windsor sausage was a treat. Normally a meal wasn't a meal unless it was meat and three vegetables. We ate in silence. The house seemed filled with the sense of loss and grieving shared with families all over Australia.

But it was only few days later that Mrs. Woodward called down the hillside. 'Mrs. Stilwell! Such wonderful news about your friend's boy! He's among the survivors! They've been landed in Sydney! His father has just rung.'

So Uncle Les was invited to tea and all the best silver and crockery brought out to celebrate Noel's miraculously safe return. There was a letter from Noel, which Uncle Les read out to us, his voice wobbling in some places, fierce and proud in others. The big attack on the *Canberra* had come just after midnight. They had spotted a torpedo coming straight at them. The captain had ordered hard a starboard and it had missed them. Then a series of Japanese star-shells had gone up. The ship had been brilliantly lit up. Almost immediately she received two broadsides and began to list and sink. The order was given to abandon ship. But most of the ship's lifeboats had been shot to pieces and only two were left. The able-bodied tried to get the wounded into these and on to rafts. Even while the ship was going down, the surgeons were going around the wounded giving morphine to those who had had legs or arms blown away. All the surgeons had to see by were torches. Then a shell hit the bridge and the captain was killed.

The survivors had been brought to Sydney on an American ship, wearing American uniforms, some of the sailor's own, which they had given them as they were rescued from the water and dragged on board. As soon as all the men struggling in the water had been rescued the American ship set sail for Sydney. Once they got back they had been issued with new Australian kit. They were given some pay and told they could each send one free telegram. Noel had sent his to his Mother. He thought 'she might have been a bit worried there for a while.' At this point, Uncle Les suddenly pushed back his chair and hurried out on to the verandah to clear his throat. Mum went briskly into the kitchen, taking us with her, and started getting the tea-things ready on the tray-mobile.

She said to Barry, 'Just slip down to the wood-heap and see if you can get me some chips to shake this fire up! Take the torch! Watch out for snakes!' Then, 'Marion! Look in the drawer for a tray-cloth! The roses one would be nice.' She laid out the tea-things on the tray-mobile, putting a lovely sponge as the centre-piece. In this fashion we tried to comfort just one of the families whose sons had survived the sinking of the *Canberra*. There were many families whose sons hadn't.

Not long after this, Mum received a letter from Mrs. Ruse to say that she and her daughter were looking forward to meeting us and would arrive the following day. 'What a quaint way of putting it!' said Mum, with a puzzled air. 'I didn't know Jack Ruse's wife all that well in the Dawson Valley. She was a quiet, retiring sort of person; rather slight, quite genteel; wore heavy glasses, I seem to recall. But we knew one another well to exchange greetings. I don't remember the daughter at all; she would have been only a girl. Still, it will suit me quite well if Mrs. Ruse is a formal polite person. I've really no wish to be intruded upon. To share the house in these difficult times is one thing, but I hope we shall all keep to ourselves.' Although the Pink Room was already in a state of preparedness Mum busied herself giving it an extra polish, misting kerosene over the lino from an old fly-spray and rubbing it well with an old singlet wrapped around the mop, to get a high sheen.

I was jubilant to move the last of my socks, bloomers and singlets from the drawers of the pink dressing-table. A freshly starched and ironed duchess-set with a thatched cottage design was put on it and all was in readiness for the arrival of the nice quiet ladies.

I was looking forward to these additions to our household. Children in books like *Norah of Billabong* and *William* always seemed to have lots of adults in their lives. Barry and I had so few in ours. Besides, there was the baby. How lovely to be able to help bath and dress it in little matinee-jackets, bonnets and booties! It would be like having Audrey's celluloid baby-doll to play with; only better.

HMAS Canberra was sunk in the Battle of Savo Island, on the 9th of August 1942; Noel Quelch was among the survivors.

Posted at the verandah-gate I waited for the squeal of the North Ward bus to herald the newcomers' arrival, at which point Mum and I would go to the bus-stop to help the ladies through the gap in the barbed-wire. We were being just like the brave people of London in the blitz, sharing our home with those less fortunate than ourselves; as Mum had reminded us, several times.

But from the beginning, this was an arrangement that was bound not to work. To start with, Mrs. Ruse and her daughter arrived in a Black and White Cab. Mum clicked her tongue in astonishment; a shocking extravagance! What must it have cost! Only the Americans could afford taxis! The ladies could easily have managed between them on the bus! They had only the two ports and the baby's folding pram!

To second with, it was not the right Mrs. Ruse.

Instead of the smallish, genteel person with glasses Mum had remembered, a large, silver-haired, flamboyant woman extricated herself from the taxi and followed sullenly by the daughter and baby and the burdened taxi-driver, came sailing like a ship under full canvas, up the terrace path, waving a jovial walking-stick in Mum's direction in greeting.

Dad had neglected to mention, if in fact he knew in the first place, that the friend of a friend from the Dawson River days had not only remarried, but divorced to remarry. Divorced! Unheard of! People simply didn't. You made your bed and you lay in it! Now, a divorced person in her own home!

It wasn't very long before long it became an established thing that 'Auntie Eileen', for so she insisted I call her, was forced by what she called 'm' leg' to occupy one of the more comfortable sea-grass chairs on the verandah while Mum did the work and I fetched and carried; mainly cigarettes and ash-trays, when they were chock-a-block with butts.'Just put it here where I can get at it, Lovie!' she would boom, meaning Dad's shiny chrome smoker's stand, the one Mum had got at the auction. Dad had never used it himself yet, 'The hide of the woman!' Mum fumed while she waited for me outside the Little House at night, our only guaranteed place of privacy now. 'Let her empty her own ash-trays if she must smoke! Unhealthy, dirty habit!' Mum had the conviction that smokers 'puffed up a suite of furniture every year.' She often told Dad so, but then he was a man and that was different. But for a woman! And in her house! 'I don't for a minute believe there's a thing wrong with that leg of hers! She can move smartly enough when she wants to get to the wireless to hear the racing results!'

Joycie, the daughter, was withdrawn and morose. Her husband, Ray, was overseas with the RAAF. She expected daily the official telegram informing her that he had been killed. Meanwhile, she kept to the Pink Room and busied herself with *Miracle* and *Oracle* romance magazines.

The baby, Rayleen, suffered from wind and cried a lot; she also had prickly-heat. Mum told Joycie to boil the nappies in rainwater; perhaps the hard town water was irritating her skin. Joycie left the rainwater tap running and wasted a rung of water. You could have cut the atmosphere with a knife that night.

Outside, the various frogs began their nightly chorus. Two called one another by their Christian names: 'Frank! Frank!' to which the other would reply, 'Andrew! Andrew! Andrew!' Tonight Andrew's voice was rich and resonant. 'That thing's back in the tank again, by the sound of it,' Barry said between mouthfuls, into the heavy silence at the table. I could almost hear Mum forming the words, 'We'll be lucky if there's any water left for him to get into, the way things are going!' But she didn't. It would have been 'infra dig'. One maintained one's dignity, no matter what the circumstance.

I was given the job of taking Rayleen for a walk each afternoon. For a little while, this was of absorbing interest. But Audrey had many baby nieces and nephews of her own. She gave Rayleen a professional once-over, remarked that she suffered from prickly-heat and that her nappies should be washed in rain-water, and showed little further interest. From then on, Rayleen's and my walks formed three sides of a rectangular pattern. We went along Alexander Street to the first corner, turned up the hill, and down again into Stanley Street to where Audrey lived. The pram would be parked under the tamarind tree, with a stone under the wheel to prevent it rolling into the gully. Audrey and I got on with the serious business of establishing who could win the most bases at hop-scotch. When Rayleen cried Audrey said that was what babies were meant to do. It was good for their lungs.

The Saunders had a garage, in which was kept a Chevrolet tourer, up on blocks because of petrol rationing and the shortage of tyres. The garage was covered with fragrant quisqualis creeper, the delicate pink flowers of which could be strung together to make necklaces and bangles. If Rayleen in her pram cried too prodigiously, Audrey and I would climb on top of the garage, lie back among the sweet profusion and sing down to her.

Audrey being in Grade Four was one of the lucky ones back at school. She dismayed me with talk of Long Division and Decimals, but taught me all the songs they were learning. If several verses and choruses of *I'll Join the Legion, That's what I'll Do* failed to put Rayleen to sleep, we would switch to *Shenandoah*, *No, John*! or *Early One Morning*. In the more vigorous ones we drummed on the roof of the garage for effect.

Another means of entertaining Rayleen was to climb the tamarind tree and rain handfuls of tiny leaves down upon her, like confetti. From within the dark interior of the tamarind tree, we could see without being seen, study cloud formations or examine the busy ant-roads trailing through the coarse bark and out along the branches. Sometimes Rayleen got tired of it all and went to sleep.

It was more pleasant to be at Saunders place than at home these days. 'Auntie Eileen' bogged into Mum's tea and sugar rations. She not only kept opening and shutting the ice-box, letting all the cold air out, but also frequently left the butter on the table so that it melted to a puddle of grease. Butter was rationed to a half a pound per person per week but was also in short supply, so that frequently it was not to be had, ration tickets or not. Mum would give an anguished cry: 'Who's left butter out?' To this 'Auntie Eileen' would reply cheerfully, 'Oops! Sorry, Ducks! Any chance of a pot of tea?'

'Oops!' was what she also said, instead of murmuring, 'I beg your pardon!' when she made loud poggy-smells after meals. She used Mum's dressmaking scissors to cut her toenails, because they were 'too tough and horny for her own', her foot up on the verandah table where I did my Correspondence lessons.

Joycie never cleaned the copper after she had boiled the baby's nappies. Mum always finished her Monday washing-day by polishing the inside of the copper with a keroseny-rag until it shone red-gold. Then it was tipped upside down over the copper-stand so that leaves and dust would not accumulate inside it. That was the sign that washing-day was over. Joycie left the water from her washing in the copper till it turned to an evil-smelling sludge in which drowned beetles and flies floated.

Neither of the ladies remembered to put the lid of the lavatory down, so that flies got in and maggots bred. Mum sloshed phenyl in to discourage them. She also sloshed phenyl, rather obviously, in the bathroom drain which suddenly had a noticeable wee-ish smell. 'Just wait until that father of yours comes home!' fumed Mum. Previously these words had referred to Barry. Now they referred to Dad!

The Duke of Kent, the King's brother, was killed on Active Service in a flying-boat crash on the way to Iceland. Because he was to have been Australia's next Governor-General, a day of National mourning was declared. Hotels and pictures closed, shops shut and people were given time off work to attend special church services. Mum made a black arm-band for Barry to wear. Didn't 'Auntie Eileen' scoff! 'The Royal Family!' she scoffed. 'More like the Royal Frumpies! Do you think that crowd would give a brass monkey's if your son was killed!' For not only were 'Auntie Eileen' and Joycie Catholics, but Irish as well! In our house where we knew to stand, to stop talking and listen solemnly while *God Save the King* was played!

Mum greatly admired King George and Queen Elizabeth. King George had spoken in a recent broadcast of how 'the members of the Empire family were standing shoulder to shoulder in these dark days.' She thought King George made a much better sovereign than the Duke of Windsor would have done. 'The Duke was just a playboy!' she would say. 'But our King and Queen set an example of devotion to duty!' She read us little bits from the *Bulletin* about them. The King and Queen had been to visit the people of Bermondsey after an especially heavy raid. A church where many people had taken shelter had received a direct hit. The King had spoken encouragingly to those digging through the rubble. The Queen had comforted those who had lost their families. Even at the height of the blitz the King and Queen had refused to leave London even though the government begged them to. No! If their people were defending London, there they would also remain! The King worked several nights a week in an armaments factory making machine-guns for fighter-planes. His foreman had said he had quite a good hand with a lathe and had never once been late for work.

'Auntie Eileen's' comments were like a red rag to a bull to Mum but she scorned to dignify them by arguing. Instead she simmered; raging inwardly. She had never come across such bigotry! The two women made a great show of taking themselves off to Mass, and 'rattling their rosary beads', but were full of scorn for the poor 'I-ties', the Italian farmers and their sons around Ingham and Innisfail who were being rounded up as potential enemies. Mum thought Italians were song-loving, hard-working people and that it was a pity more Australians didn't take a leaf out of their book. The Italians didn't really want to be in the war. They had been 'led into it by their noses by that fool Mussolini.'

'Auntie Eileen' snorted 'I-ties! You know what they reckoned after the fall of Bardia, don't you? A thousand I-ties and fifty mules were captured. The mules put up a stiff fight!' Barry guffawed and nearly choked on his shepherd's pie, unaware that he was getting one of Mum's looks. He found out soon enough afterwards. He had to wash up, also to dry and put away, all on his own.

When Jack Ruse was posted to Darwin, 'Auntie Eileen' acted as though she were carrying the responsibility of saving the country from the Japanese on her own shoulders. Jack himself wrote that he was grabbing the chance of a spot of spine-bashing to save himself going troppo. Nonetheless 'Auntie Eileen' made a great show of wearing on her capacious bosom one of the silver 'Mother's' badges that the Government gave to women who had a son on Active Service, showing a gold star for every boy. 'Well, she would be old enough to be his mother!' snorted Mum, pleased with her own little joke. 'Auntie Eileen' had a luxuriant crop of silvery-grey hair through which she poured a dipper of Reckitt's Blue water, 'to bring out the shine', after washing it on Saturdays, using rain-water, of course.

Then Jack Ruse came down from Darwin on leave. When he opened his kitbag, there, wrapped among the smelly socks and underwear which he had brought with him to be laundered, was a collection of pretty china ornaments. 'Scrounged them outa the houses! That Darwin lot, they just cleared out after the bombings! Shot through in the clothes they stood up in! Like Bondi trams!' He pushed one of the ornaments across the table towards Mum. 'Here! Have it, Nen! I thought I might as well hop in for my cut as quick as any other joker!' Mum said crisply that, really, she thought not! Jack had not endeared himself to her by using the personal name that only Dad used.

For myself, I was quite disappointed. I wouldn't have minded the sweet little china dog with his paws up begging. The thought of being able to walk around in other peoples' houses taking whatever you fancied was fascinating. I thought Jack could have saved a whole kitbagful while he was at it, if things were just being left for the Japs.

By comparison with all of this, the atmosphere at Saunders' place was calm and untroubled. Mr. and Mrs. Saunders would have been shocked at the goings-on at our place. Mr. Saunders, when he wasn't working in his little jeweller's shop under the house, sat in a chintz rocking-chair on the verandah, or pottered about the large aviaries in which he kept Blue Mountain parrots which flew to him, screeching greedily, when he went into the cages with bread and honey. Sometimes he worked among the citrus-trees, spraying them with a mixture of washing-soda and water to kill the sooty fungus on the leaves. Fruit in the shops was now beyond price because only the Americans could afford the sky-high prices. So, nearly every day Mr. Saunders would peer among the glossy foliage of his trees and pull down an orange for Audrey and me to share.

Audrey had an accomplishment that filled me with admiration. She could eat a lemon without pulling a face, dipping each quart in salt. When Mum heard this, she was horrified. 'Lemon and salt is used to get ink-stains out of clothes!' she cried.

But from Audrey I learned many useful things. If you ate a lucky wish-quart, the tiny quart sometimes found between two larger ones, in oranges and mandarins, well, it spoilt the luck if you let it touch your teeth. It had to be squashed against the roof of your mouth with your tongue and then swallowed whole for the wish to come true. And if you saw a pin on the floor and picked it up that would bring you good luck. And another thing! If you didn't close your eyes when you sneezed, your eyes would pop out. Oh! Yes! And if you ate your crusts your hair would turn curly. But Audrey's remained defiant, cut straight below her ears and across her freckled forehead in a fringe. And of course, it was a definite fact! If a girl whistled or sat on a table she would never get a husband! And – lowering your voice to even speak the words – you must never, ever, ever, put a pair of shoes on the table or – whisper it! – someone in your family would die.

The duchess in Mrs. Saunders' bedroom was large and old-fashioned with wing-mirrors on either side. Audrey and I would pose in front in front of it, viewing our profiles from the various angles or doing hair-styles with the hair-pins meshed together in a crystal bowl. 'Don't go losing any!' Mrs. Saunders would caution. 'There won't be any more until after the war is over.' Everything now was measured in manpower and materials. Even hair-pins!

Audrey learned the piano, so she and I spent a lot of time sitting squeezed together on the round stool, which was spun to adjust the height, singing songs from the album of Stephen

Foster melodies through which she was working her way. Mr. Saunders would call out from the verandah, 'Take your foot off the pedal.' We liked the way the notes clanged together with the pedal down to the floor. The front of the piano was made of pleated silk and there were brass candle-stick holders which folded in and out. In pride of place on the piano was a photograph of Victor in his army uniform, the strap of his Digger's hat firmly under his chin. Victor was fighting in New Guinea at Milne Bay. In a goldy frame over the piano hung *The Monarch of the Glen*, a proud stag deep in highland heather.

One night at home during tea, Barry told us that it was true! Yes! A party of German Prisoners-of-War, had escaped from their detention camp in Victoria. The next day when Audrey came home from school, I passed on this gripping piece of information to her. Perhaps I forgot to mention that it had happened in Victoria.

Audrey and I decided that it would be a good idea, as we knew our side of Castle Hill so well, to have a little expedition to see if there were any escaped Prisoners-of-War lurking in our area. We were always being told it was our duty to help the War Effort. This was something important we could do. If we found some escaped prisoners and turned them in we might be on the News!

On expeditions we usually carried our provisions in the calico bags that flour was sold in. Once these were washed and dried they were handy for a multitude of purposes, often as lunch bags. Audrey and I carried ours over our shoulders on string, like tucker-bags. The Saunders kept chooks and ducks in a big rambling chook-yard overgrown with giant sun-flowers so they had plenty of eggs. We usually took an egg each. We carried a billycan to make tea, which neither of us really liked but would never have admitted.

We headed off, climbing the gully which came down the hill in front of Saunders' place. Of course, in the middle of the Dry, there was not a skerrick of water in it, but the rocks were smooth and glassy and easy to scramble up. Higher up, there was a place where another gully joined the larger one and formed a large sandy pool after rain. Around this sandy basin were the remnants of an ancient stand of rain-forest, very dark and brooding by comparison with the open ironbark forest over the rest of the hill. We called this place, The Glen, after the one in the painting over the piano. We felt sure, that if there were any German Prisoners-of-War about, The Glen was where they would be found.

We kept our voices very low as we approached . We didn't want to give the game away. We were not at all sure how to go about the capture of German Prisoners of War, but the first thing seemed to be to hide our tucker-bags and billy in the shade of the rock where we often cooked dinner. The ashes of our previous camp-fires were still visible. No-one seemed to have disturbed them. They were very cunning, these German Prisoners-of-War! They knew that would be the first place anyone would look!

The cicadas chirred in the heat as we began to cast around. A rustle in the grass was a pheasant coucal scurrying awkwardly into the broken shadows, dragging its long tail like a lizard. Distantly we heard an American jeep change gears as it ground up the dirt track to the look-out. The sound of laughter and girls' squeals drifted down the hill. How surprised those idlers would be if they realised that they had driven on heedless, past such important spy-catching matters in the valley below!

And, Ahah! What was this? A flattened area in the brown grass! Someone had been lying here. And, look! An American chewing-gum wrapper! It only went to show how devious these escaped German Prisoners-of-War could be! Pretending to be Americans to put searchers off the scent, eh? Well, we saw through that one! We had both read all of Enid Blyton's mysteries about the 'Finder-Outers' and knew how important clues were. And, look! Here was something else. What on earth was it?

On the flattened grass lay a flabby, whitish object, something like a deflated party-balloon with a rubber ring at one end, containing some sort of sticky liquid. Eagerly, we picked it up and examined it. How strange! This was definitely a clue! Very likely it was a part of the radio-transmitters that escaped Prisoners-of-War were likely to have. Or spies! Barry often scanned the hill from our verandah at night for signs of spies at work. During the air-raids it was said that there had been flashing signals guiding the enemy planes in. And here was evidence! Suddenly overwhelmed by the seriousness of our discovery, we decided to head for home with all speed. Probably in our hearts we had not really believed in the possibility of German Prisoners-of-War. Now that we had found definite evidence it was time to call in the adults.

As we drew near to the front gate of Saunders' place we each lengthened our paces, both wanting to be the one who broke the news. Mr. Saunders was in the chook-yard, slipping coloured rings on some ducks' legs to identify them, holding each bird tightly under his arm like a pair of bagpipes, his glasses pushed up on to his forehead under his chook-yard hat. Audrey and I screeched to a halt before him and held out for his wonderment the sticky evidence of German Prisoner-of-War spy activity right here on Castle Hill! Mr. Saunders removed his chook-yard hat and adjusted his glasses to look.

Mr. Saunders was known to have a medical condition, something to do with his heart. He had to take things easy and not become excited. Now he clasped the middle of his singlet and looked strange. At his cry of, 'Mother!' Mrs. Saunders came hurrying as fast as bad ankles and a wonky hip would allow. She had grave fears of yet another carpet-snake in one of the bird-cages. Pesky things that they were!

On beholding our evidence of German Prisoner-of-War activities, she too turned a strange colour. She too clasped her heart. She murmured a prayer; 'Oh! Good Lord! Save us! Whatever next!'

Herding us before her like black sheep she propelled us to the garden hose. Our legs, arms and hands – especially our hands – were scoured, none too gently, with sand-soap and the outside scrubbing brush, the one for scrubbing the landing, the steps and what Saunders called the dunny. Then we were bundled upstairs, the chip-heater was lit, the bath run and an almost a full bottle of Dettol was tipped into it. Our clothes were whisked away, flung into the copper and the copper-fire stoked to boiling. The last we saw of our evidence of German Prisoner-of-War activity on Castle Hill was Mr. Saunders down in the chook-yard, setting fire to a big pile of prunings off the orange trees, and using a shovel to heave our evidence on to the top of the conflagration.

In the bath Audrey and I giggled uncertainly. We had never had a bath together before. We weren't at all sure if we had done something important for the War Effort or not. Nothing was explained to us. We simply understood that inadvertently we had stumbled across one of the mysterious things that happened only in the world of grown-ups.

When it was time to go home, Mrs. Saunders said to me, 'Mr. Saunders and I think it would possibly be best not to mention any of this to your poor dear mother. She has enough to cope with as it is.' And I never did.

The Ackland children were also having a prisoner-of-war experience. In New Guinea, the Japanese force which had hoped to cross the Owen Stanleys, capture Port Moresby and use it as a base to attack North Queensland, was being driven back. The Japanese prisoners-of-war brought to Australia for internment were off-loaded in Townsville to be sent south by train. A holding-camp had been built at Kissing Point, just across the road from Acklands' place, on a sandy bit of wasteland where the track humped over the dunes to the beach. The children saw the prisoners, slouched and woebegone, straggling round and round inside the barbed-wire fence for exercise. Very often they had to be escorted to the latrines. It seemed that Australian meat-and-three-vegetables food did not agree with them. They were used to rice. Although rice had become unavailable to civilians, suddenly the Japanese prisoners-of-war had rice. Not only had rice, but had it to waste. Shirley and the other children saw them scraping their leavings into the pig-buckets.

Mr. Ackland was horrified at such wastage. But he hadn't got to be North Queensland manager of his company without being able to recognize opportunities when he saw them. He gave Shirley and John some of his Watkins' products, cinnamon, nutmeg and other spices, and sent them across the road to barter with the camp cooks; spices and flavourings in exchange for packets of rice. Both sides were happy with the exchange. Everyone, it seemed, was learning to make the best of things; making do.

Food shortages and making-do became an accepted part of life. Barry and I learned not to grumble about junket made without sugar knowing it would lead to a lecture; children in England had to do without ice-cream!

Next thing, milk became almost unobtainable. Already, meat was so scarce that even with ration tickets there was no guarantee of getting any. There just wasn't any to be had. Sixty thousand extra men around Townsville had to be fed. Civilians just had to make do. Or do without.

Also, meat had to be shipped overseas to help feed the people of Britain who were taking the brunt of the fighting over there. So, if Mum got a scraggy bit of mutton of dubious freshness from the butcher, she sniffed it delicately, wiped it over with vinegar to freshen it up, and sniffed it again before cooking it. That was 'making do.' 'Economy Cooking' was the new thing; 'Cook your vegetables in as little water as possible, scrubbing them first instead of peeling them and cook them in with the corned beef or whatever meat you are preparing. This will save fuel.'

'Auntie Eileen' could not cope with such a change of tactics. When she cooked, it was as though she was wreaking vengeance on the foodstuffs. Cabbage had to be boiled in a saucepanful of water with bi-carb of soda for at least half an hour. 'If she had to queue for it as long as I did she might be less willing to turn it into wet dish-rags!' groaned Mum. Of course 'Auntie Eileen' couldn't do any of the queuing, because of 'm' leg'. As for Joycie, well she had the baby to look after, didn't she?

Toilet items were impossible to get, or nearly. Mum put the scrap ends of soaps in a large jar and let soften to a jelly. Then she set the jelly in patty-pan tins to make new little cakes of soap in rainbow colours. Scraps of Velvet soap were placed inside a wire soap-whisk and shaken hard in the basin to make suds for washing-up. And with no soap-powders available, washing-day meant a session of carving flakes off a bar of kerosene-soap to go into the copper. On the pretext of helping, I carved dogs' heads or chickens from the hard yellow blocks and fancied I might become a sculptor.

Starch for washing-day also became unobtainable, which was sad. It had been nice to fish around in the starch-box and find the pieces that looked like Scottie-dogs or gnomes before they were tipped into the dish, blended with a little cold water and the steaming kettle poured in to make pale translucent starch. Tablecloths, serviettes, pillow-shams, doilies and Barry's shirts all went in, and last of all the handkerchiefs and tea-towels. The 'starched things' dried as stiff as boards and were sprinkled with water and rolled like large sausages in towels before being ironed. But now these were all things of the past.

For a long time Mum had used a petrol-iron with a little tank on the back which hissed and gave off a sharp fumey smell. One day when she was in the midst of hearing my spellings as she ironed, the petrol-iron flared, a habit which petrol-irons had. Flames engulfed the handle and sizzled around the tank containing the petrol. Mum wrapped her hand in a towel, seized the iron and heaved it out the back door, to let it burn itself out.

Only then did she acquire an electric iron which having no thermostat was regulated by being turned off and on at the switch on the wall. Tuesday ironing days became recognizable by cries of dismay and the smell of scorched fabric. The scorched item was dabbed with lemon-juice and hung on the line in the sun to take the scorch out. Which it did. A little bit.

Mr. Curtin talked about the need for Austerity, asking people to have two beefless days per week. Didn't 'Auntie Eileen' complain! Why should she have less just so that the Poms could have more? Mum said that if it weren't for the British, Europe would have been plunged into another Dark Age. The Nazi terror was the most hideous blood-bath of modern times. Look at Ledice! An entire village of innocent people wiped out by the Nazis as an act of reprisal. 'Well, what has that got to do with us in Australia?' moaned 'Auntie Eileen'. 'Let the Old World fight its own battles. My forebears came to this country to get away from all that.'

'That dreadful woman!' Mum exclaimed that night, outside the Little House. 'The hide of her! 'Came to this country!' indeed! It is much more likely that any forbears of hers were *sent*!' She snorted, shaking her head. 'They'll just have to go!' But how was it possible to turn two women out on to the streets of Townsville when housing was impossible to come by? Especially when there was a baby! Mum groaned out loud about it all.

Despite sugar rationing, Auntie Eileen liked a little bit of sugar in her tea. 'Just give me an extra spoonful today, Lovie,' she would say to me. 'It might help to take my mind offa m'leg. It's that achey today!' At breakfast, the top of her porridge had a shiny crust of sugar. One of her favourite between-meal snacks was a slice of bread, heavily-buttered, thickly spread with sugar.

So Mum was horribly suspicious when 'Auntie Eileen' suddenly announced her intention of making jam for the Red Cross stalls in Flinders Street. Making jam? The woman never made anything but a mess!

The Red Cross depended on people's donations of cakes and jams to raise funds for their Prisoner of War parcels and comforts for the wounded. It would be letting down the men who had sacrificed everything if the women of Townsville slacked off in their efforts. Mum made a weekly boiled fruit cake, her specialty, which she took in to the stall in Flinders Street. As the weeks went by there were fewer and fewer sultanas and raisins in her cakes, as dried fruit became another luxury item to be queued for. Once Manahans and the other grocers had sold their quota for the week, that was it.

But there were American and Australian soldiers crowding the footpaths in Flinders Street only too keen to get their hands on any home-cooking that was going. The Red Cross knew that housewives couldn't be expected to use their own family's sugar ration to cook for the stall so anyone willing to make cakes and jams was entitled to collect an allocation of unrationed sugar from headquarters. 'Auntie Eileen' hurried into town. When she came home, gleefully hugging her acquisition of Red Cross sugar, Mum made such a point of commenting about it that 'Auntie Eileen' was forced into reluctant patriotism. She made a batch of 'sticky toffees' in paper patty-pans for the next Red Cross stall and left the burnt saucepan on the back of the stove in revenge.

In the midst of all the shortages, the weekly siren tests continued; one long blast, lasting three minutes, to make sure they were in good working order. They sounded less ominous in the daytime, but there were still people who forgot that they were only the Monday morning tests, and dived for the shelters.

One sign of the acute shortage of paper was that the *Townsville Daily Bulletin* became smaller. It also changed its familiar appearance. Instead of advertisements being on the front page as they had always been, with the news on page two inside, now the news was right on the front page. All advertisements were smaller, too. The Government said that in a time of national austerity people shouldn't be encouraged to buy things they could do without. Every pound spent on unnecessaries was a pound lost for guns, ships and tanks. People were asked to cut personal expenditure to one pound per month and to spend the money on War Bonds. Mr. Curtin said that people would not notice the difference, but would have helped their sons and brothers who were fighting to keep Australia safe.

It was almost impossible to buy soft-drink because the ingredients, particularly sugar, were no longer available. But in any case there was no longer any means of keeping anything cool. Ice was no longer available as the army had first call on all supplies and took all that the meat-works and Vardy' s Iceworks could make. Civilians found that they just had to do without.

A cool-box could be improvised by putting one box inside another, packing the space between with wet sand or saw-dust and draping wet bags over the top. As long as the bags were kept wet, evaporation kept the foodstuffs inside coolish. But it was hard on the carefully conserved water supply in the tank as the water evaporated quickly in the dry air.

For a cool drink there was the water-bag hanging on a wire hook under the edge of the verandah. Well-to-do people had ones with a little china taps. Ours had a spout with a tin cap. An enamel pannikin hung on the hook so that people would not drink directly from the bag. Mum had heard of a man who died by drinking directly from the spout when he swallowed a centipede which had got inside the bag. Or so she said. Perhaps the story was for Barry's benefit? Or for 'Auntie Eileen's.

It was one of my morning jobs to fill the water-bag by taking it down to the tank. When the bag was kept full, it beaded with evaporation on the outside and the water was sweet and chilly. When it was half empty the canvas began to dry and the water became tepid and baggy-tasting. Then I was in for it.

'Auntie Eileen' began coming home from town with mysterious long parcels wrapped in brown paper in her shopping bag. Then there would be soft clinking sounds from the Pink Room. Next she would sigh and ease herself into a comfortable chair on the verandah, a glass of nice, clean 'water' at hand. Before long she would be bursting into song; 'Eileen Alannah...', beating on the verandah floorboards with her stick to keep time. 'Ah! To be sure! M' Jack used to sing that to me!' she would announce, brimming with sentiment and Irish brogue, though for the most part her vowels were as genuinely Queensland as the next person's, as Mum would note.

'Gin!' she would hiss to me outside the Little House that night. 'The woman is common! I knew it the moment I set eyes on her! If it weren't for that poor baby....! But I am caught between the devil and the deep blue sea!' It was just as well for Dad that he had been posted to the army-training base at Redbank at far-away Brisbane.

Barry was the only cheerful face at the table at night. 'Did you hear the one about the lunatic asylum?' he would say, into the heavy silence. 'The Loonie on the inside calls out to the fellow on the outside, 'What you got in your wheel-barrow, Mate?' The fellow on the outside says, 'Horse manure.' The Loonie says, 'What are you going to do with it?' The other fellow says, 'Put it on my strawberries'. The Loonie says, 'In here we put sugar on them, and they call us lunatics!' Mum would frown. One must not make sport of those less fortunate! But 'Auntie Eileen' would snort with laughter and say that she must have another cup of tea on the strength of that one! Then she would pour it into her saucer and puff on it to cool it down. Sometimes she got the saucer to her lips without spillage on the white tablecloth.

Some nights Barry had more important items. Did we know that the Japs already had invasion money printed for when they took over Australia? Luckily our chaps were beginning to give them a good thrashing up there at Gona. And Mr. Blank said that Midway had knocked the daylights out of the Jap fleet. He reckoned Midway would be the turning point of the whole show. Sometimes his news was sad. Chester Parker, an Old Boy of the school, had been killed in action. He had been a Rhodes Scholar and had then joined the Royal Navy. He had been a lieutenant on a submarine that had gone missing. There was a two minutes silence in his memory at school assembly.

One night his face was alight with earnestness. The Grammar School Cadets were going to be training with real .303s. They were going into camp under canvas. They would be doing basic army training, the same as recruits in the army got, not just marching. Mr. Whight said that because he was tall for his age there was some chance that they might take him, even though he was only thirteen. Mum said she would write to Dad about it. When Dad wrote back it was to say that he thought it would be better if Barry waited until he was fourteen; training camps were often more than a lad bargained for.

Barry wasn't too cast down. His fourteenth birthday in January was just around the corner. In the meantime he rode the long way home from school around the Strand to keep an eye on the shipping in the bay. The convoys would form up in Cleveland Bay before heading north under escort for New Guinea waters. 'Do you know,' Barry would come bursting in to say, 'I counted forty-nine ships on the bay this arvo!' Another day it would be fifty-six, or thirty-eight. The highest number of ships he ever counted was sixty-four. When Mum and I were going into town we would see from the bus the masses of shipping, grey-painted for camouflage, stretching across the bay.

Uncle Les Quelch's job in Samuel Allen's was concerned with provisioning some of these ships. In a small motor-launch he would go from ship to ship, hailing those on board and asking what their requirements were. One night he invited us to go with him. It had seemed such an exciting adventure to look forward to, but once we were out on the dark waters of the bay it was terrifying. All the ships were blacked-out. We steered from one immense steel cliff of a hull to another, often getting the wrong ship in the darkness and being redirected further out. The launch, also blacked-out, chugged around among the anchored shipping, at times coming perilously close to crunching into a black hull which suddenly loomed out of the night. I had heard enough about convoy losses and torpedoing to feel that there was a decided possibility that at any moment a similar fate could overtake the Samuel Allen's launch. All my life-boat drill with Mumpuss and the dolls had failed to prepare my nerve for the event.

Daylight Saving was introduced to save fuel at the Hubert Wells Power Station and a system of rationing milk to civilians was introduced. Because of the petrol shortage the milkman would not deliver to individual houses but would call at certain points in the suburb where people could assemble to collect the amount allowed to them. Families with children could have an extra allowance. It became another one of my morning jobs to ride my scooter in the red glow of predawn to our collection point. The little group of people who gathered in the dawn light soon formed a bond. One morning one of the older men had a little flat case which he showed around. In it was a silver cross, the DFC his only son had been awarded posthumously after a raid over Germany. I could feel how filled with pride and love the father was as he showed it round for everyone to admire. Then in the distance the rattle of the milk-truck was heard. People started picking up their billycans in readiness. The old man gently closed the case and slipped it into his pocket. I could tell that he knew his moment of consolation was over.

In fact a number of North Ward families lost their sons; the Stewarts lost their boy, William, the Pearsons in Cook Street lost John, and the Perraux family down in Eyre Street lost Bill. Each of the boys was killed over Germany with the RAAF. But the Robert's family got the wonderful news that their son Graham, who had been reported missing presumed killed, had turned up safe and sound in a German prisoner-of-war camp. I thought how envious the mothers who had lost their sons must be, hoping against hope that the same thing might happen for their boys.

Daylight Saving meant extra hours of daylight at the other end of the day, with blue smoke trickling upwards from chimneys of the houses around the hill. The late evening of Daylight Saving made Mum homesick for England, saying it reminded her of the long twilights 'at Home'.

For Audrey and me, hop-scotch was long forgotten and done with. Sevens was in. Sevens was a bouncing game, the skills becoming more and more complicated as you progressed; first seven straight bounces, then six of bouncing, in and out of the edge of your skirt as you held the hem. Then came bouncing while clapping your hands, in front and behind, double clapping, until finally, with a twirl, you spun round on the spot, catching the ball on the full. When you had got this far you had won the game. If you dropped the ball during any of the manoeuvres it was the other person's turn.

While you waited you sat on the sun-warm gravel and observed an ant carrying its dinner-load home, or contemplated the fairy castles, the Felix the Cats or the golden galleons sailing the luminous skies over Castle Hill's darkening shoulder. Audrey was a lot better at Sevens than I was, so I spent a lot of time in contemplation. When it was too dark to see the ball anymore we watched to see the first star come out, to get the wish;

Starlight, Star bright! First star I've seen tonight!
I wish I may, I wish I might, have the wish I wish tonight.

For Barry the benefit of Daylight Saving was that there were extra hours of wireless time before 4QN and 4TO closed transmission for the day. *First Light Frazer* was back in business.

In September a rumour flew round that Belgian Garden's School had re-opened. The very next day Mum and I were on a bus heading there. Belgian Garden's was a small three-teacher school set against the northern slopes of Castle Hill. As we made our way across the empty playground, I could hear children chanting their way through the multiplication tables. Oh! Magical! Oh! Infinitely lovely! Could it possibly be true that soon I might be one of them? My heart contracted with fearful longing. Was it too much to hope for? When Mum set her mind to something she could usually make it happen.

Wild with desire to be at school, I gazed at the head-teacher while Mum talked to him. But my heart began to sink. He was saying that only those children who could actually walk to the school were being accepted for enrolment. Eagerly, Mum told him, 'But she could walk! She could walk across the hill!' My heart leapt with hope. Yes! I would walk anywhere just to take my place in that busy normal little school! The thought of walking through the bush of the hillside appealed to me as totally charming. I knew the way; there was almost a track. It would be lovely!

The head-teacher contemplated my eager face gravely. Then I was sent outside to wait on the verandah. I heard the two adults speaking in lowered grown-up voices. I caught the words 'Americans', 'Negroes', 'too risky'. I knew without having to be told that I was not going to be enrolled at Belgian Gardens. But Mum came out on to the verandah with a hopeful smile. The head-teacher had told her that very soon West End would be reopening classes for younger children. All the schools would be back to normal, soon.

We went home resolved to go to West End that very afternoon. But there, sticking out of our mail-box, was an English letter. Eagerly, Mum sat at the kitchen table to open it. Then she cried, 'Oh! Dear God! No!' and clasped her hand to her mouth. One of her cousin's sons had been killed in a Commando raid on Dieppe. She got out the box in which family photos were kept. It had a silk tassel on the front which I twiddled with, while she hunted through. I was feeling very hard-done-by. Our expedition to enrol me at West End seemed to have completely slipped her mind.

She found the photo she wanted. 'Here it is! That's your cousin! Oh! Look at him! Just a boy!' Tears flowed. In the photograph were two young men, one very tall, the other quite short, sky-larking, arms draped about one another's shoulders, for their photo to be taken in an English back-garden. 'Which was the one that was killed?' I said. Mum winced. 'Oh! Don't say it like that! But, well, that's the sad part. My cousin had only the one son of her own. That was Charles. And then they adopted another little boy, Cyril, to keep him company, I suppose. Cyril is the taller of the two. But it is Charles, their own boy, who has been killed. He would go into the Commandos! Oh! They must be distracted with grief. To lose their precious son! I must write to them at once.'

At this moment 'Auntie Eileen' called from the verandah,' What time's lunch, Love?' Mum replied that she had received some bad news. 'Well, just a sandwich will do then,' said 'Auntie Eileen' hopefully. Mum went quietly into her room and closed the door. I knew there would be no trip to West End that day.

I went down under the house to where I had a village laid out in the dirt. The houses were blocks of wood, or small cardboard boxes with doors and windows drawn on the outside of them in crayon. The village had roads and streets, a church and a school. The people who lived in the houses were interesting bolts fallen off Dad's work bench, stub ends of pencils, shells, or broken pegs. Two were squat stones who lived in a hovel apart from the rest of the village. They were the Ugly Sisters who had kidnapped a baby and kept it prisoner.

The village people led complicated lives, often quarrelling, making-up, having small triumphs or moments of distress. I knelt above them, guiding and directing their affairs, feeling a little bit like God. Sometimes there were terrible storms when the streets of the village would be pock-marked with rain. This occurred when Mum happened to be scrubbing the verandah overhead with the last of the blue-water on washing days to bleach the floorboards. But today, all the children were being sent home from school. There had been sorrowful tidings. The head-teacher's son had been killed in battle. I was so affected by the news myself that tears trickled down my nose unheeded.

Barry was jubilant at the news of the victory of Australian troops at El Alamein. The daily flights of Flying Fortresses over our house on their way to blast the Japanese at Rabaul continued. But for Townsville people there was more and more emphasis on Austerity. People were asked to do without; to make do; to use it up. Then really grave news. Mr. Curtin said it was inappropriate for a nation fighting for its freedom to celebrate festive occasions such as Christmas by spending money. Gifts should be done without. Even the winner of the Melbourne Cup was given only War Bonds. The manufacture of toys was banned as a waste of man-power and materials. People's only thought should be for saving their country from the barbarous enemy.

Advertisements promoting the sale of Christmas gifts, or the practice of giving them, were banned. Icing Christmas cakes was banned. The Red Cross planned a Sacrifice Day for Christmas Eve; people were asked to deny themselves something and give the money to the Red Cross.

Even the mango trees seemed to have joined in the Austerity campaign. The crop was very poor. Audrey and I who were allowed to climb Mrs. Woodward's mango tree, scrambled around among the dark branches or threw sticks up into the foliage in vain.

The various shark-enclosures on the beach seemed to embrace the general self-denial as well. Their rusted wire-mesh was not replaced. Mrs. Roosevelt, wife of the President of the United States, said that she would not be giving any toys or gifts to her family this year. She disliked toy tanks and guns. Instead, she would be giving her grandchildren War Bonds. Mr. Curtin thought all Australians should follow her example. Mum said she agreed. Europe was facing its hungriest winter ever. Thousands of Jewish people in Holland and France had been deported from their homes. The people of Stalingrad were starving. She had worked out from her mailing lists, that the Christmas food parcels she had sent to the English relatives would have been lost in one of the heaviest convoy sinkings of the year. There would be no Christmas for them and sorrowful ones for the families of the men lost at sea.

It looked like being a pretty bleak old Christmas all round. Barry and I did not feel exactly hopeful. If only Dad could be at home! We were glum but not all that surprised when we each got just one 'useful' present. Barry got a seat cover for his bicycle. I got a wickerwork sewing basket. It had a draw-string at the top to close it which made it very difficult to find anything inside. I knew that in Grade Three at West End, I would be required to have a sewing-basket. Audrey had told me so. So Mum would have had to buy me one, anyhow.

A sewing basket! What could be worse! No Christmas cake with threepences! No crackers! No funny hats! No decorations! No anything! 'Stinking war!' growled Barry. I nodded glumly. We felt cheated out of Christmas.

Chapter 13

SHORTAGES OF EVERYTHING: 1943

'I'm gonna buy a Paper Doll that I can call my own,
A doll that other fellas cannot steal'

Air Training Corps marching in Flinders Street. Barry, tallest, front left.

Joycie was happy, humming away to herself as she worked at Mum's sewing machine. She was making herself a siren-suit, a sort of all-in-one affair with fastenings down the front to wear when she went to Magnetic Island or up to Paluma with parties of convalescent American soldiers organized by the Red Cross. Mum had told her she would be much happier if instead of moping in her room all day she took up some war-work, such as making camouflage nets or packing parcels for prisoners-of-war. It had proved to be so. After her first few trips out with the Americans Joycie came home sparkling.

The soldiers were from the big army hospital at Black River. Joycie herself was so much recovered from her previous gloom that she took to going to the Flying Squadron Hall, to the dances held for service personnel. 'You see,' said Mum to me. 'There is nothing like helping others to make you forget your own problems. Always remember that.'

'Auntie Eileen' minded the baby. If she cried overmuch during the day her dummy was dipped in jam. Mum was horrified. The child was teething! Did the woman not consider the damage she might be doing to the child's enamel! At night Mum suspected the dummy was dipped in something stronger. After a while Rayleen's fretful cries would turn to baby-snores.

Joycie became an exponent of the art of jitterbugging. If *In the Mood* came on the wireless she would cast her work aside, leap up and begin twirling her body, doing sharp, intricate thrusts with her feet. She tried to teach Barry and me, but soon gave up on me. I was hopeless. I had no sense of rhythm. It was as much as I could do to cope with the Pride of Erin and the Gypsy Tap, which Mum taught Barry and me up and down the verandah.

But Barry had a wonderful sense of rhythm and it wasn't long before he could do all the energetic moves of the jitterbug. He spun Joycie round, snatching her hand, and whoosh! He slid her through his legs. They did quick-silver movements with their toes, pivoting and twirling. Now five foot eleven, Barry essayed to toss her round his hip, throwing her up in the air to catch her, managing to bring one of Mum's fern baskets crashing from the rafters.

One night Joycie asked Mum if it would be all right if she brought a friend home to tea on Sunday night. Mum thought she meant another one of the Red Cross ladies so of course she said yes. Sunday Night tea was special, an English High Tea. The table was set with a starched white cloth and the special silver cake-forks and tea-spoons that were kept in a silk-lined canteen the rest of the week. Mum had saved a prodigious number of Goldenia Tea labels to acquire these.

For High Tea there was delicious brawn, made from a threepenny pig's-cheek which arrived from the butcher's complete with sandy eye-lashes and floppy ear, but was cleaned and boiled with peppercorns and the flesh pressed under a weight. The salad was a mathematically precise arrangement of shredded lettuce topped with slices of tomato, cucumber and hard-boiled egg. I never liked to have the salad passed to me first as it seemed a shame to spoil the pattern. This was followed by pumpkin scones and rosella jam, made from rosellas which came from Mango Avenue where a man sold them for five shillings a sugar-bag.

On the Sunday when Joycie's friend was expected, Mum all but dropped the sponge-cake she was putting in the middle of the table when steps were heard crunching up the front terrace and there was Joycie, smiling happily, on the arm of an American soldier.

After this, Joycie often brought friends home. They were usually officers. One was even a squadron-leader! They were often Americans but not always. The one that came to Sunday Tea once and kept coming, was an Australian airman, Jerry Bushell. He was not very tall, had crinkly blonde hair and a way of taking notice of you so that even very little girls, whose brothers called them 'Skinny-legs' or 'Skin', felt better about themselves. I developed a passionate attachment to Jerry, though I thought I wouldn't like to be married to him because 'Bushell' would be such a funny name to have; like the weights-and-measures table, 'four pecks one bushel'.

One night from under my tightly tucked-in mosquito-net at the far corner of the verandah, I watched Jerry take Joycie in his arms and kiss her, bending her backwards the way film-stars did in pictures. I saw nothing untoward about it. It was just what grown-ups did and yet some instinct kept me from mentioning it to Mum.

In January the Scholarship results came out. Max Ackland had passed, which meant that he too would start at Townsville Grammar School at Rosslea when school re-opened. During the holidays the boys were totally absorbed, converting American air-force belly-tanks to canoes. Belly-tanks were fuel-tanks that were fitted externally to long-range Flying Fortress bombers to increase the distances they could fly. The Flying Fortresses flew to Port Moresby, refuelled there, flew on to Rabaul and Lae, dropped their bombs, and then returned to Townsville.

We sometimes saw aircraft looking very much the worse for wear, sometimes with one engine dead, limping heavily in across the bay on their return. Once I told Joycie that I had seen a crashed bomber on the back of a truck. She burst into almost hysterical tears, telling me to 'Shut up! Shut up!' I was quite amazed. It had seemed to me such a matter-of-fact thing to see, as ordinary as a blitzwagon or a personnel-carrier or a Chinaman's cart going down Flinders Street.

As canoes, belly-tanks were more water-tight than the sort made out of corrugated iron, but were inclined to instability. They rolled easily unless a keel was fitted. There were two types of belly-tank: the cigar-shaped ones were easier to get hold of, the larger, squatter ones were more prized as they made quite good flatties for fishing in Ross Creek. Barry called his belly-tank the *John French* after the winner of the first Victoria Cross gained on Australian territory. Corporal French had got his VC in September for single-handedly wiping out three Japanese pill-boxes near Lae by hurling hand-grenades at them and then charging with a machine-gun. Because he was a Queenslander, this was a much-talked-about feat and most small boys spent a lot of play-time rehearsing the moment of heroism. Machine-gun fire and the 'Aaaghs!' of the enemy resounded around the streets and back-yards of North Ward. The boys were also alight with excitement because Australia's crack division, the famous Ninth, was coming home from the Middle East to fight the Japs in New Guinea.

Max, John and Barry and their friends put the finishing touches to their belly-tank canoes and lugged them, turn and turn about, to the beach, pausing for a breather every so often at the cry of 'Hold on a bit! She's slipping!' Belly-tank canoes took some carrying. They got to the beach to find there was a king-tide, the water as shiny as glass and so high that even the dredge, the *Cleveland Bay* had had to stop working, the grinding clank of its buckets no longer sounding across the water. But an American Military patrol ordered the boys to keep out of the water. Two nine-foot sharks had been seen cruising along the beach. All army personnel had been prohibited from swimming. Notices had also been put up at the Swimming Basin prohibiting American Servicemen from swimming there because there had been several diving fatalities. As several panels of the shark-enclosure had been washed away during a recent storm, the belly-tank canoes had to be lugged home again. They were pushed in under Acklands' house with 'Wouldn't it rip you!'s of exasperation from the boys. They wandered off to hang about the gun-emplacements and searchlight on the Strand.

The heavy storms had also washed out big pot-holes in most of Townsville's roads through which jeeps and army traffic roared at a great pace, sending sheets of water over passing cyclists. There were many accidents because people still took it as their right to ride two or three abreast across the streets even at night in the blacked-out streets. After all, it was their town! Damned military! But at last the street-lights were switched back on and there were fewer bikes run down.

Little Patsy Flynn who lived near us was brought home from the big Children's Hospital in Sydney to which she had been sent by the American forces, having been run over by one of their trucks. But she was always a frail-looking little girl afterwards, who never joined in any evening games of Sheep, Sheep Come Home or Pins and Needles. She did not join all the other children of Alexandra Street when, after the rains, the gully was full and we went swimming in the large sandy pool just below the bridge. You could not really swim, because the pool was only waist deep. But the bolder boys could put their heads under the water as it rushed out from under the bridge over the lip of concrete. They could also crawl through to the other side, the brown water surging against their knees.

To indicate that I did not care to do such things, I would spend my time diving under water for interesting stones; ebony ones, sleek and shining, pale greens and pinks and ivory eyes of quartz. What a disappointment that, lined up for my delight on the bank, they dried almost at once to pallid dullness. But, once! A Fortune! The wonder of it!

Through the tawny water I saw what I thought was a small piece of bone. Snatching it up I burst to the surface. In the palm of my hand lay a tiny china doll. I knew that it was the sort of moment that might happen to me only once in my lifetime. To find treasure! I could hardly run home up the hill fast enough to show Mum. She turned it over in her hand and said that it had the Grecian-profiled features of the Victorian era and perhaps it had lain in the gravel for fifty or sixty years, from the days when Townsville was a new settlement. I grieved for the sorrow of the long-ago little girl who had lost it and if a mean brother had snatched it and thrown it into the gully to tease her? But now it was mine! I felt the little girl and I might have been friends and promised her in my heart that I would look after her tiny doll for her. The tiny doll was just the right size to be an inhabitant of my under-the-house village, but she was far too precious. She was put away in cotton wool to be kept forever.

After the first rush of water from the hillside the gullies became strings of crystal pools in which minute fish wavered, sketching on the rocky bottom their own translucent shapes. Next came a wealth of tadpoles. Audrey and I would squat at the edge of their watery world, eyeing them for choice specimens of tadpolehood. When a handsome one ventured solo away from the others he was scooped up in cupped hands and borne off, to be kept in a pickle bottle and exclaimed over at the subsequent development of back and front legs. Loss of tail signalled Judgment Day. Neither Mrs. Saunders nor Mum wanted hordes of extra froglets around their houses. The changelings were sloshed into a bucket and carried far down the gully to be returned whence they had come.

Because so many items of food – eggs, custard powder, rice, dried fruit – were unobtainable, tapioca pudding became something that appeared more and more on the tea table. Mum soaked the tapioca first, so that it could be cooked in a minimum of precious milk which made the grains swell to chewy globules. Barry always called it 'Fishes Eyes and Glue'. To me it looked like cooked tadpoles and I could hardly bear the feel of it in my mouth but I would not have been game to say so, as Barry's comments would have made Mum cranky enough already.

Everything was in short supply: clothing, tooth-brushes, even butcher's wrapping paper. Customers were expected to take something along to wrap their purchases in. Mum had calico squares for this which she boiled in the copper after use.

Shoes were scarce, so worn ones were mended with Kromhyde glued on the sole. If the Kromhyde came adrift while you were in town, you would have to walk with it flapping up and down. Brooms were hard to get, so to make one last longer a hole was drilled through the top end of the handle and a loop of string threaded through. Then it could be hung from a nail, instead of standing on its millet-straw all day wearing itself out.

A public meeting to protest about civilian food supplies was held on the Strand. 'Auntie Eileen' said she would go, but Mum was scornful. No matter how badly done by the people of Townsville thought themselves, they were still streets ahead of those in England whose rations had just been reduced again. As for 'Auntie Eileen'! Well! She had little to complain about when she was already making herself free with other people's butter, tea and sugar rations!

Even fire-wood for the stove was unobtainable. If I saw a fallen branch up the hill I put a lot of exertion into dragging it home, knowing how much praise would be heaped on me. Then the City Council, who always took the people of Townsville's side against the military, said they would establish a wood-depot. You had to go in to the Town Hall and pay for your load in advance. Then you could pick it up as soon as a supply became available. 'Pick it up'? How was anyone supposed to do that when no-one had petrol these days? There was more delay, until it was agreed that deliveries would be made, at an extra charge of course.

Our load of wood came. Once, the truck would have edged in backwards along the lower terrace. Now it simply dumped the half-ton load on the road in front of the gate. It fell to Mum and Barry and me to manhandle it through to the back yard. The blocks were sawn-off lengths of bloodwood and gum, about fifteen inches long. They smelt sweetly of sap and oozed ruby crystals, which hardened and could be picked off as treasure. The newly replenished wood-heap became a lovely place to play. Larger blocks became tables, smaller ones chairs. Some of the blocks had split away before being sawn clean through, giving them back-rests. They, of course, were easy chairs. Lizards sunned themselves and made nests of tiny rubbery eggs among the crannies.

One of these I kept watch on, gently removing the scattering of leaves that covered the tiny hollow. There were five miniature eggs. After ten days or so, two of the tiny eggs were broken and I thought something must have eaten them. But when I stirred the leaves with my finger, the most delicate of infant lizards, an inch and a half long, scuttled for cover. I covered the remaining eggs and checked again a few days later. This time, when I touched one of them, a small head popped out and after a moment or so the baby lizard crawled out and scuttled off. There were two more eggs to go, but when I next looked all the hatchlings had gone and the tiny nest was empty.

It was Barry's job to chop the wood every afternoon for the following day. Afterwards, it was my job to collect the chips that flew off the axe for the chip box. While he worked, I sat on the fragrant woodheap and he educated me on all the things he thought it important for a small sister to know in a country that was at war. The Americans had this new vehicle, see! Whack! Whack, went the axe. It looked like a truck but it could go on water. Whack! Yes, it could! He had jolly-well seen it with his own eyes! It looked like a barge, but had wheels sticking out from underneath. It was for invasions, for getting troops and gear on to beach-heads and across rivers. And did I know what it was called? A 'Duck'! Good one, eh! Whack! They also had a new weapon called a bazooka. Whack! In the heat, he worked with his shirt off, sweat tricking down his neck. He was good at judging the blocks that would be straight-grained and easy to split. The gnarly-looking ones he tossed to the back of the heap in the vague hope that someday Dad might be home to deal with them, or that he himself might be more of a muscle man. I had seen him flexing his muscles and looking at his reflection appreciatively in the French windows on the verandah.

One afternoon while we were busy in this way, an unexpectedly knotty block of wood jammed on the axe-head. Barry tried to jar it off on the edge of the chopping-block, but hickory axe-handles were also unobtainable and he was afraid of damaging ours. The other way to get rid of a block that had wedged itself on the axe was to break it free by making a mighty swing with the axe reversed. This would usually cause the block to jar away. So he took a hefty swing.

Unfortunately, Joycie had done the baby's washing that morning, and had somehow managed to move the clothes prop over so that the line was now directly over Barry's head. The axe with the chunk of wood wedged to it caught the line. The block broke free; down it came, right on Barry's head. As though for emphasis, the clothes prop slid along the line and dropped on to him too.

I giggled. It was just like an act, something that Fatty and Skinny in the pictures would do. They were always dropping hammers on to one another's heads, or whacking one another with ladders. They would land on the ground and pretend to see stars. Then they would leap up and chase one another, waving their fists ands shouting. But Barry did leap up, or do any running round shaking his fist. He sagged slowly, knees buckling, into an untidy heap. For a moment I stared stupidly, then waveringly I called out, 'Mum! You'd better come down! Barry's hurt himself!'

Mum came running, crying out when she saw Barry's limp form, 'Oh! Dear God! Whatever next!' Barry was helped up to the house, blood welling through his hair and trickling stickily down the side of his forehead. To staunch the flow, Mum pressed the edges of the wound together with her fingers while I ran to and from under her directions. A pressure pad was applied and his head firmly bandaged. At this, Barry began to make a mighty recovery. He would have loved to have seen his bandaged head in a mirror. Mum told him if he moved from the chair she would have him! He was given two Aspros, torn off from the waxy strip in which they came, and a cup of strong tea. I ran into Mum's bedroom and fetched the hand-mirror from her dressing-table. Barry peered into it gratefully, saying,

'Just leave it here.' When he thought no-one was looking, he had several more looks. 'You should have gone to the ambulance, but who was there to take you?' said Mum. She was right; he should have gone. The blood had soaked through the bandage already. The wound should have been stitched but there was no-one to take him in.

Barry had to sit quite still and keep his head on a cushion for several days. This was sad for him, because he was to have gone with Max and John to a special sports day organized by the Red Cross at Blue Water for all the servicemen in town. Special rail-motors were being laid on so that civilians could enjoy the day too.

I went with the Bensleys. The countryside was fresh after the rains. There was an American air-force band playing *Sioux City Sue*, *Paper Doll* and other songs. There was a mobile canteen where hot-dogs were available. Hot-dogs were really only saveloys, and nothing to do with dogs at all! There was a rodeo with mule and donkey races. There were swimming races and piggy-back fights in the water, Americans versus Australians. Barry found it all pretty depressing, when I told him about it. Mum said that to compensate, when his head was better, she would shout him to the Wintergarden to see *Mrs. Miniver* which had won the best film award of 1942. Now that he was fourteen and had his own Identity Card, he was allowed in to the pictures at night.

There were other reminders of the time when the threat of invasion had hung over the town; there were still weekly siren tests and black-out practices. There were still slit-trenches in all the streets, although these had been full of water ever since the rains. The concrete pill-boxes down the middle of Flinders Street had signs on them saying that it was illegal for anyone to use them for any purpose other than an air attack. Barry told me this meant when the soldiers wanted to have a wee and didn't want to walk all the way to the toilets on the riverbank.

When Margaretta and I wanted to go to the Ladies' toilet one day, there were three American sailors fast asleep in the doorway. Most of the concrete pill-boxes had drawings of a little man peering over a wall, and the words, 'Foo was here!' Underneath this would be, 'So was I', and other names and places such as Tulsa, Phoenix or Spokane. The names of some places were already familiar, from songs; Topeka, Santa Fe, Atlanta, Chattanooga. Everybody was singing:

Shovel all the coal on; gotta keep her rollin'

Choo Choo! Chattanooga! Here we come!

And then the schools reopened. Barry had out-grown his Grammar School uniform and no further supplies were available. The manufacture of school uniforms had been banned. The Government considered they were not essential to the War Effort. Barry's suit was passed on to Max. But Mum used precious clothing-coupons to buy navy-blue head-cloth to make box-pleated tunics for me to start at West End.

West End was a two-storied red-brick school with an impressive War Memorial Gateway. Audrey had been going there since coming home from evacuation, and had told me that there were showers for when you finished playing games. This had made it sound like 'St Clare's' in Enid Blyton's *The Twins at St Clare's*, which Mrs. Woodward had given me for Christmas. The showers at West End turned out to be merely the temporary conversion of toilets from the time when the school had been got ready for use as a military hospital. My image of coming in, flushed and excited after a victorious game of lacrosse with 'Blanche' and 'Hilary' against 'Redroofs', the deadly opponent, withered on the vine.

Miss Thomas, the Third Grade teacher, was one of the retired ladies who had been brought back to fill in the gaps caused by the absence of so many men at the front. Ladies who had been teachers before they were married were also told to come back. For the first time, feeling very strange, we called teachers 'Mrs.' Teachers were supposed to be 'Miss'!

Miss Thomas seemed dreadfully old, with a worried crinkly face, flattish, like my Eskimo Doll. She had a lot to look worried about. A class of over fifty shrill nine year-olds, seething with the excitement of being 'first-day-back' after a year off school, filled the long room, a double classroom with the folding wooden doors opened back.

Miss Thomas's means of dealing with the noise level was to have a shop-bell, the sort that customers pressed when they wanted service at a counter, fitted to her desk. When the din grew too overwhelming, she would reach out and dab genteelly on the bell. At the sound of its 'ping' the roar would lessen to a drone before mounting in intensity again.

The best thing about West End were the games at Big Lunch. Boys and girls had separate areas of the playground. In the girls' area there were always circle-games going on. Twelve or fifteen girls would circle gravely, holding hands, chanting rather than singing, a set pattern of rhyme. A favourite was

The church is made of marblestone, the windows made of glass,
And if you go inside it, you'll find a bonny lass,
Her name is [the girl in the middle of the ring – for instance, 'Nancy Smitherson']
Catch her if you can,
She married [any boy's name – say, 'Johnny Jackson'] before he was a man.
He kisses her, he cuddles her, he takes her on his knee,
And says, 'Dear Nancy, won't you marry me?'
Nancy made a pudding, she made it rather sweet.
She daresn't stick the knife in till Johnny comes home to tea.
Taste, Johnny! Taste, Johnny! Don't be afraid!
For next Sunday morning is your wedding day,
The bells will ring, and the cats will sing,
And we'll all clap hands on your wedding day!

It was expected that the girl at the centre of the ring would look appropriately coy. In fact she would be enjoying her moment to the full though with suitably downcast eyes. The whole point of the chanting was to see who would be the next one to be chosen to be in the centre of the ring. You lived in hope and dread that it might be you, but invariably it was one of the friendship group of the girl already there, although repetitions of choice were usually greeted with a universal cry of, 'She's had a turn!'

The only other moment of enlivenment in the long-drawn out chant, was the announcement of the name of the boy whom the girl would marry. This was decided beforehand by a lot of heads-together whispering. When the boy's name was proclaimed it was done with a shout and the effect on the girl at the centre was studied. The expected response was one of shock and repudiation, though if it was one of the popular or clever boys the girl would look smugly pleased. She deserved no less. It was considered unsporting to choose the names of boys suspected of having nits, or of those who had school-sores or who couldn't read.

There were similar games based on choosing sides. In one, each group would go off into a huddle to decide on some article representing fabulous wealth. Unless someone with a little imagination came up with something better these usually resolved themselves into being, 'a diamond neck-lace' ('lace' rhyming with 'face') or a 'a golden 'bayngle''. I soon learned that it didn't pay to be smartie-pants with 'emerald and amethyst fountain-pen and pencil set.' Once the choices were decided upon the game became a version of Oranges and Lemons, except that when the arched hands came down 'to chop off your, your, your, your head' the captive, would be borne way and asked in fiercely excited whispers 'What will you have? A golden bayngle or a diamond neck-lace?' According to their choice they joined the line behind one or other of the two leaders. When everyone had been through the arch and had been chosen, the two teams had a tug of war, exhorting one another to 'monkey grip' for better purchase. But that was not the real purpose of the game. The real purpose was simply to feel yourself part of a group doing these important ritual things.

There was another little girl in Miss Thomas's class who did not have any friends. She made overtures of friendship to me. I knew that she was only choosing me because no-one else would be her friend, but for that matter, no-one seemed in too great a hurry to be my friend either, so Celia and I declared one another 'best friends' and went about arms linked. Celia had a face like an everyday plate and gazed out, not very hopefully, upon the world from beneath a straight-cut fringe. Her hands were much painted with blue-bag, or iodine, because of warts. In Sums, we would exchange tiny folded scraps of paper to compare answers. If my answer didn't agree with hers I would hastily scrub it out and change it. Celia was clever.

The large playground behind the school had zig-zag lines of air-raid slit-trenches. Regular air-raid practices were held. Bells rang, whistles shrilled. We all scampered down the staircases and pelted to our Grade Three trench under the Moreton Bay fig-trees. There we crouched, heads between our knees, hands clasped over the backs of necks. Each child had to have a cloth bag in which were kept a wooden dolly-peg to grip between our teeth and cotton wool to be stuffed in our ears to lessen the effects of bomb-blast. It was all a bit of a game, especiallv beholding Miss Thomas easing herself down awkwardly into the trench then fanning herself with her lace-edged handkerchief. She would no sooner have made it, than the whistle would go to signal the end of the practice. Several boys would eagerly offer to help her out, hauling away even though she was off balance and her hair-pins coming out. They genuinely wanted to help and were not revenging themselves for the many whacks with her ruler that would have been dished out to them on the backs of their legs for neglect of spelling-homework, blots in copy-books or dropping of slates.

Paper was so scarce that all schoolwork was done on slates. The only books written in were the meagre Government-issue ones kept in the press, in which Compositions, Exercises and Mapping were done. Compositions were written on the slate first, corrected, then copied in. Exercises had decorative headings done in Old English enclosed in a fancy scroll. Maps were of 'Australia – Physical Features', or 'Queensland – Towns and Railways'. For 'Physical Features', mountain ranges were shown as lines from which spikey strokes rayed outwards. The effect was as of a continent infested with centipedes. The coastline had to be inked and then outlined with a crinkly blue-pencil line. That part was pleasurable. Nothing could go wrong. The worst moment came at the end, for then you had to firm-in the margin with red ink. The slightest slip with the ruler and Woe! Complete spillage of the bottle of red-ink was not unknown, to which the long desks bore witness. The blue ink, however, was safer, in china inkwells inserted at the top of each desk. These were kept filled by those select persons, the Ink Monitors, recognizable by having right arms that were blue to the elbow from stirring the ink-powder into the bucket of cold water.

It was forbidden to play in or around the air-raid trenches but this did not prevent the wild leapings and jumpings that went on during the boys' games of Red, Red, Rover or Bedlam. There were baldy patches where the gravel embankments were packed down hard. The teacher-on-duty lurked nearby to catch culprits who were then sent to the Office for 'four'; four cuts of the cane on the hand. I was flattered that, hearing that I learned the violin, the boys asked 'gis a bit o' y' resin'. They had it on good authority that resin rubbed on the palm of the hands would magically prevent pain. Lacking resin they spat on their palms as they trailed towards the Office, and would return, flicking their hands to lessen the sting, or nursing them under their armpits.

The next day the same games across the air-raid shelters resumed. The trenches were too wonderful a challenge to be resisted. The top end of the play-ground was an American army camp, a mass of dull, greenish khaki tents, set out in rows like a town. It was strictly out of bounds. It seemed as normal for the camp to be there as it was for the cemetery to be at the other side. Beyond the camp rose Castle Hill with rocky outcrops marching in precise formations across its shoulders radiating the brilliant heat of summer.

Grade Three sums now involved additions and multiplications of pounds, shillings and pence, under the answer-line of which little boxes had to be ruled where the totals of the various columns were shown. Half-pence had to be divided by two to turn them into pennies, pennies by twelve to turn them to shillings and shillings by twenty to turn them to pounds. I could never work out which bit went where and after a few frantic scrubbings-out and tears I gave up, to sit gazing out the window at the patterns in the grass high on the hill as the wind swept freely across under the plate-blue sky.

No-one any longer felt that the Japanese would invade North Queensland. Despite all the shortages, spirits were brighter. Our side seemed to be doing well. The Australians had captured Buna in New Guinea after heavy fighting. And B-25s, A-20s and Australian Beaufighters had sunk a Japanese transport fleet leaving Rabaul. There was a lot to be cheerful about. Only Mum sighed over the Luftwaffe damage to Canterbury Cathedral and the continuing death-toll in raids on London.

Heatleys in Flinders Street had a window display of Japanese souvenirs from the New

Guinea campaign; gas-masks, coins and paper money – the invasion-money that Barry had talked about – leaflets, mess-plates and bayonets. People stared in silence. So these were to have been our conquerors then! Cheeky baskets!

Barry also had a collection of souvenirs. The top-hat section of his chest-of-drawers was chock-a-block with pieces of shrapnel and bomb-fragments. Children were not supposed to have these. A boy near Cairns had been killed by an unexploded hand-grenade which he had collected from a firing-range. A little girl down south had been blown up by a souvenir mortar bomb brought back from the Western Front by her uncle. But there wasn't a boy in Townsville who didn't have a shrapnel collection, swapping with others for bigger and more deadly looking pieces at every opportunity.

Barry was still hoping that the war would last long enough for him to be in it. He was now in the Grammar School Cadets, and on Thursdays went to school dressed in full Cadet uniform, including the Digger-hat. The night before he would sit on the back-steps and polish the army boots to a mirror-like finish. Dad had once said that if you shone your shoes well enough and often enough the time would come when you didn't have to do it anymore. Both Barry and I fell for it. Barry would spit into the tin of Kiwi polish, before he began because that was what Dad had always done.

What he really wanted was to join the RAAF. He studied aircraft recognition charts endlessly, lecturing me while we carried meagre buckets of left-over household water to the garden, or helped fill the copper with rainwater for Monday morning's wash. He felt it imperative that I should know the difference between an Avro Anson and a Kittyhawk; that a Hudson had twin oval tail fins and tapered wings and that fighters were smaller and swifter than reconnaissance planes. The Mosquito, with two Rolls Royce Merlin engines, well! Nothing could beat it!

The only ones I was absolutely sure about were the big B24s that went over the house, sometimes so low that we could see the Walt Disney insignias painted on the fuselages. My favourite was Goofy. Sometimes I felt sure that the crew of Goofy waved back, when I rushed out to wave a tea-towel as it roared in over the verandah. I could also tell the difference between Sunderlands now that the Sunday service to Sydney had been resumed, and Catalinas, for both kinds landed on the bay. There was a base at Palm Island for repairing the Catalinas so we saw more and more of them. They were easy to tell because they had the wings on top like huge dragonflies, and a blister, or perspex dome, halfway along the body.

In his spare time Barry sat at the dining-room table with a balsawood kit of a Lancaster bomber which he had saved up to buy. The components of the Lancaster were printed on a sheet of balsa wood. Each was carefully sliced out with a bit of broken razor-blade on the back of the bread-board. Then the pieces were glued painstakingly together to form the air-frame of the fuselage. The aircraft began to take shape. It was a work of art. Every so often Barry would lift the construction and sight along it lovingly to make sure it was not warping in the heat.

Lancasters were his love. 'Gee! Listen to this!' he would exclaim, reading from the *Bulletin* yet another account of how a Lancaster had performed some feat of daring over

Europe. A Lancaster had looped the loop, fully loaded with bombs. It was over an important target, avoiding fighters in a steep dive, when a large shell had exploded right underneath it. The Lancaster had been turned over on its back. The pilot had completed the loop with a dive that had taken it to nearly four hundred miles an hour. 'That just shows what the kite can do!' he whistled, 'The size of her! And fully loaded! You wouldn't think it was possible! And then she goes on to finish the bombing-run, too!'

On Monday nights, he cycled off to the Morse classes that were held at the back of the Post Office in Flinders Street, preparing himself for the time when he could join up. When Bluey Truscott, the Australian air-ace was killed, it was to Barry the loss of a personal hero.

This keenness was to pay off. The blood-poisoning that he had had as a little boy in Eyre Street began to tell against him. He found it difficult to finish the route-marches which the Army cadets had to do as part of their basic training. The injured leg had never been as strong as the other one, something which he had disguised, never complaining when it was playing up. Not even Mum had realized. At fourteen, although he was still under age, because of his height and build and, as Mum liked to think, because of his good looks and breeding, he was allowed to transfer to the Air Training Corps. His cup of happiness overflowed.

When the Dillon family down in Rose Street lost their son in the RAAF over Germany, Barry spruced himself up, jumped on his bike and rode down to ask if there was anything that he could do for them. He made a point of calling on Mr. Strange along Alexandra Street when his son won the DSO. He felt himself part of the whole show now and that it was just a matter of time until he could get a crack at the Huns. And the Nips!

In May there was dreadful news. It was too horrible! The hospital ship the *Centaur* was torpedoed off the Queensland coast. It was Mum's birthday and we were to have had a day at the island to celebrate. But when the news came through that the Japanese had sunk the *Centaur* everyone was stunned. To sink a hospital ship! It was unheard of! Hospital ships were protected by the Geneva Convention! Even the Germans had never stooped to such barbarity! Hospital ships were immune from attack! They always had their lights full on and had prominent Red Crosses painted on their superstructure to show that they were ships of mercy. But now the *Centaur* had been torpedoed forty miles off the coast from Brisbane. Of the crew of three hundred and sixty three, including doctors and nurses, only sixty four had survived. Most of the others had been trapped below decks by fierce fires in the gang-ways. Remembering the night on which we had lurched around the harbour with Uncle Les in the Samuel Allen's launch I shuddered. There *were* submarines about! To think Mum had kept shooshing me! Imagining the patients, doctors and nurses trapped below decks, and the padre who could have escaped but chose to remain with the wounded, I could feel the horror as they were engulfed in swirling black water.

When Mum said that she didn't think we should go to the island after all because it wouldn't seem right to be in holiday mood, it came as a relief. Supposing the island boat was next! Instead, we went to the Memorial Service at Central Methodist. Mr. Prouse said that the civilized world would share a sense of revulsion at this unnecessary act of barbarity.

Hospital Ship Centaur, sunk 14Th May, 1943, off Stradbroke Island, with the loss of 322 lives.

It showed the sort of enemy our young men had been called upon to fight so that love and peace and mercy might prevail. Barry, in the pew beside me, looked grim and determined. When the first hymn was *Fight the good fight, with all thy might* Barry sang loudest of all, just being careful on certain notes because his voice was breaking.

One Saturday afternoon not long after this I was busily at work under the house trying to arrange secret quarters for Mumpuss to have her next batch of kittens. The poor thing, she was desperate! No matter where she had her litter Mum would always find the place and the kittens, despite my tears and pleadings, would be put to sleep with chloroform. Mum said that we simply couldn't be over-run with cats. But, oh! Their dear little blunt butting heads and sealed eyes! I thought I would arrange an IXL jam box facing away from where anybody would see and put some dry grass in for her. I introduced Mumpuss to this haven and waited for her reaction. She dabbed a couple of times with her nose at the arrangements, seemed about to make herself at home, then changed her mind and went stalking off to throw herself, tail twitching, among the galardias edging the front path. Her bulging side had knobbles where the kittens' heads were.

Mum had gone out dressed in her best white linen suit with red appliques on the pockets. It was a special occasion. The ladies from the Red Cross and Comforts Fund at the Town Hall were to meet Lady Wilson, the wife of the Governor of Queensland. From within the quiet house overhead I could hear Joycie availing herself of Mum's absence to make herself a play-suit on the Bluebird. I heard the floorboards creak in what was Mum's bedroom which meant that 'Auntie Eileen' was on the prowl again. I knew she couldn't resist poking into Mum's things whenever she had the chance, although, fearing trouble, I had never mentioned this to Mum. Grown-ups were strange and life was an overwhelming mystery. No sooner did pieces of the puzzle seem to fit than they would slide out of control again. To make it more difficult I often felt that I was half of someone else, as well as being myself; a someone who had walked a steep village street swinging a lantern, a someone who had loved a particular stone staircase leading down into a garden and a someone who had gone running across a battlefield towards a darkling enemy. At times this other person would feel just as present to me as I was to myself.

Suddenly I saw Jerry Bushell coming up the front path. He was carrying a pack which he held rather awkwardly, away from his side. It was almost as though he wanted to avoid having the pack touch his skin. He let himself in at the front verandah gate. 'Auntie Eileen' came hurrying forth from Mum's bedroom, bold-facedly cheery. Joycie ceased sewing and made a glad exclamation of surprise. But there was something unusual about Jerry's response. There was none of his accustomed banter. No light-hearted cheek to 'Mother Mc Rhea', as he called 'Auntie Eileen'. 'Make us a cup of tea, Darl, for Christ's sake!' I heard him say.

Curious, I crept up under the edge of the verandah where I could hear and not be seen. There was a place where I could climb the rock retaining-wall and crouch just below the floor boards.

I heard Jerry gulp his tea. Then he told his tale. A Catalina had crashed into the bay. It had been coming in for what had looked like a perfectly normal landing. Suddenly it had reared up and dived vertically, disappearing before the watchers' horrified gaze. Of course, one of the air-sea rescue boats that cruised the bay constantly, had been there like a shot, but – his voice shook – 'Bloody Hell! The poor bastards!' At this point Jerry said, ' God! Have you got something a bit stronger, Darl! It was that bloody awful!' Footsteps hurried, and there were clinks and gurglings of liquid being poured from a bottle. Then Jerry gave a sigh, 'Oh! That hit the spot!' before going on.

With growing horror, I heard him telling the story. There had been eleven men on board the Catalina. The pilot and the navigator had escaped through the cockpit window and been picked up. The others had been trapped in the rear compartment from which the only means of escape was the perspex blister. There had been a big fat bloke who had tried to get through the blister first and had got jammed. The others were trapped behind him. 'They were drowning like trapped bloody rats! They all but ripped the poor bastard's legs clean off! God, it was that awful!' There was a long pause, and then 'Any more where that came from, Darl?'

I crouched, frozen. The unseen grown-ups got up and moved away down the verandah, laughing now a little and talking about a moonlight cruise to Picnic Bay that the Red Cross were putting on. My shocked stillness deluded a nobby-lizard which ran up the rocks then paused, smiling a leathery smile. The story was as stuck in my mind as a nugoora burr; the desperation of the trapped men, the drowning, experienced in my own body. Trapped under water! Stuck in the blister! Nearly had his legs pulled off! Trapped! Trapped!

Mum came home, pleasurably excited from her afternoon of meeting the Governor's lady. I was pale and ill. She peered at me with something very like exasperation. If it wasn't just like me to be sickening for something and spoil the occasion for her!

The pack which I had seen Jerry carrying so awkwardly up the terrace path turned out to be a parachute from the ill-fated Catalina. Mum, having been regaled with the story by Joycie, recoiled from the pack in horror. 'Oh! I don't want it in the house!' she cried. But Joycie was spreading the parachute on the line to dry. Its very presence seemed to bring the trapped and drowning men into our midst. Joycie was impervious. She thought she could make some lovely silk scanties for herself.

As it happened this turned out to be impracticable, for all the silk was cut on the cross, in

R.A.A.F. Catalina Flying Boats were based at Townsville during the war.

long narrow panels. Joycie was frustrated. Jerry had so wanted her to have nice lingerie!

Another person who did not scruple overmuch about a souvenir that was brought from the ill-fated Catalina was Barry. Jerry gave him a Very pistol, used to send up distress flares. The mouth of the barrel was so large that it looked like a pirate's blunderbus. It still smelt of the grease with which new weapons were coated before they left the factory. Mum shuddered when she saw it. 'Oh! Put it away out of my sight if you must keep it!' she cried. And of course Barry had to keep it. What a prize! No-one else he knew had one. The Very pistol was added to the collection of shrapnel in the top-hat drawer. But even he seemed to recognize that it was associated with horror beyond our comprehension. Perhaps the worst of it was for him that he had been cautioned by Jerry to 'keep his mouth shut' about it. What was the use of having a Very pistol if you couldn't let on about it and do a bit of skiting!

The silk parachute was to signal the end of 'Auntie Eileen' and Joycie's little gallop at our house. Mum felt she could no longer be expected to put up with their presence, wartime conditions, servicemen's wives, or not. Anyone who could calmly sit at her 'Bluebird' trying to make herself scanties from material that had come from the very spot where nine men had drowned! The two women were told that really, wasn't it was time that they found other accommodation? 'Auntie Eileen' said cheerfully that, OK, Love! They knew when they weren't wanted. In any case, young Jerry had been able to get a flat over in Railway Estate for Joycie to move into, just as a house-keeper, mind you! She herself would be going to help look after Rayleen, because Joycie had got herself a job at the Wet Canteen at the Base. It was all settled.

The end did not come without one more bit of drama though. On Sunday evening, when the table was set for High Tea, and I was wriggling in Mum's grasp as she tied a bow into my hair, we heard raised voices from the dining-room. 'Divorce! A mortal sin!' and 'Ha! Look who's talking!' Suddenly, there was a splintering crash of china and glass-ware. Mum went dashing in with me close behind, despite her hissed imperative, 'Stay here! I will deal with this!'

In the dining-room Joycie and 'Auntie Eileen' were locked in combat while Jerry struggled to separate them with grunts of 'Come off it, you two! Fair go, Darl! Get a hold of yourself!' On the floor was the starched tablecloth with the ruins of all Mum's precious Sunday china; the pretty Shelley tea-set that she had got at the Auctions, the two-tiered cake plate that the scones had been on, the long sandwich dish, the crystal salad bowl.

Mum's hands flew to her mouth and she gave a cry from the heart. All her pretty things! Mumpuss came running in and crouched greedily over the upturned dish of brawn. Growling in her throat she began to eat, scarcely believing her good fortune. Barry stamped his feet at her and sent her flying. He got the dustpan and broom and began, in the total silence, to sweep up the broken china. Jerry said 'Come on, then, you two! Get your gear together! We'd better clear out.' The two women went in to the Pink Room and began to pack their belongings.

Barry made several trips with the dustpan out the back. I heard him hurl the contents into the darkness. Then he came back inside and put the plunger on to make Mum a cup of tea. She was sitting at the kitchen table, silent. 'Get her some hankies!' he hissed at me. I went to get the sachet of starched handkerchiefs from the top drawer of Mum's duchess. As I was going into her bedroom, 'Auntie Eileen' pushed past me hurriedly.

The next day at school we had to write a composition about what we had done on the weekend. Although my heart was burdened with the guilty knowledge of these adult goings-on I wrote how Audrey and I had tied pieces of cotton to the horns of the rhinoceros-beetles that we found in the poinciana-tree to make them fly. We had swung them round our heads to get them started and then run, following their ponderous flight. The warning 'Scisss! Scisss!' of the gentle giants was plain in my ears as I wrote, blotting out the memory of grown-up women belabouring one another and the dining-room floor littered with smashed crockery.

After school I went down under the house to my village in the dirt, removed the two blotchy stones that were the Ugly Sisters and hurled them far down the hillside. I allowed the sweet, motherly beach-coral widow to adopt the pink baby-stone. I also intended at the first opportune moment to crawl in under the bouganvillea bush where Barry had thrown all the fragments of china and save all the pieces that had roses, forget-me-nots or bluebells on them. Such items were treasure! I knew I must never, ever let Mum know how I had profited from her loss. The treasure must be hidden away in a secret cranny in the rocks.

It was lovely to have the house to ourselves again. When Mum cleaned out the Pink Room, giving it a thorough going over, she found the ashtray that Jerry had made as a gift for Joycie from the melted-down aluminium of the ill-fated Catalina. She put it out to be taken to the Comforts Fund rooms. They were always short of ashtrays. Barry pounced on it and hid it away under the shrapnel in his top-hat drawer. It was too remarkable a war-relic to part with.

A few days later when Mum was tidying out her bedroom cupboards I heard a cry of dismay. I ran in to find her standing before her open wardrobe with an expression of stunned disbelief. Her war-bonds were missing! She had always kept them underneath the newspaper lining of the towel shelf. But they were all gone! All her scrimping and saving for the last three years! Gone!

The thought flashed through my mind; how many times from beneath the house had I heard 'Auntie Eileen' moving stealthily round in Mum's room. I remembered the way that she had pushed past me rudely on the night of their departure. Should I tell? Quickly, I calculated the benefits against the disadvantages. There would be the sensation of the moment of disclosure, of knowing something that an adult didn't know, the titillation of adding fuel to Mum's fire about the two women. But, equally, might there not also be trouble for me? Why hadn't I told her before? Surely I must have known that it had been my duty to tell? Did I have no sense of right and wrong! I could mentally rehearse the lecture that would follow.

I did not want any more troubles just now. I needed Mum to feel well disposed towards me for I had important information, information that nobody else in the whole wide world knew! I had been hugging it to myself, waiting for one of those golden moments when Mum was composed and comfortable to be with. Nothing must go wrong to spoil it. Nothing must stir her up against me. Not when I had the most precious of all secrets! Mumpuss had had her kittens and I knew where she had hidden them!

I gazed up sympathetically into Mum's distraught face. 'There must have been a burgular!' I said.

Chapter 14

ONE OF OUR AIRCRAFT IS MISSING: 1943

'Though there's one motor gone, we can still carry on,
Comin' in on a wing and a prayer.'

Mum and Dad at the Front of the Alexandra Street House, 1943

Dad came home newly promoted to Warrant Officer, First Class. He had been away so long that I felt awkward and strange with him. But I decided that he looked acceptable, even handsome, in his officer's uniform with a leather Sam Browne belt across his chest and a swagger stick made from plaited leather. One of his men, in peacetime a stockman on a western station, had made the swagger-stick for him. It had a .303 bullet embedded in the tip. The only thing that did not look good about his uniform was the tropical rig of baggy shorts called Bombay Bloomers. Dad had been gassed in the trenches in World War One and one of the effects of this was that he had no hair on his legs. I found Dad's shiny legs embarrassing.

He had one week's pre-embarkation leave because he had been posted overseas. Off Mum and he went on a trip by Pioneer Bus around the Atherton Tableland, the only holiday they had ever had. Then we all went to City Studios to have a family photo taken for Dad to carry in his wallet. Mum declared the photo spoiled by the photographer making me stand on a box to be the same height as Barry. She railed at both of us for not having smiled nicely.

But Dad didn't go to New Guinea after all. Instead he was appointed Quarter Master in Charge of the big camp on Bayswater Road. From there he could quite often get home by borrowing a bicycle. He taught Barry and me the words of *In the Quarter Master's Store*

'There was ham! Ham, mixed up with the jam! In the store; in the store;
There was ham! Ham! Mixed up with the jam, in the Quarter Master's Store!'

When it came to the best bit,

'There was beer! Beer! Beer you couldn't get near...'

Mum would shake her head warningly at him and say ... 'Bert!' but we would go rollicking into the chorus of

'My eyes are dim I cannot see,
I have not brought my specs with me,
I ha-ave no-ot brought my-eye specs with me.'

Dad would sing the baritone part, and Barry the high part, and we would all laugh, including even Mum.

Dad usually managed to smuggle out some army treat for us; tins of prunes or bitter orange juice, which were to help the troops in New Guinea fight off malaria. Suddenly, tapioca pudding became tapioca and prunes. Fresh fruit was unobtainable, except for custard-apples which Americans did not like because of having to spit out all the seeds, so no argument was brooked about whether the army prunes were to be eaten or not. They were fruit. You ate them.

One night, not long after we had finished clearing away the tea-things, Dad arrived with a haversack on his back. 'Guess what I've got in here!' he said. As he turned around slowly, it seemed likely to be more prunes. But from under the flap a small black and white nose could be seen peeping. For years, whenever I had asked 'Where are you going, Dad?' he would reply, 'Oh! Just to see a man about a dog.' I had never lost faith that one day he would actually see the man concerned. And here the dog was! I almost fainted with delight.

Gently Dad tipped the little dog out of his haversack on to the shiny kitchen lino. It sat, its feet gradually sliding further and further from beneath it, looking searchingly up into each of our faces in turn. 'Oh, Bert!' said Mum, 'It's a she!' 'I know, but the poor little beggar's been hanging round the camp for days. Some so-and-so must have abandoned her when he got posted north. Perhaps one of the chaps that have been sent up to the Finschafen show. She's a nice little thing.'

By this time I was down on the lino with my arms full of little black and white dog. She recognized in me a friend she needed and began licking my ears and throat frantically. Then Barry hoisted her high on his shoulder. She balanced there as though that was where she had expected to be, and sat, eyes rolling with happiness. 'Well, Nen! What do you think?' said Dad.

Mum said, 'Don't let her lick you on the mouth! Dogs have worms!' This was Mum's way of saying that the dog could stay. It remained only to name her. 'Bess' or 'Spot' were too common; 'Pixie' was for a Pomeranian. Is there anything nicer in life than thinking of a name for a new dog? Finally it was Dad who decided. The little dog had been wandering around the Bayswater camp without a home, like a gypsy. What about 'Gypsy'? It was perfect. I heard the name as 'J-i-p-s-y' and ever-afterwards spelt it that way in compositions, no matter how often Miss Thomas made me write it out as a spelling correction.

There was much to write about. Jipsy could play Dead Dog, lying prone on the floor with her paws held stiffly. She could jump over a broom-handle. She could ride like Darby Munro on Barry's shoulders as he crawled around the floor. She could balance on the footboard of my scooter when I rode to the shop on messages. She liked to look around the handle, the better to help me steer. She could balance on the carrier of Barry's bicycle. At the beach she rushed into the waves to retrieve sticks. She dived like a seal for stones or pieces of coral.

Barry thought that such enthusiasm should be harnessed to good purpose. 'Listen, Skin!' he said. 'How's this for an idea? I'll go down to the wood-heap and give her a piece of wood. You stay up here and call her. Then I'll call her back down. We'll train her to bring the wood up!'

Jipsy did not have her clever brain for nothing. She soon saw through this. After carrying one or two pieces of wood up, she sized up the situation and flopped down in the cool damp patch where the copper had been emptied after wash-day, tongue lolling. Each time that Barry went labouring past up the steps with an armful of morning-wood she thumped her tail encouragingly.

Jipsy soon had some affectionate dog-friends around the neighbourhood who dropped in for purely social visits. Her best friend was Boxer Bliss, the diminutive Foxie from along the street. There was also Nigger Nutt, a big liver-coloured retriever belonging to Rosa Nutt, who 'came-in' daily to help at Mrs. Woodward's. Nigger would escort Rosa to Woodward's door then drop in shyly but determinedly to see how things were going at our place. Of her callers the most aristocratic was Prince, a handsome Alsatian who sauntered all the way down from Castle Hill Road.

Dad would frown if he saw Prince. He disliked Alsatians intensely. They reminded him of when he had been a prisoner-of-war in Germany in the Great War. The camp had had Alsatians as guard-dogs. Dad and two other men had escaped from the camp by saving their meagre rations and using them to lure the guard-dog into the latrine. They had slit its throat, dropped its body down the pit and escaped across an open field. The other two men had been shot; only Dad had made it back in safety to British lines. He had a letter from King George V, in the King's own handwriting, congratulating him on this feat. Prince understood and bore no hard feelings. Whenever Dad was home he would keep his visit brief and depart with dignity.

But Jipsy turned Quisling; she betrayed the whereabouts of Mumpuss's hideout. A week or so before, Mum had said to me, 'This cat has had her kittens. You must bring them to me, or we will be over-run with cats.' It was no use pleading. If I didn't bring the kittens, then Mumpuss herself would have to go. 'Go' meant to the lethal-chamber in South Townsville where stray animals were gassed. This threat hung over me like a doom.

Gulping tears of sorrow and guilt, I went to the rock under which was Mumpuss's secret lair, reached in and drew out the four kittens. Mumpuss made growly mews and tried to nudge my hand away. I had not the heart to do it. I would run away from home! I would not go when I was called for tea! I would sleep out on the warm flat rock. I would refuse to do my violin practice! Then a thought occurred to me. Supposing I left just one kitten?

Mum would never know. When it was big I would find a home for it. Perhaps Miss Thomas would like a kitten? I could ask all the teachers at school! Surely somebody would love a kitten?

Bunching up my play-tunic at the front, I carried three of the kittens down the hill to Mum. I left the handsome black one. Mumpuss curled around him ecstatically. She seemed not to mind so very much the sudden diminution of her family.

A few days later, Mum said, 'Well, you would think Mumpuss's milk would have dried up by now. I do hope the poor old thing is all right.' Then Jipsy gave the game away. She stood in front of the little cave, high on our top terrace, barking happily and waving her tail. Mum looked at me sternly. 'Bring it down!' she said. By this time the handsome black kitten was at the peak of kitten perfection. One look and Mum was won. 'What shall we call him,' I asked with false eagerness, wanting to get the deed signed and sealed without delay. Mum looked thoughtful for a moment, then she said, 'Why, I think it must be, Kelly', she said. 'Ned Kelly was an outlaw living in the hills. Yes, Kelly!' So began Kelly's long life of getting under Mum's feet when she was serving up, draping himself elegantly on verandah chairs and revelling in the knowledge that he was Mum's favourite. He would box Jipsy firmly on the nose to remind her of her place. He was King Cat.

The only thing that Jipsy could not tolerate was to have a stick or a broom pointed at her. When this happened, she would put her tail between her legs and run squealing with terror. Dad said that perhaps whoever had owned her in the first place had tried to shoot her when his unit was moved up to New Guinea. Or perhaps drunken louts had taken pot-shots at her. I loved her all the more to make up for it.

As the Dry Season progressed Townsville once again had a time of severe water problems. Work was started on a second weir and a reservoir at Stuart. The new reservoir on Castle Hill improved pressure in the taps for a time. But civilians were asked to have 'waterless nights' when the supply was switched off at eight o'clock and turned on again at five in the morning. People were warned against using kerosene tins for storing drinking water; lead soldering could be poisonous. Some days the water was switched off from ten in the morning until after four o'clock in the afternoon. Even the Military were made to toe the line. Water was disconnected from one establishment when a corporal was seen washing down an officer's car with a hose. Citizens who used hoses were fined and their houses disconnected 'without respect of persons'. School children had to take a bottle of water to school. There was a lot of talk about building a pipeline to connect Townsville to a dam at Mount Spec, but the cost would be three hundred thousand pounds. An unimaginable amount of money!

There was also talk that, to make a better harbour, the Americans might dynamite Castle Hill and join Cape Pallarenda to Magnetic Island. An outrage! How dare they! Castle Hill was Townsville! But no-one doubted that if the Americans decided to, they not only could but they would. But as though a sign of its everlastingness and its scorn of silly human-beings and their plans, there were grass-fires on Castle Hill at night, and in the morning air, the hawks circled lazily, on the lookout for a breakfast of scorched lizards, just as they had been doing since the Aborigines hunted there for hundreds of years.

Mrs. Eleanor Roosevelt, the wife of the American President, visited Townsville. She was the head of the American Red Cross which had recreation rooms for their men near Hayles Wharf. She also went out to Black River to visit the big American hospital there, where the wounded from the fighting in New Guinea were brought. Barry rode into Flinders Street on his bike to see her, and reported that she had been wearing an American Red Cross uniform with a peaky cap and that the WAAAFs had made a pretty smart guard-of-honour for her outside the Services' Club; not too bad for women!

Across the road from West End School was the main north-south railway line. All the school children were accustomed to troop trains going past. The troops, especially Australians, would lean out waving and chiacking. If it was Big Lunch, we would crowd the fence or cling to the bars of the Memorial gateway to wave back. One afternoon, just as school was being let out, a troop train was passing, heading north. Then, suddenly, brakes screeching, it clanked to an unexpected halt. Men began leaping down from the train. Others were leaning out of the windows of carriages looking shocked. There were shouts and yells. Train-crew and military police pounded along the line. Troops tumbled out of the carriages and milled around. A couple of them turned to vomit near the little fig-tree. The guard came racing along the cinders, shouting angrily and waving his arms at the children swarming across the road. It was soon obvious that something very dreadful had happened.

The dreadful thing was that one of the soldiers had fallen off the train and been run over. Perched on the railing of the little wrought-iron platform at the back of the carriage, he had overbalanced and fallen beneath the wheels. The several hundred children surging through the school gates began to charge across the road, I among them, part of the mass decision to look, borne along almost against my will. I didn't know what I expected to see, except that it was something horrible. But if everyone was looking, then I must too. But, suddenly, planted in front of me, right in the middle of the road, was Mr. Poulsen, the Fifth Grade teacher. In a strong, firm voice, looking me steadily in the eye, he said, 'You don't want to see that!' In fact I did. I wanted to see what all the others were seeing. But Mr. Poulsen had singled me out. It was important enough to stop me in my tracks. Relieved of the responsibility to move with the crowd. I went docilely towards the bus-stop, only glancing back once, curious but absolved of guilt, at the mass of soldiers and children seething like blowflies around the dreadful spot on the railway line opposite West End school.

Celia's and my friendship had reached that point where a diplomatic exchange of Saturday visits takes place. Celia had been to my place and been shown my wealth: a new litter of kittens, my Capstan tin collection of Sunday School tickets, the ring made out of perspex with a tiny red stone set in it that Dad had got someone at Bayswater Road to make for me. Jipsy had jumped over the broom handle and played dead-dog for her. I had shown her the Look-out Rock at the top of our steps. I had even extracted from its hidey-hole, the tin of pretty fragments of Mum's china, though I did not explain their origin. Together we marvelled over the largest piece which showed an almost complete coach setting out from a thatched inn.

Then it was my turn to visit Celia' s place. She gave me her address on a scrap of paper so tiny it was difficult to make the words out. I gave it to Mum in the kitchen. Dad was skinning cumquarts ready for Mum to be make into marmalade for the Red Cross. I was on the verandah reading *Children of the New Forest*. Suddenly I heard my name being mentioned. It is strange how your own name will leap out, as though in large print, from an otherwise jumbled mass of conversation. I listened carefully, head bent over my book. '...can't possibly let her go' '....make some excuse...never know what goings-on...' They were talking about Celia. I wasn't allowed to go to Celia's place. Nothing was explained to me and for years I would not understand. Celia's address had been, 'just behind the Causeway Hotel'. The particular row of little houses 'just behind the Causeway Hotel' would have been well-known to many of the troops stationed around Townsville. Celia seemed to understand when I told her I was 'not allowed'. She nodded, gravely and with dignity. I had the feeling that there had been other times when her invitation had been turned down.

Barry was looking forward to the promised visit of a Lancaster bomber which was to fly around Australia on a fund-raising mission for the Fourth Liberty Loan. It was going to fly in low over every town, then park at the aerodromes and be open for inspection. Anyone who bought a one hundred pound Liberty Loan Bond would be entitled to a flight. Those who bought a ten pound Bond could go through it on an inspection.

Barry's model Lancaster was very close to completion. The fuselage was almost covered with the required number of layers of pasted tissue-paper to simulate aluminium. He could not, of course get the hobby-paints to paint it, but the kit had come complete with stick-on roundels and air-force markings. All that remained was to connect the piece of elastic that was the source of power for flight. Mum had sacrificed elastic intended for a pair of pyjamas she was making herself. The elastic had to be hooked inside at the back of the fuselage, using one of Mum's crochet-hooks, and then connected to the propeller. When the propeller was turned it would give the model sufficient power for its first flight. It was a moment of great satisfaction for Barry. Such a lot of time and effort had gone into it. He could hardly wait but he wanted Dad to be there for the great launch flight. Mum promised she would make a batch of her special pilelets to celebrate. Dad said, 'Right, Son! Next time I'm home!'

One of the nice things about having Dad at the Bayswater Road camp was that he was able to get home quite often to do things about the house that had long needed doing. The first thing was that he cut a door through the end room so that we had access to the bathroom without having to go outside around the end of the house. As there was no timber to make a door, Mum improvised with a curtain on a wire. This meant that if you were in the bathroom it was best to keep singing to give people fair warning not to come barging in.

Dad also decided that, as we had such a huge backyard and fresh eggs were impossible to get and the dried variety nasty to eat, it would be a good idea if we kept chooks. The Government said that it was everyone's patriotic responsibility to dig a garden and to keep poultry to boost food production. I promised to be the one who would look after the hens. Dad resurrected the chook-house that Barry had raided for corrugated-iron for the roof of the air-raid shelter. He said that hens didn't need a lot of roosting space, for the less timber there was, the less area for lice to infest. I listened intently to everything he had to say. I saw myself as gaining in importance from being the keeper of the hens. It fitted the secret part of myself that felt it had lived in a village in England.

I felt well-qualified for the task, having observed much about chooks at Acklands' and Saunders'. I knew that the bran and pollard mash tasted quite nice if you took dabs of it during the mixing, that is, before the scraps from the kitchen were added in. I also knew that nice red combs were a sign of a good layer, that china eggs from Buzzacott' s had to be placed in the nesting boxes to fool the hens into laying, and that a broody hen could turn nasty if disturbed, sometimes if only looked at.

Dad and Barry went off on their bicycles with sugar-bags to Teitzel's Poultry Farm out at Aitkenvale, and returned with five Rhode Island Red hens and a handsome rooster. We gathered to watch when they were tipped out of the bags into the new chook-yard. They blinked stupidly for a moment or two and then one of the hens, more daring than the others, ventured a pace or two and gave a tentative scratch. When she purported to have found something of interest, the others darted forward to snatch it from her. The rooster fluffed out his green and bronze feathers, shook himself and strutted after the hens. Then he leapt on the back of one of the hens and bore her to the ground, grasping her neck feathers to maintain his balance. 'Oh! Bert!' exclaimed Mum, 'Was a rooster really necessary?' 'It's all right, Mum!' I said, all knowledgeable. 'It's called the pecking order. Mr. Saunders told us so.'

Bran and pollard were put into two forty-four gallon drums under the house. We had had the drums from the time when all households had been issued with them to store water for incendiary bombs. Dad made a wooden lid to fit each of them. Fowl-feed was another commodity in short supply so Dad told me to be sure to let the fowls out each afternoon after school, for 'green pickings' to supplement their diet. He also told me, 'Feed the fowls early every morning, and always feed them at the same time. They are just like you and need a good breakfast.' Barry was sent off to the beach to bring home some of the piled up shell-litter at the tide line for shell-grit, so the eggs would have tough shells.

The hens soon settled in and there came a day when I had that most delightful of feelings: reaching into the nesting boxes for freshly laid brown eggs. The ritual question would be asked, 'How many today?' to which I would have the satisfaction of replying, 'Three,' or 'Four!' The date had to be pencilled on each egg so that Mum would know which ones to use first. They had also to be placed in the bowl pointy end down because this kept the yolk in its place instead of it rising up and touching the shell. In this way they stayed fresh longer. When we had more than we could use, Mum rubbed them with Ke-peg to make them last. She gave some to Mrs. Woodward because she was kind about passing messages on from the phone and was very old. Fresh eggs were a very important addition to our diet. None were available in the shops as the military took all the local farmers could supply.

Dad also got up on the roof with some nails borrowed from the army and secured the iron for the next wet-season, just in case he got another posting before the rains came. Nails were another item that were unobtainable in Townsville, so other people had to hammer out old nails in order to reinforce their roofs. He built kitchen shelves, a corner cupboard for the Philip's wireless, and realigned the copper stand. He put on his old boots and dug over the garden beds. 'There's not much goodness it. The soil has had it. What it needs is a good dose of manure and sea-weed. That would put a bit of spark into it', he said. But with Townsville's critical water-shortage, how could a garden ever be possible?

Dad also decided the bougainvillea bush was overgrown and needed cutting back. I was glad that I had crawled in while the going was good and collected all the delicate pieces of broken china. I had put them in the Mickey Mouse toffee-tin from the last proper Christmas and found a secret place under a rock on the top terrace to hide them. I didn't tell Mum about this. I realized she would be hurt to think I could take pleasure from reminders of her loss. Now, Dad got in with the saw and gave the bougainvillea a good hair-cut. He stacked all the trimmings in an open space, patted his pockets for his matches, touched a light to the pile and stood back to make himself a well-earned smoke.

Upstairs, Barry was putting the one last round of finishing touches to his model Lancaster. Inserting the elastic band had been the trickiest bit. It had been dodgy to hook in. After all, the surrounding fabric was only tissue paper. There had been many 'Tchhhs!' of frustration, and a few swear words, carefully under his breath, before finally it was latched into position. The last identification-number transfers had been soaked in a saucer and slid into place, RAAF roundels positioned. Finished! At long last! He gave it a couple of experimental casts, lovingly, the length of the verandah to test for balance. It glided smoothly and landed with convincing realism on the floral couch. Yes! She was ready for a proper test flight! He decided that one flight would be enough. Just to prove he had done it. That was all. He would have made something that could fly. After that, he might just hang it from the ceiling in his room and lie in bed and look at it. He had put too much work into it to take any chances. 'Come and look at this, Mum! Mum came hurrying from the kitchen. 'Where's Dad? Dad! Hey! Dad! Get a load of this!' The propeller was wound. The elastic tautened. The air-frame quivered with desire to be gone. He called, conning tower to ground crew, 'Dad! Are you looking?'

Enjoying his quiet cigarette in the back yard, Dad looked up expectantly. He called, 'Yes, Son! Let her rip! I'm all eyes!' The flames of the rubbish heap were just beginning to lick upwards. Within a few moments they were leaping through the dry kindling and curling higher. Dad took a few paces back from the heat and shaded his eyes to watch the Lancaster's inaugural flight.

Well, who would believe such a moment! The Lancaster, fruit of so many months hard work, had all North Ward across which to fly. From our verandah it had the perfect take-off point. It could glide towards the shining curve of the bay. It could find an up-draught and soar to the heights of Castle Hill. Its destiny was of its own choosing! Faces bright with expectation, its youthful maker and proud family watching, the model launched itself over the neighbouring houses as though bent on some great mission. It cleared Bliss's mango tree, travelling well. It banked around Saunder's wireless aerial smoothly as a dove. Shading our eyes, we followed the graceful curve of its flight. Curve? Curve! Alarums and consternations! It was coming back! It was homeward bound! For our place! For our yard, wherein, as though a purpose-built beacon of weighty significance, smoked Dad's bonfire! Cripes!' yelled Barry, rushing for the back door.

'Oh! No!' cried Mum, clutching her hands to her breast. I nearly fell over the verandah rail in agitation.

Dad was pretty athletic; he had boxed for his regiment when young. Wielding the garden rake like a tennis champion he rushed towards the oncoming Lancaster, batting at the air.

It was a noble effort! But to no avail! The Lancaster was not to be deflected. It had determined its course. Nothing could alter its flight-plan. It was drawn to the smoke and leaping flames as a moth to a lamp.

All that could be said was that the end was mercifully quick. One moment the model was a thing of beauty, lovely in grace and comeliness. The next, a flowering of incandescence. The bit that had been the elastic for Mum's pyjamas spiralled slowly downwards, last of all, with a whiff of burnt rubber. No-one spoke. Aghast, we stared at Barry. He, without a word went leaping down the stone steps two at a time. Grabbing his bike he jumped on and went tearing down the hill, legs going like pistons.

That night, Mum went in and sat on his bed. She told him, that when the fund-raising Lancaster arrived in Townsville, he could be the one from our family to have the privilege of the inspection tour which her ten-pound Fourth Liberty Loan Bond conferred. He was comforted. When the Lancaster arrived we all went out to the aerodrome to watch him go aboard. But the crew didn't care who had Bonds and who hadn't. The queue stretched far back across the tarmac. Mum and I were also allowed to join the queue and see through it as well. While we waited, we marvelled at the tiny Spitfire which had been positioned for contrast under one of the giant bomber's wings. Mum pressed her handkerchief to her lips in awe at being so close to the Spitfire. The Spitfire was the heroic little fighter that had saved England in the Battle of Britain.

And when Barry at last emerged from the maze of metal, dials, instrument panels and webbing that were the insides of the giant Lancaster, he swung himself down the narrow ladder and landed on the tarmac as though that was the moment he had been waiting for all his life. On his face was the abstractedly soft look of a young man newly in love.

The Grammar School at Rosslea was temptingly close to the many air-fields on the western side of Townsville. There were times when Barry felt called upon to inspect the latest developments that were taking place at these, rather than be present for rehearsals of *The Merchant of Venice* which his English class was preparing for a performance at the Theatre Royal. And how could the battle strategies of Oliver Cromwell hope to compete with the return from a raid on Lae of a flight of Lightnings, the amazing P-38s? Or the pale flame of a bunsen-burner in the school laboratory with a ground-crew's cutting away sections of under-carts savaged by Japanese shrapnel?

Barry told me nothing of this. I would have been more than ordinarily interested, for I was in a modest way experimenting with the freedom of playing the wag myself. My wagging was from Music Theory lessons. These were held at Mr. Kennedy's place in the corner of Rowe's Bay where his corrugated-iron house crouched in the shade of crowding mango-trees. Theory Lessons! What a wearying business! What a dreary waste of time! All Saturday morning gone and what for? Did it matter that two quavers made a crotchet, or what would be the result if you raised d-natural by one semi-tone? All the other children seemed to think so. They sat at little tables in the deep coolness of the mangoes, heads bent industriously over theory books in puzzlements of harmony and composition. It was the mathematics that did for me. Was a composition in three-four or five-eight time? How many demi-semis of this equalled a bar-rest of that?

Across the road was the shining curve of Rowe's Bay, a mirror-bright glitter to the eyes. To the north there were islands, fading, one behind the other, to an infinity of blue distance; Great Palm, Orpheus, Phantome and on clear days the massive heights of Hinchinbrook. Closer at hand was a small creek nosing its way into the bay through the heavy silence of mangrove swamps. Moored in the creek was a rowing-boat, a flattie, probably owned by one of the old chaps who had corrugated-iron humpies amongst the ti-trees where the swamp turned to sand-dunes. This flattie just happened to be tied to the bank by the merest bit of stringy rope. It even had oars shoved under the seat. What could be more natural than to give theory lessons the heave-ho, to have a little borrow of the flattie and to drift with the tide, rallentando, untroubled by dotted minims or inverted quavers, until the morning should be fled, the flattie returned to its mooring, and I to trudge home through the quiet of Saturday noon, wearied as though from mental exertion?

It was not long before I was joined by one or two other deserters. Together we grew familiar with water-logged mud as we poled along the creek, with mangroves walking on stilt-legs or thrusting up peg-like fingers through the sand. We studied fiddler crabs that scuttled down burrows at our approach but which would come out again and start to feed if we were quiet. They seemed not to be alarmed by voices, only movement. The most obvious ones were purple with white-tipped claws and with eye-stalks sticking up from the front of their shells. They fed by sifting through the mud near their burrows, leaving behind pellets like tiny mud-pies. If we waited quietly enough, they would rise on their front end and go in for queer and frequent beckonings, as though semaphoring to a mate. These would be seen just after the tide had retreated and the mudflats were newly exposed.

In the trees along the bank tiny animals lived in safety above the smothering mud, miniature snails and barnacles. The barnacles clung to leaves hanging out over the water, a risky business because their time was up when the leaf dropped. The trees were alive with small insect-eating birds from the Common which darted in and out among the bright dappled stillness. And, hung from branch to branch, were the large round webs of orb spiders, a trap for unwary flat-bottom boat adventurers. If, from time to time, with a thunderous roar, a flight of Marauders limped in from the north, or a Catalina landed droning on the bay, we would glance up, but only momentarily. Aeroplanes were just the war. The war was what grown-ups did. It was nothing to do with us.

One afternoon at home, Barry beckoned to me from the mulberry tree. I crawled into the speckled shade and drew myself on to the branch beside him. He regarded me solemnly. 'So! Young Skin! What have you been up to?' I considered. I had climbed on the roof after the tennis ball and the guttering had come away from its mountings. But nobody knew about that. I had given a piece of my violin resin to Cyril Lovelady at school because he was always getting the cane. But nobody knew about that either. I felt innocent and looked at him doe-eyed. 'Don't come the Old Soldier with me!' snorted Barry, using one of Dad's pet sayings. 'I happen to know things! You're gone a million! I know, for instance, that you've been going ack-willy from Theory lessons! And Old Kennedy is on to you!'

True horror must have registered on my face. I knew ack-willy was what soldiers said instead of 'Away without leave'; in military terms a crime. Another word for it was 'Awol'. It was a court-martial offence. Some fellow-feeling must have begun to work on Barry at that point. He brought out a letter hidden inside his shirt. 'This is from Old Kennedy. It's to Mum. He says you haven't been at Theory for a month of Sundays, and wants to know why.'

Shocked and frightened I was about to make a clean breast of it, working myself up to the necessary tears in a bid for mercy, when Barry added, 'Don't get your tail in a twist! I'm in strife up to my ears, too.' It seemed that Mr. Whight at Grammar had matted him for going 'Awol' from school. The Headmaster had given him a good dressing-down, finishing by saying that a letter had been sent home to his parents. So Barry had been lying in wait for the postman each day, bent on making a tactical interception. 'I'm playing for time, see!' he told me. It won't be that long before the Old Man gets posted back to Geelong or somewhere. I just want to stall till he's gone.' He laughed. 'So when this formal-looking letter showed up I thought it was from Old Whightie! I grabbed it to get a geek at what he he'd said. Nothing like having your ammo ready. Like Dad says, 'The best means of defence is to attack!' I'm gonna say I don't give a pig's about stupid old Shylock and that lot. I'm only a courtier in it, anyhow; and I don't go for wigs and all that! It just makes more sense to be getting boned up on air-force stuff. I'm dead serious about joining-up. It's only three more years now. I'll bring in about defending the Empire and all that stuff. Mum will swallow that. But Dad mightn't. Him and his bloody army! Foot-slogging round in the bush in big boots! Blow that for a lark! The RAAF is the thing!'

Heads together, we shared a nervous laugh. It would definitely be better if these matters could be held off until Dad was out of the way again. It was like the old times when Barry had pulled me out of the dam at Stainburn and not told, or when we had gone Guy Foxing with my violin; 'Us' against 'them'. Parents were OK and you had to have them, but it paid to be on your guard a bit. After all, they were grown-ups.

The week-end before Dad left for Geelong we went to the Wintergarden to see *Fantasia*, for children were now allowed in to pictures-theatres as long as they were accompanied by an adult. It was the first time I had been since before the invasion scare. Part of the programme was Community Singing, during which the words came on the screen and a ping-pong ball bounced along so that everyone would keep in time. The most popular song of all was *When the Lights Go On Again, All Over the World.* The soldiers in the audience really let rip with that one. People were beginning to feel that there might be an end to the war some day, after all. The King in his last message had talked about 'the dark clouds beginning to lift'. In Flinders Street the shop lights were on and advertising signs flashed on and off. Even the street names and the name on the railway-station were back.

After the pictures, as we waited for the North Ward bus we stared curiously at Funland, an amusement parlour, which had been built where Pennys had burned down in March. There were American soldiers clustered round outside it, but not many Australians. Diggers did not have the same money to flash around. The doorway was outlined in electric lights that rippled on and off as though being spilled from a container. The name Funland in red, white and blue with stars and stripes around it, was lit up over the building. Dad looked at the Americans and said without envy, 'Flash beggars! More money than sense!'

On the Sunday night we pulled our chairs around the wireless to listen to a special programme broadcast direct from the BBC in London, Calling Townsville. It was to be made up of messages from boys in the RAAF and other services stationed in England, to their parents or wives and sweethearts in Townsville. Everybody would be tuned in. Mum was flushed with pride when the broadcast began with the chimes of Big Ben and the announcer's voice saying, 'This is the British Broadcasting Commission calling Townsville, Australia.' Mum might have been sitting in her usual chair with Kelly on her lap and crochet in her hands, but in spirit she almost disappeared clean through the silk front of the wireless. Dad reached over and put his hand on hers. 'All right, Old Girl?' he said. We all hoped the English relatives would be listening. Perhaps even Cousin Graham on his ship in mid-Atlantic? It made us feel linked to all those other far-off members of the family.

The men who came on the air to speak didn't make much of a fist of it. It was as though they were so excited that when the time came words deserted them. Most of the messages ended up being almost exactly the same. 'Hello, Mum. Hello, Dad. Hope you're all doing O.K. I'm doing O.K. They're looking after us real good over here.' When their time was nearly up they would get a rush on, as though they suddenly remembered all the things that they had wanted to say in the first place.

We had a moment of stunned silence when the announcer said, 'And our next call goes out to Mrs. Joyce Benson, and is from her husband Sergeant-Pilot Ray Benson,' and Joycie's husband came on, sounding self-assured and affectionate. His message finished 'And give my love to little Rayleen and tell her that her Daddy will be home soon, and will give her lots of big hugs and a kisses.' Almost immediately afterwards Mum said it was about time for our beds, and Dad said that, Yes, he had to make an early start in the morning. As we went through to our rooms I heard Dad say, 'The poor blighter! You mean she hasn't broken it to him yet?'

I did not mind so very much when Dad left for Geelong. Even the colored post-card of the Geelong floral clock left me unmoved. For at North Ward Sunday School we had an American soldier teaching us; Rex Tutt, from California. I and all the other little girls were almost in love with him. Well, there weren't all that many other little girls. For some reason the Sunday School seemed to be composed mainly of boys, four of them Acklands. I had given up going to North Ward Presbyterian after an unfortunate incident at the Anniversary Concert there. Audrey and I had sung *Jesus Bids Us Shine*, each of us holding a lighted candle. During the performance my candle kept going out, no matter how many times the Superintendent creaked on tiptoes across to the stage to relight it. One of these extinguishings coincided with the line, 'Well He sees and knows it, if our light grows dim'. Someone in the audience sniggered. I was sure of it! I left North Ward Presbyterian, never to return.

But Rex Tutt had everyone at North Ward Methodist in thrall. It was not so much that he was good-looking, because he wasn't, not really. He had round shiny spectacles, thinish sandy hair and a tendency to tub. But he shone! He was the shiniest person I had ever known. When he talked about loving one another because Jesus loved each one of us and if we asked him into our hearts then we would be able to love everybody, even our enemies, I could feel my heart swell. If Rex Tutt said so, then I would! I would be loving enough to burst. I would love everybody in the whole wide world!

Miss Edgar was still the Superintendent but Rex Tutt was the star. Each Sunday Miss Edgar laboured out all the way from Central Methodist like a 1943 Saint Paul. She supervised while we got busy and lined up all the little folding chairs into rows beneath Lowes' house, where the Sunday School was held. Then, while we waited for the wonderful moment when Rex Tutt would arrive, she pumped the pedals of the harmonium while we sang, *When He Cometh*; *Jesus Wants Me for a Sunbeam* and *Shall We Gather at the River*. I was always sure the river to be gathered at was Black River with its wide sandy bottom and big paper-bark trees.

One day Rex arrived with a bundle of small black-bound books and placed them on the white tablecloth of the table at the front. He preached more inspiringly than ever, saying things that made us gladden with pleasure: what wonderful boys and girls we were to know and that he prayed we would all grow up to be fine men and women who loved the Lord; how special his time with us had been to him; it had made the fighting in the war worth while just to have known us; then, Bomb-shell! He told us that he had been posted to New Guinea and would not see us again. The small black books were those issued to American servicemen; *Guide to Christian Living*. There was one for each of us, our names inscribed on the fly-leaf. The words 'who served his country in....' had been crossed out. Each was signed 'from Rex Tutt, California'. We were stunned with grief.

For days, whenever an American transport plane flew over our house heading towards New Guinea, I rushed out on to the verandah to devour it with my eyes, shading my face until it disappeared as a dancing speck into the north, loving all the men on board as Rex had told us in case he was one of them. That year the evening star Venus was very brilliant because it was on an exceptionally close orbit to the earth. We heard that at sea, survivors from torpedoed ships adrift in lifeboats and rafts often mistook it for the lights of a search-plane. For some time after Rex Tutt had gone to New Guinea I would lean on the verandah railing at night, drawing comfort from the thought that at that very moment he too might be looking at the brilliance of Venus in the night sky and thinking of the children he had cared about in Townsville.

Barry got to see a lot of the early morning sky. It had become almost impossible to get ice for the kitchen ice-box. Often the ice-works had run out of supplies by seven o'clock in the morning. Barry had to get up earlier and earlier to get a good place in the long queue. Even then, the supply did not meet the demand. He would set off at five, take his place in the queue, spread his sugar-bag on the pavement and like most of the other waiting customers, doze off to sleep again. It didn't make it any easier that, having waited so long, the civilians would often find that the military pushed in ahead of them and commandeered all the supply. Once, having waited two-and-a half hours, he still came home empty handed. 'I was only three from the head of the queue when this big Yank tore up in a Jeep and said he would take all the rest' he said wearily. After the ride to the ice-works and the long early-morning wait, Barry then had to get ready and ride out to Rosslea to the Grammar School.

Without the supply of ice, the food rations of meat and butter and milk went off quickly in the heat. The inside of the ice-box smelt dank and nasty. Then Vardy's Ice-works announced that it would serve civilians and military on alternate days. A regulation was also passed that the military would have to take their turn and not push in ahead of civilians in the queue. Still there were problems. Sometimes the ice-queues stretched for two blocks back along the street. One lady used to arrive at half past two in the morning to make sure of a good place in the queue. People were desperate. Finally the Town Council said that they would establish a Municipal ice-works. It was also announced that the American forces were going to import refrigeration equipment and make their own ice.

It was about this time that my career as a violinist came to an unexpected end. Mr. Kennedy had re-scheduled my lesson to half-past seven at night. After the lesson I had to walk down from the old QATB Building in Sturt Street to Flinders Street and catch a North Ward bus home. One evening I arrived at the bus-stop just in time to see the tail end of my bus trundling off. Violin case banging against my knees I tore after it in desperation only to see it gather speed and disappear amidst the Jeeps, blitzwagons and army-trucks jamming Flinders Street. I was in despair. Is there anything worse than being alone and far from home on a city street at night?

Townsvillites queue for their block of ice.

The street was crowded with servicemen. A two-up game was in progress, the roars from the men's throats like Romans watching Christians being eaten by lions. Some American sailors had climbed on to one of the pill-box air-raid shelters and were harmonismg, *Don't Sit Under the Apple Tree*. When they finished they tossed their beer bottles into the empty flower-beds, with the sound of splintering glass. An Aussie voice yelled, 'Go home! Bloody Yanks!' Fighting back tears, I longed to be snugly in bed with *Treasure Island*. When would another bus come along? Supposing there wasn't one!

Then, seeing the brilliantly lit entrance to Funland I brightened. Maybe it would make the time pass more quickly if I crossed over and looked in. I knew Dad had said never to go where there were servicemen, but this was different. There were servicemen everywhere. Servicemen on both sides of the street. There couldn't be any harm! Dodging a couple of Jeeps and a canvas-hooded truck I crossed the road and planted myself in the middle of the footpath outside Funland. Violin case in hand, I peered in. I saw garish lights and games. I heard the juke-box music and the shouts of laughter. So totally absorbed was I in the spectacle of flashing lights, glitter, male laughter and streams of coins pouring from machines that I did not see the American soldier staggering along the footpath towards me. All I knew was that, suddenly, without warning, a man's arms had been thrown around me, there was a puff of alcohol in my face, and that I was in the grip of strong, muscular arms. I froze with horror.

In an instant an Australian soldier appeared from nowhere. Throwing himself upon the American, he plucked him off me, held him the full length of his arm, drew back his fist and, snarling, 'Garn! Yer bloody mongrel! Leave the kid alone! Keep your dirty Yank mits to yer-bloody-self!' punched him full in the face. With a dropped-watermelon sound the American's mouth flowered red with blood. He sprawled backwards across the footpath into the door of the fun-parlour, just as a group of laughing Americans were coming out. They were just in time to take in what had happened and to get some of the blood spurted on to their silvery, well-ironed trousers. There was a barrage-exchange of curses; 'Australian scum!' 'Yankee bastards!' Other Australians came running, steel-capped boots pounding. Americans still inside Funland came pouring out on to the footpath. There were shouts and yells. Fortissimo! Crescendo! Every serviceman in Flinders Street, Australian and American, began to converge on the spot. Within moments there was a free-for-all that extended the length of the block and was growing by the moment.

Clutching my violin case to me like a mother her only child, I fled across Flinders Street. I was all but skittled by a military police van, honking furiously to get through the traffic. The two-up game, thinking the MPs were after them, broke up in disarray. Soldiers yelling, 'Provos!' pelted in all directions, ducking under the rails the City Council had put to stop people straggling across Flinders Street, vaulting over the bonnets of jeeps and staff-cars. An Aussie soldier barged into me, spun me round and set me back on my feet, and pounded off after a mate. Whistles shrilled. The brawl spilled, boiling like porridge from a pot, off the footpaths and across the road. The length of Flinders Street had become a heaving turbulence of thumping, punching, kicking, swearing, sweating, grunting, bloodied mass of Our Brave Servicemen and their equally bloodied Brave and Noble Allies.

Far down Flinders Street I glimpsed the sight of the North Ward bus lumbering, turtle-like, through the melee. The Second Coming could not have been more welcome. I climbed on board shaking with fright. Of course I dared not tell Mum what had happened. She would have gone over and over the number of times she had told me never to go where there were troops. Hadn't she told me? Expressly! Hadn't she? I dared not even tell Barry. Somehow I knew without being told that the awful street fight had been All My Fault.

'Mum,' I said a few days later, when I had got over the initial shock and had decided what had to be done, 'I don't want to learn the violin any more.' Mum was terribly cast down. She put down the knife she was cutting up the pumpkin with and dried her hands on her apron. 'But, why ever not? You have such nice hands for the violin! And Mr. Kennedy says you are coming along quite nicely, really!' I knew that myself. I was just beginning to enjoy it. There were moments as I drew the bow across the strings when my heart rejoiced at the tremulous sweetness so mysteriously produced. But now I shrugged. 'I just don't want to learn any more,' was all I could think to say. Then, on a sudden inspiration, to make it easier for her, I said, looking earnestly into her face, 'I want you to save the money for the War Effort and, and, and most of all, I want to concentrate on my school-work. I want to be top of the class.'

So the violin was taken to school and sold to Mrs. Cullanane, the Grade Two teacher, for her son. I felt a twist of jealousy at the thought of him handling the instrument that had been mine. Mrs. Cullinane gave me the four-pounds and ten shillings and Miss Thomas minded it for me in her desk until Last Bell, because it was such a large amount of money. I felt genuine pain that I would never see the honey-voiced violin again.

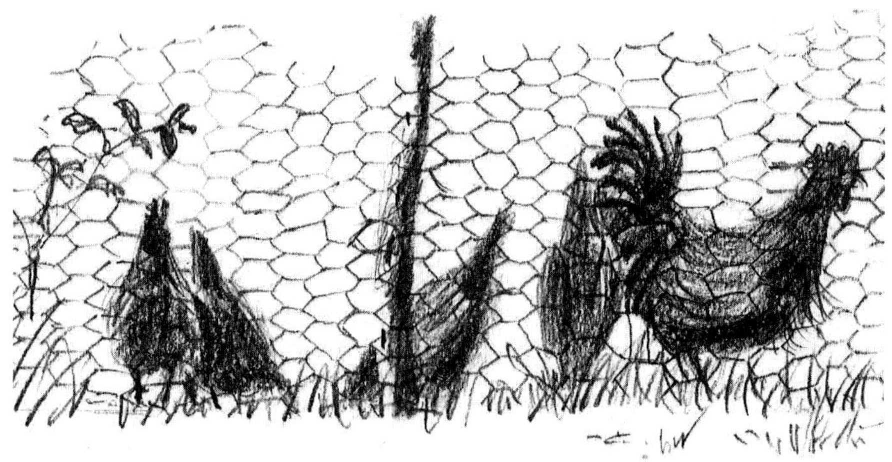

Chapter 15

SUMMER OF '43

'Give Me One Dozen Roses. Put my heart in beside them,
And send them to the one I love.'

Townsville, as the major Allied Base for the South Pacific, became a sea of military camps.

The heat of the summer of 1943 approached. Water was desperately short. Vegetables and fruit were things of the past. People who had struggled to grow a bed of lettuces or a trellis of beans had to keep a sharp eye on them or they would develop legs and walk during the night.

But the Bensleys had roses. The song *Give Me One Dozen Roses* was on everyone's lips and Mr. Bensley had spotted a business opportunity. If the Americans wanted roses, roses they would have. For a price! The front and back yard of Bensley's place were given over entirely to growing rose bushes, battalions of them. The ventilator of their air-raid shelter stuck up like an ack-ack emplacement from squads of roses. Mum had private thoughts on how the ranks of bushes were kept watered, suspecting Mr. Bensley of midnight skullduggery in the matter.

There was every reason for ant-like industry in the production of roses. Hardly would the blooms have opened their velvety faces to the heat of Walker Street than they were snapped up by eager purchasers with Texan, Atlantic City or Philadelphian accents, charming manners and ties deftly tucked into silver-khaki shirtfronts. Rolls of bank-notes would be produced and notes of large denomination peeled off and flicked carelessly in Mr. Bensley's direction. The rose-bushes were magic money-trees, quietly and efficiently producing gold, like gnomes in fairy stories.

Then, alarums and consternation! Morning after morning, numbers of the velvety beauties were missing. Someone was hopping the fence and helping themselves to roses during the night. Mr. Bensley was sure it was the Sydney-side element among the Australian troops. 'Two-bob Sydney lairs!' he would explode. 'Big-timing themselves with the sheilas at my expense!' When roused, Mr. Bensley had a habit of chomping on a piece of grass; when very roused, of running his fingers rapidly through his hair, as though 'tearing his hair' like the man in the Bible. After the first rose-napping he chewed on a stalk of grass. After the second he tore his hair. After the third he said he was getting a watch-dog.

The next time I went to Margaretta's to play, there I was, tripping along from the bus-stop, pertly conscious of my new floral dress and matching bloomers and thinking how nice it was going to be to meet the new dog. I let myself in expectantly through the front gate. As it clicked behind me I had just time to see, coming towards me at a very great speed, travelling low and very close to the ground, something blue-grey and snarly. The next moment a blue heeler hit me in the middle of the chest and I was bowled head over heels, the dog still attached, slathering terribly, into the nearest rose-bed.

Brand-new dress and matching bloomers were but minor impediments to the dog's progress into my thigh. My screams of genuine terror brought the Bensleys running. Mr. Bensley lacked assurance as to how to handle savage blue heelers. He thought to turn on the hose as a means of rescue. In fact this was very effective. The blue heeler is a scruffy breed not overly given to bathing. It unfastened its grip upon my thigh and made off behind the potting sheds at a very great rate, a sliver of floral bloomers like a battle pennant in its jaws.

I was helped, sobbing and hiccoughing, inside the house, petted, fussed over and patched up. It was consoling to see how much sticking-plaster the Bensleys were prepared to invest in my recovery. In such matters Mum was over-frugal. And there is something about scarlet mercurochrome, liberally applied, that does the heart of the sufferer much good. As to the matter of the torn dress and ripped bloomers, which were now my main concern, I was to think nothing of it.

Margaretta had such things by the cupboardful! I could have some of hers. To myself, I thought that is all very well but you don't know Mum! She has just finished making them!

When Mr. Bensley drove me home my heart was in my boots, expecting sparks to fly. I could not begin to imagine what Mum would say about the ruination of not only a new dress but bloomers to match. The crisp brand-new one of Margaretta's that I was now wearing seemed to signal 'Here's a to-do!' I limped up the terrace path towards the front verandah a little more painfully and stiffly than was strictly necessary, grateful that in Mr. Bensley's presence I would be spared the worst of the wrath to come.

Mr. Bensley said he would like to speak with Mum privately, so Margaretta and I slid into the mulberry tree and strained our ears. We heard Mr. Bensley's apology for the necessity of the watch-dog, in terms of the packet that the Sydney riff-raff were costing him. He explained he had got the dog off old Alfie Gurnie across the road in Walker street who had been going to throw it in the creek with a stone around its neck. Alfie's missus was taking in washing for the Americans now and didn't want the customers being put off by a cantankerous blue heeler. The Gurnie's dog ! The one that had bitten me when we lived in Walker Street! There had seemed something familiar about its bullet head! Somehow it felt better to have been savaged by a familiar dog rather than an unknown one.

Margaretta was smiling smugly and secretively. She knew what was afoot and was not letting on, enjoying immensely the drama of the revelation about to come. The Bensleys were going to Melbourne after Christmas; they wanted to take me with them as company for Margaretta. Odd words drifted across to our lurking place; 'hotel', 'museum', 'theatre'. The trip to Melbourne would be the Bensleys' way of making up for the dog's attack. At this point Margaretta and I broke from our cover and ran, unaccustomedly hand in hand, as little girls in 'Heidi' might, to join the grown-ups.

'But what about the Border-hopping restrictions?' Mum was saying. Townsville was a war zone. Civilians were not allowed to travel unless they had priority rating. It had to be for something important such as a funeral or a wedding or a family emergency. Even then, a permit did not always come through in time. Mr. Bensley scoffed. 'There are ways and there are ways!' was all he said, patting first the side of his nose and then his hip pocket.

And so it was decided; I could go to Melbourne. After the Bensleys had departed, leaving Mum and me feeling rather stunned, I said tentatively that I had been told to keep Margarettas's dress but I knew it didn't make up for the lovely one that she had made. And the bloomers. I even tried putting my little hand touchingly into hers. Mum said, 'Put your head forward!' She studied the label inside the dress and said with satisfaction, 'This one is worth a dozen times as much. Don't worry. We have got the best of the bargain.'

'I wouldn't mind letting a blue heeler have a go at me, if there was a trip to Melbourne in it!' said Barry that night; said jokingly, but I could tell he was jealous. Melbourne was 'down south', where recruiting was done. Barry was longing to be on his way.

As the end of the year drew near, Mr. Curtin again asked the Australian people to have an Austerity Christmas. There were to be no Christmas advertisements and giving presents was discouraged. The manufacture of toys was still banned but women used precious coupons to buy felt for making toys. Mum made kangaroos and rabbits for the Red Cross stall, cutting up old singlets and stockings for stuffing. I hung over her as she stitched up the final gaps, hoping to come into possession of one of these nice little animal-people for my school on the verandah. Mum said with some asperity that little girls being taken on marvellous trips to Melbourne could hardly expect any other gifts for Christmas. I resigned myself to socks and handkerchiefs. In a flash of insight it dawned on me that Mum was also jealous.

The following Saturday morning, the stuffed toys were taken in to the Red Cross stall on McKimmins' corner. The tables were already piled high with Raggedy-Anns, golliwogs, and felt animals. There were wooden trucks and rifles and tanks and ships that obliging husbands had made as their contribution. There was a red fire engine with mounted ladders, and clowns on sticks and painted cockatoos that could loop the loop over their perches. While Mum and the ladies were getting everything in order and preparing the small change in their biscuit tins, a crowd of customers pressed forward, waiting for the signal. The moment the stall was declared open they descended in a rush. Raggy-dolls, ships, painted clowns and bunny-rabbits were snatched up with 'But I saw it first!'s and 'Don't give me that! I'm having it!'s. Within minutes the stall had completely sold out and the tables were down to the bare white sheets with which they had been covered. It seemed that people thought that this business of Austerity Christmases was all right as far as it went, but doing little children out of toys for their Christmas morning was pushing it a bit too far.

Just before Christmas it was announced that the American Army had installed a refrigeration plant capable of making six tons of ice per day. Six tons! All that extra would be available to the people of Townsville! Ice-depots were to be established in each suburb so that people would no longer have to form long pre-dawn queues outside the ice-works. The depot for North Ward would be at Coates's Store. Each family could register their name at a depot and be entitled to four blocks of ice per week. Any family caught registering at more than one depot would be removed from the register altogether. So instead of the long ride to the ice-works in town, Barry would get an extra hour's sleep-in every morning. On Christmas Eve one block of ice per family would be available between 6am and 8am and again on Christmas Morning. People were told not to plant extra family members in the queues as this would be doing other families out of their share.

Then there was an announcement that a quota of soft-drinks would be available at the soft drink factories; twelve bottles per family. Excitedly we sat at the kitchen table to list which flavours we would have. Barry wanted Horehound. I wrinkled my nose. Cherry Cheer! Mum preferred Creaming Soda. Barry was allowed three bottles as his choice, as he would have to ride to Cobb's Cordial Works to collect it. Each person had to arrive at the factory with empties already cleaned. Bottles were scarce because the troops made a habit of pelting them out of trucks so that Townsville had become a sea of broken glass.

Barry came back from Cobbs' Factory with the dozen bottles in a sugar-bag balanced on the handle-bars of his bike. Eagerly Mum and I helped him unload. It was a long time since we had had anything so pleasurable to do. Mum had filled the smaller of the two corrugated-iron wash-tubs with Reckitt's blue-water as the best way to keep drinks cool. The bottles, hot from the sun, were plunged in and then covered with wet bags for evaporation to bring the temperature down. All the labels soaked off and it became a lucky-dip. They were all so cool and refreshing it didn't matter. 'What a treat!' sighed Mum. 'But clean your teeth afterwards! All that sugar!'

At the factory Barry had spotted several pairs of brothers in the queue, pretending they had never seen one another in their lives before. They were after an extra whack. Some like the wily Frizwells had got away with it. Others had been spotted and sent packing, with 'Hop it! And if you try it on again you'll cop a flea in the ear!'

No one could blame them for trying. There was very little else that was to be had in Townsville that Christmas; no fruit, no vegetables; in some areas not even bread, as the bakeries ran out of flour. The Town Council announced that it would have a stall selling cabbages outside the Town Hall on Christmas Eve, but it was sold out within half an hour. There was also very little water, though everyone was pinning their hopes on better things to come with the announcement that the wall of the new weir was almost complete and would be capable of storing water in the coming rainy season.

Knowing the adults were resolved on another Austerity Christmas, Audrey and I consoled ourselves by playing Christmas. We made decorations for the cubby-house, twisting strips of orange crepe-paper between our thumbs and fingers or folding them in criss-cross patterns. We cut paper stars that were never quite the right shape, and coloured them with crayons. Mrs. Saunders had a little hoop pine growing in a pot which became our Christmas Tree. It was so heavily decorated that it became an orange-coloured cone. Nobody told us that the proper Christmas colours were red and green. We gave one another almost identical gifts of pink soap wrapped in pink face washers.

But what could I give Mum? It had to be something special. I decided I would make her a peg-bag. I could cut it from the bottom half of a sugar-bag, and decorate it with a wash-day scene; a clothes-peg-lady hanging tiny little clothes on a washing-line. Fortunately Audrey was handy with a sewing needle and could bite off threads in a most grown-up manner. Frowning with concentration, she did most of the spade-work on the bag while I got on with dressing the clothes-peg doll and cutting out miniature garments to go on the line. When it was finished I felt it a most satisfying present. On Christmas morning I carried the over-decorated Christmas tree into Mum's room and gave her the present. I had hoped for surprise and delight and I was puzzled and a bit hurt. I thought she would love the peg bag and exclaim over it with wonder. I could not understand her reaction, which was strange. I didn't know if I was imagining it or not but it almost seemed that for some reason or other she felt a little bit ashamed.

Mum made up for any disappointment I might have felt about Christmas by flying into preparation of my wardrobe for the trip to Melbourne. As clothing coupons had to last until June, two frocks were made from two of her own by cutting them down and adding lacy Peter Pan collars and cuffs. She also made me a long, floral housecoat and pyjamas. Mr. Bensley had told Mum I would have to travel under the name 'Bensley' so as not to arouse suspicion if our travel permits were checked. A cardboard label saying 'Marion Bensley' was cut out and attached to the handle of the little brown port I would have to carry myself when we crossed into New South Wales. This secret crossing of state boundaries was called 'Border Hopping'. There had been quite a lot about it in the newspapers, saying that 'trafficking' in Travel Permits was becoming a 'racket'. Mum said it was just that Australians never took rules and regulations seriously.

When in my journeyings with the Bensleys we eventually got to the New South Wales border late one night, we had to crunch along the cinders beside the railway track in the dark, each carrying our own things in strict silence. It should have been exciting and adventurous, but was done quite matter of factly. After tramping along in the dark with night sounds all about, we came to the edge of a road at the side of which we had to wait. Mr. Bensley disappeared into the night.

Crickets chirruped and a mopoke called, 'More pork! More pork!'. We were tired and gritty feeling. After a while a car approached, showing no headlights. We piled in and were whisked across the border to the New South Wales town of Tenterfield. I felt it was a very significant moment of my life to be in a different State but in the morning when I looked out from the hotel verandah it was exactly like Queensland. Even crossing the Murray River at Wodonga, Australia still looked like Australia. And at last we arrived in Melbourne.

Mum had imagined my journey to Melbourne would be the cultural experience of my lifetime but the Bensleys were not cultural people. We did not go to Art Galleries, and the only theatres we went to were the moving picture type. These were almost a cultural experience, with an organist who ascended grandly from some unknown depths, playing a great Wurlitzer organ for the audience's entertainment during interval. The decor of theatre was almost an entertainment itself, with dawn and sunset effects before and after interval and a ceiling spangled with stars and constellations. It was almost as good as the open-air Olympia in Townsville had been before it was shut down during the Invasion scare.

We did go to one museum just to see Phar Lap, the most famous of all Australian racehorses, who had been poisoned by gangsters while racing in America. He stood, proud and magnificent in his glass case, one foot slightly forward as though stepping out on a last victorious race, scarcely looking stuffed at all. His glass eyes seemed to shine with kindly intelligence and reminded me of Felix at Stainburn.

The rest of the time we went to places like Luna Park. Margaretta and I also spent a good deal of time riding up and down in the lift cages of the Victoria Palace Hotel, clanking the sliding grill-doors open and shut for other passengers, many of them high-ranking American officers or country people down from western properties. Once I said to Margaretta, 'Remember that episode of The Dead End Kids when they were stuck in the lift-shaft?', but she had forgotten. Each time the lift descended I hoped that no-one was trapped at the bottom.

The thing that impressed me most about Melbourne was the number of Darrell Lee chocolate shops, their windows filled with chocolates as though Mr. Curtin had never mentioned Austerity. Just before Christmas in Townsville there had been an allowance of chocolate but only for children not adults. It had seemed an incredible luxury and yet here in Melbourne there were shop-windows with chocolates piled in profusion, spilling over from containers and displayed in every kind of decorated box. I spent a long time choosing the very small box that I could afford as a take-home present for Mum.

On the day we were to return to Townsville I was so nervously excited that I was sick on the carpet of the hotel lounge. We were flying home and part of the journey would be by Sunderland Flying Boat. Perhaps some distant memory of the Catalina disaster triggered off the moment of mortification. Mr. Bensley looked aggrieved. I felt that, more than the inconvenience to the hotel staff, his concern was lest we should have been made to look like country bumpkins because we came from Townsville.

The Sunderland from Sydney to Townsville was luxurious, with arm-chair seats and cabin stewards formally dressed. Landing at Townsville, seemingly so smooth and effortless when watched on Sunday afternoons from the beach at Anzac park, was in reality, noisy and alarming. We might have been landing on the rocks of the breakwater. There was a series of sharp, heavy smacks and an unnerving sound like the loud ripping of fabric. Once we were on the water the aircraft settled quietly, like a nice old dog lying down. We motored towards a launch into which we scrambled to be taken up Ross Creek.

I felt incredibly shy at seeing Mum and Barry again. Mum kept saying, 'Well! Tell us all about it!' in a way that made me completely tongue-tied. Barry, I could feel, was in a rage of jealousy that I had flown not only in a Dakota but a Sunderland as well. The box of chocolates, so impressive in the Darrell Lee shop in far-off Melbourne, had sagged in its travels and seemed to represent but poorly all the wonders I had seen and done.

The Fort on Magnetic Island

During the weeks I had been away there had been an outbreak of typhoid fever in Townsville. In South Townsville, where the outbreak was worst, people had been given free vaccinations. The level in the weir was so low that drinking water had to be trucked in from Rollingstone. Mum boiled ours. She also boiled the milk which made the skin rise to the top and crinkle in nasty wrinkles on which dust settled. Even worse, it would stick in your throat. All our meals were eaten from beneath throw-overs because of the flies. Even when the rains came and the weir filled, the water was sludgy with the run-off from the surrounding hills. Then it couldn't be pumped because of a shortage of coal at Hubert Wells Power Station. Sometimes water was only available for two hours a day and spurted out from the taps like runny mud.

Once when I went to take the eggs to Mrs. Woodward, I found her sitting on the verandah fanning herself with a large fan woven from pandanus. She had her feet in a dish of cool water and a wet towel over her shoulders. Mrs. Woodward was probably quite old but kept her hair dyed jet black. She said, almost panting, 'Never in all my born days have I have I known anything like this heat! And the way these storms build up and then disappear! It is all these aeroplanes flying about! I'm sure of it!' Whisk! Whisk! went her pandanus fan, while she waited for me to agree. She reminded me and herself that it was nearly the anniversary of Cyclone Leonta, which had destroyed Townsville in 1908. She remembered it quite well; even the new brick Grammar School had tumbled down. 'With this heat,' she went on, glad to have even a little girl to talk to, 'I wouldn't be the least bit surprised if we got another cyclone just like Leonta! And then we shall see what we shall see! Mark my words! With all these military huts and igloos about, won't there be some iron flying!'

I loved Mrs. Woodward's stories about the olden days. When she was a little girl, there had been a forest of pandanus between North Ward and Belgian Gardens. Once she had been looking for a stray cow and had met some Aborigines armed with spears and boomerangs. She hadn't been afraid of them but their dogs had attacked her. I could identify with that. 'Luckily I was carrying a smudge-pot to keep the mosquitoes at bay. They were bad that year! I swung the pot at them! Got one right one the nose! Didn't he yelp! Then they all ran so I was safe!' Whisk! Whisk! went the pandanus fan.

'Belgian Gardens was called German Gardens then.' They changed the name during the Great War. That was to show sympathy with the poor Belgian people. They were having such a bad time of it. The Germans were eating the babies, so we were told! It possibly wasn't true, but in wartime the newspapers are full of strange tales. But, Oh! We did feel so sorry for the Belgians just in case it was. So that's how Belgian Gardens got the name.' Deep in remembrance she suddenly added, 'The beach was much further out in those days, you know. It seems to keep moving further back every year.'

At the beginning of February there was a tremendous storm. There were hailstones, a rarity for Townsville. All night the rain thundered on the roof, sweeping in sheets across the verandah. In the morning the stone steps at the back of the house were running like a waterfall, frothy with brown water. Jipsy, who had hollowed out a little cave underneath the house in which to have her puppies, was flooded out. She had carried each puppy to a dry spot, high under the floor boards at the back of the house. The sightless pups squirmed in the dust, emitting tiny bleats while she nosed them to stay in one group and curled herself around them reassuringly. We flew to her rescue and soon she was established in a warm, dry tea-chest turned on its side.

In the chook-yard the water had backed up behind the debris that had washed against the fence. My favourite little bantam rooster had been drowned, his fine feathered legs protruding from the flood as he circled slowly round and round on his back. On Castle Hill every rock-face had turned into a waterfall. Water cascaded down, sometimes curving out from the surface of the rocks in bows which glittered with colour. The air was filled with the roar of tumbling water. The gullies ran bankers. Over two and a half inches had fallen in North Ward.

The weir was filled to overflowing and water had backed up from Aplin's Weir to Gleeson's. The stock-crossing was nine feet under. After these rains, the worst of the typhoid scare was over. But the rains meant that air-raid shelters and slit trenches all over Townsville were again filled with water to the brim, so there were mosquito plagues, including *anopheles* the malaria-spreading kinds. The *anopheles* were easy to recognize because, when biting, they stood on their front feet with their back legs in the air as though doing handstands. Many of the troops in New Guinea returned to Townsville on leave with yellowish skin caused by the Atebrine tablets they had to take to prevent catching malaria so any *anopheles* on a leg or an arm were swatted viciously. No one wanted malaria in North Queensland.

The tide of war had turned in New Guinea and almost daily there were photos in the paper of captured Japanese prisoners-of-war, sometimes being carried along the muddy tracks on the backs of Australian soldiers. It was decided that it was high time the air-raid trenches in Townsville were filled in. Barry got busy and filled in our backyard air-raid shelter. It became merely a bare hollow patch where rubbish was burned off.

Barry had passed his Junior Public Exam, the point at which nearly every child who had continued on to secondary education left school. Very few went beyond Junior which was considered to be a high standard of learning. Although Barry had only just turned fourteen in January he had to register with the National Service Authority because manpower regulations controlled all employment. He was directed to work as a Junior Clerk for the Allied Works Council which had its head-offices on the Strand, with a starting salary of one hundred and seven pounds per year. But to Barry the job was just a means of killing time until his seventeenth birthday when, because of his Air Training Corps background, he could get into the RAAF as air-crew.

'I don't know, Skin,' he said to me when, bare-legged, we had just finished hosing the verandah, now allowed because of the new weir, 'I don't know that I could cop it, if this show is over before I get a bash. Things are looking too good over there for my liking. The RAF and the Yanks are doing these thousand bomber raids on Berlin and Stuttgart and polishing them off. The Luftwaffe have had it. It'll all be over soon, if I don't look out.' To ease his anxiety he played a fine spray from the hose on Kelly, luxuriously asleep on Mum's verandah chair. Kelly woke with a start, shook his head in annoyance, then darted along the verandah keeping to the furniture for cover. Old Mumpuss, wiser in these matters, had fled at the first sight of the hose.

There was a feeling that the war was going our way. The King in his last message had spoken about 'the clouds of war beginning to break' and that 'fresh hope was springing up in every country'. Auntie Elsie Quelch and Ronnie returned from evacuation in Warwick. At first Ronnie seemed like a stranger, but it was not long before we were on our bikes, riding out with the Acklands through the chinkie-apple scrub beyond Aitkenvale on an expedition to see the new weir. A sheet of green water about fifteen inches deep was sliding over the wall. Men were at work on the downstream side, reinforcing the banks. The boys had a swim, taking it in turns to push or throw one another in, but Shirley told me that a boy had been drowned when he cast a bait-net which was tied to his wrist and dragged him down by its weight. I thought it would be horrible to swim where someone had been drowned. I liked to be able to see the bottom.

At school I had Miss Thomas for a teacher again though the huge class had been divided and a little man named Mr. Reynolds had the other half. Mr. Reynold's half did not learn a lot as he was deaf and read the paper most of the time. By now in Miss Thomas's class we were so accustomed to the pinging of the little bell that no one took the slightest notice. The uproar only subsided when Mr. Jones, the Head Teacher, was on the prowl. As he stalked along the corridor, he might perhaps find us, heads bent over Transcription, copying out a passage from the Reading Book in copperplate writing, thin ups, heavy downs, on each stroke, into a special Transcription book. Or perhaps we would be all concentration, heads down, arms hooked around our pads, at Dictation, writing a passage with correct punctuation while Miss Thomas read it aloud, phrase by phrase. At first she would tell us where to put commas and full-stops but after a while you had to judge them for yourself to get 'a feel for the English language'.

The relative silence of Dictation and Transcription, broken only by the click of a pencil or ruler being dropped to the floor, were a balm to everyone's nerves. The actual marking was done by others in your long desk, on the command 'Change pads!' so it was important to have friends to make any necessary amendments. If they applied ticks in red pencil and inscribed 'ten out of ten', it enabled you to scramble on to the form on the command, 'Stand, Tens!' 'Nine' was also acceptable. 'Eight' was marginal. Anything less and you felt the heavy doom of failure.

Social acceptance went with position in class, determined once a month by examinations, after which you piled all your possessions on to your slate, filed out around the edge of the room and waited, tense with dread, to learn where you had 'come'. For the rest of the month you sat according to whether you were 'first', Top, or 'forty-second', Bottom. As they took their seats at the ends of the long back desks, 'Top Boy' or 'Top Girl' were followed to their places by eyes vicious with envy. I hated the Japanese enemy less than I hated Bobby Skau for beating me for top place by a half a mark. He had known how many yards made one rod, pole or perch in measurement and I had got it mixed up with chains and links.

So it became a matter of life and death to know every Avoirdupois, Troy, Capacity and Linear Measure, and to fire questions about gills in pints or quarters in hundredweights at one another as a means of recreation at Little Lunch and Big Lunch on Exam Day. What these terms meant, Miss Thomas did not explain. Or perhaps she did and only the children in the front row heard, her voice being so powdery-soft. For me a 'perch' remained something a budgerigar sat on: a rod, pertained to people in the Bible; Moses making water come out of rocks by striking them with his rod, or Psalm 23, 'Thy rod and Thy staff, they comfort me'. The only measure that was a little less obscure was 'chain', the length of a cricket pitch and that twenty-two yards, sixty-six feet and one hundred links made one of them. A link of course was something in a dog-chain, but the length of a dog-chain was anyone's guess.

Then there were the mysteries of 'be, been, and being'. Miss Thomas did not explain these either, merely telling us to learn 'The Parts of the Verb To Be' by heart. We chanted with a will; 'The parts of the Verb To Be are; am, is, are, art, was, wast, were, wert, be, been and being'. There did not seem to be a lot of call for 'wast' and 'wert' except when they made their appearance at exam time; 'Wist thou not that I wast o'erwhelmed?; Analyse into Subject and Predicate and parse the underlined words.' We only knew that, somehow, to know these things off-by-heart was part of the secret code of growing-up.

Safer by far were the journeys of the Explorers. The comfortable days of the arrival of the *Duyfken* in the Gulf of Carpentaria and of Blaxland, Wentworth and Lawson Crossing the Blue Mountains were behind. We were into serious matters: with Sturt down the Murray; the journeyings of Major Mitchell; the depots of the hapless Burke and Wills; John Forrest's party raising their hats to cheer the Overland Telegraph Line. On the walls of the room were framed lithographs of these high points in history.

It was entirely possible to get twenty out of twenty for knowing these, as well as the names of the Northern Rivers: 'Tweed, Richmond, Clarence, Hunter', the products of Birmingham: 'railway rolling-stock and small-arms' and the Home of the Rivers, 'Buckland's Tableland', by committing to memory every page of *Brookes' School History* and *Brookes'*

School Geography. There was nothing else to be learned. That was the entirety of knowledge.

Happily, Sewing was not included in the examination results. On Wednesday afternoons, the boys were marched off down to the basement area to Woodwork where they learned to make impressive pin-trays and nail-boxes. Girls from Mr. Reynold's Grade Four crowded into our room for Sewing. Because of clothing rationing the lessons consisted of working sampler-stitches on a strip of calico. A long queue of busy fingers formed at Miss Thomas's table, waiting to have French Seams approved and to move on to Run-and-Fell. Some even attained the heights of Smocking. It was possible, by courteously offering my place to newcomers, to never actually get to the top of the queue at all and to be permanently arrested in the limbo of Tacking Stitch. To pass the time there were the lithographs of the Explorers to reflect upon. What would it feel like to climb a mountain at the heart of the continent and hoist the Union Jack? Or to see across the desert the Overland Telegraph Line? And fancy Leichhardt not setting a sentry when he knew they were being trailed by hostile blacks! Poor Gilbert! About to get speared while fast asleep in his blanket! None the less, Leichhardt remained my favourite, because I also sometimes got things terribly wrong; got 'the bull by the horns', as Dad called it. Also, Leichhardt was nice-looking, despite his whiskers.

Eventually the sewing class progressed to bloomer-making. Miss Thomas did the cutting out. There was acute embarrassment in being measured for crutch and waist. Having recovered from that, the next shock was the sight of the enormous distances involved where actual hemming was concerned. It was not humanly possible! Like a rare species of heron, ducking my head and keeping my legs moving, I lurked at the tail-end of the queue. Long before the bloomers were anywhere near completion I had well and truly out-grown them.

The only other kind of lesson was Religious Instruction, which dedicated ladies came to teach, usually in pairs for safey's sake, from the various churches. I thought it strange when they declared to us passionately that Jesus was such a young man when he had given his life for us: only thirty-three. To me thirty-three was terribly old. As old as Mum! We were also quite used to the idea of people giving their lives for us. Hadn't the Anzacs? And the Ninth Divvie at Tobruk? And Corporal John French, V.C.? But as Methodists we did a lot of cheerful singing: *Build on the Rock* and *My Cup is Full and Running Over*. These were Action Songs because you made appropriate movements to suit the words. With arms stretched wide you showed how great was the Saviour's love, 'wide, wide as the ocean'. Squashed six or seven to a form, the boys wasted no time in seizing the opportunity to topple one another backwards on to the floor.

A scheme to give every school-child one-third of a pint of milk a day was introduced. Being Milk Monitor now outranked being Ink Monitor. The boys vied eagerly, with straight backs and fingers clicking, to be the elite. Not only was there the prestige, but the bottles arrived in wire crates across the top of which were scattered a few lumps of ice. These became the perks of the Milk Monitors, to be sucked to the last envied drop. At Little Lunch we sat on the concrete beneath the school and the Monitors dealt out the milk. At home, drinking milk with or without the skin on top was impossible, and led to gaggings, some faked, some genuine. At school it became easy. You lifted the cardboard lid of your appealing little bottle, tore a small hole at the edge, replaced it and sucked through the hole like a baby's bottle. Everyone, even boys, did.

When the monthly exam results were known, Mr. Jones would sometimes pay a ceremonial visit to the classroom, an occasion for sitting, backs straight, arms folded tightly behind. Questions were fired. If the poem in the Reading Book had been *Only One Mother*, it might be 'Hands up! Who loves their mother?' Up would go every hand, mine included, though guiltily. I knew there were times when I didn't. Didn't anybody else's mother get shrill and say, 'For pity's sake leave your nails alone!' or make them drink disgusting senna tea for their bowels? Or take fishy-tasting Hypol for their chests? Sometimes Mr. Jones's visit developed into a pogrom of those at the bottom of the class. They were made to stand on the form and the class invited to 'Just look at them!' while Mr. Jones peered into their ears and pretended to wince at what he saw, or sent them home telling them not to come back until they had got their hair cut. They endured their humiliation stoically, seeming to accept that it was their lot in life.

In March some of the troops from the fighting in New Guinea started coming home on leave. Among them was Victor Saunders, Audrey's brother. The Saunders planned a big Welcome Home party for him. I was invited and went skipping off to it very excitedly, with a bow tied in my hair and a plate of pikelets to put on the table. It was going to be my first grown-up party. I knew from my induction to such matters by Margaretta that there should be caviar and trays of long stemmed glasses of drinks called 'Martinis' and 'Manhattans'. Streamers and balloons would be an optional extra but none the less appreciated.

But it was not that kind of party. The Saunders were a large family and it was a clan gathering. The dining-room table, which was normally shrouded beneath a green woven cover with bobbles round the edge, was now spread with a snowy cloth. It was loaded with food; sponge-cakes each higher and lighter than the next and oozing frothy cream, plates of sandwiches, egg and lettuce, corned-beef and pickle, and 'Burdekin Duck' made of bacon and tomato and cheese squashed up. There were butterfly cakes and lamingtons and, in the centre of it all, a large iced cake like a twenty-first birthday cake, with 'Welcome Home Victor' and the colour patch of his battalion done in angelica and coloured coconut. No-one had stinted on their coupons. I hardly liked to squeeze Mum's plate of pikelets in among the feast of deliciousness.

Victor was looking tanned and fit; his snowy hair cropped short. There was just the slightest tinge of the yellow from malaria tablets about his skin. I had somehow expected to find him dressed in jungle greens and muddy boots with the vicious glint of a seasoned jungle fighter in his eye. It was something of a let-down that he had an ordinary shirt and tie and was leaning casually against the windows of the verandah with the other men, a cup of tea in his hand. All the ladies were seated together in the lounge.

Audrey and I were told we could work the gramophone for the music, which sounded promising. Audrey knew how to lift the silver arm and to insert the tiny needle after each record had been played and how much to wind the handle on the side of the cabinet so that it would be neither over-wound nor too slow and groany. But all the shiny black records belonged without exception to Ron, another brother, an admirer of brass band music. An infinite number of Sousa marches later, we were heartily sick of the job and wished we could go outside on the road under the lamp-post and play 'Sheep, Sheep, Come Home' with the other children.

After supper we were able to make our escape, as the piano was opened for a sing-song. One of the older sisters went to the piano-stool, gave it a few spins to bring it down to her height and commenced to play all the old favourites. Everyone linked arms around the piano and joined in. They sang especially hard for the new song, *There's a Boy Coming Home on Leave*;

There's a boy coming home on leave;
There's a girl wants him home on leave.
We'll meet him right at the station;
There'll be a grand celebration,
When he comes home on leave.

They wanted her to play it over again for a second and third time which she did, going very loudly on the 'Oom pah, oom pah's in the left hand. Victor, who was leaning against the doorway, just grinned and shook his head sheepishly. Another brother, passing by gave him a heavy clout on the shoulder and Mr. Saunders in his rocking chair swayed his stick backwards and forwards in time and looked proud. One of the little twin cousins, Billy or Gordon, ran up and deliberately went 'tramp, tramp' on Victor's shiny shoes. Victor seemed glad of the chance to chase after the twins along the verandah to rough them up, turning them upside down till they roared for mercy.

When the next song was, *When the Lights Go On Again all Over the World* the whole family, arms about one another's waists or shoulders, swayed backwards and forwards in unison and raised their voices to the roof. Mrs. Saunders, out in the kitchen piling plates into the sink for Alwyn to wash, seemed to be quite bothered by perspiration around her eyes. Quite a few times I noticed she had to lift her spectacles to mop them dry.

There were many Townsville families who would never be able to stage Welcome Home parties for their boys. Each week the list of Roll of Honour names in the *Bulletin* grew longer. The name of the dead soldier or airman would be accompanied by a photograph of him in uniform. It seemed strange to think that when he had gone to have the photo taken at City Studios he would not have thought of it being in the paper in the Roll of Honour, and himself dead and buried far away. Sometimes there was a short verse which the family had chosen to go with it.

Tell England we died for her,
And here we rest, content.

or,

Help me, Oh God, when death is near,
To mock the haggard face of fear,
That when I fall, if fall I must,
My soul shall triumph in the dust.

Most often it was simply,

Not just today, but every day,

In silence, we remember.

Sometimes it seemed as though the family were using the opportunity to write a letter to the son or brother they had lost: 'We miss you, Jim. We will never forget you. Love, Mum, Dad, and Loving Sisters Dorothy and Lou.'

Some of the names we began to remember from year to year: 'Private Jack Bird, Tobruk' was one of them. Barry had started off by cutting out the Roll of Honour for his war scrap-book but after a while the lists grew so long and so frequent that he got further and further behind and gave up.

Mail from England now took up to four months to arrive, so when Mum's mother died she did not know until four months later. I came home from school one day to find Mum sitting quietly at the kitchen table looking infinitely sad. She had not seen her mother since the middle of 1927, when she and Dad had run away together to be married. Dad had looked like Rudolf Valentino, the star of the Silent films in the Twenties. Grandfather Greenleaf had not approved of the match so they had eloped. Mum had been just eighteen; Dad considerably older. All had gone well until Dad bought a gold mine in Central Queensland that had been 'salted' to make it look a good prospect. The family fortunes had never recovered, especially as Dad had then tried his hand at farming. The Soldier Settlement cotton farm in the Dawson Valley had also been a failure, the farm not large enough to be viable. There was a major flood that ran four feet deep through the tent home, pests which destroyed the crops, and no markets during the Depression. Mum had always hugged to her heart the dream of going 'Home'. But now with her mother gone, there would be no home to return to. She knew she and her stern father would never be reconciled. Grandma Greenleaf had died because she could not get the medications and diet she needed as a diabetic in wartime England.

There was an old couple who lived in Mitchell Street who every year grew white chrysanthemums, Mother's Day flowers for sale to the children of North Ward. If you arrived with two shillings Mrs. Shepherd would move among her fragrant bushes cutting a lovely bunch of creamy-hearted white blooms for you. On the afternoon Mum got the letter about her mother's death, Barry rode down to Mrs. Shepherd's. It wasn't yet Mother's Day but it seemed nicer to get the flowers a bit earlier this year. I also gathered all the giant sunflowers that grew prolifically in the waste area behind our Little House. Mum cried when she saw the flowers. She hadn't cried at all at first but at the sight of the flowers she did, and didn't seem to know how to stop. Barry and I looked ruefully at one another, uncertain what to do next. Mum said that she wasn't crying just for her own mother but for all the mothers that had been killed in the raids on London or died because of the war; for all families and war and separation.

Barry was eyeing me uncomfortably while she spoke and raising his eyebrows at me. I knew that he had arranged to meet Cliffie Frizwell at the Wintergarden to see *Road to Morocco*, starring Bing Crosby, Bob Hope and Dorothy Lamour, a picture everyone was talking about; it's 'Let's meet on the road to Morocco, instead of the tunnel of love…' so cheerful and catchy.

When eventually he blurted this out, Mum said that he might have stayed at home one night out of respect for his grandmother. Barry said, 'Oh! Come off it, Mum! She's been dead for four months! And I didn't know her from Jackie Jackie!' He might as well have dropped the Royal Doulton Haywain plate. In the total silence which followed, he slunk out and rode off, mud-guards rattling, into the night. Mum and I were left to the chrysanthemum perfumed solitude of sorrow.

Later that night, Barry's bike was stolen from outside the Wintergarden. It was a common practice among servicemen who found themselves far from camp when their leave pass was up, to commandeer the nearest bike and dump it when they had finished with it. Barry had to hoof it home. Mum's eyes gleamed with something very like satisfaction when he had to catch the bus to work for several weeks. Eventually the bike turned up, dumped in the guinea-grass outside the anti-aircraft battery at Signal Hill.

Even after the D-Day landings, when Barry and Mum were both glued to the ABC News to hear the latest developments, they were still cold-shouldering one another. Barry put up a map of the Second Front, showing the beaches where the landings had taken place: Caen, where heavy bombardments were going on, and the Allied push inland towards the Falaise Gap. He would have liked Mum to take notice and comment, but she refused to let bygones be bygones. It was not just Barry's tactless words that had cut her to the quick but the knowledge that they were true. It was part of the price she had paid for coming to Australia. I would not have known my own grandmother either, had I met her, but I was not the one who had blurted it out. Mum turned her grief into mourning for the victims of a Nazi massacre that had taken place at a little French town called Oradour where all the villagers had been herded into the church and burned to death, except one little boy whose mother had pushed him out of the church window and told him to run for it.

Mum was not inclined to take much notice of my complaint that there were not going to be a proper Sunday School Picnic because of lack of transport; no train ride to Black River, no sitting on the back of a truck with legs dangling over the side to go to Pallarenda, no crowded boat to Magnetic Island. The Annual Combined Sunday School Picnic would be held at the Botanic Gardens. Egg and spoon races and lining up for lemon buns without any of the adventure of getting there. What a let-down!

I had other worries of my own with Kennels to run. There was a series of books by Albert Payson Terhune about his Sunnybank Kennels where he raised purebred Collies. After reading them I came to the conclusion that, although Jipsy was not quite a purebred, there was no reason why I should not have a similar establishment. The name was immediately obvious: 'Rockybank Kennels'. Jipsy, of course, became 'Rockybank Jipsy Queen'. In an old ledger-book I kept diary notes of each puppy's progress, the remarkable feats it had performed, the intelligence it had displayed. Their given names had to start with 'R' to sound well with 'Rockybank': 'Rockybank Rover', 'Rockybank Rascal', 'Rockybank Rilloby Rill'. Sometimes I found rude comments pencilled in by Barry: 'Rockybank Ratbag' or 'Rockybank Rank-piddle', which I ignored. Once, he had written 'Anymore dog-poo in my sand-shoe and Look Out!'

For the current litter I had started to run out of Rs. The largest and most handsome was therefore called 'Monty', after Field Marshall Montgomery, Commander-in-Chief of the

British forces and the hero of El Alamein. We had decided to keep Monty ourselves.

The other two went to good homes. When each litter of puppies was old enough I put a small advertisement in the *Bulletin*. 'Wanted homes for beautiful fox-terrier puppies. Almost purebred. Price, five shillings per puppy. Apply Box number ....'. When letters of inquiry started to arrive, I would ride secretly to inspect the given addresses to satisfy myself that they looked like worthy establishments. Any sign of busy roads, broken-down fences or nasty-looking boys and the applicant had no chance.

Chapter 16

THE TIDE OF WAR MOVES ON: 1944

'Would you like to Swing on a Star?
Carry moonbeams home in a jar!'

Military Hospital, Cape Pallarenda.

A 'Doodle Bug' – one of the new German flying bombs – had hit Auntie Kitty's house in London. A direct hit! For the second time the indomitable old lady had been dug out alive from under the rubble. When the bomb struck she had been just about to pour herself a cup of tea and when found ten hours later she was still clutching the tea-pot handle in her hand.

Uncle Horace wrote of the way the 'Doodle Bugs' could be heard motoring along overhead. 'As long as we can hear the engine, it's all right. Then we know some other poor blighter is going to get it. It's when the motor cuts out that it's unnerving. That's when it's coming down. There's silence for about fifteen seconds, then a bang and some poor devils have bought it.'

Londoners were being evacuated again just as in the bad days of the 1940 Blitz. Nearly two thousand people were being killed each month, many of them children. The Flying-bombs were intended to demoralise the civilian population so the targets were random. Even one of the hospitals had been hit. A journalist friend on Uncle Horace's newspaper had received a telephone call at work to say that his wife and twin sons had been killed in their home at Croydon. Another friend who was a fire officer said that as they were carrying one little boy out of his burning home, he had been saying over and over 'My little Willie! My poor little willie! It's gone!' and feeling for the place where it had been. Uncle Horace seemed to think it was a mercy the little boy had died later in hospital.

To cheer Mum up, Barry said 'Never mind! The Yanks have got these new Super Fortresses now; B-29s. They'll belt the living daylights of the Huns, just like they did with the Nips at Tokyo and Yokohama. And the RAF and the Yanks have been doing these thousand-bomber raids over Berlin. It's a round trip of over a thousand miles but they use belly tanks for the extra fuel. Just like they did for the raids on Rabaul from here. So that ought to teach the Huns a lesson or two.'

To Barry it was unspeakable that the Germans had executed fifty Allied officers who had escaped from a Prisoner of War camp. It was an officer's duty to try to escape! By this act the Germans had sunk to the level of the Japanese in his opinion.

One night he came home from work, his eyes alight with the desire to tell a funny story. 'Did you hear about the RAAF chap who gets shot down over Normandy and has to bale out? Well, he lands in the middle of all these Yanks, see. They don't recognize his RAAF uniform. They think he's a Hun and they don't know whether to give him the bullet or take him prisoner or what. He keeps yelling 'I'm British! I'm RAAF!' Finally he yells 'Look, youse bloody mugs! I'm a bloody Aussie!' Straight up, they know he's fair dinkum! No bull's wool!'

He laughed hugely at his story, dealing a death blow to a large mouthful of corned beef and pumpkin in the telling. I dared not laugh. I had seen what I thought was a warning glint in Mum's eye. He had gone too far. Men might swear in their own company but never in front of women and children. I kept my eyes down and tried to wangle some unwanted squashy-peas under my fork. To my amazement I heard Mum not only laugh, but laugh with enjoyment. Things were certainly changing.

Mum was in good humour because she had had another Airgraph from Uncle Horace. Cousin Graham had taken part in the landings in France, delivering not only troops but supplies of ammunition on the beaches. Another heartening piece of news was that the pilots of the RAF had developed the knack of tipping the wings of the Doodle Bugs so that they turned around and went back out to sea, even back to Germany some hoped! Barry explained; 'The trick is they manoeuvre the wing-tip of their Spitfire or Hurricane so that it's just under the wing of the Flying Bomb! Then they give it a bit of a nudge, see! They don't actually touch the wing. Hell! No! That would be too risky! But, see! There's a cushion of air between the two wings that does the trick, rip snorter! They just tip it up and that put the bastards off course. They crash out at sea. Hundreds of the buggers have been sent packing! And, you know what! Those Mosquito Fighter Bombers, they get up there and shoot the bastards down! Shoot them out of the air! Over six hundred, they reckon!' His eyes shone with fierce delight in the telling.

Mum was so enthralled that she let the language pass. She was thrilled to hear that of over eight thousand German 'Doodle Bugs' launched at London, only two and a half-thousand had actually reached their target. The Auntie Jessies of England would be so much safer.

In July the first news began to seep through about the German's use of Gas Chambers to exterminate the Jews. 'The Germans are placing themselves outside the pale of civilised nations!' cried Mum, her face stricken. 'Oh! To think! Mozart and Beethoven and Goethe! The genius of the race! And now they descend to barbarity of this scale! It is monstrous!' After that, neither Barry nor I dared to demur about the endless pumpkin that was put on our plates. If we didn't appreciate good wholesome food in a world where countless people were being starved to death then we could go without.

Subdued talk of the Gas Chambers replaced games at school for a few days. Little groups huddled together, skipping-ropes forgotten, going over and over what we had picked up from hearing adults telling one another, endlessly repeating the grim details of thousands of people being marched into dark sheds from which there was no escape, doors being clanged shut, and gas turned on. The fact that the doors were sometimes opened again for a moment to throw any spare babies or toddlers in worried everyone most of all. In the hot sunshine of the school playground we grappled with the notion that the horror was real, not just the pretend-horror of The Return of the Zombie, or The Mummy's Revenge.

Horror pictures were almost a relief. There had been a run of them; Frankenstein, The Cat People and several generations of Zombies and Mummies. Because I was not allowed to go to see any of them, Margaretta would re-enact the plots for me, showing how the Mummy had limped, dragging his bandages, to burst through the door of the heroine's bedroom; how the blood had trickled under the door when the Cat People were abroad, or how the lid of the coffin had creaked open, slowly, slowly, when the Zombie rose from the dead. I would have been better off seeing the actual pictures for myself. The imagined monsters took root and grew to horrid proportion in my mind's eye, lurking just beyond the corner of my vision on the dark verandah at night. The lurching mummy in particular. There was something so graphic about Margaretta's demonstration of his yawing gait. Mum tried to explain that real mummies were first embalmed and then wrapped all in one piece and couldn't go wandering about the countryside, arms free to strangle people, even if they wanted to. I knew that she knew such things. I also knew that she did not know that, in the dark of any night, a monstrous shape might happen upon us down Alexandra Street, lurching horribly, arms out-stretched, bandages flapping, towards the side of my bed.

But in the reassuring, practical world of daylight, it had become my job, on the way home from school, to buy the meat, the two-shillings tied in the corner of my handkerchief all day. I felt the weight of this new responsibility as I stood in the queue for half an hour waiting to be served. I did not have to worry about ration-books because the cheaper cuts of meat; tripe, liver, brains, tongues, kidneys and ox-tails were not rationed. The note wrapped around the money in my handkerchief never said rump steak.

While waiting in the queue I marvelled at the precision of the butcher in his blue-striped apron at his chopping block, a massive section of a gum-tree tree-trunk. No wonder he had two fingers missing, I thought, as the chopper flashed up and down faster than the eye could follow. The sawdust of the floor was littered with odd scraps of bone and fat and meat. I half expected to see a finger or two among them. As soon as our meat was in my calico meat-bag, I asked for 'A pennyworth for the dog, please'. The butcher would gather up a generous handful of scraps off the back of the chopping block and toss them into a piece of newspaper. People who asked for 'threepenceworth' got the same amount. I was sure the butcher remembered that I had mentioned to him once or twice what a remarkable dog Jipsy was.

And Jipsy was a remarkable dog. She may have been the first dog in the whole wide world to climb up the cleft between the twin precipices of Castle Hill. It was a climb which neither Audrey nor I had set out intending to do. We had been wandering across the hillside on an afternoon when the grasshoppers were silent in the grass and even the lizards sought shelter from the heat, when Audrey said 'Let's climb up the cliffs'. She was a much better climber than I was. She never seemed to get stuck half-way along a ledge and have to say the Lord's Prayer in a hurry before she could go on.

So we worked our way through long stiff guinea grass around to the foot of the cliffs which reared overhead, enormous, pink and bulging. The smooth granite thrust upwards from the ground and rose vertically for five hundred feet. We had to throw our heads back to look upwards and even then we could only see the sheer rock-face receding towards the flat blue of the sky, but not to the top of them. As a whisp of cloud drifted over, the cliff-face seemed to topple forward.

At this very point I would have conceded defeat and settled for what Dad called 'a tactical withdrawal'. 'Let's go home!' flashed, unbidden, to my mind. Home, the red tin roofs of which we could just see through the crowns of the ironbark trees around the curve of the hill, seemed suddenly very dear. And safe. But Audrey had the sort of dogged persistence that won lands for the Empire. Having set out to climb the cliff she was not about to turn back. 'Discretion is the better part of valour' – Mum's saying – was not for her.

We forced our way round the base of the cliffs, searching for the foot of the cleft. It seemed that no-one else had been there before us, or not for a very long time. Under a ledge where the rock seemed to have split away, Jipsy nosed out the skeleton and horns of a large old billy-goat. I remembered the goats that Barry had gone chasing from Walker Street and the big old billy that had been their brave leader. Were these his remains?

Getting into the foot of the cleft was hard. There was a bulging-out exposed section of rock, like a puffed out cheek, with nothing to grip on to but slight niches and crevices; nothing to actually put a grateful foot into; just a matter of pressing close to the warm rock and not thinking that you were getting level with the tree tops and going up and up. Because Audrey was there up ahead. Not only Audrey but Jipsy, too! Jipsy was proving to be a cheerful climber. Well, she had toenails that clicked and clung on to the rock. And she had four feet to do the clinging.

But once into the cleft it all began to feel much safer. Just like a very steep, upwards gully, like a rocky ladder, really. There were stunted bushes and tufts of spiky grass to hang on to and the higher we got the deeper the cleft became, so there was the reassuring sense that unless we were silly enough to stand on the edge, we couldn't really fall. Or so I kept telling myself.

We were simply aware of one sheer wall on the right dropping away into an immensity of sunlight and air, and the other, against which we pressed as close as we could, towering majestically overhead. Jipsy dug her claws in and scrambled mightily, only needing a push on her eager bottom or a haul on the collar in the very steepest of places. There was a rock-face up which Audrey and I had to drag and shove one another. Jipsy found her own way by skirting with quick confident little steps along the very rim of the outer precipice, tail waggling, face grinning, panting 'I'm ahead of you! Why are you so slow!' down into our faces. She had found she had a very good dog-head for heights.

We had got more than halfway to the top when suddenly, clattering and bouncing, there were rocks falling! By the way they curved out overhead we knew they were being thrown by someone on the lookouts above. Hardly anybody that went to the lookouts could resist the temptation to hurl a few stones over for the thrill of hearing them smash and bounce after a few moments of silence, on to the rocks below. Somebody was doing it now. 'Hoy!' we shouted, with a certain degree of emphasis. 'Hoy! We're down here!' Our voices bounced off the rock-wall and echoed upwards. 'Hoy! Hoy! Oi! Here! Here! 'ere!' diminishing into the blueness of sky and heat. We shouted again, shrinking back against the foot of the cliff. And waited, hearts thumping.

One or two more rocks clattered nearby and then there was silence. We counted on the fact that most of the loose stones near the look-outs had been hurled off long since. People could only throw as many stones as they had carried in. In this we knew, lay our hopes of survival. We were right. There was silence, broken only by the wind soughing up the cleft. We waited, breathing tensely. But only silence and shimmering heat. We ventured out, peering nervously upwards, and reassured, continued climbing. Emboldened by the moment of danger faced and overcome, I remembered Barry's song, and began to feel myself very much like the bearer of 'a banner with a strange device, Excelsior!'

The cleft narrowed and was jammed by a rock fall to which a stunted gum-tree clung. We hauled ourselves past, emerged from the cleft and found ahead an upward sweep of short spiky grass and beyond it the summit. Jipsy went bouncing through the wind-combed tussocks as though she climbed cliffs every day, while, red and sweaty in the face from heat, exhaustion and triumph, we looked back and could see, in the granite V of the cleft up which we had crawled, the streets of the town like a toy village, the silvery bow of the creek, the harbour no longer packed with war shipping and Cape Cleveland, pale with distance across the shimmering bay. Yes! Excelsior!

This was to be Audrey's and my last adventure on Castle Hill. Not long after this she left school and got a job as a sales-assistant in Fostars' Shoe Store. Although we had played cubby-houses and gone climbing together right till the very end, once she started work it was no longer the same. She was now a grown-up and I was just a little girl at school. Barry and other people of their age had parties at which, 'Spin the Bottle', 'Consequences' or 'Sardines' were played. The aim seemed to be for the boys to make a name for themselves as exponents of mouth-kissing, taking the girl in their arms as they had seen done by Errol Flynn or Clark Gable in the pictures. I could only watch in fascinated horror thinking 'Eerrck!' and be glad that it wasn't me. I never wanted to be fourteen!

Changes were in the air. The war was moving on. One of the signs that the high tide of the American presence in North Queensland was on the ebb, was that the American Red Cross Recreation Rooms near Hayles' Wharf closed down. Also that sometimes small advertisements would appear in the 'Personal' section of the paper; 'Wanted: Loving home for baby girl', or 'baby boy'. One young girl trailed around Flinders Street with a battered perambulator in which was the most beautiful little black baby boy, exactly like the black-baby doll I had always longed for. The baby was always crying, squirming in rage because its bonnet had worked down over its face and the young mother was too inexperienced to realize it needed comforting and attending to. Mum would click her tongue in exasperation and sympathy. 'Can't the silly girl see that it needs changing!' The pram was very often parked outside one of the Ladies' Lounges of the hotels in Flinders Street.

Each town was still being asked to fill its quota for the Victory Loan, for which Honour Pennants were awarded. Posters showed Japan exploding like a fire-cracker. The slogan was 'Now for the Knock-out! Invest all you can!' It was said that the war was costing one million pounds per day. Mum wondered,'Where are they going to get the money when peace-time comes to pay all these loans back?' More and more there was talk of 'after the war' and 'when peace comes'.

General Montgomery said that the end of the war was in sight. There was talk of making a start on an Australian film to be called *The Overlanders*, about one of the longest cattle droves in history, from the Kimberleys to Queensland, for the War Effort. There were auction-sales of the huts and igloos the American army had used, and of equipment such as dixies and stretchers and the amazing new 'bull-dozers' which had been used to build air-strips. The steel matting which they had used to surface the temporary airstrips was found by many Townsville people to be useful for backyard fencing, especially chook-yards, as once it was firmly dug into the ground chooks couldn't scratch their way out.

Through Jipsy I had become an unofficial off-sider to Mr. Denny, the Vet who lived at the far end of Alexandra Street. When Jipsy's pups were the correct age, ten days old, I gathered them into a basket to be taken to Mr. Denny to have their tails docked. The fragile little appendages called dew-claws on the inside of their forepaws had also to be clipped off. Mr. Denny showed me how to do these operations, pulling the skin of each tiny tail firmly back before making the snip so that afterwards it would slide down and cover the stump. This method gave a nice feathery effect to the tip of the tail when the puppy was grown. Afterwards he didn't put any iodine or mercurochrome on. He said 'A dog's saliva is healing and it doesn't do children's sores any harm if a dog licks them, too.' A theory with which Mum did not agree.

After a while I could perform this operation myself and helped Mr. Denny when he was pressured with work. Mr. Denny said it was extremely cruel to cut dogs' tails off on the woodblock in the back-yard the way many people did. And as for some of the other home grown cures, such as cutting a dog' s ears and nose and letting it bleed, if it had been bitten by a snake, or swinging it round and round by its tail if it had taken a glass-bottle bait, well, he was speechless!

One of the young women whom Mum knew from Red Cross had married a soldier. They had no hope of finding a house or flat so they had bought two of the army 'hut-ments' that were put up for sale at the Allied Works Council's auctions, to make a home. Mum and I were invited to visit and went, taking a fern in a pot as a house-gift. Barry had made the handsome pot by cutting down a kerosene tin with Dad's tin-snips and then creating a decorative edging of curlicues by tightly winding down the strips of tin around the edges, and painting the whole thing green. He had actually made it for Mum, but when she said 'This young couple have nothing and they are just starting out', he was persuaded to let it go to the newly-weds instead.

Mum and I found the place. It was on a bit of waste ground near the salt-pans beyond the Show Grounds. There was quite a little settlement of similar establishments. The tiny home was the essence of cosiness. It was like the best imaginable cubby-house, with curtains at each window, mats of hooked-rags on the lino and cut-out pictures from magazines and calendars on the walls. The curtains were of the cheese-cloth with which army meat was wrapped, but tied back with ribbons they had a pretty effect. There were paper-flowers in pickle bottles which had been painted and on which cut-out pictures of pears or plums from tinned fruit had been pasted to turn them into vases. The bed was covered with a shining white bedspread which the bride's grandmother had crocheted as a wedding gift. Under the bed could be seen an enamel jerry-pot. The bride said there was a community lav. which the men had dug, but at night she did not like to go there alone.

The ground around the door had been swept so that it was like concrete. The bride said she scattered the used tea-leaves around each day before sweeping it over to keep down the dust. There were pots of ferns and of the little mauve-coloured flowers known as stink-ing-billies, making quite a pretty show. On a duchess made of two kerosene cases around which a pretty flounce had been draped, was a picture of the couple, the husband in his army uniform and the bride in her AWAAS's, on their wedding day outside the West End Methodist church. They had been married only six weeks when the bridegroom had been posted to Milne Bay. As he was an assistant pay-sergeant and not a jungle-fighter, it seemed very likely that he would return in due course to the little home filled with so much love and cheerfulness.

Mum said, as we trailed around the edge of the salt-pan back to the bus-stop, that it had all reminded her of the pioneering days when she and Dad had been Soldier Settlers in the Dawson Valley. They had lived in a home which they had built themselves, a tent at one end and a bark-hut at the other, while they cleared the brigalow-land the Government had allocated to them, acre by acre, all by hand. 'Your father made all our furniture from kerosene cases and I stained it with Condie's Crystals and polished it with boot-polish! Even your cot was made from a whiskey case! We didn't have a penny! It was the middle of the Depression.'

We trudged in silence for a few minutes. Suddenly, Mum added, 'When I knew I was on the way with you, it was the last straw. I could see no way that we could possibly manage. At one stage we were reduced to living on turnip-tops. The actual turnips were for the cattle, to keep them going doing the drought. Grandfather Greenleaf sent one hundred pounds to see us through but, would you believe! The government took it all in unpaid lease fees! They were completely heartless! And your father all through the trenches at Ypres and the Somme! So much for the Land Fit for Heroes! We had not one penny! Nor had any of the other settlers. I tried everything I knew to end the pregnancy. Everything!' Brushing away the persistent flies, I absorbed this information, which I realized was more to do with remembering out aloud than actually talking to me.

Far from being cast-down at the news that I had been an unwanted baby, I found myself feeling rather clever. Fancy out-smarting them all! Surviving the 'everythings' so darkly referred to! I did not think of myself as formless, a mere cluster of cells, but like the china doll found in the gully pool, tiny but perfect. But what a quick-witted little thing I must have been, like the good Grade Six and Grade Seven skipping-girls at school who, clutching tight to the hem of their dresses, could do 'One! Two! Three! Pepper!' and not be 'out' until the rope-turners arms had tired. To think I had been like that! As we approached the bus-stop, Mum interrupted my thoughts with a deep sigh. 'That poor young woman! She will find that 'Love flies out the window when poverty walks in at the door.' There was never a truer saying.'

But, everywhere now, there were signs that the war was drawing to a climax. Barry had a map on the wall with little flags made of match sticks to mark the various stages of the Allied progress across France. As the tide of war rolled on, the flags sometimes gave up the ghost and fluttered to the floor like dead moths. But when the Allies broke through the Siegfried Line in October he made a large triumphant flag and secured it in position with shoes-tacks. He could remember the dark days at the beginning of the war, when the defiant song had had been *We're Going to Hang Out the Washing on the Siegfried Line*. The Siegfried Line was a line of defence fortifications which the French thought would defend their country from the Germans but it had soon been over-run and France surrendered to the invaders. Now the allies had regained it and had freed France from their enemies. The picture in the *Bulletin* which Barry cut out for his scrap-book showed British Tommies actually hanging their socks and singlets on the fortifications of the Siegfried Line, with Mr. Churchill looking on, puffing on his cigar. Barry had to explain the meaning of the joke to me several times before I cottoned on that 'line' could mean a defence position as well as a washing-line.

The great German battleship *Tirpitz* was sunk by RAF Lancasters. Even so, Hitler announced that Germany would never surrender. 'That man must be the most hated man in the whole of human history!' cried Mum who had been reading of the losses of the British Empire alone; over one million killed. And since the D-day landings alone over four hundred thousand Germans had been killed. Barry's eyes glittered with envy when it was known that the Germans were now recruiting boys of fourteen and fifteen for their armies and sending them straight to the Front. He told me as we rode home from the beach one afternoon 'Don't let on to Mum, but I'm thinking of shooting-through to Sydney. I might be able to pull a swiftie on them down there about my age. I'm pushing six foot now, so they might fall for it. It's worth a shot. If I don't get a move on this whole shebang will be over before I get a crack at the bastards!'

The thought that immediately sprang into my head, quite uninvited, was that were he bravely to enlist then I would be able to have his room, the cosy little one with the sloping ceiling. I would inherit his desk, his wall-map, his bookshelf, his drawerful of war-relics and his door opening out on to the hillside. Jipsy would be able to sleep under my bed without Mum knowing. 'No, I won't say anything,' I promised loyally.

But Dad was posted back again to the big camp on Bayswater Road, the army using his common sense and flair for organisation to sort out any problems that occurred with supplies to the troops. Mum would sigh heavily 'That man could have made a fortune working for the Americans! Everyone else's husband is simply raking it in!' With Dad home, Barry's plan of 'shooting through' to join up in Sydney had to be dropped. It was almost like being a proper family to have Dad home again, even though it was only for a day or a night, every so often.

The first thing he decided was that I should have a bike so that I could ride to school instead of having to catch the overloaded buses in which people jammed two, three or four deep, hanging out of the doors. There were times when the North Ward bus, creaking over the rise in Wickham Terrace, would miss the gears and roll backwards. Each time it did this I was sick with fright. I had never been able to forget the men trapped in the Catalina. The only moment of relief from my dread of the overloaded bus was looking out for the bees which came and went from one of the air-vent grills in the base of the Custom's House. But, now! A bicycle! For me! I could hardly believe my swift ascendancy up the scale of things. A brown lady's bicycle was bought at the sale of twenty-seven unclaimed ones at the Police Station, dumped by servicemen, as Barry's had been.

That night Dad planned a safe route for me to ride to school to avoid the traffic of Flinders Street, drawing a little sketch map on a scrap of paper. This is the Cutting, see? I could ride to the foot of the Cutting, and then walk beside the bike on the footpath until I got into the quiet backstreets of West End; then, and only then, was I to mount and ride the remainder of the way to school. Did I understand? Yes, Dad! I must always place the bike in the school bike-racks by its back wheel. Putting bicycles in racks by their front wheels caused the front wheel to buckle. Did I understand? Yes, Dad! I must never ride standing up on the pedals, as that caused the chain to stretch. Right? Did I understand? Did I promise? Yes, Dad! Oh! Yes, Dad! Yes!

It was just as well that no placing of hand and swearing on the Bible had been involved. On the first day I did all that was required of me. On the second day I felt sure I could get half-way up the Cutting if I stood on the pedals and zigzagged, as I had seen Barry do. On the third day, I felt a compulsion to reach the same mark again, or to pass it. I swiftly forgot about the back wheel having to go into the bike-rack, not the front one. Everybody else put theirs in front-wheels first, all the bikes drooping uniformly. How could I be different? As for the quiet back-streets of West End, perhaps even Dad realized that there was an element of fantasy about that.

Within a very few days I was skillfully negotiating a passage for myself amidst the traffic snarls of Flinders Street West with the best of the blitzwaggons and Chinamen's carts. There even came a time when, judging the right moment, I could catch hold of the iron-bound edge of the flat tray-back of one of the brewery-trucks to be towed effortlessly along, steering with my left hand and keeping a skilled eye on the big solid-rubber wheel of the truck rumbling along beside me.

Dad also decided he would get the gardens started for us, vegetables at the back, flowers at the front and tiny strips of lawn between the rocky beds. The water restrictions had been eased and watering of gardens was permissible as long as someone was holding the hose. The someone was me. When Dad was in camp, it was easy enough. The merest sprinkle, shaking the hose so that the stream of water made figure eights and other intersecting patterns in the air and the job was done. But if Dad was home he would get a bit of stick and investigate. 'Ah! Snookie! You don't call that watered, do you?' he would chide. The long shadows of late afternoon would be spilling down the hillside, the parrots exploding in colour as they screeched homewards and longed-for playtime receding further and further before I was free to go.

Sometimes release only came with the welcome theme tune of the ABC Children's Session, the Argonauts' Club, based on the legend of Jason and the Search for the Golden Fleece. I sent in my postal note for two shillings and back came my badge and pledge:

I promise to seek adventure,
And having discovered
Aught of wonder and delight, of merriment or loveliness,
To share it freely with my comrades,
The band of band of Happy Rowers.

I was allocated to the ship Xerxes. The 'rowing' was all imaginary. You rowed for your ship by sending in stories or poems or letters. Many of the other Argonauts' letters seemed to be about dogs that had saved owners from snakes or babies from drowning. I regarded Jipsy with a critical eye. How was it that she had not yet performed one of these point-winning actions? But Jipsy would yawn hugely and move herself to a cooler spot on the verandah. The late afternoon sound of the theme song,

Row, mighty Argonauts, bending to the oars,
Today we go adventuring to yet uncharted shores...

signalled the end of the cares of the day. This was my time to curl up on a dining-room chair as close to the front of the wireless as possible and enter into a world of myth and legend and escape from the ordinary. I really believed that I was part of a noble quest. There were dragons to be overcome. Wrong would bow to right. There was laughter and fellowship, song and story. Excellence was not only expected but achievable. It was a magical counter-balance to the unlovely rowdiness of Miss Thomas's Grade Four.

Dad had decided that the pale and listless soil of the terraced garden beds needed some cow-manure to revitalise it. If the Ackland children were riding out to the Common to collect 'cow-pats', I should go with them. Townsville Common was an area of lagoons, sand-dunes and salt-pans with belts of paper-barks and pandanus, behind the sickle-curve of Rowe's Bay where people who had dry house-cows or horses could put them out to spell for a few months. The Town Council had installed a wind-mill and troughs to which the stock walked in every day to drink. The cattle stood around after drinking in meditative groups enjoying the companionship and occasionally lifting their heads to roar cow-hellos to an acquaintance in the far distance. The paddock was liberally covered with hard round platters or cow-pats of dried manure known as 'buffalo chips'.

With Jipsy on my carrier, a packet of sandwiches, a bottle of water and an empty sugar bag, I would set off with the Acklands and Ronnie. Barry was no longer involved in our activities. Now that he was fourteen he saw himself as a man involved with Air Training Corps and National Fitness.

The bitumen ended at the Three Mile bridge. After that we had to stand on our pedals to heave the bikes through the loose hot sand. Once the tip of the windmill came in sight there was a bush track which turned off into the sand-dunes, winding through the paper-barks and around the edges of the lagoons. During the Dry most of these were waterless and the lush vegetation around them was brittle and dead. An occasional group of wallabies would start up, regarding us with paws held neatly at the ready before bounding off through the scrub, tiger-striped with paper-bark shadows.

When the windmill-paddock was reached, collecting the buffalo chips began. It paid to be circumspect and carry a stick. Underneath many a circular cow pat dwelt a scorpion or centipede, thinking itself secure in its fortress of damp and darkness. It had to be disabused of this notion and whacked, writhing, into oblivion before the cow-pat could be claimed for the bag. It was also best to tap each cow-pat with the stick to ensure that it was in fact well sun-dried. No one wanted to be involved with the green slimy consequences of ones that weren't. Even the boys drew the line at throwing these at one another. Once the bags were full we tied them up with string and propped them under a black-wattle for later collection. The rest of the day was our own. We could head further into the interior of the Common to where the vegetation gave way to the aerial roots of mangroves fringing the tidal mud-flats and creeks of the Bohle or weave our way through cattle-pads and bush tracks to the foot of Many Peaks Range. Overhead was an immensity of sky and cloud, and always there were birds.

Brolgas probed for tubas by the drying lagoons, strolling, heads down, companionably, sometimes breaking off the quest to bow and curtsy graciously to one another with occasional sideways leaps of pleasure. Magpie geese congregated around the remnants of waterholes. Sometimes these would take exception to our arrival and start up, beating the air with scratchy wings as they formed wedges that honked off to the south-east. Along the white rims of the remnant water-holes plumed with rushes and bottle-brush, stalked egrets, spoonbills and ibis, prodding the tea-coloured shallows for their lunch. Wise old pelicans sailed in pairs, conversing gravely in pelican-talk. They were like old married couples, always communicating; a serious 'Wark, wark!' to which the answer would be a grave 'Wark, wark, wark!' The straw-yellow grasses were alive with finches, red-backed wrens, bee-eaters and double-bars; overhead, in an infinity of cloud and sky, drifted dark motes that were kite-hawks.

Often a sand-goanna would waddle across the track into the tawny-grey undergrowth, his tongue flicking abuse. There were boomerang-shaped markings in the pink sand, where a snake had thrust its weight forwards. There were dingo tracks; never a dingo, or any that allowed themselves to be seen.

At the foot of Many Peaks Range where the baking mud-flats skirted the scrub, we had a favorite rock which we called Sphinx Rock, because it looked like a huge carved head with eye-sockets and mouth. Perhaps a million years before, it had rumbled down from the thirsty escarpment and parked itself at the edge of the salt-pans. The seaward side was fretted with pockets and cavelets into which we scrambled, calling out to one another like prisoners in a row of cells while the billy boiled for dinner and the smoke drifted upwards among the pandanus.

Then it would be time to head for home, collecting our bags of buffalo chips along the way. Once when we were nearly back to the Three Mile Bridge and the air was shrill with late afternoon bird tumult, John suddenly realized that he had left his sandals behind. Worse, he couldn't remember where! They were new ones and he had taken them off to save wear and tear, playing and climbing barefoot. Smitten with group anxiety, guilt and fright we clung to the wooden railings of the bridge and exhorted him to, 'Think!' At last he remembered. He had put them in the fork of the paper-bark near Sphinx Rock. Max, as the elder brother and therefore the one who must hold himself responsible, said 'You lot go on home. I'll go back with John. See you later, then,' every bit the bomber pilot who must hold his craft steady while the crew parachute to safety, accepting the risk because it went with the rank.

The two boys headed back into the long shadows of late afternoon. It would be almost dark before they got there and long after dark before they got home. A good hiding from Mr. Ackland's razor-strop was sure to await them both. You did not lose things, especially things that had cost good money. You looked after things that had been provided for you. You had to learn to be responsible.

Christmas approached and it seemed that our family might be together for the first time since 1940. Dad would be home. He brought some things from the army canteen for us;

tinned apricots, boiled lollies, tinned orange juice and, marvellously, some potatoes for Christmas Dinner. Mum made a cake, giving each of us a stir so that we could make a wish for the coming year. She scrubbed some silver threepenny bits with sand-soap to be put in. We knew that in the bottom of her wardrobe there were presents wrapped. Barry had a look and a feel. He told me; something flat and hard, something with a handle. Some sort of bat?

Dad stood outside the chook-yard fence speculatively, trying to gauge exactly which one of the hens it was that wasn't laying. One of them was for the chop. Eventually one of them was herded into the corner, seized and borne protestingly forth. On to the wood-block went her head. Whack! Down came the axe. No messing about with Dad. If a job had to be done then it was done. No use sentimentalising over a chook. A chook that wasn't laying had come to the end of her productive life. She couldn't expect to go on eating her head off for nothing. The decapitated hen ran frenziedly around the woodheap before flopping down on to her side, legs scrabbling at empty air.

But, Oh Dear! When gutted, this chook proved to contain a clutch of orange-coloured shell-less eggs, each one smaller than its predecessor, receding back to tiny match-head sized ones, the promise of eggs for months to come. The entrails were very speedily drawn and the feathers disposed of. Dad paused at last to pat his pockets for the 'makings' of a smoke and his tin of wax matches. 'Now you won't go dobbing me in with your mother about this, will you?' he said off-handedly, watching me over the cigarette paper attached to his dampened lip while he pinched out the correct amount of shredded tobacco. I shook my head gravely, registering with interest that adults could not only get things wrong but want to cover their tracks as well.

Mum and Dad between them put up the Christmas decorations, criss-crossing them across the dining-room table. We had a little gum-tree from up the hill for a Christmas Tree. The paper-chains on the verandah blew down almost as soon as the afternoon sea breeze got up but things certainly looked Christmassy. Then, late on Christmas Eve, came the news from Clyde, Mrs. Woodward had died. Just sitting in her chair with her hands folded on her lap! My heart sank. I knew Mrs. Woodward was old but I didn't think she was old enough to go dying! And did it have to be at Christmas!

Christmas became very subdued, punctuated by frequent 'Sshh!'s and 'Keep your voice down!'s from Mum. The hard-and-flat present in the wardrobe turned out to be a Shuttle-cock set which we were allowed to play with on the verandah, quietly. Quiet Shuttlecock proved to be a contradiction in terms. The hurroo when the feathered cock wedged itself into the gap between the corrugated iron and the rafter was the last straw. The set was put away and only Chinese Checkers indulged in for the rest of the day. At four o'clock we tuned into 4TO Townsville to hear the Funeral Notices, always introduced by Handel's *Largo* and the words 'The relatives and friends of the late...' It did not seem possible that they could mean our Mrs. Woodward, who we now discovered had been an 'Angelina'. Could a very old lady be 'Angelina'! It seemed a name for a little girl, or a beautiful Mama doll, the sort with long curly hair and blue eyes that closed when she was tipped backwards.

'Mrs. Woodward was a good woman and a wonderful mother,' said Mum. 'A fine example of womanhood. But it is no longer popular to hold up her type as an example. These days, to be admired, women have got to have legs like Betty Grable or blonde hair like the Andrews Sisters. Whether they are good wives and mothers doesn't seem to count any more.'

Mum and Dad went to the funeral at Stokes Street Presbyterian Church on Boxing Day. Barry and I were told we could take ourselves off to Kissing Point. There was a king tide, smoothly and silkily breathing up and down around the tips of the stakes and piles of the shark-enclosure. The water was crowded, the air full of laugher. Screaming children jumped up and down or fought piggyback fights and young boys did somersaults or jack-knives from the new diving-platform that had been built. Even the little rock-pool in the foot of the cliffs had been cleaned of all the broken bottles that had been flung into it and was safe to use again. It was just like the old days. At least that was something good that had happened this Christmas; both the City Baths and Kissing Point had been repaired by the Council, after the long years of neglect.

T NEWMAN

Chapter 17

VICTORY IN EUROPE: 1945

'Maizy Doates and Dozie Doates and Little Lambsie Divie,
A kid'll divie, too! Wouldn't you?'

Victory in Europe Celebrations, Anzac Park, May 1945.

Townsville was in need of a good sprucing-up! The energetic Council set about doing it. First of all the sandbags from around the Post Office were got rid of. The bomb-blast walls, five-ply structures filled with sandbags, in front of the Government offices in Wickham Street, were taken down. Shops, businesses, the Ambulance Station and the Police Station followed the lead. Any remaining slit-trenches were filled in. The footpaths were cleaned up. The flower-beds along the centre of Flinders Street, which had been trampled out of existence, were dug over and planted with thousands of dusky-pink acalyphas.

Anzac Park had taken an awful hammering. It had been a popular place with off-duty troops for two-up schools, 'canoodling', drinking and sleeping-off the after-effects. The lawns were threadbare, in places turned to sand. The Council began replanting colourful crotons and grass. She-oaks and coconuts were planted round the foreshore of Rowe's Bay. There was an added incentive for all this. Australia's new Governor-General was to be the King's brother, the Duke of Gloucester; he and the Duchess were to visit Townsville in early June.

There were other signs of a return to normality. On Sunday afternoons, the white sails of the skiffs and V-Jays of the Sailing Club bedecked the bay. The private schools, St Annes's, St Patrick's Convent and Townsville Grammar returned from exile to their proper establishments. A poll on whether to build a pipe-line to bring water from Mt Spec was discussed and argued about. Even children took opposing views and waxed loud and heated as they had seen their elders do, chanting in groups 'No! No! No!' or 'Yes! Yes! Yes!' angrily at one another.

Return to school for First Day Back of 1945 was a day of anticipation and dread. Who were all these new clever-looking faces in our class? Grade Five was the beginning of preparation for Scholarship. From now on school was a serious affair. We knew that such matters as Compound Interest, Relative Pronouns and Isosceles Triangles lay ahead. West End had a reputation for good results in the Scholarship exams. Almost every year one of the top ten passes in the State, the first of whom was awarded the Lilley Medal, would come from West End. This year it had been Beverley Allan, the sister of one of the new girls in the class. We all filed into Assembly to see her receive her book prizes and to be showered with praise. Even the teachers seemed obeisant in the presence of one who had come fifth in Queensland. Only four places behind the Lilley Medalist! I viewed her sister, Elizabeth, in my new class, with vast alarm. Another contender for top place! As though Bobby Skau and Jimmy Butler weren't enough to worry about!

The Scholarship teacher Mr. Butcher, famous throughout Townsville for his examination results, never let his class out before five o'clock in the afternoon. People who had clever children and wanted them to do well in Scholarship, sent them to West End for Grade Five, to be sure they got Mr. Butcher when the time came. Grade Five was the beginning of this struggle to the death.

Our new teacher was Mr. Goodwin, tall and bony with crinkly black hair and horn-rimmed glasses which made him look like a daddy long legs spider. Each morning he arrived on his bicycle, clips around his trouser-legs, little brown school-port on one handle-bar. Those wishing to earn favour would cluster near the memorial gateway and chant 'Good morning, Mr. Goodwin!' as he rode through.

We were glad to have him as our teacher, not one of the temporary ones. There was status in being in Mr. Goodwin's even though he was known to be 'tough', hurling chalk with great accuracy at anyone not paying attention to the blackboard, prowling the aisle, cane in hand, while holding forth on nouns-in-apposition, or the derivatives of the Latin root, 'gradior, gressus'. When the class grew languid in the afternoon heat he would snap us back to reality. Wham! The cane came down on a blackboard duster, a storm of chalk-dust flew up powdering those in the front desk. 'If you want to do Scholarship, brighten your foot-work!' he would roar. It was good to have a tough teacher. It made you feel significant; on your way up the ladder of things in life.

Sometimes he would be more tranquil. Legs propped on his desk, he would disappear behind the *Bulletin* while we got on with Sum Cards. These were kept in a linen-covered box on his desk. Good pupils could fly through a card at a sitting and earn a nod of approval between turnings of the pages of the paper. They ostentatiously marked their sums from the Answer Sheet, selected a new card and ruled up a new page. I laboured over one card for a week.

There were twenty sums on each card, ranking in difficulty from addition and subtraction through those involving money, then measurements: Linear, Avoirdupois, Troy and Square, growing progressively harder. Required amounts of carpet for rooms, areas of odd-shaped playing fields, problems about trains that left different stations at different times travelling at different speeds; 'At what time would they pass?' There were others about filling baths with water flowing at a certain rate of gallons per hour. If the plug had been left out so that a given number of gallons of water escaped, how long would it take to fill the bath. Why would anybody want to? What about water restrictions! Desperation filled me at the senselessness of it all.

The only gleam of hope lay in Sum Number Twenty, which was usually a 'Bill' to be set out as a business account with the working shown in a column on the right hand side. 'Fourteen and a half yards of muslin at one and sevenpence halfpenny per yard' and similar purchases of buckram, flannel or crepe-de-chine. Sometimes the items were more masculine: 'Sixteen bales of hay, seven pairs of boots, one dozen pitch-forks, a hundredweight of flour and two cases of jam' all at various prices, seldom without the irritant half-penny on the end. We might have been stocking some isolated property or equipping an expedition into the interior.

Once, while the class was so occupied and Mr. Goodwin relaxing behind his newspaper, there was a sudden alert: Mr. Jones's heavy tread coming up the staircase! With admirable coolness Mr. Goodwin swung his long legs off the table, surveyed us casually as though momentarily interrupted, and began to read aloud. '...a hitherto undiscovered valley, the inhabitants of which had never before set eyes on white men. An air-strip was built, with the co-operation of the native people themselves, and the rescue was carried out by glider, flown in by a volunteer, and hauled to safety by a rescue plane, one of the most daring feats in the history of air-navigation.' Mr. Goodwin was explaining the meaning of the term Shangri-la when Mr. Jones made his entrance and the class thundered to its feet. Shangri-la, according to Mr. Goodwin, was a place where the men all had sixteen wives and never did any work but sat and talked all day while the women did everything. The two men exchanged glances which they thought well above our heads.

This tactic proved to be so successful that from then on Mr. Goodman read aloud quite frequently from his newspaper while we did Sum Cards. In this way we learned not only that the Americans had taken Iwo Jima, that Guy Gibson, who had led the Dam Busters attack, had been killed and that President Roosevelt had died, but also that giant cane toads from Hawaii were eating bees out of hives at Mysterton Estate and that someone in Ingham thought it might be possible to invent a machine to cut sugar-cane. I was not surprised about the toads; I had seen their ugly black tadpoles in the rock-pools of the gully.

He did not read aloud the increasing numbers of atrocity stories. There was no need to; everyone knew. Day by day, everyone in the playground gathered, heads together, play suspended, to discuss the latest hideous revelations: crematoriums stoked with corpses, vats of bodies rendered down to make soap, pits in which hundreds of skin-covered skeletons had been dumped, corpses stacked in piles like the timber at J C Butler's timber-yard. Belsen! Auschwitz! Buchenwald!

Mum said to me 'This is the reality of what we have been fighting against!' We knew the stories were true of some distant place, but not of proper life, not life in Townsville. There were other parts of the world where such things were possible. They weren't possible in Townsville. In some of the photos the dead people had faces you might have seen at the Municipal Fruit Mart or Manahan's or on the North Ward bus. Ordinary and yet not ordinary, the faces of people doomed to die like this: to become corpses, sticking out from a pile, mouths open. You could stare. You could know it as a fact. But it could not be understood.

After a long subdued discussion someone, wearied of being unable to understand, would sing out 'Who wants a game of Bedlam?' Everybody would leap up. Lunch tins were slammed into school-bags, school-bags thrown under seats. Let the rest of the world do horrible things; in Townsville they didn't happen; that was all that we needed to know.

Bedlam was rough; even violent. Pockets were torn from shirts, sleeves ripped off, knees and elbows gravel-rashed. When the bell rang there was no time to cool down before Parade. We marched, steaming, into school, to the accompaniment of *Colonel Bogey*, faces scarlet, chests heaving. The classroom smelt like a cattle-truck. It usually took only a day or so for Mr. Jones to announce from the elevation of the front steps 'Bedlam is banned! Anyone caught playing Bedlam will come to the Office for the cane!'

Bedlam was wild, thrilling, exhausting, the best of games. There were two teams, chosen by leaders who 'picked sides' turn and turn about, until only the feeble and the overweight were left shamefacedly waiting. 'In' and 'Out' was decided by tossing a stick in the air. The leaders caught it and grabbed upwards, hand over hand, to the top of the stick. Whoever got the top would choose to run free and be hunted. The others were the hunters. They drew a large semi-circle against the front fence for a prison, over which some of them mounted guard, while the rest set out to hunt in pairs, bringing prisoners back to base. Captured prisoners could be freed by any member of their team being game enough to tear, full pelt, through enemy base, yelling, 'Bedlam!' At this the prisoners could escape with triumphant whoopy-ings as they scattered.

Hunting continued until all were caught, the last one being exhorted with screams to 'Struggle!' At this point the seams of clothing were likely to come adrift or pockets be ripped off. The next day there would be irate notes written by mothers.

The game made it easy to understand why war-heroes performed acts of self-sacrifice. Even though you risked capture and imprisonment, it was impossible to resist the challenge of attempting to rescue your team mates. Keeping to the cover of the African Tulip trees and Miss Thomas's parked Baby Austin, you crept as close as you could into enemy territory, before, casting caution to the you winds, you made your run for it. The out-stretched arms of the base-keeper and his cronies might form a wall ahead of you, but this was your moment. Death or glory! Capture could be eluded by sheer momentum. Flailing arms provided fire-power. In the exultant yell, 'Bedlam!' and at the sight of your team-mates scattering in freedom, you knew you were as close as it was possible to get to the fierce thrill of the

Spitfire pilot at the moment of kill.

Then it was March and the Rainy Season and right round the ranges purple and black water-bag clouds were building up. Down came the heaviest rains for years. The water ran five feet deep over the weirs. A train was washed off the Burdekin Bridge and four passengers floated miles downstream on a log before they made it to the bank. The Three Mile Bridge on the Pallarenda Road was partly washed away. From now on it would only be possible to ride out to the Common by carrying the bicycles down a bouncy plank over the green water. Mum, concerned about the young wife in the make-shift army-hut home, sent Barry out on his bicycle to check. He came back to report that the huts were four feet deep in water. Everyone had fled.

I viewed the flood waters racing out to sea with lugubrious eyes. One of the many books in the Town Library was about a scheme by Dr Bradfield to turn the wasted waters of coastal streams to better use by damming them and redirecting the floodwaters inland for irrigation. Not only did I know this, but I had got ten out of ten for a Composition on the subject. I had discovered a fact of life; if you are not actually clever, the next best thing is to delude people into thinking you are. To do this all that is necessary is to become an expert on topics designed to astonish the less well-read.

This crafty extremity was forced upon me as a survival tactic born of knowing myself to be worse than a dud at Arithmetic. It was a family joke that Dad had tossed me up as a baby in the tent home, hitting my head on the ridge pole and squashing the part of the brain that did sums. In order to claw to my place near the head of the class I had to get extra marks in other areas. So while the others were sniffling over their *Girls' Crystal* magazines I was hopping into H.V. Morton, not so much for enjoyment but because it would pay off. The next time the Composition was about 'A Place I Would Like to Visit', everyone else would write about Magnetic Island or Mount Spec. I would get down to the task of knocking Mr Goodwin sideways with insights about the Scottish Covenanters or the Ladies of Llangollen. In this way I built up a reputation as a brains-trust. My compositions were read aloud. I kept my head modestly lowered and tried not to let on that I knew how much the others were loathing every fulsome word and darting malevolent looks in my direction. I shivered in my shoes thinking that once again I had outsmarted a grown-up. Precious marks had been scored. Secretly I wondered how long I could keep it up. Surely I would soon be revealed as a fake? Or worse, Elizabeth Allan would discover the Town Library!

There were moments of less stress. Someone high in the ranks of the Department of Public Instruction had decided that in the post-war world, Queensland children would need a better standard of physical fitness. A new system of Physical Education was to be introduced; West End School was to be its point of introduction. Teachers from all over the north arrived to be initiated into the new scheme. Our class was to be the demonstration model; the boys stripped to the waist, the girls in brown bloomers and short tunics with a slit at the front for greater freedom of movement. We felt very daring the first time we appeared. Before long every school in Townsville had adopted the Physical Education tunics as their uniform, each in its given colour.

Under the Moreton Bay fig-trees we marched, formed teams and learned to respond to coded whistle blasts and signals, doing things with military precision. Any Sar' Major would have approved of our daily School Parades. We 'fell in', 'dressed ranks', ' at ease'd and 'tentioned!' with the ease of long familiarity. Every morning, shoulders back, we saluted the Union Jack by numbers; 'One!' Right hand smartly to forehead; 'Two!' Right hand smartly to side, fingers curled, thumb tucked in. If it wasn't done crisply enough, we practised until Mr. Jones was satisfied. On Monday mornings it was done to *God Save the King*. We marched, arms swinging, elbows straight, eyes forward, into school to *Colonel Bogey*. Among the boys, being Music Monitor to start the gramophone for the loud-speaker, became second only to being Bell Boy.

Now, medicine balls, skipping ropes, baskets of tennis-balls and cane hoops were dispersed around the grounds. Hoops were for performing rhythmic drills, not for doing the hula, and what a surprise, skipping ropes should be turned backwards not forwards, to correct round-shoulderedness. Shirley Townsend saw it as a chance for us to develop our bosoms, which was rich! She was already well endowed and in such matters. I hardly registered. Medicine balls were heavy and could bend fingers backwards painfully. Basketballs smelt of hot leather and sweat. One long blast of the whistle, the teacher's right arm was raised and given a sweep like an umpire signaling four. You replaced the equipment you had just been starting to get the hang of, 'fell in' behind your Team Leader and trotted off to tackle the next lot.

Finally everyone formed up into squad ranks, raised and lowered on tip-toes, breathing in, breathing out through the nostrils to restore their pulse rate and to calm their thoughts. Secretly you were wondering if you could beat everyone to the drink-troughs and if you got there first, would somebody behind you break your front tooth by shoving you against the bubbler.

Another aspect of Physical Education was Folk Dancing. This was more than the boys had bargained for. They were quite amenable to barefoot drop-kicking of a footie in long slow arcs across the grounds during school-hours or even practising catches with a cricket ball, occasionally getting a finger or two dislocated and blackened in the process. But to ask an actual girl to be a partner, hold hands and hoof it round a circle with her! Come off it! Not bloomin' likely! How would you be!

Staunchly a true believer in the merits of the Scottish Reel, young, blonde and what the boys called a bit of all right, Miss Saunders shouted 'Circle left, eight steps! Circle right, eight steps!' and, to the tune of *Wi'a Hundred Pipers an' a' an' a'* we were away. There were collisions between couples that had counted eight steps for the change, and those who hadn't. Most hadn't. Whenever a movement called for dancers to place their hands on their hips, link arms and circle-skip round one another nicely, boys would seize the opportunity to unbalance the girl entirely by swinging too fast or would allow his neighbour to run painfully on to an extended elbow. Movements requiring partners to trip together beneath an archway of linked hands were sure to be punctuated by 'Aaagh!'s as arms were dropped in perfect time to catch friends' or foes' wind-pipes. Unfortunate breakings of wind, and guffaws in the livelier movements, were only to be expected. Feet shuffled. Dust rose. Happy he who, insufficient girls being available, got to partner another of his own kind. Attempts could be made at elbow-wrestings or foul trippings of the few natural gentlemen in the class, Bobby Skau, Mervyn Cox, Ray Smith and Jimmy Butler. The fact that at the end of each dance, partners were expected to bow and curtsy to one another was the last straw. None the less, before long we were all exponents of the intricacies of the the Durham Reel, the Circassian Circle, and sundry other Cobbler's Dances and Square Dances. I thought them infinitely preferable to the jitterbug, or that strange new fad which Barry had demonstrated at home, the Hokey Pokey.

The war in Europe was drawing to a climax. Mum listened avidly to every news broadcast on the ABC, head pressed to the silk-front of the wireless set. If I wanted to have a hem put down or a diphtheria consent-form signed, I would be waved away irritably with 'Not now! They have released the Dunkirk Prisoners of War!' or 'Berlin is surrounded!' or 'Mussolini is dead!'

At school there was much discussion of Mussolini. No one knew exactly why he was hated so much. We simply knew that it was so. It was fitting to exult in his death, that his body had been dragged around and put on display. 'One Italian mother fired five bullets into his corpse,' said Shirley Townsend who always knew such things; 'One for each of her five dead sons.' Shirley had a photo from the paper of the dead Dictator and his mistress. We all stared hard. The dead Dictator simply looked like a fat man lying untidily on the road-side.

On the same page was a tiny paragraph that Flying Officer Basil Roberts of North Ward had been declared Killed in Action after being listed as Missing in Action since the previous October. As more Prisoners of War camps were released by the Allied armies there were frequent memorial paragraphs about young men who had previously been listed as Missing in Action but who were now known to have been killed. There were many sorrow-filled homes.

But, Oh! The pleasurable excitement when it was known that *Lassie Come Home* was to be shown at the Wintergarden Theatre. As part of the publicity build-up, the theatre management announced a competition; a prize would be awarded to The Most Faithful-looking Dog in Townsville, as a tribute to the beautiful collie star of the film. And, No! Entrants didn't have to be collies. They could be any breed of dog: all they had to do was look faithful. Well! I thought. We've got this in the bag! Jipsy will wipe the floor with them! Faithfulness! Where was there a dog to match her? Didn't she wait for me at the gate, every afternoon, when I came home from school? Mum said it was uncanny. She seemed almost to know the time. Faithful dog! She would outshine them all! The others hardly need enter!

On the day of the competition I got up early to bath and prepare her, even pouring a dipper of Reckitt's Blue-water over her to make her white parts shine. I forgot that the Reckitt's Blue would make the water cold, so that, aggrieved by surprise, she tore off down the hill and rolled in the faint remains of the sand-bag heap. It was a matter of aggravation that the Chinaman's cart had called the previous afternoon and that his horse had filled in the waiting time in the way which horses usually filled in waiting time. To Jipsy this was as 'Evening in Paris' perfume is to humans; Jipsy made sure to apply a dab behind her glossy black ears on either side. None the less, she remained, without a doubt, the certain prize winner. Just look at that faithful face! Where was there a dog to match her!

Mum said not to get my hopes of winning the Faithful Dog competition too high; the judges were bound to be prejudiced in favour of a boy. Not only was this always so, she insisted, but because part of the prize was to be a publicity photo in the *Bulletin*. In the film, the boy-hero of the story was played by Roddy McDowell. Naturally they would want a boy to win, one that looked like Roddy McDowell.

In that case, I decided, I would go disguised as a boy. Roddy McDowell was a bit sissie-looking, anyhow. I borrowed an American GI 'giggle hat' of Barry's and pushed my curly hair out of sight. Wearing shorts and a shirt and sandals and scowling as boys mostly did, I set off for the Wintergarden, Jipsy, as the star of the occasion, riding on the seat of the bicycle, and I doing the pushing from the carrier. As we flew down the Cutting, the wind carried her ears outwards like Spitfire wings.

The fore-court of the Wintergarden was swarming with dogs and dog-owners in various stages of amiability. The air was filled with barking, woofing and yapping. Jipsy pressed herself very faithfully against my legs. I surveyed the assembled throng, and thought 'What a lot of also-rans! Not a faithful face among them! We have got this in the bag!' Margaretta was there with her Pekinese 'Bambi'. Bambi had crossed front teeth which he bared in a most alarming manner at anyone who approached, especially if they cried 'Oh! Isn't she sweet! And what's her name?' They would soon be anxiously examining their wrist and moving on. Two large cross-breds stood on hind legs and made 'Ggnnr! Ggnnr!'s at one another's throats for some time before their owners, assisted by the Theatre Management, were able to separate them. In the process, a tiny Pomeranian was trodden underfoot, and dog and owner complained bitterly. I surveyed them all loftily. I thought to myself, 'This will be the first time I have ever had my photo in the paper! And Jipsy in it too!'

But it was not to be. True to Mum's prediction, a boy won. His dog did not look the least bit like 'Lassie', but was a rangy-looking back-yard dog with the most unfaithful-looking face that I had ever seen on a dog. Personally I thought the judges had not given the occasion the time and consideration it required. They had hurried past with anxious faces. They weren't concentrating, not one bit! They hardly paused to even look at Jipsy, so missing the most obvious winner of the lot.

As for the film of Lassie, the only moment I truly believed was when Roddy McDowell was given a new pencil-case for a birthday present, instead of getting Lassie back, but managed to smile bravely and say 'Aye, Dud. It's chumpion.' It made tears come to my eyes and run down my nose. Too embarrassed to wipe them away, I let them trickle till they reached my chin and them scrubbed them away angily, feeling I too was getting to know about moments of life that didn't work out the way they should have.

At the beginning of May there was a rumour that Hitler was dead. Could it be true? The 'most hated man in history' dead, just like anybody else? Surely he hadn't existed inside a human shape with toe-nails and a bottom and a belly-button, like ordinary people? Surely he was like Frankenstein or the Devil, with a monstrous existence independent of mere body. 'He shot himself. And that Eva woman of his! Well, she took poison! Then they threw petrol over them and burnt them both.' Shirley Townsend seemed certain enough that

Hitler had been only a mortal. There were earnest discussions whether Hitler was now in Hell. When I asked Mum she said bitterly 'It is devoutly to be hoped so. He was the cause of unmitigated suffering to millions.' When she thought I had turned away she said, under her breath 'A thousand years could not be enough for him!' and chopped savagely at the pumpkin.

Because of the continued clothes rationing, a lady Mum knew at Red Cross had given her a red crepe-de-chine dress saying that she might be able to cut it down for me. Mum saw little likelihood of my needing a dress made from red crepe-de-chine. But as it became obvious the war in Europe was drawing to a close she could scarcely contain herself. Out came the red dress to be made into a banner for the front of the house.

She had envisaged a large Union Jack, but she made the discovery that Union Jacks are extraordinarily complicated in design, something I could have told her from trying to do them in pastels at school. Just about everybody's pastel-book had a page that was a Union Jack. Finally she compromised with decorations for the letter box and verandah and a larger one backed on to an old sheet, that read 'Peace – DG', all of which were to be hung the moment the news came through. 'DG' stood for 'Thank God', deo gratia in Latin. Mum added 'DG' or 'DV', for 'deo volente – God willing' to most statements. It was her way of saying 'touch wood'.

But when at last the news was officially made known that the Nazis had surrendered and the war in Europe was over, instead of being happy and excited Mum was infinitely sad, tears streaming down her face as we stood around the wireless to listen to the King's words. 'Let us not forget the sacrifice of those who will not come back, and salute the living who have brought us to Victory...the men and women, armed and unarmed, who have fought, striven and endured to the utmost.' We heard Mr. Churchill, 'Even as a bird out of the fowler's net escapes away, so is our soul set free.' 'Long live the cause of freedom. God save the King!'

Feeling subdued at seeing Mum so upset, Barry and I hung out the prepared flags, but it was not the joyous occasion we had expected. As he climbed up on the verandah railings to tie up the string of little pennants, Barry said bitterly, 'So, the Show is over. Bang goes my chance of getting into the RAAF!' He could not hide his terrible disappointment. Since he had been a little boy he had been waiting for the moment when he could join up. He simply could not believe his bad luck in being born one and a half years too late. 'Mind you, this ding-dong in the Pacific has a bit to go yet! I could still make it, with a bit of luck. If only I was down south!'

For the first time ever the *Townsville Daily Bulletin* had a coloured head-line. In red letters two inches high it proclaimed CEASE FIRE IN EUROPE. Churches rang their bells. Flinders Street was decked with the flags of every nation; shop-fronts were adorned with red, white and blue, verandah posts with crossed palm fronds. 'The place hasn't sparked up like this since the Coronation!' people said. Everyone milling joyfully, there was a procession of bands and marches to the War Memorial in Anzac Park. There were speeches and prayers of thanksgiving. The Community Singing began with *Till the Lights of London Shine Again*, then when it came to

We're marching on! Marching on!
From the land of the southern sea,
So keep your chin up Mother England,
We're marching on to Victory.

the crowd faily bellowed, threw their hats in the air and hugged one another joyfully.

The Acting Prime Minister announced that over one thousand Australian prisoners of war had been released from German prison camps and would be brought home as soon as possible. A public holiday was given throughout the Commonwealth, which meant two holidays in one week as there was also Labour Day.

To celebrate Victory in Europe Day we went to Magnetic Island with the Quelches. The island launch, the *Melita* was decorated with red, white and blue from stem to stem and loaded to the gunnels. Anyone who had a flag waved it over the rails as we chugged out of the inlet. The Quelches were jubilant, hoping that now Noel would be demobbed early and be able to go on with his Law degree.

At Arcadia Uncle Les reclined against the trunk of a hoop pine beside the picnic rug and spread his paper. It was full of pictures of even more Nazi atrocities; of General Eisenhower looking at piles of stacked corpses, of crates containing thousands of wedding rings removed from the Jews before they were gassed, a stack of children's shoes including tiny baby-sandals from the bodies of children that been marched to the gas-chambers. 'How will it be possible to lift the Germans out of the pit of barbarism into which they have plunged themselves?' Mum was saying, as Ronnie and I, pelting one another with wet seaweed, raced up from the edge of the surf.

On the second of the two public holidays I went with the Bensleys to Bluewater. Their car was decorated with bunting for the occasion and Margaretta and I hung out of the window holding our flags into the wind. The picnic ground at Bluewater was alive with people in holiday mood. Margaretta and I had long passed the stage where we had to be piggy-backed out to a shallow sand-bar by Mr. Bensley. We could not only swim but line up to take our turns to play 'Keep the Kettle Boiling' on the diving plank fixed into the fork of the paper-bark tree. On this special holiday the queue was long, children wrapping their arms about their bodies and jiggling up and down, chilled and excited, while waiting their turn. I decided on an experiment; my first dive off the bridge.

The concrete coping of the bridge was hot underfoot as I balanced, looking down into the blue depths. I hugged my hands under my chin and jigged from one foot to another. Could I do it? The bridge didn't seem so high when you looked at it from a distance, but suddenly, the water seemed a long way down. I wished I was back in the line waiting for a turn on the diving plank. But there could be no backing out. It would only give Margaretta the chance to say 'Scaredy Cat!' Apart from being best friends, we did not really like one another very much. Arms over my head I poised a moment, screwed my eyes tight and launched outwards into a dive.

As the cold water closed over me there was a searing pain in my head. 'I have hit a stick. There must have been a stick underwater,' was my only thought. My head felt impaled. When I came to the surface I swam feebly to the under-part of the bridge and crawled out of the water. Hardly knowing what I was doing for pain, I groped my way towards the Bensley's car and crouched on the running-board making small moans. Mr. Bensley found me when he came to lift the picnic things out for lunch. He had no idea what had happened. I was in too much pain to explain. 'We will take you home. Can you hang on until we have had a bite to eat?' he said.

At the hospital Mum sat with me on one of the long wooden benches, the same ones on which I had sat to wait when Barry's leg had been poisoned. The Royal Family, in their Coronation robes on the wall were a comfort. The young doctor who saw me, Dr Green, had thinnish, sandy hair and a concerned face. Even in my pain he reminded me of Rex Tutt, so I tried to not to squirm when he thrust a silver nozzle into my ear and announced that I had burst an ear-drum. I was led away upstairs to a long high-ceilinged ward with rows of iron beds, each with its own mosquito net, which seemed to recede into the distance along opposite walls. I was the only child. The next morning a nurse shook me awake and ordered me to 'pass a specimen' into a large metal bedpan. I had no idea what 'pass a specimen' meant. When, from the various ssss-ing noises along the ward, realization dawned, I knew I would die of utter humiliation.

During the weeks that I spent in hospital I was treated with an amazing new drug called penicillin. Dr Green told Mum that during the war, penicillin had saved thousands of servicemen's lives and that I was one of the first, if not the very first, civilian in Townsville to be treated with it.

Every morning the snowy wooden floors of the ward were scrubbed by the younger nurses, vigorously applying sand-soap in wide arcs before them, scrubbing it into swirling patterns of creamy suds and then sopping it up with a wrung-out floor cloth, moving backwards on kneeling pads the length of the ward. Afterwards the air would be filled with the sweetness of freshly scrubbed pine floors. There were high French windows opening on to the front verandahs and views across the wide blue bay.

The new drug proved very effective and once convalescent I was allowed to sit out in a deck chair on the verandah looking out over the bay, to sniff hungrily at the smell of mashed pumpkin, boiled cabbage and corned silverside which heralded lunch. The pudding was always blanche mange with a dab of plum jam.

One day I was horrified to see two black-clad nuns approaching along the verandah, heavy garments swaying, rosary-beads and crucifixes swinging. Each had a short black strap hanging from a leather belt. Overwhelmed with fright I watched as, saying a few words to each patient in turn, they drew closer and closer. I tried to make myself invisible but it did not work. I felt utterly defenceless. There was no escape. Then they were by my side. Blue kind eyes in tightly wimpled faces, soft Irish voices 'And wesh t' little girl getting' better, an' all?' They were pleased to hear she was. 'Wesh tere anyt'ing she had t' need of? Well, t'en, wasn't she t' lucky one wit' t' lovely verandah t' be sitting on, an' all! An' t' lovely view! An' didn't she have t'pretty curls!' The good Lord and his Mother Mary were invited to bless and keep me. And they were gone, with a glimpse of black lace-up shoes and ribbed stockings as their skirts swung round the corner of the verandah. So that was what Margaretta's Sister Selvetia who said we stank like dead horses when we died was like! Not so very terrible after all!

A lady who lived permanently on the verandah and who had to wash her own knives and forks and dishes after meals because she had TB gave me an encouraging smile. 'Old black crows, ain't they just! Scare the living daylights outa you! But they don't mean no harm. They're good bodies, in the main.' I smiled back, nodding in agreement. I was burdened for this lady. I had seen her crying when she thought no one was looking; no one but the nuns ever seemed to visit her.

Barry came to see me, sitting in awkward silence on the metal hospital chair. Then too loudly he said, 'Listen, Boof-head! You should have waited a bit before you pulled this stunt. As soon as the war is over they are going to be starting work on a new hospital. All brick and glass. I've seen the surveyors and their off-siders taking the levels. This old dump has had its day!'

After an interval, during which he stared impudently at the young nurses, he said, 'Want to hear a joke? It's dinkum! Well, the Japs are using these suicide-planes, y' see. Kamikazes, they're called. It means 'Divine Wind'. They're loaded up with bombs and the pilots try to lob themselves on to our ships. They're getting away with it, too. Did the *Bunkers Hill* in. A direct hit in her magazine! The Jap pilots know they are going to get it in the neck! But, that's OK by them. They reckon they go straight to heaven. Anyway, the British fleet was getting a hammering. The flagship, the *Indomitable*, copped one, fair and square, on the deck. The captain of the *Formidable* sent a signal 'Little yellow bastard.' Like a shot Admiral Vian signalled back, 'Are you referring to me?' As usual I didn't get the point. Barry had to explain it to me laboriously, telling the story a second time, so that I could come in with the laugh at the right moment, though still not really getting it.

That was the last time I was to hear one of Barry's jokes for many years. By the time I came out of hospital he had taken off for Sydney, hoping to wangle his way into the RAAF. Mum said his first step had been to get a job on a freighter heading for the United Kingdom with frozen meat. She had hurriedly packed the small brown port that had been got ready as our evacuation port during the invasion scare and which had gone 'border-hopping' with me to Melbourne, filling it with foodstuffs for her family in England on the off-chance he might be able to deliver it.

Once the freighter got to Sydney, Barry didn't have the correct papers and was put ashore. The RAAF soon tumbled to the fact that he was only fifteen and sent him packing. He got himself a job in Sydney and from time to time Mum received photographs of him; on the promenade at Manly, in the Blue Mountains, usually with his arms around not one, but several, 'brassy' looking girls, which made Mum shake her head sadly. In one photo he was wearing one of the baggy Zoot Suits which had come into vogue among the Americans, though they were banned by the Australian government for requiring too much cloth in the long baggy jackets. The Government knew that the war in Europe might be over but that in the Pacific it was still far from being won.

Chapter 18

'AND PEACE EVER AFTER' : 1945

'Then there'll be time for things, like wedding rings
And peace bells will chime.
When the Lights Come On Again,
All over the world.'

Townsville Railway Station, Victory in the Pacific, August, 1945

So I inherited Barry's snug little room with the sloping ceiling and the door that opened out on to the hill. I was able to smuggle Jipsy in to sleep under my bed unless Mum was alerted by the click, click of her toenails as she crept across the lino. I also inherited all Barry's jobs, for Dad was now stationed at Canungra, the jungle-training camp outside Brisbane.

Four mornings a week I rode in the pre-dawn to Coates' Store for the ice. You had to go early so the ice wouldn't melt before you got it home, strapped in a sugar-bag on your carrier. Even so, it tended to drip down inside your ankle as you pedalled. Waiting for the ice-truck was a companionable time in the early light. Each person had a card which the ice-man marked off so there could be no cheating. When I got home Mum would have the ice-box wiped out ready to receive it from my chilled hands. Then the ice-bag had to be rinsed and pegged on the line.

Another early morning job was getting the bread from the Greek baker in Eyre Street, waiting hungrily with John or Colin Ackland and other children for the baking to be finished and the loaves in their blackened tins to be fetched forth from the oven on long wooden shovels, the morning made fragrant by freshly-baked bread. One of the privileges of this job was breaking off the crusty edges of the loaf as you rode home with it; commonly warned against as 'Don't pick the bread!' Some of the boys thrust the hot loaves down the front of their shirts and had one all but hollowed out before they got it home, despite the knowledge that a clip around the ear would await them.

There was also the wood to be chopped and brought up. There was a poem in The School Reading Book called *The Australian*, which began,

He swings his axe in the early morn,
The blade rings wild and free.

Chopping the wood made me feel very Australian and capable of anything. I remembered Barry's strategy of selecting only the blocks with a true straight grain that would be easy to split and in no time at all had developed a discerning eye. Like Barry I tossed the tough knotty ones to the back of the heap for that some-day-never when Dad would be home.

Then there were the fowls and the garden to be taken care of. I imagined myself running a little farm, almost like Jalna in the series which Mum and I were reading our way through, and myself as Renny Whiteoak, the 'man about the house', making decisions as to when or whether it was time to root out all the tomatoes or whether we needed more bran and pollard.

There was a famine of fowl-feed at Buzacott's, the Stock and Station Agents, so it eked out supplies when a plague of grass-hoppers descended, the fowls scuffling noisily round the hillside after them, the only drawback being that the egg-yolks turned a bright off-putting orange. Another problem was that from time to time I found large cane-toads floating spread-eagled in their drinking bowl. The Poultry Notes in the *Bulletin*, which I read word for word, warned that this could poison the fowls' water. And no Barry to do the disposing of them! He would have used the garden fork.

June the eighth was announced as Victory Day throughout the British Empire. Mum had been busy at her Bluebird, attaching some red, white and blue paper to the hem of a white skirt for me to wear in a concert at school. We were going to march around on the stage, weaving in and out as we sang patriotic songs. But in the letter-box there was an English letter which I carried up to the house, studying it back and front. I could tell it was not from Uncle Horace or any of the aunts. The handwriting was a very beautiful copperplate. When I handed it to Mum she gave a startled gasp. 'It's from your grandfather! Something must be wrong!' The dreadful news was that my little six-year-old cousin, Sheila, had been killed. She was Uncle Horace's and Auntie Win's little girl, born after they had given up hope of having a second child, when Graham was thirteen. She had been killed by an army truck after getting off the bus on her way home from school. Auntie Win, who always met her at the bus-stop, had been delayed for just a few moments and the little girl had run across the road towards her, straight under the oncoming vehicle. 'But there wasn't a mark on her body,' Grandfather Greenleaf had added, as though somehow that had been of some comfort to him and would be to us.

Wiping her eyes, Mum said, 'It is so tragic! That beautiful little girl! To think she was born just after the outbreak of war, and survived all the air-raids and the flying-bombs, and now this! To be killed after peace in Europe has been declared. It is unbearable! They adored the child!'

Mum read and re-read the letter. It was the first time her father had written since she had left home against his wishes sixteen years before. There had been nothing but embittered silence since. Sheila's death changed that. From now on he began to write regularly as though he realized how brief life can be. In one letter there was a hand-tinted photograph of Sheila with tousled golden curls, holding a beach-ball in an English garden. The photo was framed and put on the side-board next to Graham's in his Merchant Navy officers uniform. Mum would sigh as she dusted them, 'How ironic for Graham to survive four years of Atlantic Convoy duty under constant attack and little Sheila to be killed in front of her mother's eyes. Life can be so cruel.'

Mum urged me to keep up Barry' wall-map of the war in the Pacific, but without Barry's enthusiasm the war seemed remote and unreal, even though the American forces were forging their way towards Okinawa to within bombing-range of the Japanese mainland and the prime target, Tokyo.

We heard how important it was to the Japanese people not to lose face. The boys at school were fascinated by the concept that Japanese officers committed ritual suicide, called 'hara-kiri', if they lost a campaign. Once the mechanics of the procedure for hara-kiri were made known, the plunge of the sword into the stomach, the twists and cuts, it was not long before boys in Grade Five could do a pretty good imitation, kneeling among the fallen leaves under the Moreton Bay fig-trees to stab imaginary swords into their entrails, make the required number of cuts and then falling on their faces in death with grimaces of stoic agony, loud 'Aaghs!' and much eye-rolling.

During the first week of the August holidays I was playing at Ronnie's place where a fierce game of tip and run cricket was going on. At the batting end there were proper stumps which had been part of the cricket set, but at the bowling end the wicket was Auntie Elsie's clothes prop. The prop happened to be in use for its proper function, propping up the washing line. Ronnie was bowling and lobbed a short ball. I swung at it and clipped it into the ferns under the back steps. I scampered along the pitch for one run, and was on my way back for a second when I real-

ized that Ronnie was only pretending to be searching for the ball. He had it in his hand and was intending to stump me out. I spun round, made a frantic return scramble to the crease and with a loud cry of 'Wickets!' gave the base of the clothes prop a great whack. The clothes prop jolted to attention and under the weight of its long line of washing, began a slow, irreversible slide. Before our horrified gaze, the entire lineful of freshly-starched tablecloths and shirts collapsed in a deep curtsy into the black soil.

There was a moment of dreadful silence. The other players remembered that they were needed at home, or had messages to run, or little brothers to look after and melted over the fence and away. Taking the opportunity to scowl mightily at the dint which the prop had inflicted upon his bat, Ronnie quavered in the direction of the back landing, 'Mu-um!'

Auntie Elsie had been getting ready to go to Ladies' Morning Tea at Hermit Park Methodist, and had her hat with the little veil and gloves on. Now, lips pressed, she marched down the stairs, forbidding as a pocket-battleship going into action, magnificent in her silence, her face saying it all; 'Suffer the little children.'

Aware of our huge disgrace, Ronnie and I slunk under the house and got out our marble bags. Barry's marble bag, including his precious Tomboler, was something else I had inherited with his departure. Ronnie avoided my suggestion for a game of 'Droppies', wary of the Tomboler's smashing fire-power. We had played Big Moonie and Little Moonie till we were tired of them. Twisting his marble-bag on its string while he decided, Ronnie opted for 'Poison', at which he was an expert. 'Play you for keeps!' he said challengingly. I agreed, striving to appear nonchalant.

We got the holes for Poison gouged out in a well-spaced diamond pattern, grinding round and round with our heels in the dirt. The battle for of the first hole was well joined and we were engrossed in manoeuvres for possession to render it 'Poison', when Auntie Elsie's legs appeared at the top of the steps. 'Ronald! Ronald! This is important! Listen to me!' Ronnie and I eased back onto our heels and eyed one another resignedly. We knew we had been let off lightly regarding the clothes-line. No doubt some tiresome duty now awaited us in retribution.

Auntie Elsie peered through the railings 'Ronald! This is something you should know about. It has just been on the ABC News. It could come up on your Scholarship paper. Are you listening!' He hadn't been. He had been using the opportunity to nudge his blood-eyed aggie closer to the first hole. He did not think that I had had noticed. Auntie was saying 'Ronald! The Americans have dropped this very big bomb, bigger than many, many tons of TNT on a city in Japan called Hiroshima.' Faces raised obediently, Ronnie and I listened. Ronnie was made to repeat the name several times so it would sink in. We were made to spell it; 'H-i-r-o-s-h-i-m-a'. I made a mental note of it too. I had my reputation as a fountain of all knowledge in Mr. Goodman's eyes to consider.

As soon as Auntie Elsie had gone back upstairs, I hissed fiercely 'Rotten cheat! I saw you give your taw a nudge!' I demanded rights to the first Poison hole in compensation. Ronnie said, 'Come off it! What do you think this is? Bush Week?' Our voices raised in accusation and protestations of innocence, Hiroshima was soon forgotten.

Within days came news of Nagasaki. For a while the new American bomb was the sole

People who had cars or trucks had decorated them with flowers and palm-branches and Victory V's. One covered in bougainvillea had a little girl in white on the bonnet with a banner 'The Angel of Peace'. I had a momentary pang of envy as she was cheered past. A British Bulldog, dressed in a Union Jack waist-coat, hung over the side of his owner's motor-cycle side-car, panting happily. 'Winston' had been a star feature of many wartime parades and I always looked out for him. A crowd of boys had decorated their bicycles, threading coloured paper in and out of the spokes and tying bunches of streamers on the handle-bars. They rode arms about one another's shoulders. A South Townsville boy rode past in a decorated billy-goat cart drawn by a wily old billy who had to be hauled out of the garden beds every few paces. On one float the women and girls were got up as sections of the American flag and a very tiny boy about four years old was dressed as Uncle Sam. They were given a rousing cheer.

Every float, every band, every contingent was cheered and applauded, but the Garrison Battalion got the loudest 'Hurrah!' of all. They weren't even marching properly with fingers clenched and arms straight, but were sauntering along kissing girls that ran out to meet them or putting their arms in a brotherly fashion around little boys who fell into step beside them. Some had flowers stuck in their hats. Some had toilet paper wrapped around them. Some had no hats at all. One had a little dog riding on his shoulder.

As the tail end of the procession came in sight, everyone fell into step with the bands and began to follow along to Anzac Park. As we were swept forward with the crowd Mum said to me urgently 'Now keep up! Don't get separated!' I squeezed along behind her, pressed in on all sides by cheerful noise. A man with a little girl on his shoulders crossed in front of me. A stout lady with a tiny pug dressed in red, white and blue jacket and tie, wheezed and paused to catch her breath. I turned my head for one moment to look at the pug. When I looked back Mum had disappeared. All that could be seen was a wall of people pressing forward, bearing me along.

Breaking into a trot, I squeezed in and out of the packed throng with 'Excuse me, please!'s of desperation. I dropped into the gutter to make better headway. The thought struck me, maybe Mum was not in front but behind! I passed the man piggy-backing the little girl. People pressed by on all sides, laughing and talking. I squeezed into a shop doorway and jumped up and down to see over their heads. Not a sign of Mum! Suddenly the warm evening seemed cold. I felt like a party balloon let down with a whoosh; all my air had gone out.

The entire width of the street was one mass of people pressing towards the Strand to secure good places for the open-air concert and speeches. From somewhere near Hayles' Wharf could be heard the mixed strains of *Scot's Wha' Hae*' and *Three Cheers for the Red, White and Blue* as the Townsville Ladies' Pipe Band closed with the Townsville Citizens' Brass.

Mum might as well have disappeared off the face of the earth. There was nothing for it but to follow the crowds. In any case there was little choice. The entire population of Townsville was moving in one direction and I had no hope of moving in the other. Nervous fright was replaced by fear, not of being lost, for all I had to do was to catch a bus home, but fear of what Mum would have to say.

Borne down by misery I heard in the distance the whistles and squeals of microphones as the mayor on the flag-draped podium got ready for his speech. The words '...tribute to our brave fighting men...courage and self-sacrifice...ever-lasting gratitude... brave American Allies' reverberated through the dark trees as I skirted round the fringe of the crowd, searching. When the mayor came to the part about 'those who have lost their loved ones being more sorrow-filled than rejoicing in this hour' he could have been speaking of me. I caught sight of John, Shirley and Colin perched aloft on the shiny barrel of the field-gun from World War One. 'Have you seen my mother?' I called, hard-put to keep the quaver out of my voice. They shook their heads, sorrowful for a moment, understanding only too well the trouble that lay in store for me. 'Stay with us,' urged Shirley, all motherly concern. 'We could take you home.' I shook my head. My mood was too dismal to accommodate their high spirits.

Round and round the crowd I trailed, even when all hope was gone. Mum had been wearing her white linen dress. I ran up to anyone in white, my heart wild with hope. Each time it was someone else. Several times I was almost sure I saw her moving through the crowd ahead of me, but by the time I got to the spot she would have disappeared. I even peered up into the branches of the dark trees crowded with youths, to make sure she was not among them.

There came a moment when my legs would carry me no further. Utterly worn out and dispirited, my mind registered the thought 'Go home!' I turned my back on the happy crowd and set out. There was a bonfire blazing on Castle Hill and others had been lit around the curve of the bay, the orange lights flickering and gleaming in the dark water. The crowd behind me was just warming to the task of *Bless 'em All*, when I heard the squeal of the North Ward bus coming round the Custom's House corner. As I climbed on board all I could say to the driver was 'I've lost my penny.' I had said the same thing many times in happier circumstances, having spent it on an icy-pole, or a packet of seeds at Woolworth's.

'She'll be right, Love' said the driver. It was little Mr. Piper from our street. 'Hop on! The war is over! It's the Peace!' The empty bus, burdened only by me and my huge unhappiness, lumbered along the darkness of the Strand leaving the crowds to their bonfires and celebrations.

Hours later when I was deep in the blessed relief of sleep, I was aware of the bedclothes being flung back. A rain of slaps, hard and angry, fell upon me. Like infuriated wasps, angry words darted about my head; 'looking for hours!' 'been to the police'... 'frantic!'... 'murdered'... 'out of my mind' ... So tired and wretched was I that either I didn't wake properly or had the sense to realize that sleep was a kind of sanctuary. I acknowledged to myself the fairness of it. I should not have got lost. It was my own fault. Rotten Peace Celebrations! Phooey to them!

Once the holidays were over and school reopened we got well and truly into preparations for the All School's Sports Carnival and Peace Tableau. Mr. Poulsen was by now resorting to outright bribery. If we marched properly and got it right he would see to it we got our photo in the paper. We squared our shoulders and stepped out. 'Lep! Right! Lep!' It was a vast improvement that there was a gramophone record of *We'll Make a Bonfire of Our Troubles* to swing along to. When the wind was in the right direction you could almost hear it.

The day came, 31st August 1945. The Grand Stand at the Sports Reserve was packed with parents and spectators. People were in a mood to celebrate. First there was an athletics programme with sprints and relays. This was followed by ball-games for the girls; circle-dash, tunnel ball and corner spry. Then came a display by the boys; vaulting, somersaulting and pyramid-building. West End's pyramid was topped by Cyril Lovelady, the smallest in our Grade Five. There was not a sound from the crowd as, placing his bare feet on the knees and shoulders of the boys in the base of the formation, he reached the top, paused for a moment to get his balance, grinned and threw his arms out wide in triumph. There was a burst of appreciative applause.

Then came the climax of the day, the moment for which everyone had been waiting. We had been lined up school by school chittering with nervous excitement at the back of the grandstand. When all was ready the signal was given. The loud-speaker crackled to life, *Colonel Bogey* blared and 'Lep! Right! Lep!' we were moving. The children of every school in Townsville in perfect step marched on, rank upon rank, fingers curled, thumbs pressed down, arms swinging shoulder-high. Eyes were to the front except for perfectly natural squinnyings up into the Grand Stand. Was Mum looking? Had Dad come? Was that Grandma?

Rank upon rank we advanced, marked time and wheeled, until one by one the letters P... E... A...C...E had been blazoned in living white across the green lawns. Then came a single whistle blast. We knew what to do. Soundlessly we dropped to a kneeling position and put our heads on our hands. For a brief instant it was like the air-raid practices of the early days of the war. There was a moment's perfect silence, followed by astonished applause from the spectators. At a second whistle fifteen hundred children leapt to their feet, drew out white handkerchiefs and fluttered them wildly above their heads. P E A C E came alive with happiness and excitement. In the grandstand, out came a thousand Box Brownies to click the moment of history into family albums. In this respect West End was most fortunately situated. Our letter being 'A' was dead centre. But that was only fair. After all, it was our Mr. Poulsen who had organised it all.

Then came Folk Dancing, the grand finale. We Durham Reeled and Oh! Suzannaed to perfection. Who would think there had been ever been mumblings and mutinies. There were Ron Hacket, Bobby Skau and Cedric Keast circling eight to the left, eight to the right, skipping on the spot, hands on hips, tripping under archways with every nicety of execution. Such verve, such dash just proved they loved every minute. Not a collision, not an elbow-gouge in sight. When the music drew to a close, we bowed and curtsied as though, being children of Townsville, we were born to grace and elegance. In that moment we almost believed we were. The applause of the assembled parents was thunderous. Without a doubt it could have been heard high on the eminences of Castle Hill where, it was hoped, Mr. Poulsen's photographer was lurking.

At school it was only to be expected that we would have to write a Composition: 'What Peace Means to Me'. In Mr. Goodwin's Grade Five we chewed the ends of our pencils and scowled in perplexity. No one was sure what Peace entailed. None of us could clearly remember when there had not been a war. We had spent a childhood without lollies, chocolates, ice-cream or entertainment. Toys had been few and far between, but we had played our games and had our fun. None of us wished our childhoods had been any different. None of us was aware they could have been.

Mr. Goodwin wrote some ideas on the blackboard to get us started. What about the long lists of names of Prisoners of War that were being published in the paper every day? Those men would be home soon, wouldn't they? Eight thousand of them. We should mention them. I knew Cousin Graham's ship was in Singapore bringing some of the Changi prisoners home. Well, that was one idea. I could bring that in. Then there was the swimming pool on the Strand. Perhaps work would start again on it now that the war was over. There was talk of naming it the 'Tobruk Memorial Pool.' We could put that in too. Anything else?

'Sir!' said Jimmy Butler, clicking his fingers, 'The pill-box shelters in Flinders Street! My father reckons they're going to bull-doze them and use the rubble to fill in the old Swimming Basin!' Mr. Goodwin was startled. This was a new one on him. But Jimmy Butler ought to know. His father had been Chief Warden all through the war. 'Well! Well! It's hard to imagine the Strand without the Swimming Basin. Or Flinders Street without the pill-boxes, for that matter. The town won't seem the same!' he said.

Elizabeth Allan's hand was raised. 'Sir! What about all the new roads in the North since the war. Perhaps they will build a road to Brisbane now!' At once, I was on my mettle. Elizabeth Allan was now one of my best friends. We had a secret club called the Bushrangers with a cubby on the hill, club badges and a secret password. But now We are being clever, are We! Right!

While others flustered and frowned over what to put for that crucial opening sentence, I was away. First of all I had Mum and I going on a cruise 'Home' to England, to see Grandfather Greenleaf. A couple of lines from *Daffodils* came in handy here. For a moment I toyed with the idea of having us actually fly, but that was stretching it a bit too far. Ordinary people didn't fly; especially not to England. But as a return salvo for Elizabeth Allan's marvellous road systems, I got in another bite of the Bradfield Scheme cake. Perhaps the government would dam the mighty Burdekin and turn its waters to irrigate the inland? And perhaps some of the Displaced Persons of Europe for whom we had collected money and clothes, well, perhaps some of them could be brought to Australia as settlers!

Then for the big conclusion. I knew the value of the tug at the heart. What could be more telling! I played an unbeatable trump: '...but it will not seem that Peace has truly come until my father returns home to us again.' Even writing it I felt a phoney. It was how I was supposed to feel; I knew that. The truth was, I didn't. And knowing that made me uneasy and guilty. In my heart of hearts I was not at all sure I wanted Dad coming home soon. I was used to Mum and me being on our own; to being Mum's off-sider. If she had a worry or a problem she consulted me. We didn't need a third person butting in and coming the Boss Cocky. Mum was the one who told me what to do. No one else. 'Until my father comes home to us'. I hesitated before committing the words to paper. Still, I knew it was the popular notion. A child should be longing for the day her father came back from the war. *Dear little child, when you kneel down, to say your evening prayer...* and all that. And what an unbeatable closing sentence! Ten out often, for certain! Elizabeth Allan's father wasn't even in the forces; he was the manager of a fertiliser company!

Mr. Goodwin looked through my finished work and gave me a long and sympathetic look. There was, I felt, something almost of fondness in it. Admiration, even. Under his gaze I sat erect, chin firmly lifted, an appropriate amount of melancholy clouding my eyes. Noble-hearted girl! All the long war years without a father!

Playground talk was more down to earth. Everyone thought the Peace would mean something concrete; a new house, a holiday shack at Magnetic Island, maybe a trip to Brisbane on the *Manunda*. The Bradfield Scheme and cruises to England having served their purpose, were consigned to oblivion. In fact I felt I would settle for a peacetime featuring a Cold Flame refrigerator. No more early morning trips to the ice-depot for the ice! I knew about Cold Flames because Barry was working down south in the Cold Flame factory. Yes! A kerosene fridge! That and the sound of Mum in the kitchen, beating-up mashed potato, creamy with lots of milk, banging it round and round in the pot, scraping the sides to make the butter melt. That would be Peace.

Almost without exception the most popular option was a car. Boys especially. 'Yeah! My Dad reckons we're gonna get a car! Not an old rattle-trap. A proper car, like them Yanks have in the pitchers!' Everyone nodded sagely. Their Dads had said the same thing.

No matter how unlikely some of the dreams were, no one was brought down to earth with a thump. No one said, 'Yeah! Come off it, y'dill! That'll be the day! Now pull the other one!' Everyone was allowed their say, listened to with wide-eyed interest, even awe. It was a time of wonder, a time for dreams. After all, this was the Peace. And who knew? Anything was possible!

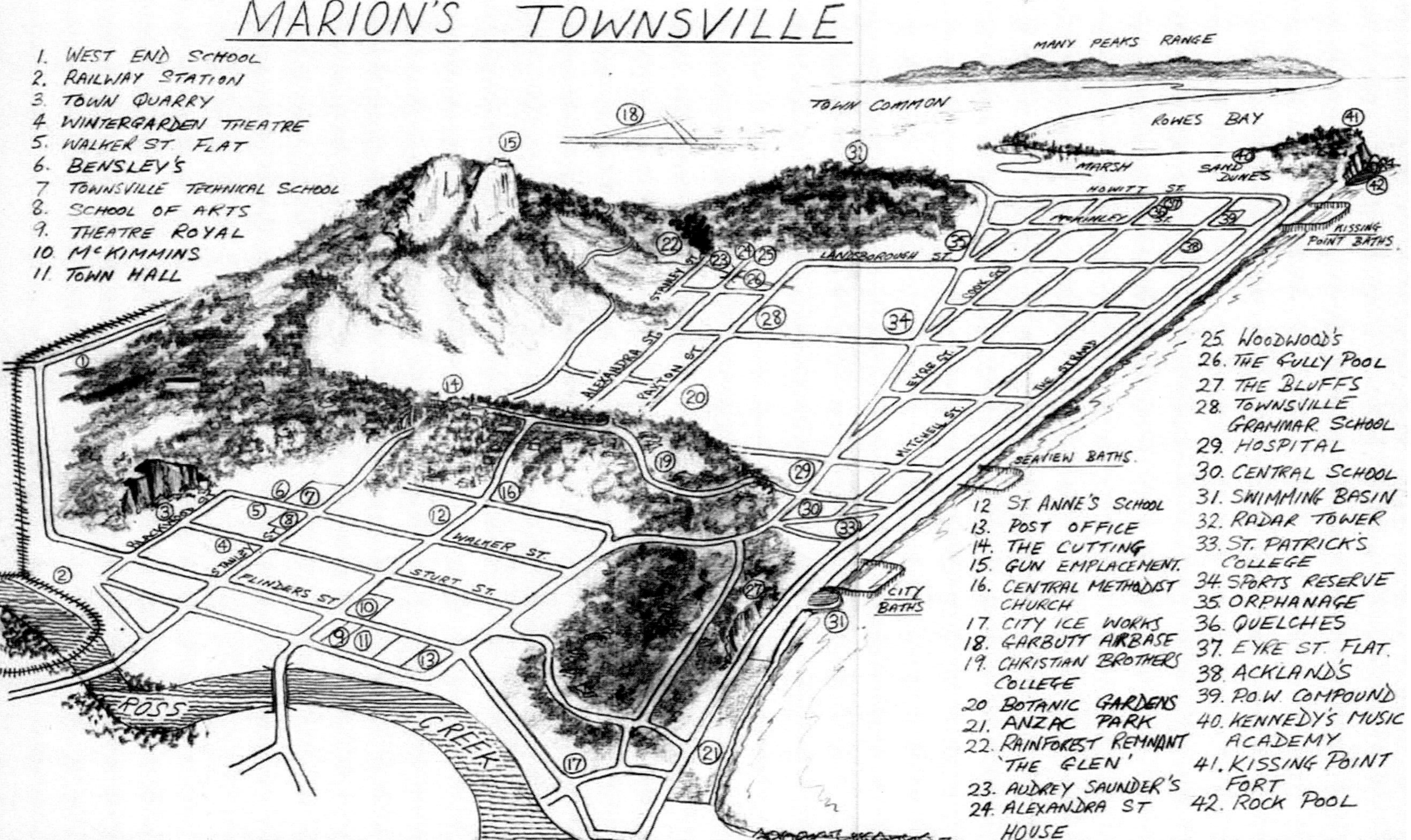
MARION'S TOWNSVILLE
1. WEST END SCHOOL
2. RAILWAY STATION
3. TOWN QUARRY
4 WINTERGARDEN THEATRE
5. WALKER ST FLAT
6. BENSLEY'S
7 TOWNSVILLE TECHNICAL SCHOOL
8. SCHOOL OF ARTS
9. THEATRE ROYAL
10. McKIMMINS
11. TOWN HALL
12 ST. ANNE'S SCHOOL
13. POST OFFICE
14. THE CUTTING
15. GUN EMPLACEMENT.
16. CENTRAL METHODIST CHURCH
17. CITY ICE WORKS
18. GARBUTT AIRBASE
19. CHRISTIAN BROTHERS COLLEGE
20 BOTANIC GARDENS
21. ANZAC PARK
22. RAINFOREST REMNANT 'THE GLEN'
23. AUDREY SAUNDER'S
24. ALEXANDRA ST HOUSE
25. WOODWOOD'S
26. THE GULLY POOL
27. THE BLUFFS
28. TOWNSVILLE GRAMMAR SCHOOL
29. HOSPITAL
30. CENTRAL SCHOOL
31. SWIMMING BASIN
32. RADAR TOWER
33. ST. PATRICK'S COLLEGE
34. SPORTS RESERVE
35. ORPHANAGE
36. QUELCHES
37. EYRE ST. FLAT.
38. ACKLAND'S
39. P.O.W. COMPOUND
40. KENNEDY'S MUSIC ACADEMY
41. KISSING POINT FORT
42. ROCK POOL
MANY PEAKS RANGE
TOWN COMMON
ROWES BAY
MARSH
SAND DUNES
HOWITT ST.
McKINLEY ST.
KISSING POINT BATHS
LANDSBOROUGH ST.
STANLEY ST
ALEXANDRA ST.
PAYTON ST
COOK ST
EYRE ST.
THE STRAND
MITCHELL ST.
SEAVIEW BATHS.
WALKER ST.
STURT ST.
FLINDERS ST
STANLEY ST
BLACKWOOD ST
CITY BATHS
ROSS
CREEK

Books by
Marion Houldsworth

The Morning Side of the Hill

Barefoot Through The Bindies

Red Dust Rising

From Gulf to God Knows Where

Maybe It'll Rain Tomorrow

The Immigrant Boy